THE AMERICAN MOSAIC

The United States Committee of the International Council on Monuments and Sites (US/ICOMOS) is one of 68 national committees of ICOMOS forming a worldwide alliance for the study and conservation of historic buildings, districts and sites. It is the focus of international cultural resources exchange in the United States and shares preservation information and expertise with other ICOMOS committees around the world. US/ICOMOS, 1600 H Street, N.W., Washington, D.C., 20006, U.S.A. (202) 842-1866.

This project was supported in part by grants from the National Endowment for the Arts, a federal agency; the American Express Foundation; The J.M. Kaplan Fund, Inc.; and Jane Blaffer Owen and the Robert Lee Blaffer Foundation.

Book design by DR Pollard and Associates, Inc.

Jacket design by DR Pollard and Associates, Inc. from a design by John T. Engeman.

Printed by J.D. Lucas Printing Company, Baltimore, MD

Printed in the United States of America
91 90 89 88   5 4 3 2

Library of Congress Cataloging-in-Publication Data

The American mosaic: preserving a nation's heritage/edited by
  Robert E. Stipe and Antoinette J. Lee.
    p. cm.
    Bibliography: p.
    ISBN 0-911697-02-0 (pbk.): $19.95
    1. Historic sites—United States—Conservation and restoration.
  2. Architecture—United States—Conservation and restoration.
  3. Cultural property, Protection of—United States.   4. United States—
  Cultural policy.   I. Stipe, Robert E.   II. Lee, Antoinette J.
  (Antoinette Josephine)   III. International Council on Monuments and
  Sites. U.S. Committee.
  E159.A3854   1988   88-9447
  363.6′9′0973—dc19   CIP

Distributed By
The Preservation Press
The National Trust for Historic Preservation
1785 Massachusetts Avenue, N.W.
Washington, D.C.   20036
202-673-4058

THE AMERICAN MOSAIC

PRESERVING A NATION'S HERITAGE

Edited by Robert E. Stipe
and Antoinette J. Lee

US/ICOMOS
United States Committee
International Council on Monuments and Sites
Washington, D.C.

DEDICATION

This book is dedicated to America's historic preservation pioneers, especially those who came just before us, setting the stage for our challenges and accomplishments. All would understand German theologian Paul Johannes Tillich's view of the relationship of the past to the present and to the future, expressed in his book,

The Religious Situation:

"To understand the present means to see it in its inner tension toward the future . . . there is such a thing as spiritual perspective, the possibility of finding amid all the infinite aspirations and tensions which every present contains not only those which conserve the past but also those which are creatively new and pregnant with the future." (Translated from the German by H. Richard Niebuhr. Henry Holt and Company, 1932.)

Frontispiece:
Kitchen, No. II Dormitory
New Harmony, Indiana
(Doane Studio, Mt. Vernon, Indiana)

TABLE OF CONTENTS

ACKNOWLEDGMENTS

The editors wish to express their thanks to the Design Arts Program of the National Endowment for the Arts for its financial assistance in the preparation of the manuscript. NEA program director, Adele Chatfield-Taylor, and program officer, Allen Payne, provided guidance and advice throughout the project. For financial assistance in the publication of the work we are most indebted to Joan K. Davidson, president of The J.M. Kaplan Fund, Inc., New York City; Stephen S. Halsey, president of the American Express Foundation, New York City; and Jane Blaffer Owen and the Robert Lee Blaffer Trust of New Harmony, Indiana.

The following individuals reviewed all or portions of the manuscript: Jerry Rogers, James Charleton and Barry Mackintosh of the National Park Service; Hester Davis of the Arkansas Archeological Survey; and David Brook of the North Carolina Division of Archives and History. Stephen N. Dennis of the National Center for Preservation Law provided valuable insight. The editors also appreciate the efforts of the many employees of the National Park Service and state historic preservation offices who responded to requests for information, in particular, Steven Newman and Betsy Chittenden of the National Park Service.

Diane Maddex, Director, Preservation Press Books, National Trust for Historic Preservation, was a consultant from the concept of the book in 1984, to its final production three years later. Russell V. Keune, US/ICOMOS director of programs was project director of the book. Hope Headley, US/ICOMOS program officer, and Barbara Bowen, US/ICOMOS volunteer technical aide, were its production editors. Candace Clifford of the Advisory Council on Historic Preservation helped in identifying and collecting illustrations. Margaret Davis and Margaret DeLaittre of the National Trust provided answers to many questions.

Andrea Cheatham, Erin Muths and Monica Rotchford of US/ICOMOS contributed much to the publishing effort. For favors too numerous and varied to be described here, we extend our most profound thanks to Allan Olson and Josie Stipe.

FOREWORD

*T*he American Mosaic was published on the occasion of the 8th ICOMOS General Assembly and International Symposium hosted by US/ICOMOS and held in the nation's capital October 7–15, 1987. "Old Cultures in New Worlds," the symposium theme, was interpreted for the more than 600 participants by 101 speakers from 31 countries. Presentations under four subthemes ranged from "The Ancient Great Wall in a New Era," by Hou Ren Zhi, People's Republic of China, to "Monitoring Air Pollution Impacts on Anasazi Ruins at Mesa Verde National Historic Park," by Donald A. Dolske and William T. Petuskey, U.S.A.; "The Vistula Mennonite House in Poland, the Soviet Union and America," Jerry A. Dick, Canada; to "Earth Architecture of South Morocco: Problems of Conservation," by Jean-Louis Michon, Switzerland.

Interpreting "Old Cultures in New Worlds" from the American preservation experience, *The American Mosaic* traces past and present developments and forecasts future directions of U.S. preservation from early-day archaeology and historic museums to today's adaptive use and tax act projects.

The American Mosaic actually had its origins many years ago in the imagination of one of its editors, Robert E. Stipe, a US/ICOMOS Fellow. Believing that the United States had much to learn from the preservation practices of other countries, he found himself traveling throughout western Europe in the late 1960s, while a Fulbright fellow at the University of London, meeting and talking with European preservationists. At that time and again during later travels in the 1970s, he encountered more often than he likes to remember the view among European preservationists that the United States is a young country with no real past, not much of an architectural tradition and no historic preservation program of which to speak.

To address the proposition that Americans have much to learn from other countries, US/ICOMOS has already published several volumes edited by Bob about historic preservation programs elsewhere: Great Britain, the Republic of Ireland, France, the Netherlands, Denmark, Federal Republic of Germany, Austria and Switzerland. These publications—which for several countries constitute the only ones available in the English language—are the work of Antony Dale, retired Chief Investigator of Historic Buildings of the British Department of the Environment and Margaret Thomas Will, an American scholar and preservationist who makes her home in Munich, Germany. A new volume covering Turkey will be published this fall, and another on Greece will be forthcoming next spring, both prepared by Martha Jo Ramsay Leimenstoll, a North Carolina architect and a graduate of the International Centre for the Study of the Preservation and the Restoration of Cultural Property. Other volumes in the US/ICOMOS series, *Historic Preservation in Foreign Countries*, which Bob continues to edit, are in progress.

To address the second proposition, that the United States is a young country without much to preserve and only the rudiments of a preservation program, Bob has long wished to prepare a book that would present the

American preservation story to a wider English-speaking audience, both in the United States, and elsewhere. He and Antoinette J. Lee, a distinguished young scholar-practitioner in the fields of preservation and American studies, began their collaboration on this volume two years ago, with the goal of having the book available for the 8th ICOMOS General Assembly in Washington, D.C.

Anniversaries are always a propitious time for such publications, since they inevitably evoke a perspective that the rush of day-to-day events obscures for most of us much of the time. This book looks back not just to the passage of the National Historic Preservation Act of 1966, but to earlier times. It recounts for many who have never heard it, a brief history of the American preservation movement.

To simply display the chronological experience would have been a relatively simple task. However, the American preservation movement, like the history of the country itself, has evolved quickly over a relatively short period of time, and its strength lies in the diversity of human motivations that drive it. It is a young and exuberant movement, accepting all who see value in the past. At one side of the pendulum stroke lies sound scholarship and appreciation of the traditional associative values of history and architecture. At the other, the preservation movement celebrates fashion, modernity and sometimes even whim. At one side are the Williamsburg restoration and the tradition of Ann Pamela Cunningham; at the other are a late-1930s rehabilitated Main Street bank building, Saarinen's Dulles Airport and the Society for Industrial Archeology.

The most striking changes in the American preservation movement during the last 20 years reflect those of the larger society—among them, the civil rights movement and new immigrant streams into the country from Asia, Central and South America. A new spirit of tolerance, the coming of age of a younger generation unmarred by the scars of a Great Depression and a World War—but with scars of other events—have forced Americans to take a new look at what is regarded as important to preserve. Now there is cultural pluralism, the value of the intangible cultural heritage, the importance of landscapes for their own sake and not merely as the surround of buildings. New and vaguely uncomfortable— or uncomfortably vague—concepts like "heritage" and "conservation" take their place beside such accepted and secure values as "preservation" and "restoration." As the world shrinks, terms from the international preservation vocabulary like "monuments bureau" and "lists" are applied with increasing frequency to American preservation programs and practices.

It is these changes, in the context of a book that looks as much to the future as to the past, that give special meaning to the individuals and organizations who have made this publication possible.

First among these is Jane Blaffer Owen, wife of Kenneth Dale Owen, a direct descendant of Robert Owen, the Welsh-Scot industrialist-philanthropist, who purchased the Harmonist colony known as New Harmony, in Indiana. Mrs. Owen was an early patron of the National Trust, when the staff, lead by Richard H. Howland and Helen Duprey Bullock, numbered only six. In 1957, she contributed funds to redesign the National Trust logo, its letterhead and its magazine. Today, 30 years later, there is a US/ICOMOS staff of six, and she has again joined in pioneer efforts—in America's first opportunity to host the foreign preservation leaders and to share preservation concepts and standards that Mrs. Owen helped establish.

Mrs. Owen and the Robert Lee Blaffer Trust have been generous in their financial support of this book. This has a special ring of appropriateness, given that New Harmony blends not only the best of an older tradition of building restoration for museum use, but adaptive use for contemporary life as well. At New Harmony are the collaborative efforts of architect Philip Johnson and sculptor Jacques Lipchitz that produced the Roofless Church. It is the final resting place of 20th-century theologian Paul Johannes Tillich, in a landscape designed by Robert Zion. A National Historic Landmark, New Harmony displays not only the old, but also emphasizes the importance of adapting the best of the old to new uses—a living town open to social experiment, where elevation of the human spirit to new levels of integration can take place. Appropriately, also, New Harmony gave birth in 1978 to an increasingly important aspect of the preservation movement itself, the Alliance for the Preservation of Historic Landscapes. As it gave birth to a social movement under Robert Owen in the 19th century, so in the 20th century New Harmony, Mrs. Owen and the Robert Lee Blaffer Trust help to give birth to a book that tells the story of the American preservation movement to the rest of the world.

One of the compelling aspects of the American preservation movement since passage of the Preservation Act of 1966 has been a new alliance between historic preservation and the private sector, and—with consequences for the future that even now can only be imagined—the impact of tourism and the preservation of monuments and towns on one another. These developments give special meaning to the support received by US/ICOMOS for this book from the American Express Company and the American Express Foundation, through its President Stephen S. Halsey, long-time member of US/ICOMOS Executive Committee.

Twenty years since the Preservation Act of 1966, preservation has begun to come of age as an important aspect of everyday life, and therefore has become an increasingly important value to be taken into account by decision-makers in both the public and private sectors. That this book speaks directly to those decision-makers both in preservation and the larger world of day-to-day affairs renders symbolically important the support this project has received from the J.M. Kaplan Fund of New York City, through its president, Joan K. Davidson, a trustee of the National Trust.

And for all of these reasons, we are pleased to acknowledge the assistance of the Design Arts Program of the National Endowment for the Arts and its Director, Adele Chatfield-Taylor, former executive director of the New York Landmarks Preservation Foundation.

US/ICOMOS owes a special debt to the individuals who have prepared the individual chapters of this book. Greg Andrews, John Fowler, Myrick Howard, Tom King, Toni Lee, Liz Lyon, Brown Morton, Bob Stipe—have, in each of their own special subject areas, been counted among the leading practitioners of the preservation movement for, collectively, well over a century. Readers will quickly note that each one has a personal perspective and a personal style—often times strong ones—and that one writer does not always agree with another. The editors have made a special attempt to respect these individual opinions, styles and even disagreements. That US/ICOMOS is deeply grateful to these individuals for their work and perseverance goes without saying. A brief biography of each is found at the end of the book.

It is our hope that this book presents useful information about the growth, development and prospects for the American preservation movement to our friends in the English-speaking community at home and abroad. We hope also that it is an agreeable and helpful introduction to American preservationists, students and professionals alike, and that it will help them gain a fresh understanding and new insights into "the American Mosaic" of historic preservation.

Terry B. Morton, Hon. AIA
Chairman, US/ICOMOS

October 1987
Washington, D.C.

Postscript:

Less than a month before this book was to come off the press, I sat proofreading the galleys in Nicholas Biddle's library at Andalusia. The young nation's most powerful early 19th-century banker, he was also a poet, editor, architectural authority, experimental farmer and political and financial adversary of President Andrew Jackson. "This is one of the country's great evocative libraries," declares Roger Moss, architectural historian and director of the Philadelphia Athenaeum. "Nicholas Biddle was one of the most articulate and learned men of his time, and this is his library. It was assembled by him and it is still his library. Andalusia has passed through seven generations of one family, but the furniture, objects, books and bookcases are unchanged." Nicholas Biddle was the official editor in 1811 of the Lewis and Clark journal and the manuscript, with his editing notations, remains on the Andalusia library shelf.

Today James Biddle is the busy lord of the manor. Few Americans have experienced as many preservation issues discussed in this book, have contributed so directly to their resolution and have given direction to the preservation movement as it is today, as has James Biddle. Former curator of the American Wing of the Metropolitan Museum of Art, second National Trust president 1968 to 1980 and chairman and member of the boards of many preservation and museum organizations, Mr. Biddle's dream is to create an adequate endowment and secure for all time this property, which is considered by many to be the finest example of Greek Revival domestic architecture in the United States.

T.B.M.

Andalusia, on the Delaware River north of Philadelphia, Pennsylvania, was begun in 1797 and expanded in 1806 and 1835 by Benjamin H. Latrobe and Thomas U. Walter. Other buildings on the grounds, maintained in the 19th-century tradition, include the Gothic Revival cottage and grotto, the temple-like billiard room, and the graperies, now the rose garden. (Historic American Buildings Survey, Jack E. Boucher)

PREFACE

How To Read This Book

While this book has been written specially for the 8th General Assembly of the International Council on Monuments and Sites, it has been designed in ways that the editors hope will enhance its usefulness to many audiences over a relatively long period of time. These audiences include the beginning preservationist as well as the experienced professional, the preservation policy-maker as well as the doer-technician, and a domestic as well as an international audience. And, of course, the student.

The book is divided into three parts. Part I describes the structure of the American preservation system, what happens at each level of government and how each part relates to the other levels. Part II describes what is preserved and why, and how the American preservation movement has arrived at its present situation. It contains several essays of special interest and central importance in the American preservation movement as it currently exists. The third part, consisting of a single chapter, looks briefly at the strength and weakness of the present system and raises some issues important to the future of the movement.

The beginning reader possessing either a limited or a rusty knowledge of the workings of the American federal system will wish to begin with Chapter 1, which describes the legal and governmental setting of the American federal system within which the preservation movement resides. A basic understanding of the American government's role is fundamental to everything else. The second half of Chapter 1, summarizing and introducing the subject matter of Chapters 2, 3, and 4, may be skipped by the experienced reader. However, all of Chapter 1 will be essential to readers in other parts of the world who find the U.S. preservation system of divided responsibilities and authority confusing. Thereafter, the beginning reader may wish to proceed to Chapter 5, which begins with a brief history of the American preservation movement up to the present time, describing what is preserved and why and providing a context for the chapters that follow.

Those readers who are familiar with the American federal system may wish to proceed immediately to the essays contained in Chapters 2 through 4, which describe in detail the responsibilities and perspectives of the federal, state and local components of the U.S. preservation system as seen through the eyes of the individual authors. Chapters 6 through 8, describing aspects of the American preservation movement that have come specially to the fore in recent years, and which will be of interest to the advanced practitioner, may be viewed as free-standing essays by specialists at different levels in the system or by the masters of particular subjects.

Readers' comments and suggestions for additional works in this area will be welcome and should be addressed to the publisher.

The Editors
October 1987

CHAPTER ONE

HISTORIC PRESERVATION: THE PROCESS AND THE ACTORS

ROBERT E. STIPE

HISTORIC PRESERVATION: THE PROCESS AND THE ACTORS

ROBERT E. STIPE

Introduction

To visitors from abroad as well as to many Americans, the American historic preservation system must seem terribly complicated. It is much like that of the fabled blind man and the elephant, each touching a different part, but unable to comprehend the whole; it depends in part on our view of preservation, our place within a federal system of government, whether we are layman or expert in some aspect of preservation and on special professional interests. Unlike many other countries in which preservation is viewed as a specialized branch of art or architectural history, roots of the American movement lie in the area of history. While its roots are both broad and deep, the sweep of the movement's concerns has increased vastly since passage of the National Historic Preservation Act of 1966.

While the business of preserving buildings and neighborhoods is partly a matter for government, the movement to a large extent is driven by private organizations and individuals within the controlling forces of private market decisions and the overall state of the American economy. When government does become involved in preservation, there are often three governments, local, state and national, with which to deal. Adding to the confusion, each of these has some significant measure of legislative, judicial and administrative control over the processes of preservation. The powers that they exercise vary according to the level of government.

While most Americans understand the parts better than the whole, there exists nonetheless a preservation system in the United States that is coherent, comprehensive and comprehensible. But, like the elephant in the fable, before it can be understood, there must be a basic familiarity with the parts and how they relate to each other. That is why this book begins with an introduction to the preservation process, its context, the actors who operate the system, and an explanation of how responsibilities for preservation are allocated or shared among them.

If historic preservation is thought of as a simple three-part process of inventory, evaluation and registration, universal in its application to preserving almost any resource, the details of the preservation process become understandable. If the ups and downs of historic preservation before and after 1966 are understood as part of a mixed-market economic phenomenon, then not only is the outcome of various preservation problems easier to predict, but better preservation strategies may be selected in the first place. Finally, understanding how authority, power and responsibility are shared among several levels of government, shows not only where to take problems, but how to manipulate various parts of the system to produce a desired result.

This chapter begins with a description of the American preservation scene both before and after 1966 and looks at our preservation machinery as it has evolved since then. This is partly a matter of historical and political accident, but also a response to the nature of the threats to our cultural resources. There is a brief description of basic preservation processes, followed by an outline of basic governmental powers, principal sources of preservation laws and procedures at each of the three levels of government and their application to current preservation problems. The chapter concludes with a summary of the people and institutions applying the laws and operating the system.

The 1966 Setting

A report commissioned and published by the National Trust for Historic Preservation and a Special Committee of the U.S. Conference of Mayors, *With Heritage So Rich,* was published in 1965. It called for a substantially expanded national program of historic preservation and recommended a comprehensive survey of historically and architecturally important buildings, sites, structures, districts and objects to be included in a national register. The report called for a new preservation partnership to be developed among federal, state and local governments and a planning system to help insure that federal projects would not harm cultural resources. It also urged the creation of a system of financial incentives to bring development and preservation processes into better balance. The committee's principal recommendations were signed into law by President Lyndon B. Johnson in October 1966, as the National Historic Preservation Act. Since then, all of the committee's recommendations have been put in place in some form.

The year 1966 was a time of optimism and a new beginning for preservation. The 89th Congress was praised as The Preservation Congress for this and its other historic preservation initiatives of that year. But optimism was imperative in 1966, since by that time the country had experienced almost an entire decade of destruction of historic resources which had been brought on by heavily subsidized post-World War II federal programs of highway building, inner city urban redevelopment, reservoir impoundments and a flight to the new suburbs.

The American preservation community was then relatively small. Much of it was located east of the Mississippi River and tended to be concentrated in states that comprised the 13 original colonies. The focus of its attention was high-style architecture up to the time of the Civil War, battlefields and memorials—places associated with great leaders and founders of the Republic. By 1966 a new concern for preservation of neighborhoods and even entire towns was made manifest by the Williamsburg, Virginia, restoration of the 1930s, and by post-war museum village restorations such as Sturbridge Village in Massachusetts and Old Salem in North Carolina. There were also experiments with historic zoning districts in Charleston, South Carolina; Boston, Massachusetts; New Orleans, Louisiana; and a few other places. However, most preservationists concentrated on individual buildings and full-scale restoration for museum purposes. Restoration tended to be regarded as a somewhat higher and more noble objective than preservation. Terms such as conservation and adaptive use had not yet been coined.

In 1966, local preservation projects involving the restoration of buildings of local or statewide significance were mostly financed with local money, and sometimes state appropriations. There were no more than a few dozen local historic zoning districts. The attitude of state courts toward aesthetic regulation tended to range from suspicion to outright hostility. Legal tools for preservation were limited. Local ties to state and federal programs were for the most part weak or nonexistent. With a few notable exceptions, state historic preservation programs were focused on state historic sites and buildings operated as museums, on the erection of historical markers and highway plaques and, occasionally, on appropriations for local projects. History tended to predominate as an associative value. In the East, state preservation programs tended to be lodged with state archives, museum and records management programs, and, in the Midwest and West, with state historical associations, state departments of recreation or natural resources.

1966: The Big Leap Forward

As a result of the 1966 federal initiative, there has been an explosion of interest and programs in historic preservation during the last 20 years. While no accurate statistics exist, an estimate would be that there are 2,000 to 3,000 preservation organizations actively engaged in public education, advocacy, preservation and restoration projects of various kinds, many of them operating revolving funds. In terms of geographic interest, distinctions among the regions are no longer drawn. Membership in the National Trust for Historic Preservation grew from 10,700 in 1966 to 185,000 in 1986. More than 35 university graduate professional and technical courses directly related to historic preservation were created in the interim. It would be reasonable to estimate that more than 5,000 jobs were created in the administrative aspect of preservation alone.

With few exceptions, all of the 57 states and territories responded within a few years to financial incentives provided by the 1966 legislation and commenced the preparation of statewide surveys and required preservation plans. While a new view of state historic preservation offices as the overworked, underpaid enforcers of federal tax and environmental laws has been the subject of growing controversy in recent years, it is impossible to overstate the stimulative effect of the 1966 amendments and its 1980 amendments.

At the local level, historic preservation programs have also mushroomed since 1966. This is partly the result of financial and technical assistance made available to local governments through state participation in the federal program, but it has been reinforced by other events as well. These include the

American Revolution Bicentennial observance in 1976, and the rise of environmental protection and consumer movements of the 1960s and 1970s. A number of preservationists now take for granted the idea that historic preservation is an essential and integral part of the environmental movement. Watergate, Vietnam and the civil rights movements also played a part, if only indirectly, in democratizing the preservation movement as they did the larger society.

The ultimate consequence of this flowering of interest in preservation has been that a relatively simple structure with a small, narrowly focused set of characters acting more or less locally and independently of one another has been replaced by a large, complex structure encompassing a wide variety of preservation interests. The groups of which it is comprised sometimes compete, but they are politically and financially interdependent, and strongly linked to one another through both governmental and nongovernmental programs. A simple, easily understood, straightforward approach to preservation was replaced by a complex and often confusing one in which all three levels of government are important players.

Preservation as a Market Phenomenon

The American system of preservation is more easily understood if one accepts at the outset that the core of the problem of preserving old buildings and neighborhoods is simply a matter of economics. If preservation efforts are to succeed, respect for what is called the owner's bottom line is of paramount importance. Unlike many other countries, in which land tends to be regarded as a scarce resource to be treated with care and respect, Americans always tended to view real estate as a marketable commodity whose principal purpose is to provide capital gains or income to its temporary owner. This view of land tends to insure that most of our important buildings, and the neighborhoods in which they are located, are lost as the result of two extreme economic situations, each being equally damaging.

In a bullish market, that is one in which land values are high and rising and where developers are actively searching out new building sites, it is almost inevitable that as soon as the value of any given site equals or exceeds the value of the structure on it, there will be inexorable pressures on the owner to tear the building down and replace it with a more profitable use. Often, the cost of maintaining a vacant building, when added to the potential liability for accidents upon the premises or the danger from fire, will be seen as justification for its demolition and clearance of the site, merely for the purpose of enhancing its marketability.

At the opposite extreme is the historic property located in an area where real estate markets are stagnant or bearish. There is not enough economic activity to keep a responsible tenant on the premises and the last tenant leaves. Windows are boarded up, roofs leak, weather and vagrants settle in and the building begins the inevitable long, downhill slide. Again, the real estate market is the principal culprit.

The same basic rules of economics that apply to buildings apply as well to neighborhoods and large areas. Real estate markets, whether in Hoboken, New Jersey, or San Francisco, California, are driven to a substantial extent by fashion. Run-down, undesirable neighborhoods suddenly become desirable. There are various reasons, including easy access to center city jobs, an appreciation of the architecture, reasonably priced houses for young couples and changing market conditions. In the same way, the problems of preserving rural buildings and landscapes essentially arise from a depressed agricultural industry.

Often many of the best buildings are owned by institutions or individuals least able to maintain them: such as financially pressed local governments, universities, churches and other charitable, nonprofit enterprises which have special problems. Endowments do not produce the same income as when interest rates were high; the cost of renovating while meeting handicapped and other code standards rise ever higher; and someone always needs the parking space to be gained by demolishing the building. Universities are strapped for cash; central-city church congregations move to the suburbs; and the old sanctuary or Sunday school building sits on increasingly valuable urban land. With few exceptions, most local governments in the United States place a low priority on preservation. Most would strongly prefer to demolish the old city hall for a new office building. In all these situations, however, the result is the same. The building is lost.

Fighting Fire with Carrots and Sticks

The response of the American preservation system to these basic problems, particularly during the period 1966–86, was to fight fire with fire, by trying to find viable financial solutions for hard-pressed historic property owners. The solution lies in moderating the worst effects of the economic extremes outlined above. The basic thrust of the system was to try to improve the owner's financial position through subsidies of one kind or another. It was an effort to increase the owner's return on equity to the point that sale, removal or demolition is a less desirable alternative, enabling the historic building to compete on its own terms in the market.

Recently, it has been recognized that an effective system will also attempt to improve the larger market context in which the owner is situated. Neighborhood improvement programs aimed at providing housing and amenities, in addition to preservation projects, are an example of this. In addition, there are the currently popular Main Street programs which seek to revitalize small town central business districts faced with growing competition from outlying shopping malls.

Regardless of the purpose of any subsidy, the system can deliver it to the owner in essentially one of two ways. The first is an up front, outright cash grant, matching or otherwise, or an affordable below-market rate loan that takes money from the public treasury and places it at the disposal of the owner. The second approach might be called an indirect subsidy in the form of tax relief. This method allows the owner to keep funds that would otherwise be sent in the form of taxes to the city hall, the state capital, or Washington, D.C.

The federal component of the preservation system delivered direct preservation grants from about 1968 through 1980. These were cut off at the beginning of the Reagan administration, except for a brief time in 1982 when a small amount of emergency job funds were available. The relatively small appropriations provided by the U.S. Congress, the administration notwithstanding, have been used largely to support the American preservation infrastructure, that is the federal and state, and as of 1986, local, professional and administrative staffs. Advantageous preservation loans were authorized by the 1980 amendments to the Preservation Act of 1966, but these were never funded by the U.S. Congress.

Indirect subsidies in the form of accelerated depreciation schedules for certain types of rehabilitation work on National Register properties were available from 1976 through 1980, when these were changed to more advantageous credits of up to 25 percent against actual tax liability for rehabilitation work. Since 1986 they have been held at 20 percent, an outcome of the tax reform measure of that year. The tax subsidy approach was successful beyond anyone's wildest dreams, generating more than $8 billion of preservation work since 1976.

The subsidy system is not limited to the federal government. Since 1966 an increasing number of state and local governments provided grants, loans and tax subsidies of one kind or another in increasing numbers and variety. This sometimes follows the general criteria or procedures established in federal programs, but is usually tailored to circumstances of a particular state. Whether subsidies come from local, state or national governments matters little, since on the owner or investor's book of accounts the result is the same as an outright grant. What is important is that all front and back-door subsidies add up to an economically satisfactory alternative to demolition.

Public subsidies, direct or indirect, are essentially a carrot approach to the problem. They take the costs of preservation and divide them among the larger community, reducing the owner's burden by a corresponding amount. The reverse approach, which might be called the stick, is seen in the form of the increasingly popular historic district, landmark and other preservation regulations at the local government level. These, of course, operate in ways that impose higher standards and costs of construction or maintenance in preservation work or delay demolition for stated periods. The use of uncompensated regulations in this fashion thus shifts some of the costs of preservation away from the larger society and back to the owner.

Protecting the Larger Environment

While neglect and demolition resulting in the loss of building fabric represents the ultimate preservation threat, the harm done to historic buildings by inappropriate changes to their immediate surroundings may be equally damaging. Preservation implies protection not only for the building or structure itself, but also preserving the integrity of the larger environment in which the building is situated. Some sense of this is revealed in the regulations of the Advisory Council for Historic Preservation that define harmful effects as ". . . the introduction of visual, auditory, and atmospheric elements that are out of character with the building and its setting." This setting may be as small as an individual lot or it may include a large area. Thus, the walling in of the Vieux Carré Historic District in New Orleans, Louisiana, with an elevated expressway or the construction of a large prison complex in a rural environment of great natural beauty is regarded as no less damaging to essential fabric than a badly designed addition to a private house in an 18th-century historic neighborhood.

Tactically speaking, the trick in every case is to insure that potentially damaging effects of this kind are disclosed as far as possible in advance, so that regulatory or political processes may be put to work to save the situation. The responsibility to accomplish this in the private sector is on the estimated 2,000 historic district and landmarks commissions around the country. The heart of this approach is a local regulation requiring the property owner to submit plans and elevations of any proposed work to a local review board which has the authority to approve or withhold a certificate of appropriateness. This depends on what the review board believes the impact of the work will be on the historic building and its surrounding area. However, this process was established primarily to deal with buildings and has, therefore, been less successful with regard to larger environments.

The requirement of disclosure in advance of construction is an essential preservation tool in the public sector as well, and here it has had more success. Examples are seen in the National Environmental Policy Act of 1969 and its state-level counterparts, and in Section 106 of the Preservation Act of 1966, requiring that the Advisory Council be given an opportunity to review and comment on the effect of federal, federally assisted or federally licensed projects affecting National Register properties or districts. As will be seen in a later chapter, Advisory Council procedures have the potential for greater effectiveness because they lead to a legally enforceable settlement under which a federal agency is required to mitigate or reduce a harmful impact on a historic property. The approach of the Environmental Policy Act of 1966 is somewhat less satisfactory, for the reason that disclosure, without direct follow up and enforcement, is about all that can be required. These approaches reflect to some extent a fairly recent preoccupation with planning processes as a device to minimize harm and a relatively new interest in mediation as an approach to resolving disputes. At heart, however, they are products of the environmental and consumer movements of the 1960s and 1970s emphasizing the importance of advance disclosure and product labeling.

Saving Historic Resources: The Basic Process

The system for preserving cultural resources in the United States is essentially no different from systems elsewhere. In fact, the procedure for preserving historic buildings, neighborhoods or cultural sites generally is no different from the system involving the preservation of other scarce resources—a rare and endangered plant or animal, community or an artifact of importance to society.

Viewed as a sequence of rational steps, the process can be broken down into the following steps: (1) locating or finding the resource, fixing its location and describing it in prescribed language; (2) evaluating the importance of the resource according to predetermined criteria and listing or otherwise formally designating it as something worth preserving; and (3) applying one or more of a number of planning or protective measures to insure that it does not disappear or suffer harm.

The First Step: Finding and Describing the Resource

This stage simply involves the collection of information. In the context of American preservation, history and architecture predominate as the important associative values. The federal program, which sets the limits of state programs, also includes prehistory, engineering and culture, although not tightly defined. Values, such as landscape, townscape or other environmental factors, might also be taken into account, depending on the nature and purpose of the survey. More often than not, however, these are of secondary importance.

Good surveys and inventories and professionally competent evaluations of the relative worth of that which has been surveyed are the mainstays of any conservation or preservation program. While thorough coverage, detailed investigation and competent scholarship are important for their own sake, the potential legal consequences of faulty or sloppy work are equally if not more important. Most of this work is undertaken by historians, architectural historians and where appropriate, archaeologists, folklorists and cultural geographers. At times, volunteers undertake surveys with professional guidance.

While technical distinctions might be drawn between surveys or inventories, here it refers to locating and describing a particular resource. When such survey or inventory data are arrayed, the result is simply called a survey, inventory or list to indicate that items in the survey have been brought together as a collection.

In the American system, lists are kept at all three government levels but since 1966 the National Register of Historic Places, maintained by the National Park Service, is generally regarded as the most significant. It is an extension of the Historic Sites Survey, begun under authority of the Historic Sites Act of 1935, and, as noted earlier, containing since 1966 properties of national, state and local significance. Since 1980 historic properties of national significance receive a somewhat greater degree of protection in federal planning processes but all are treated equally in terms of eligibility for federal tax credits and subsidy.

The bulk of survey and inventory activity in the United States actually happens at the level of state and local governments. Here confusion begins, since many of them also maintain their own state registers of important sites. Prior to 1966, a number of states maintained registers of historic places including those of local significance. When the National Register was expanded in 1966 to encompass places of state and local significance, as well as national importance, some states, recognizing that there was little point in maintaining two sets of registered properties, dropped or abandoned their own registers in favor of the national list. Presently, some states are talking about reinstating the state registry programs, in anticipation of a reduced federal program.

State survey and inventory activities are often supplemented by local surveys, which may be done as part of a state program, to identify National Register nominations, or undertaken locally for the purpose of designating local landmarks and historic districts or administering local grant, loan, tax credit or other preservation incentive programs. The National Register survey and documentation procedures increasingly dominate state and local survey procedures and standards, regardless of the ultimate purpose of that work.

The deterioration of a building in Wilmington, North Carolina, is the result of an economic downturn in a neighborhood, the loss of tenants and the abandonment of real estate. (Robert E. Stipe)

The construction of elevated urban highways through American cities in the post-World War II era caused massive disruptions in older neighborhoods and contributed to the growth of the historic preservation movement. (Elliott Erwill, Magnum, *God's Own Junkyard,* Peter Blake, Holt, Rinehart, and Winston, Inc.)

An active economic market can also promote the disuse and deterioration of buildings, seen here in Raleigh, North Carolina, where the value of land exceeds that of its buildings. Parking and greater density development are the natural outcome of such forces. (Robert E. Stipe)

The approaches to many American cities are littered with fast food restaurants, motels and convenience stores, erasing the distinction between city and country. (National Trust for Historic Preservation)

The Second Step: Evaluation and Registration

Next comes an item-by-item evaluation of what was found and included in the inventory. This involves an evaluation of each item in the survey to decide whether or not it meets the standard. This evaluation will usually be of two orders. One is a threshold level of decision to list or not list a particular resource. A second order evaluation will be to grade or classify the resource, usually of national, state or local significance. The first order qualifying evaluation will explicitly place the building or other resource in a special category from others, not listed or set aside. A variety of terms is used for essentially the same purpose, which is listing, scheduling or registering.

The act of designation or recognition is accomplished in various ways. Sometimes it is done more or less automatically, in the absence of objection, following a legally published notice of intent to list. This is the procedure followed by the National Register of Historic Places and some state registers. Local landmarks might also be designated in this fashion, if authorized by state or local law. Typically, however, local designation is accomplished by passage of a statute or ordinance. At one time or another all three levels of government followed this procedure. Occasionally, designation or registration is accomplished through some action of an administrative or elected official, a mayor, governor or even the president.

A variety of consequences flow from the act of official designation. The property or area may qualify for some special treatment, such as a plaque, government grant or loan, tax benefits, special regulations regarding use or design or delay of demolition. Sometimes the listing is merely for planning or honorific purposes, such as the placement of a plaque. Such listing has little or no affect on the value of the property, imposes no restrictions and requires no special level of effort or expenditure on the part of the owner. In these instances, the consequences of being listed are unimportant for all practical purposes. However, where the consequences of listing affect the value of the property or the owner's pocketbook, standards and procedures by which properties are included or excluded take on greater significance. As a general rule, the more impact the listing has on the pocketbook, the more political and legal considerations enter the picture.

Sooner or later the expenditure of public funds or the imposition of public regulations on a particular building or site may be called into question in a court of law. This may be the result of a taxpayer's suit challenging the appropriateness of an expenditure, or some protest action brought by an owner contesting regulations as they apply to the property. At this point it becomes essential that the expenditure be justified as fulfilling a public purpose in the constitutional sense, and that public regulations regarding design, maintenance or demolition not impose an undue burden on the owner of a historic property. A court will usually require reassurance that something more than political whim has been brought to the processes of survey, evaluation and listing.

A confusing aspect of our federal system is that the act of listing by one unit of government may serve to trigger some regulatory or other action by another unit. For example, a local government might designate one or more landmark buildings for purposes of enforcing a local landmarks ordinance, qualifying properties for local government preservation grants or tax benefits. A state might add these properties to the state register so that they qualify for state appropriations or to activate some state environmental protection law. Some of these properties may also be eligible for listing in the National Register, qualifying them for the benefits of matching grants for acquisition and development, and Section 106 review.

The Third Step: Protective Strategies

The purpose of inventory and survey, evaluation and registration is to apply protective or preservation measures of one kind or another to the resource, whether it is a building, site, structure, district or object. Viewed broadly, there are only two general categories of threat to a cultural resource. One is from the hand of man; the other is from the hand of time.

Protection against the hand of man is usually protection against demolition, extensive alterations amounting to a defacement of architectural fabric or historical association, including the interior. It also includes anything done to destroy or harm the surrounding environment, whether done by the owner of the building, adjacent property owners or a unit of government.

In a tactical sense, one may think of protection against the hand of man as involving a range of actions, from gentle to severe, not relying principally on the expenditure of public funds to achieve a result. In the most gentle category would be the stop, think, disclose or mediate approaches involved in the Environmental Policy Act of 1969 or Section 106 of the Preservation Act of 1966. From here, increasing the pressure on the property owner, getting tougher, would additionally involve compulsory design review procedures backed by sanctions and perhaps coupled with restraints of up to a year on demolition and removal. Dealing with the larger environment would presumably also encompass some combination of the above measures. The third and highest level of pressure on the owner might involve compulsory acquisition and ownership of the resource itself by a government or agency to hold and protect the property when the private owner is unwilling or unable to do so. Indeed, some preservation strategies go beyond the effective limits of persuasion or the outer boundaries of permissible regulatory activity, such as permanent prohibition of demolition, protection of the larger environment or restrictions on change or the removal of valuable interiors. These strategies may only be enforceable through acquisition strategies. The political situation will always impose limits on regulation. The availability of funds for purchase or condemnation of threatened properties will restrict the possibilities of public ownership as a protective device.

Protection against the hand of time encompasses the notion of harm to or loss of essential fabric, whether suddenly as the result of some natural disaster, or more slowly over a long period of time. Remedial measures in this instance would customarily involve work on the fabric itself, ranging from stabilization and repairs to preservation and restoration. This kind of protection invariably involves expense. One or more public or private sector programs are aimed at assisting the owners through grants, loans or other forms of subsidy, from whatever source. The sources of authority for all of these tactics will be explored later in this chapter.

11

The Basic Powers

Anyone wishing to understand the American preservation system must have a basic understanding about the nature and sources of governmental power in the United States. Each level, federal, state or local, has by tradition and in law defined and limited authority to act. While there are certain governmental powers that are fundamental to governments generally, it is important to understand where these come from and how they are allocated in the American federal system.

For a government to exist it must possess at least three basic powers. They are: (1) the authority to tax citizens and to spend the proceeds for their general welfare; (2) the authority to regulate or limit the conduct of individuals and their use of property, without compensating them for rights that they give up as the result of such regulations; (3) the authority to acquire, hold, manage and dispose of land and buildings and to undertake other basic legal actions allowed any private individual or business, to enter into contracts, and sue and be sued. In general, everything done by any federal, state or local government falls into one or more of these basic categories. Some have included the power to plan as a fourth great power of government.

Taxing and Spending

The first power of government is the power to tax its citizens and to spend the proceeds where there is a public need or purpose. Taxes, of course, come in many forms: income, payroll, excise, sales, estate, inheritance, licenses, property and many others. They usually represent the involuntary giving of the citizen's money to the government. The system itself encourages charity by allowing deductions against income for certain gifts and these kinds of gifts have always played a major role in historic preservation efforts, for the federal government seems to have a lock on personal and corporate income tax. It is also an important source of income for states and, increasingly in recent years, for local governments. Taxes on property, generally for historical reasons, tend to be the prerogative of local governments and, to a lesser extent, state governments. The American system of taxation is a hodge-podge, based more on historical accident and the ease with which revenues may be collected, rather than upon any rational scheme.

An important aspect of the tax system is that certain taxes will often be levied by one unit of government and subsequently returned to another in the form of grants, loans or other sharing mechanisms. There are literally dozens of programs through which federal revenues are returned or shared with states and local governments, as well as hundreds of schemes among states by which revenues collected by states are returned to local governments and private individuals.

Revenues collected by the government may be spent for a variety of historic preservation purposes. Sometimes the expenditure is a direct subsidy in the form of a grant or loan made directly to the owner of a historic property for its restoration or a related purpose. At other times, governments may subsidize preservation indirectly, by allowing the property owner to keep sums that would otherwise go to the government in taxes. The subsidy may be a deduction against income on which federal or state tax is paid or it might be a more valuable dollar-for-dollar credit against the tax bill itself. It might be a partial remission or forgiveness of city property taxes to help with the maintenance of a listed landmark. All of these tax incentives can be regarded as forms of government spending. Funds directly appropriated and spent from the treasury are the first form; taxes not collected in the first place are the second form. By a curious twist of logic, the latter are sometimes called revenue losses.

Once raised, there is little question in ordinary circumstances about the authority of governments to spend money on historic preservation or any other legitimate function. So long as the expenditure is explicitly authorized by legislation, there is a public benefit, and the expenditure is not otherwise prohibited. Such an expenditure, made possible by some provision of the federal or state constitutions, will be discussed later. The use of tax deductions and credits as incentives for preservation or any other socially desirable objective, as distinguished from appropriations, is often criticized on grounds that the public cost of the activity is not in the budget and therefore hidden from public scrutiny.

Regulation

The second of basic governmental power is the power to regulate citizens in their conduct and use of property through uncompensated regulation, referred to as police power regulations. Provisions of a zoning ordinance requiring a front yard in which nothing may be built is a good example. The yard is effectively taken out of use for building purposes, but the owner is not paid for land that is given up. Such laws must be specific and understandable by ordinary citizens; they must apply with equal force to everyone; and they must have a believable relationship to the objective of promoting public health, safety, morals or general welfare. Most importantly, they must not go so far in their application as to deprive the owner of too much beneficial use of the property. Since there is never enough money available to acquire all historic properties and to preserve them as museums at public expense, the use of regulatory authority to shift preservation costs from the general public to the individual owner becomes a matter of absolute necessity, especially where the preservation of areas and neighborhoods or other large areas is considered.

Acquisition of Property

The third basic power enables governments to acquire, hold, manage and dispose of property, just as any individual or business does. Normally, property is acquired by individuals and governments through gift, purchase or inheritance, which are voluntary transactions. But an essential difference between private citizens and the government is that the latter has the power under certain circumstances to go beyond bargaining and to acquire property compulsorily for certain public uses, even when the owner does not wish to part with it. In other words, to take it away from a private owner, there is a special court proceeding called eminent domain or condemnation. For this to happen, four requirements must be met: (1) fair or adequate compensation must be paid; (2) there must be specific statutory authorization for the taking; (3) acquisition procedures must be rigorously followed; and (4) property acquired must be put to a public use. Compulsory acquisition became increasingly important to preservation in the United States during the last 20 years, but more in as tactical than in any real sense. In actuality, the mere existence or availability of the power of eminent domain is a strong inducement to sell at a reasonable price, whether or not it is actually exercised.

Before going further, it is important to understand that there are different degrees of ownership or dominion over property held by government or anyone else, however acquired. All or part of a property can be owned. If, for example, a historic property were to be acquired for permanent use as a museum, then lawyers would say that the fee simple or fee, representing the entire bundle of property rights, would be needed.

However, as an alternative to acquiring all ownership rights, it will often be just as effective to obtain only those actually needed to preserve a property. For example, there is no reason to buy the entire bundle of ownership rights if all that is needed is the single right to control its exterior appearance. There are several advantages to this approach. One is that buying specific or limited rights is usually cheaper than buying all of them. Another is that they can be tailored to individual situations, unlike regulations that must apply equally to everyone similarly situated. A third is that such restrictions can go beyond the permissible limits of regulation; for example, they may have effect inside the building to save an important interior, where regulations might not. A fourth is that the owner or seller of rights is paid for what is given up. This is not the case with regulations where no compensation is made.

Revolving funds depend heavily on the ability to use such rights in buying and selling historic properties. An older, now largely disused technique was to buy a property outright, fix it up and put it back on the market as a shell or a fully restored building. It would be subject to preservation restrictions covering the restoration and maintenance. However, this approach was seen as slow and inefficient, tying up capital for long periods of time. Now the more common approach is for the revolving fund to acquire an option on the property, prepare a preservation plan and market the property aggressively. When a buyer is found, the fund exercises its option, buys the property and then sells it immediately to the purchaser, subject to restrictions assuring its preservation by the buyer and all future owners.

These so-called less-than-fee-arrangements are ancient and complex legal devices, varying widely in their wording, practical application, consequences and enforcement from state to state. Thus it is not necessary to go into any more detail about them here. To understand the system, however, it is necessary to remember that whether temporary or permanent, full fee or less-than-fee, these techniques for transferring the ownership of real estate have become major tools in the preservation of cultural property in the United States in recent years. Many states have passed laws to do away with old common law restrictions on their enforcement. They currently add significantly to the ability to save historic buildings in the private sector.

Preservation Planning

At this point this narrative takes a slight diversionary but necessary tack. Many writers and scholars have referred to a fourth power of government, as the power to plan. This term is not found in constitutions or law books, but the idea of preservation planning has come into the picture with such increasing frequency and different meanings during the last 20 years that it is necessary to say a few words about it.

A first level of preservation planning is essentially voluntary. Its purpose is typically to draw the attention of the owners of historic buildings to their true value or potential, and to instill a desire on the part of owners or the public to restore them. Examples are seen in preservation projects that emphasize before and after drawings of historic buildings and neighborhoods, and adaptive use projects. Such plans are often purely advisory or educational in approach.

A second level of preservation planning refers to attempts to introduce preservation strategies as official components of local or regional comprehensive land use plans, usually in the form of policy statements, maps, drawings and diagrams. In this context, preservation plans take an official place with plans for public utilities and facilities, housing, transportation and land use. Such plans not only provide guidelines for new development but also establish a framework for historic district and landmark regulations, deal in a coordinated way with potentially troublesome public projects, such as highways and urban renewal projects, changes in land use and related matters. This kind of preservation planning is especially helpful as a means of inserting historic preservation goals into a city's capital improvement and operating budgets and as a basis for regulatory activities. Virtually unheard of prior to 1966, it has been on the rise during the 70s and 80s, following pioneering studies in Providence, Rhode Island, in the 1950s and in New Orleans, Louisiana, in the 1960s. California is typical of the few states that specifically mention historic preservation as a comprehensive plan element. They depend on local initiation for their preparation and execution.

The preservation planning efforts just mentioned flow essentially from the plan-as-design and planning-as-policy thrusts of the planning profession in the 1950s and 1960s. A third approach arises from the consumer and environmental movements of those years and has come into widespread use. In essence, it requires the administrators of large-scale federal and state projects to consider the potentially harmful effect of projects, such as dams, airports, prisons and urban renewal. Administrators are also required to disclose the potentially harmful effects of projects to the public through a system of environmental impact reporting. Some go a step further, requiring the submission of projects to a special tribunal that may have an opportunity for review and comment, or even better, there may be a chance for a negotiated settlement that reduces the worst impacts of the project. The Environmental Policy Act of 1969 is an example of the former and Section 106 of the Preservation Act of 1966 is an example of the latter. These planning procedures that have many state-level equivalents can be complex and time-consuming. Because of this they are referred to as the MAD technique of planning which stands for maximum administrative delay. The American preservation community had used these procedures with adroitness at times.

A fourth and final kind of preservation planning is known by the acronym RP3, a rather specialized planning procedure introduced several years ago by the National Park Service to put a more rational base of thinking under the state preservation plans. Described in more detail in chapter 3, it requires state survey and planning activities to proceed according to study units or historical themes. State decision-making in these matters necessarily requires a degree of flexibility to accommodate political priorities and these two goals sometimes conflict with one another.

Preservation and the American Federal System

Within the public sector, it must be understood that each of the three levels of government in the federal system has different origins, and that powers available to it, for preservation or other purposes, will differ from the other two. The starting point is to recall that in the American system, the states were the first units of government to exist. They, in turn, created the other two, the national federal government and a variety of local governments. As the sovereign units of government, states inherently possess all of the basic powers just described: to levy taxes and spend the proceeds; to acquire, hold, manage and dispose of a variety of interests in land, by eminent domain if necessary; and to control personal conduct and the use of land through uncompensated regulation.

Fundamental to understanding the American system is to recognize at the outset that the states created the national government, and not the reverse. In doing so, the states invested the federal government, in the Constitution of 1787, with a limited range of specified powers. A few of the more familiar ones were to create a national system of coinage and money, to make treaties with foreign countries, to declare war, to regulate commerce among the several states and, in general, to do those things the states could not do effectively on their own. The federal government was also given the power to tax and spend for the general welfare and to acquire and hold property. The key point to be made here, however, is that in order to carry out any program of activities, including historic preservation, the federal government must be able to point to some express authority in the federal Constitution. What states did *not* delegate to the federal government in the Constitution of 1787 was any type of regulatory authority other than in the field of interstate commerce, which is by now the justification for almost all federal attempts at regulation. Thus, while the federal government has the authority to control conduct on federal property (which is the basis for protecting archaeological sites on federal lands) and to regulate interstate commerce, the general or inherent authority to adopt and enforce policing regulations, was retained by the states in the 9th and 10th amendments to the U.S. Constitution. The power to make and enforce police power regulations (generally those resulting in a fine or jail sentence) remains as an inherent power of the 50 states and is not delegated to the national government.

While it may lack inherent regulatory authority, the federal government enjoys significant power of another sort, the power of the purse. By virtue of its ability to raise vast sums of money through personal and corporate income taxes and to share those proceeds with state and local governments, subject only to conditions of its own devising, the federal government is able to encourage specific programs that it regards as important to the nation as a whole. Since the federal government captures such a large share of the national wealth by comparison with revenues available to state and local governments, its power of the purse is extensive as well as powerful. In this sense the common term federal regulations is something of a misnomer, since regulations are in fact nothing more or less than conditions on the receipt and use of federal funds. Violation of these federal regulations does not carry the penalties that customarily accompany a breach of the police power but simply denies access to federal money. Thus, a key aspect of the American federal system is that the federal government cannot force states to do anything. It can only use its vast financial resources to create a climate in which it, in partnership with state and local governments, can induce others to carry out programs that it, the federal government, favors.

If states are the sovereign units of government in our system, possessing all the inherent powers of government, and the federal government is one of delegated powers given to it by states, what of city and county governments? Like the federal government, these are also creatures of the states and have no inherent powers of any kind. They are created by the state, may be abolished at will by the state and may exercise only those powers given to them by the state itself. One prevailing rule of law declares that local governments may exercise only those powers explicitly granted to them by the state, those necessarily implicit therein and no others. As will be seen in a later section, states have authorized an extensive and wide range of preservation powers to cities throughout the nation, most of it since 1966.

Two things must be kept in mind, however. One is that when states authorize local governments to undertake a given activity, they merely enable or authorize it to be carried out. Except for a few basic activities, it is not usually required that they do so. Thus the initiative for preservation remains at the local level rather than that of the state. Common experience in preservation and other areas reveals that what a city is authorized to do as a purely legal matter and what it is willing to do as a matter of practical politics are not always the same thing.

The second caution is that in discussing what local governments may do, it is necessary to distinguish between cities and counties. From a historical perspective, American counties, following the British tradition from which they arose, have historically had a limited range of duties or functions. These included such basic functions as the conduct of elections, running schools, building roads, enforcing the law and keeping jails, holding courts, keeping real property records and caring for the poor. For many years, counties were regarded as local branches of state government, located geographically throughout a state for the more convenient transaction of the state's business. Cities, on the other hand, were created by the state more for the purpose of providing services required by people living in close proximity to one another: police, fire and other protective services; maintaining hospitals and libraries, garbage collection, park and recreation programs and water and sewer services. While these traditional distinctions between cities and counties have now largely died out, rural counties tend to be relatively poor and strongly conservative by comparison with cities. This has practical consequences in terms of their willingness and ability to mount historic preservation programs.

Sources of Preservation Law
Constitutions

Having looked at the three levels of government that comprise the American federal system, it remains to look briefly at the sources of law from which the three levels take their authority. These sources are not only more diverse than most foreign visitors, and most Americans, realize, but each contributes an essential part of the American preservation system. The limits of permitted preservation activity are defined by the overall framework of the federal and state constitutions and by the legislative enactments of the U.S. Congress, the state legislatures and local governing boards. Of increasing importance since 1966 have been the regulations drafted by nonelected federal and state civil service employees. All of these, including constitutions, legislation and administrative regulations, are subject to the scrutiny of federal and state courts.

The U.S. Constitution would not normally be viewed as a source of historic preservation law, but it underlies every action taken by government in every field. The 5th and 14th Amendments to the federal Constitution establish what is called a due process of law framework that emphasizes the basic concept of fairness in the application of all laws, preservation and otherwise. In a substantive sense, the Constitution insures that property is not confiscated for public use under the guise of regulation. Due process also requires that property owners be treated fairly in a procedural sense. For example, they must receive notice of any action involving them, both in adopting and enforcing historic district regulations. It has been thought from time to time that the 1st Amendment, prohibiting the establishment of a state religion and insuring free speech, might limit the authority of state and local governments to regulate signs and billboards in historic areas or, possibly, to prohibit grants for the restoration of historic churches. So far this has not proven to be the case.

Thus, these basic constitutional guarantees, such as due process and equal protection, become a part of preservation law and the American preservation system because they apply to all aspects of the relationship between the American citizen and his or her government. The relationship between public preservation policy and these basic rights is not a mere academic matter.

To take one example, following the Preservation Act of 1966 and prior to passage of the Tax Reform Act of 1976, the listing of a property in the National Register was generally regarded as being of no more than honorific importance. The owner was protected to some limited extent against harm from federal projects and had some chance, although remote, of obtaining a federal grant to preserve or restore the property. In all, National Register listing had no significant impact on the value of the property. This changed with the Tax Reform Act of 1976, which penalized an owner who demolished a National Register property. This penalty, it was argued, affected the value of the property. At this point the owner's right to have a say in the listing process became a matter of due process.

Another example arises from the common provision in most local landmarks ordinances requiring the owner of a listed property to postpone the demolition of a listed building once an application is made to do so. The question then becomes: What is a reasonable delay period? When is it so long and burdensome to the owner that a court would say that the property has been taken without fair compensation? Determining the point at which the burden of the ordinance is too heavy is a matter for courts.

Other constitutional issues may easily arise. For example, federal and state constitutions limit expenditure of public funds to public purposes. At one extreme, it is quite likely there would be no difficulty in finding, in a taxpayer's suit challenging the expenditure of local property tax revenues to restore the local headquarters of George Washington, that there was an adequate educational public purpose in preserving the property. By the same token, there may be a real question whether the expenditure of public funds to preserve a 1950's diner would fall into the same category. Similarly, the requirement of periodic public access to a building restored by government grants-in-aid is, at heart, an attempt to convince a court that there is a public benefit derived from a grant of money to a private owner to restore it.

Most people are surprised to learn that these basic protections are also found in the constitution of every state. While the enforcement of the 5th and 14th Amendment guarantees is principally a matter for federal courts, enforcement of similar guarantees in state constitutions is a matter for individual state courts. Here, subject to the federal Constitution, they are interpreted according to the traditions of each individual state. With minor exceptions, state constitutions do not address themselves more specifically than this to historic preservation issues.

Legislation

Whereas federal and state constitutions set the general framework, details of any government activity are found in legislation passed by elected officials: statutes of the U.S. Congress and the 50 state legislatures and ordinances passed by local governing boards. Here it must be emphasized that basic state enabling legislation for any governmental function, preservation included, is governed by the U.S. Constitution and historical and political traditions of each state. While there are basic similarities in the preservation laws of states, exact duplication of laws from state to state, except in situations where one is literally copied from another or from some national model, is purely coincidental. Each state, as a sovereign entity, makes its own laws.

The other thing to keep in mind is that federal and state laws represent an accumulation of government policies over time. For example, the Preservation Act of 1966 expanded the national survey of historic places established under authority of the Historic Sites Act of 1935, and the 1976 and 1980 amendments expand and bring the 1966 law up to date. These, in turn, are tied to other federal laws, such as the Internal Revenue Code and a variety of federal environmental laws. The same general pattern of relationships will be found in state preservation laws, the most recent supplanting or changing earlier laws. Thus, it is not sufficient to look merely at the most recent preservation legislation, since earlier laws remain on the books until changed or repealed.

Administrative Regulations

The enabling acts of the U.S. Congress and of each state, while worded more precisely than constitutions, are nonetheless usually general, and must be supplemented by federal and state regulations regarding the administrative proce-

Federal government plans to demolish the late 19th-century Old Post Office in Washington, D.C., sparked protests in the early 1970s and led to the creation of a citywide preservation organization, and the eventual preservation of the building for government offices and a shopping arcade. (John J. G. Blumenson, National Trust for Historic Preservation)

Actors in New York City rallied to persuade property owners and the city government to save Broadway's historic theaters. (Herbert Eisenberg)

Rallies at the foot of the U.S. Capitol in Washington, D.C., encouraged the U.S. Congress to save the historic west front of the nation's most recognized building. (Lisa Berg Photography)

The Board of Trustees of the National Trust for Historic Preservation sets policy for the nation's largest private, nonprofit preservation organization. (Carleton Knight III, for the National Trust for Historic Preservation)

dures to be followed in their execution or enforcement. Although administrative regulations are prepared by nonelected officials, they are no less legally binding. These are proposed or drafted by members of the civil service and posted in a journal of public record, best known to laymen as the legal notices. In the case of the federal government, it is known as the *Federal Register*. After allowing a period for public comment, they take effect automatically at the end of the prescribed period. Virtually all of the details of National Park Service and Advisory Council preservation programs and procedures are thus created by the agencies themselves, pursuant to the broader mandate enacted by the U.S. Congress. Accountability to the U.S. Congress and to state legislatures is insured through annual budget hearings and through periodic special legislative oversight committees.

Occasionally an administrative code or procedure is found at the local government level. More frequently, however, the local equivalent of these regulations is found in the rules of procedure, sometimes called bylaws, of local boards and commissions. Such rules deal mostly with how things are done, rather than substance. For example, bylaws of a historic district or landmarks commission might spell out procedures for the election of officers, steps to be followed in vetting applications for certificates of appropriateness, how public notice of hearings is to be given, the taking of evidence, reporting of decisions and similar details. While they appear to be relatively unimportant, rules of procedure are just as binding in a legal sense as though they were located in the local ordinance, the state enabling legislation or the state or federal constitution itself.

Executive Orders

This is the appropriate place to note several other sources of authority in the American system of government. One such important source is called the executive order. While not law in the ordinary sense, executive orders can be equally important in terms of results. An executive order is nothing more or less than an instruction or statement of policy from the head of an agency or institution. Executive orders, which spell out administration policy on particular topics, are issued by the president, by state governors and occasionally by mayors or managers at the local level. The penalty for failing to follow or carry out an executive order is not jail, fine or civil action, as would be the case with a statute or an ordinance, but disciplinary action by the head of the governmental unit involved. In our system, such executive orders may be the precursor of later legislation, as was President Richard M. Nixon's Executive Order 11593 of May 1971, spelling out a variety of preservation procedures to be carried out by federal agencies. The substance of this executive order was later embodied in the 1980 amendments to the Preservation Act of 1966.

"Rulings" of the Attorney General and Other Lawyers

In the interpretation of existing preservation laws, there is a final source of authority that must be considered for a full understanding of the American preservation system. This is popularly referred to as rulings of the attorney general, who is the principal paid legal advisor in federal and state governments, whose local counterparts are city and county attorneys. These individuals represent the governmental unit in all legal matters, including representation in court. They are the first individuals called upon for legal advice when the meaning of a statute is unclear, when there is a question about the authority of a local preservation commission, and similar matters. While their decisions may be binding as a practical matter, since they must represent the particular unit in any subsequent litigation, their opinions are nothing more or less than that and have no force in a court of law. When asked by a mayor or manager for advice on preservation matters about which there is reasonable room for disagreement, these legal advisors tend to voice opinions that are on the more restrictive or conservative side, positions often not helpful to historic preservation interests.

The Courts as Sources of Law

Any law that was so perfectly written as to apply unambiguously to an infinite variety of situations would be so long and technical that no one could understand it or enforce it. For this and other reasons it is necessary to go to the courts for answers to ascertain the meaning or application of a law when its meaning is unclear or its impact upon an individual property owner is allegedly too heavy. Again, unlike many foreign systems where appeals from administrative decisions to courts tend to be more restrictive, access to the American judicial system in preservation and other matters is relatively open. The principal requirement is that one wishing to enter the fray against a city (for, perhaps, the refusal of a permit) be aggrieved in the sense of having a personal or property interest that has allegedly been damaged or violated.

Generally speaking, American federal and state courts have been favorably disposed to historic preservation interests in a wide variety of situations. From the first U.S. Supreme Court decision in 1896, upholding the right of the federal government to acquire land through eminent domain for the purpose of operating a battlefield memorial, to its most recent preservation decision denying the right of a developer to ruin a historic railroad station by building a skyscraper on top of it, federal courts have yet to deny preservation interests in any significant way. The same has been true of the state courts in dealing with issues arising under state constitutions and state preservation enabling legislation.

There are several issues that have been troublesome for the preservation community. One that lingers on in a small number of states, for example, is whether aesthetic regulations go beyond the permissible limits of state regulatory authority. This was regarded as a major issue in 1966. Since then, most state courts that have faced the question have come to a more modern and positive view holding aesthetic regulation to be permissible under state and federal constitutions. A second issue, one that courts are always careful to look at in individual cases, is whether or not regulations delaying or prohibiting the demolition of historic buildings amounts to the confiscation of property without compensation. All regulations impose some costs upon property owners, but American courts have tended to hold that until such regulations destroy all or nearly all of the owner's right to make any reasonable use of the property, or realize any economic return whatever, they are not invalid. Other issues have been whether or not legislative authority has been improperly delegated to non-legislative bodies without sufficiently detailed standards to limit administrative discretion or couched in terms so vague that the property owner cannot know what conduct is permitted and what is not. Again, the courts have held that even such general standards as not incongruous with the historic character of the area had only to be interpreted by local administrative bodies to be sufficiently specific to pass constitutional muster.

It must be remembered that in the American system, historic district regulations are usually part of a local zoning or related land use regulations, or are treated as if they were. These are issues with which American courts are comfortable. Since most state preservation legislation is post-1966, it has tended, within each state, to be drafted with limits of judicial tolerance in mind. The system thus avoids many vexing issues at the outset. For example, a law authorizing permanent restrictions on the demolition of a listed building through regulation would normally be accompanied by some requirement of financial relief to the owner and the extent of this requirement might be discerned from cases presenting comparable issues. While there are unquestionably many local laws or ordinances on the books throughout the country that would probably not pass constitutional muster, they continue to be enforced. This is partly because many laws enjoy widespread public support, legal or not, and partly because the process of testing them in court can be time-consuming, aggravating and expensive.

It should not be assumed from this that all basic constitutional issues that might be imagined have already been dealt with by courts. For example, it is assumed that the 1st Amendment prohibition against the establishment of a state religion would probably not be interpreted so restrictively as to prevent federal or state grants for the restoration of churches. No final assurance can be given on such matter until a court of last resort has ruled upon the specific issue.

On procedural matters, when it is alleged that a property owner was not given proper notice or that a hearing affecting the owner's property rights was not properly conducted, courts tend to be more rigorous and less favorable to the side of preservation. However, this is more the result of judicial policies that favor the protection of the individual's right to due process of law than any intrinsic bias against preservation. Federal and state environmental laws, which with increasing frequency include historic preservation as a value to be protected, have also tended to be favorable to preservation, but more often than not they turn on issues having more to do with procedural compliance than with substantive values.

Preservation Legislation
Federal Legislation

What the federal government has always done best in the preservation system is to use its vast financial resources to create a climate in which state and local governments can carry out national programs in the national interest. Federal legislation since 1966 has had several major thrusts: (1) the creation of an expanded national registry or official list of cultural resources; (2) the creation of a system of direct and indirect subsidies to assist the owners of historic properties and to engage preservation interests as major players in the private real estate market; (3) the creation of an extensive network of professional preservation activity at the state level; (4) the establishment of federal agencies and processes to review and mitigate the potentially harmful effects of federal and federally sponsored activities on cultural resources; and (5) the establishment of other related programs in the fields of environmental review, housing, transportation and archaeology. It is thought that the Preservation Act of 1966 had a broad base of public support. Actually, it was put in place by a small number of individuals who knew how to work the system.

The National Register continues to expand and the states are accepting more responsibility for nominations having state and local significance. During the last decade direct preservation grants of the early years have been largely replaced by tax credits and the movement privatized to a significant extent as a result. The state network has taken on a life of its own, sometimes challenging federal interests. The project review process established by Section 106 is more sophisticated and stronger, but stewardship of properties owned by or under the jurisdiction of the federal government, while better than 20 years ago, is still far from perfect.

The national survey of historic buildings was commenced under the basic authority of the Historic Sites Act of 1935, which served as the statutory basis for the National Historic Landmarks program as well as the Historic American Buildings Survey and the Historic American Engineering Record (HABS and HAER). These programs are essentially documentation efforts concentrated on properties of national significance. The Preservation Act of 1966 expanded the existing Registry of National Historic Landmarks to create the National Register of Historic Places, which for the first time included properties of state and local significance. The new National Register was to include not only significant buildings, but sites, districts, structures and objects as well. The Register is the official list of places worth preserving. Including properties in districts, there are an estimated 750,000 entries. The inclusion of properties was originally an honorific gesture. Now it not only triggers certain federal protective efforts, but, increasingly, action by state and local governments and the private sector.

The Preservation Act of 1966 authorized direct subsidies to public and private owners of properties included in the Register. Annual allocations under the program for the acquisition and restoration of properties began in 1968, but were never large. Direct grants were discontinued by the Reagan administration in 1981, and congressional appropriations since that time have been used principally to maintain the technical and professional infrastructure of the program, assist state survey and planning efforts and administer the program. Except through the Full Employment Act of 1982, no federal funds have been available as matching grants to preserve the fabric of historic buildings for seven years.

During the early and mid-1960s through the early 1970s, some federal preservation assistance was made available through the U.S. Department of Housing and Urban Development (HUD) by way of urban renewal and community development, planning assistance, urban beautification and open space programs. These provided relatively small amounts of preservation money through direct grant programs, but they were folded into the Community Development Block Grant program in 1974. That program turned authority about how HUD funds were to be spent over to local governing boards concerned with more basic needs for housing, employment and related programs, and with whom the preservation community had less political clout.

The direct grants system began to be replaced with indirect subsidies in the Tax Reform Act of 1976, and by 1981 grants had disappeared almost entirely. The tax incentives were sweetened by the Economic Recovery Tax Act of that year, which substituted a yet more generous 25 percent investment tax credit for the earlier system. The Tax Reform Act of 1986 reduced this subsidy to 20 percent. The federal tax incentive program can only be described as extraordinarily successful in dollars and numbers of projects. Nearly 17,000 projects, valued at $11 billion were carried out between 1976 and 1986. However, a less happy consequence of this privatization of the preservation market through tax subsidies has been that many nonincome producing properties, among them private residences, estates and archaeological sites have been excluded.

The condition for participation in the new 1966 federal program was approval, by the National Park Service, of a state-wide plan for historic preservation, drawn up by each state, spelling out an appropriate preservation philosophy, projecting long and short-term preservation goals and the pulling together of a compendium of existing state legislation and inventory of known historic resources. Also required was an annual work program specifying how the periodic allocations of federal money to the states would be administered by a professional staff headed by a state historic preservation officer (SHPO). The requirement of statewide preservation plans was not particularly new or innovative. In requiring these, the U.S. Congress merely followed a pattern created earlier for such federal-state cooperative efforts as highway building or hospital construction. In recent years these state plans, which were based originally on priorities established by the states, have been dominated by federal planning procedures, which, while building a higher degree of rationality into state programs left less room to accommodate the requirements of state politics and other state priorities and expectations. This shift has been at the center of an increasingly acrid and noisy state-federal debate.

The system contemplated by the Preservation Act of 1966 was based on the idea of a federal-state partnership. In it, the federal government would establish national standards and guidelines for preservation to maintain the integrity of the National Register, while state governments would conduct statewide surveys and inventories and feed nominations into the Register. For survey and planning work, states received 50 percent matching grants, later increased to 75 percent. As time passed they took on added responsibilities for environmental review and the processing and certification of private sector projects stimulated by the 1976 tax incentives program. Under the 1966 Act National Register nominations might originate anywhere, that is in a federal agency, a local preservation group or property owner or some other source. However, the principal filter through which all nominations had to pass was a state professional review board, presided over by a state historic preservation officer appointed by the governor of each state.

The program was a magnificent conception, but in recent years it has begun to show signs of strain. Since 1966, the work required of state historic preservation offices has grown significantly. The conduct of the statewide surveys, National Register nominations, administration of the federal tax incentives and environmental review programs, in addition to state-mandated programs and assistance to local governments and private groups, has outstripped the capabilities of state staffs. The federal government has established increasingly higher standards for planning and administration, but federal funds for staff support have not matched the increase in work requirements. Some of the states, observing federal program limitations in recent years, tended to cut their own appropriations as a response. Presently there is tension between state and federal preservation agencies, each of which is doing its job in an entirely commendable way. How these tensions will be resolved is, as yet, unclear.

The Preservation Act of 1966 also established the Advisory Council on Historic Preservation to monitor the impact of federal activities on National Register properties. This was to be an independent agency of the executive branch, comprised mostly of cabinet members and Presidential appointees who would consider any potentially harmful effects of federal projects on National Register property. These comments would, it was hoped, be taken into account by the sponsor agency. In recent years the Advisory Council's review-and-comment process, presided over by a professional staff, has evolved into more of a mediation process. Its membership has become more broadly representative of the preservation movement itself. The Council was, also, given other duties in the 1966 Act, mostly to serve as the eyes, ears and conscience of the preservation movement.

In some respects the Advisory Council might be viewed as an offshoot of the consumer movement of the 1960s, depending for its effectiveness on public or political reaction to the enforced disclosure of projected harmful impacts on historic resources rather like labeling the harmful ingredients in a food product. The Section 106 procedures are roughly akin to those of the Environmental Policy Act of 1969, which covers preservation in addition to environmental values. However, since the Advisory Council has developed a legally enforceable mitigation process, it tends to achieve a somewhat better result than the Environmental Policy Act's processes, which are basically limited to disclosure. Section 106 does not occur in any case unless there is federal involvement in a particular project. Also, at the conclusion of the process there are no sanctions, the law providing only the authority to require that the rather elaborate commenting process itself be completed.

A somewhat stronger approach than Section 106 of the Preservation Act of 1966 is found in Section 4(f) of the Transportation Act of 1966, which prohibits the use of parks, wildlife refuges and historic sites for transportation projects unless there is no feasible and prudent alternative, and unless there has been "all possible planning to minimize harm" from such use. As interpreted by the courts in a number of decisions, these are high standards indeed. In 1966, National Historic Landmarks were folded into the National Register as properties of national significance, which did not provide them with special status over and above other National Register entries. The requirement of special planning steps to minimize harm was included in the 1980 amendments to the 1966 Act to provide an extra measure of protection for National Historic Landmarks.

A final aspect of the developing federal program which began as the 1971 Executive Order 11593 was intended to require the federal government itself to act as a more responsible steward of its own properties. It required the head of every federal agency to identify and nominate eligible properties to the National Register, to maintain them and to insure that, if disposed of, adequate measures were taken to insure their preservation. The response of federal agencies has been reasonably good but uneven from the beginning. Executive Order

11593 was elevated from executive order to law by the 1980 amendments to the 1966 Act. These stewardship responsibilities related to those of the Federal Surplus Property Act of 1949 and the Public Buildings Cooperative Use Act of 1976, requiring special attention to preservation values in the acquisition, leasing, management and disposal of federal historic property.

Federal housing and agriculture programs have had profound effects on the preservation of cultural resources. The devastating effects of post-World War II slum clearance, dam building and highway construction programs are common knowledge. Increasingly sensitive to these criticisms, federal legislation of the first half of the 1960s attempted in small but important ways to deal with the preservation problem. Important preservation studies demonstrating the linkage between preservation and housing and urban revitalization activities were completed. Those in Providence, Rhode Island, and New Orleans, Louisiana, had considerable educational value for other cities. The Model Cities Act of 1966 recognized historic preservation activities as proper to urban renewal projects. By this time a number of preservation-related HUD programs of urban beautification, open space and the like were also in place. However, so many federal categorical grant programs were created during Lyndon B. Johnson's presidency (1964–68) that coordination among them became a major issue. In the early 1970s various revenue sharing and block grant programs began to replace them but were a mixed blessing for preservation. Some housing assistance programs were capable of being used for the rehabilitation of existing dwellings, while the HUD community development programs had potential for encouraging neighborhood preservation and revitalization. But under the 1974 Community Development Block Grant program, ultimate decision-making regarding the expenditure of federal funds was placed with local governing boards. But these inclined strongly to favor development and meeting basic human needs over preservation.

The federal position on archaeology has changed very much since 1966. The focus of the American preservation movement since its inception in the mid-19th century tended to be on buildings, and, in recent years, on neighborhoods and larger areas. Nonetheless, federal preservation initiatives really began with archaeology at the turn of the century, and the two movements have been close partners since the beginning. Motivated in part by the depredations of pot hunters on Indian lands in the Southwest, the Antiquities Act of 1906 authorized the president to designate certain federal lands as historic monuments, within which a permit for archaeological excavation would be required. The next step to protect archaeological resources was not taken until 1949, when the Reservoir Salvage Act was passed. This required no more than the survey and reporting of archaeological finds on federal dam projects to the Secretary of the Interior. However, the National Park Service had little in the way of funds for archaeological salvage projects. The Moss-Bennett Act of 1974 authorized the expenditure of up to 1 percent of project costs for data recovery. The Archeological Resource Protection Act of 1979, replacing the Antiquities Act of 1906, established the present permit system for the investigation and removal of archaeological resources on federal lands and their entry into interstate commerce, with heavy criminal penalties for violation. Archaeological remains are, of course, routinely entered into the National Register of Historic Places, although they constitute a relatively small percentage of entries.

26

State Preservation Legislation

There is a tendency to think that state historic preservation programs were the result of the Preservation Act of 1966. Not so. All but a handful of states already had preservation programs in 1966, a few admittedly being limited. Change in state preservation programs since then has been more in size than in substance. Again it must be remembered that as sovereign units of government, each state program has the potential to be exactly what it wishes to be and, if need be, differs in both substance and extent from other state programs. While there may be 50 different state preservation programs, there are common elements among them all.

Within state governments, historic preservation programs have been lodged at the cabinet level or just under it. Arrangements vary widely. In some, mostly in the eastern United States, they exist as independent agencies or commissions or they are combined with state archives or museum programs. In the Midwest and the West, they tend to be associated with state departments of natural resources, parks or outdoor recreation or, occasionally, with a department of transportation. In a few situations, they are run by a state-chartered, quasi-public corporation or historical association. There is typically an advisory board or commission, sometimes with rule-making authority, appointed by the governor. Directors of state agencies are also usually appointed by the governor or by a cabinet secretary. While they serve at the highest level of the civil service system and may be protected by it to some extent, their decisions regarding what is to be saved, and how, are almost always politically sensitive. In this respect, they are always vulnerable.

Pre-1966, state programs tended to focus on the operation of state museum, historic site and highway marker programs. Where state appropriations were available for local projects, administrative, supervisory and technical services were also provided. Historical research and publications, archaeological surveys and the maintenance of statewide inventories and state registers of historic buildings were also sometimes undertaken by individual states.

In addition to operating statewide programs, the states also authorized local governments to undertake their own historic preservation programs. A few states authorized cities or counties to pass historic district or landmark regulations, either through a direct delegation of the state's police power or through home-rule charters. Some authorized the expenditure of local funds for preservation activities or made state funds available for this purpose. During the late 60s and 70s, many states passed state-level environmental protection laws not unlike the Environmental Protection Act of 1969 in their application to buildings and places of historical and archaeological importance. After the mid-70s and the growing importance of the private sector in preservation, a number of states authorized tax breaks for preservation projects in the form of credits against state income tax levies or against local property taxes. A number of states passed legislation making it easier to use various forms of preservation easements and deed restrictions as aids in the execution of preservation programs.

As was hoped by the planners of the 1966 national program, extensive and significant changes in state legislation and programs came about during the following 20 years in response to the Preservation Act of 1966. Chief among these was the appointment in every state of a SHPO to administer the program, including the preparation of a statewide preservation plan, the execution of a statewide inventory, the nomination of properties to the National Register, participation in the review process established by Section 106, and certification of properties and projects to qualify for the tax incentives established by federal laws in 1976 and 1981.

New state legislative initiatives, while ultimately based on the political and fiscal situation in each state, tended over the years to be copied from one another, or based upon model legislation provided by the Advisory Council on Historic Preservation. Increasingly, the listing of a property or district in the National Register triggered a state-level protective response. A number of states, for example, have enacted legislation providing that no state-funded or state-licensed project having an adverse impact on a National Register property may proceed without state-level review akin to that provided under Section 106 of the federal legislation. Similarly, properties in the National Register may be protected under state coastal zone or other regional or state-level environmental protection laws.

Before 1966, state preservation programs might for the most part have been characterized by their limited scope and their diversity in size, content and approach. By 1986, however, these same state programs are now essentially similar in content and purpose. They are led or driven, as some state preservation officials would put it, by the incentives, direction and philosophy of the national program. It is safe to say that all state programs are now substantially dependent on continued federal program funding.

Local Preservation Legislation

The starting point for an overview of local preservation legislation as part of the larger system is to recall that cities are created by the state and that generally they have only those powers specifically granted to them by the state. They must not only stick to the substance of what they are authorized to do, but also to do it exactly in the manner prescribed by law. They have been authorized to appropriate funds for a wide variety of preservation purposes and to spend the same; to acquire, restore, manage and dispose of property; and to adopt a wide range of regulatory measures. As is the case with state governments, almost everything done in the name of preservation will involve one or more of these powers, usually in combination.

There is, of course, no way to account for the amount of local government spending on preservation activities; records of this kind are simply not kept. Suffice it to say that there has been a substantial increase over the last 20 years as a result of the need to match federal, and often state, grants for preservation. Indirect subsidies in the form of relief from local property taxes have been authorized in more than 12 states. Where preservation and neighborhood revitalization schemes have been undertaken, public subsidies for both preservation and infra-structure facilities and improvements has been common. However, the role of local governments in preservation, especially during the last decade beginning with the HUD Community Development Block Grants and Urban Development Action Grants, has been a mixed bag. Cities have often been willing to sacrifice important historic buildings for a new civic center, for more municipal parking or a new city hall. Here a distinction may be drawn between what a city is legally authorized to do, on the one hand, and what it is politically willing to do on the other. This has given rise to the assertion that what happens in state capitals and in Washington is not much help from a preservation standpoint unless there is strong political support at the local level.

From a regulatory standpoint, the most widely used preservation tool has been the historic district or landmark ordinance. In 1966 there were probably fewer than two dozen such ordinances in effect in American cities. Presently, the number is probably pushing 2,000, most of these having been adopted within the last decade. Few, cities have ever repealed such an ordinance. It seems reasonable to assume that the number using them will continue to increase rapidly in the future. This will be especially so if federal and state financial assistance for preservation diminishes with time and there is a correspondingly greater need to approach preservation through the less expensive route of uncompensated regulation.

While no two historic district or landmark ordinances are exactly alike, there is a common thread running through them. Typically they involve the creation of a separate historic district commission, sometimes called a preservation or landmarks commission, comprised of a few knowledgeable preservation specialists and citizens. They are appointed by the governing body to draft regulations and to recommend them and the boundaries of the district to the governing board for adoption, either as a special zoning district or as a separate ordinance. When adopted, the regulations are applied to all properties within the district or to those designated as individual landmarks, and these may not thereafter be altered, demolished or moved without approval of the commission. Such approval is in the form of a certificate attesting to the appropriateness of the owner's plans and proposals, usually required before other zoning and building permits may be applied for.

People may reasonably disagree about such regulations. Conservatives argue that in theory they burden the artifacts that reflect the traditions of a free enterprise society and that in practice they tend to trample over the basic constitutional guarantees of the individual property owner. Others say that they are essentially benign, in the sense that they do not come into play until the owner proposes to do something with a property. The regulations do not protect valuable interiors, and hardship variances, rightly or wrongly, are all too easy to obtain. Architects are not infrequently heard to assert that the regulations stifle innovation in design. Landmark ordinances, which apply to individually designated historic properties, have been subject to the same criticisms.

Perhaps a more telling criticism of preservation at the local level is that even now, in 1987, preservation remains at the fringe of local government conservation and development processes in many cities. Preservation issues are treated essentially as aesthetic issues, by a separate historic district or preservation commission, rather than as part and parcel of the more compelling land use and development problems, which are dealt with by planning agencies located closer to the heart of local government and its political processes.

The basic authorities needed for a traditional municipal preservation program would include a historic district and landmarks ordinance, provision for the appropriation and expenditure of funds for historic house museum operations and the authority to engage in or support the work of local citizens and groups engaged in preservation work. How much more would be needed depends on the local program. If, for example, the local preservation program is coordinated with neighborhood conservation efforts, a wide variety of other regulations would come immediately into play. A list of these would include the use, density, off-street parking and other requirements of the local zoning ordinance; the building code governing new construction; and the housing code establishing minimum standards for dwellings. Still others would be nuisance control and abatement ordinances, sign and billboard regulations and controls covering sanitation, the protection and maintenance of trees and noise.

Fiscal support from a city might be as uncomplicated as periodic direct appropriations to support the work of local preservation groups or individuals. Or it might be as elaborate and sophisticated as that of a partner in revolving fund activities, or as a participant or guarantor of neighborhood housing improvement schemes. As noted earlier, cities may not only be authorized to make direct grants or loans for preservation and restoration work, they are able in a growing number of states to offer indirect incentives in the form of tax concessions to the owners of listed buildings for rehabilitation and preservation work.

A general criticism of local programs is that too much reliance tends to be placed on a limited range of regulations, thereby missing the opportunity to deal in a coordinated way with building, housing, area and neighborhood revitalization, zoning, site planning and other planning and land use controls that should be integrated to achieve significant environmental results. There are notable exceptions to such criticisms throughout the United States and while they are partly a function of a city's size, resources and the sophistication of the local planning system, they are valid, mainly. Whether this situation will change as the result of the new Certified Local Government Program is conjectural.

The Actors

It is often said that the American government is one of laws, not men. But we know that there is always a substantial gap between the law in books and the law in action, and the difference is people. We know instinctively that the outcomes of preservation plans and controversies often reflect the personal and professional biases of the men and women who run the programs, their position in the federal-state-local hierarchy, and their institutional affiliations. For this reason it is important to close this introductory chapter with a brief description of some of these individuals and organizations and their relationships with one another.

In 1966 there were probably no more than 800 individuals employed full-time in preservation programs throughout the country. A reasonable estimate would put that figure at more than 8,000 today—a one hundred-fold increase. The number of organizations with which these individuals are affiliated has also grown. For sake of convenience they can be grouped into several categories, most of which exist at all three levels of government. In general they can be categorized as (1) official bodies created by law to administer particular programs, (2) quasi-public organizations with a public purpose, usually receiving some form of direct government subsidy, (3) specialized preservation organizations, (4) professional interest organizations, and (5) subject-oriented groups. No other country in the world sustains such varied public and private involvement in preservation.

The Washington Preservation Mafia

Since 1966 and until recently, preservation leadership and authority have concentrated in the capital city, Washington, D.C., although it is now spreading throughout the country.

The American equivalent of the European monuments bureau, the National Park Service, has been lodged in the U.S. Department of the Interior ever since its creation in 1916, except for the brief interlude of 1976–1980, when it existed as a separate entity within the U.S. Department of the Interior. Its principal mission was to establish standards and guidelines for the implementation of a national preservation program in partnership with the states. The National Register, the Secretary of the Interior's Standards for Rehabilitation and the standards for planning and archaeology, represent for all practical purposes, the essentials of acceptable preservation practice throughout the country. Notwithstanding the explosive growth in the number and extent of the Park Service's preservation responsibilities since 1966, especially as a result of the tax incentives program, it stands in size and organization now about as it did then. The core of its professional staff is historians, architectural historians, historical architects and archaeologists, numbering in all about 500, including those at 9 regional offices throughout the country.

The location of the national preservation program within the Park Service has been both a blessing and a curse. It is a blessing in the sense that the Park Service is probably the single most popular branch of national government in terms of public support, but a curse in the sense that the Park Service has never regarded historic preservation as its primary mission.

If the Park Service is the standard setter of the national preservation effort, its conscience is the Advisory Council on Historic Preservation, whose mandate stems largely from Section 106 of the Preservation Act of 1966 and other policy and leadership responsibilities assigned to it by Congress. The staff of the Advisory Council has generally the same professional makeup as that of the Park Service, but is somewhat smaller in number. It exists not as a bureau within a larger service or department, but as an independent agency of the executive branch. Since membership in the 19-member Council is by presidential appointment, except for a number of ex officio positions, administration policies and policy changes occasionally come to the fore, even though it has, for all of its history, been essentially apolitical. Even though the Advisory Council has never had a save-everything philosophy, it has in recent years become more representative in its membership of preservation interests.

A third federal government agency that has made substantial contributions to the American preservation movement, although rarely credited with having done so, is the National Endowment for the Arts. It is a branch of the National Endowment for the Arts and Humanities, created by Congress in 1965 for the purpose of providing federal subsidies for arts and humanities projects. Hundreds of its projects have directly or indirectly supported preservation. These have taken most often the form of demonstration projects, books and monographs, films, exhibits and other programs related to the environmental arts and design.

Of nongovernmental organizations (NGOs), that is organizations that are essentially private but funded in part by the government in recognition of their public purposes and objectives, there are the United States Committee of the International Council on Monuments and Sites (US/ICOMOS) and the National Trust for Historic Preservation. US/ICOMOS is a small membership organization comprised for the most part of preservation professionals. It receives a small subsidy through the National Park Service in support of the World Heritage program, for other international programs and for its advisory and technical services. It has a cooperative agreement with the National Park Service and a number of international student and professional technical exchange and training programs.

The largest of the NGOs is the National Trust for Historic Preservation, chartered by Congress in 1949 to facilitate public participation in the preservation movement. Notwithstanding that it is a private member organization, it receives approximately $4 million annually on average from the U.S. Congress in support of what in 1985 was a $17 million budget. Most of its income is received from membership dues, gifts, endowments, tours and contractual services. Unlike national trusts in other countries, it owns and operates relatively few museum properties, concentrating instead on publications and organizational services to members and member organizations and is governed by a Board of Trustees. It maintains regional offices in Denver, Colorado; Charleston, South Carolina; Boston, Massachusetts; Chicago, Illinois; San Francisco, California; Philadelphia, Pennsylvania; and Fort Worth, Texas.

Washington is also the seat of a number of private preservation organizations. Among the best known and most energetic of these is Preservation Action, which since 1974 has carried on an extensive and successful lobbying effort in the U.S. Congress on behalf of preservation. There is also the Americans for Historic Preservation, a political action committee that directly supports congressional candidates who are strong preservation advocates. The National Conference of State Historic Preservation Officers represents the collective interests of state programs. The National Council of Preservation Executives represents occupational and preservation interests of the executive directors and leaders of state and local preservation organizations. The National Center for Preservation Law provides a weekly service updating legal matters related to preservation. The National Alliance of Preservation Commissions provides a newsletter and other educational services to local members of historic district and landmarks commissions. Partners for Liveable Places is a coalition of design professionals and organizations from a variety of fields who are advocates for the amenities as an essential aspect of public life. Corresponding perhaps more closely than other American organizations to the British Civic Trusts, Partners has been a constant and effective advocate for preservation since its establishment in 1977. Most of these organizations run on relatively small budgets and have small staffs. However, in their areas of specialty they are lean and effective.

As might be expected, the individual professions whose members' work directly involves them in historic preservation all have strong support programs. These include the American Institute of Architects, whose Historic Resources Committee will celebrate its 100th birthday in 1990; others are the Society of Architectural Historians, the Association for Preservation Technology, the Society for American Archeology and the American Society of Landscape Architects. Interest in landscape preservation prompted the formation in 1978 of a multi-disciplinary Alliance for Historic Landscape Preservation. All of these groups sponsor journals or publications, periodic meetings and seminars and other educational programs for their members and the public. Historians involved in preservation activities would normally identify with the American Historical Association, the National Council on Public History and the American Association of State and Local History.

It is no secret that Americans have a special tendency to join and support organizations that promote their personal interests. In the field of preservation, a list of such organizations would include the Victorian Society of America, the Friends of Cast Iron Architecture, the Friends of Terra Cotta, the Society for Commercial Archeology, the Society for Industrial Archeology, the Vernacular Architecture Forum and the League of Historic American Theatres. Many, many more could be added.

People and Organizations at the State and Local Level

The official state representatives of the preservation movement tend to be the upper level policy members of the SHPO's staff, and, state-level arts agencies that have an interest in architectural preservation. State chapters of national organizations, such as the American Institute of Architects and the Society of Architectural Historians, also provide input into state preservation plans, policies and programs. The SHPO is regarded as the leader of the movement in individual states, although as the result of the officer's delicate political situation, discussed earlier, there are exceptions to this.

The great majority of states now have private statewide historic preservation organizations equivalent to the National Trust. They sponsor state-level educational meetings, sponsor and lobby for legislation, publish newsletters, provide technical and leadership training for their members and sometimes support or oppose candidates for state elective office. In the West, statewide programs in Oregon and Utah have long been regarded as strong. In the Midwest, the Historic Indiana Landmarks Foundation is widely respected; and in the East, the programs in Florida, Georgia, North Carolina, New York and Maine are often emulated. These are organizations with many members. The first statewide revolving fund was established in North Carolina in 1975. It has been involved with more than 85 properties and generated more than $12 million in preservation work since its founding. It works closely with local preservation revolving funds and also serves as the statewide preservation education and promotional organization as the result of a merger in 1982 with the state's older Antiquities Society. Active statewide revolving funds, a recent phenomenon, now exist in eight states.

Locally, the official representatives of the movement are often the preservation commission and the local historical or preservation society. There are now approaching 2,000 commissions around the country. There are approximately 4,000 private societies, many of them formed in response to a crisis involving threats or demolition of a favorite local building. Except in large cities, organizations on the local government level depend more on volunteers than professional preservationists.

Networks

The informal networks among these individuals and organizations are as important as formal lines of communication. In Washington, for example, the leaders of the movement meet monthly at the Arts Club on Pennsylvania Avenue for lunch, to exchange gossip send up trial balloons and to pass along and receive news and information about political and other developments of interest to the preservation community. There is no fixed agenda, no dues, no membership formalities. These events and the invitation list are managed informally by a few senior members of the national preservation leadership who divide administrative tasks among themselves from time to time. It is no less real for being informal. Those not invited know that they are on the outside of things and sometimes speak of it. This informal management and direction of a movement by a few senior insiders or elders is not limited to Washington, D.C., but it is reported as a rather common phenomenon in many state capitals and local areas. In such instances a few individuals are seen as core members who always manage to get things done. In the case of a movement where volunteer leadership and political skills are important, however, this kind of insider participation and involvement is not necessarily a bad thing.

It happens frequently in America that a crisis atmosphere is precipitated by real or perceived threats to an important building or buildings. The informal protest movement that follows may lead to the formation of a historical society, which, in turn, takes on a permanent activist coloration as threats continue or recur. In time an ordinance is passed and the activist members of the community are appointed to the official commission. This is seen by the larger community as representing preservation values to the exclusion of others. In time, investment and development communities come to understand that their best protection is personal involvement in both the official and the unofficial preservation structures, leading to yet other kinds of struggles for influence. This story, with variations, is told in local communities throughout the country. In small communities, with limited access to professional preservation skills, politics and emotion tend to drive the movement. How this pattern plays out as the preservation movement becomes less national and more local will be interesting to observe.

CHAPTER TWO

The Federal Government as Standard Bearer

JOHN M. FOWLER

THE FEDERAL GOVERNMENT AS STANDARD BEARER

JOHN M. FOWLER

Introduction

The partnership that lies at the heart of the historic preservation program in the United States traces its origins to the earliest efforts of the federal government to establish their role in protecting historic properties. The current blend of federal, state and local government activity, which guides and encourages private citizens, businesses and organizations in day-to-day preservation, evolved from the initial leadership role that the federal government assumed in historic preservation. After its inception in the 19th century, that role expanded and changed to reflect the maturing preservation consciousness of the American people. Likewise, the involvement of the federal government and its relation to the other players developed in response to the changing forces that spur historic preservation in the United States. In many ways, the evolution of the federal role is a mirror of the past century's growth in historic preservation.

The Federal Role Before 1966

While the earliest efforts of the federal government to protect historically significant sites can be traced to the establishment of Yellowstone National Park in 1872, the concept of a truly national approach to preservation did not emerge until early in this century. Federal activity prior to 1906 was primarily limited to the preservation of Casa Grande, an ancient Indian ruin in Arizona, and the acquisition of Civil War battlefields to ensure their permanent protection. While limited in scope, it formed the basis for later development of the federal role in historic preservation. However, it was far removed from today's comprehensive effort to preserve a broad range of historic properties throughout the nation.

At that time, federal involvement had three notable characteristics. Firstly, the federal government concerned itself solely with properties of significance to the nation as a whole, an emphasis that ebbs and flows throughout the history of the preservation program. Secondly, attention focused exclusively on sites of military or prehistoric interest, limiting the impact on historic resources. Fortunately, this was simply a stage, one that is repeated as the federal government from time to time responds to threats to a particular kind of historic property. Thirdly, the sole preservation technique employed was federal ownership, which could not be expected to have bearing in shaping a broad-based program for preserving the full range of significant historic properties in the United States.

Antiquities Act of 1906

Responding to increasing destruction of prehistoric sites in the Southwest, the U.S. Congress in 1906 enacted the nation's first general historic preservation legislation. The Antiquities Act of 1906 authorizes the President to designate as national monuments "historic landmarks, historic and prehistoric structures, and other objects of historic or scientific interest" situated on federal lands. Such monuments would be set aside for federal protection. The act authorizes the government to accept donations of private lands, but confers no other acquisition authority. In addition to the protection afforded designated monuments, the act also established a permit system for the excavation of archaeological sites and the collection of artifacts on federal lands.

The Antiquities Act of 1906 continued several of the 19th-century characteristics of federal preservation activity. Protection of nationally significant sites, primarily of prehistoric interest, through government ownership was at the core of the legislation. However, the act did introduce an important innovation that is central to the federal government's role in preservation today. Prior to the act, the U.S. Congress, by individual laws establishing protected areas, had exercised the power to determine which historic properties warranted protection. Now the act entrusted the president with such determinations. This transfer of authority from the legislative to the executive branch was essential to establishing a program to identify the full range of historic resources. Reaffirmed in subsequent preservation legislation, the basic concept of executive branch responsibility eventually evolved into today's administrative system for the identification, evaluation and designation of a historic property.

The National Park Service Established, 1916

The U.S. Congress established the National Park Service as a separate bureau in the U.S. Department of the Interior in 1916. Its initial mission and continuing focus was the administration of the national park system, which in time included the majority of properties owned by the federal government and designated historic. While the 1916 legislation contained no new provisions for preservation, it is key to the shape of today's federal involvement in historic preservation. As subsequent legislation expanded the scope of the federal role, primary administrative functions were entrusted to the Secretary of the Interior and delegated to the National Park Service.

The National Park Service has had the central role in administering the national historic preservation program since passage of the National Historic Preservation Act of 1966. Its traditional role as custodian of the national parks contributed to the quality of its professional leadership, although its dual responsibility of property management and external program administration have inherent contradictions that frequently surface. Nevertheless, the current national preservation program and the federal government's role in it is largely the product of almost three-quarters of a century of National Park Service leadership and administration.

The Historic Sites Act of 1935

The Historic Sites Act of 1935 further committed the federal government to historic preservation, advancing the national program in several significant ways. In this act, the U.S. Congress first articulated a national policy of historic preservation:

> It is declared that it is a national policy to preserve for public use historic sites, buildings, and objects of national significance for the inspiration and benefit of the people of the United States.

Viewed 50 years later, this statement, along with the substance of the act, is significant for its characterization of the federal role. The act continued the concept of national significance as the touchstone for concern. This notion, that the national government should consider only those properties of national significance, was embodied in previous laws and changed only with the advent of the Preservation Act of 1966. Failure of the federal government to be sensitive to historic properties significant at the state and local level contributed to the massive loss of historic buildings and sites in the post-World War II period of widespread highway and dam construction, urban renewal and suburban development.

The policy declaration and primary provisions of the Historic Sites Act of 1935 also perpetuated the policy of public ownership as the primary federal tool for preserving significant properties, but public acquisition of historic properties in the 1930s, the years of the Great Depression, was not an act frequently employed. Hence the federal impact on preservation remained limited.

Where the Historic Sites Act did have an important long-term impact on the federal role in preservation was the creation of the administrative infrastructure. Responding to the need to provide work for architects, historians and related professionals during the Great Depression, the act directed the Secretary of the Interior to:

> • Secure, collate and preserve drawings, plans, photographs and data of historic and archaeologic sites, buildings and objects.
> • Make a survey of historic and archaeologic sites, buildings and objects for the purpose of determining which possess exceptional value as commemorating or illustrating the history of the United States.
> • Make necessary investigations and researches in the United States relating to particular sites, buildings, or objects to obtain true and accurate archeological facts and information concerning same.

This continued and expanded the concept of executive responsibility for historic properties that was first established in the Antiquities Act of 1906, and became the foundation of today's federal preservation program. An immediate consequence was the creation of the National Survey of Historic Sites and

Buildings in 1937, to identify and evaluate nationally significant properties on the basis of themes in American history. Another was the establishment of the Historic American Buildings Survey, a comprehensive effort to record the nation's historic structures through measured drawings and photographs.

The programs initiated under the Historic Sites Act of 1935 have a dual significance for current preservation activities. At one level, the administrative apparatus to carry out these duties shaped, and in some cases developed into, the organizational components that carry out the program today. The National Survey spawned the National Register program when legislation in 1966 expanded the scope of the federal government's concern for historic properties. The Historic American Buildings Survey recently celebrated its 50th birthday and in 1969 founded the Historic American Engineering Record, modeled after HABS, to record the nation's engineering heritage. More importantly, the organizational structures, and often the veteran personnel, were used to put new preservation programs of the National Park Service into operation.

At a slightly different level of impact, the methodology, standards and criteria developed to implement the Historic Sites Act of 1935 formed the basis for the practices followed today. For example, a comparison of the criteria of evaluation established for the 1937 National Survey bears a remarkable resemblance to those used today for the National Register of Historic Places.

Federal Government Initiatives, 1935–66

The period between 1935 and 1966 witnessed few new federal laws or advancement of the federal government's role in preservation. The impetus given by the 1935 legislation and the employment programs of the Great Depression which supported historic preservation was overcome by the exigencies of World War II. Then, during the economic boom that followed, little attention was paid to expanding the government's role in historic preservation. In 1949, however, at the behest of the National Park Service and others, the U.S. Congress passed legislation chartering the National Trust for Historic Preservation. It was an important step toward today's program, and one supplementing the federal role but not directly affecting it. The creation of the National Trust was intended to provide a focal point for stimulating public involvement in preservation, through educational programs and the management of historic properties. This reliance on the private sector throughout the 1950s and into the 1960s was characteristic of preservation in the United States, with the federal role remaining narrowly limited to programs identifying, commemorating and documenting nationally significant properties.

By 1960, there was growing awareness of the shortcomings of the national historic preservation program, notably its failure to stem destruction resulting from unprecedented post-war economic growth. That year a modest attempt was made to compensate for these losses when the Reservoir Salvage Act of 1960 required federal agencies responsible for constructing dams and reservoirs to notify the Secretary of the Interior when significant archaeological data was likely to be lost as a consequence. The Secretary was then authorized to undertake appropriate data recovery, although there was no mechanism to stave off destruction nor were there any significant amounts of money authorized to conduct the salvage work. While admittedly a step forward, the Salvage Act was a modest one. Within a few years the preservation community was clamoring for more comprehensive legislation to protect historic properties, as well as for substantial changes to the 1960 legislation itself.

The National Historic Preservation Act of 1966

Spurred by public reaction to the widespread destruction of historic properties by urban renewal, the interstate highway system and other massive public works projects in the 1950s and 1960s, the National Historic Preservation Act became law on October 15, 1966. The first comprehensive historic preservation legislation in 31 years, the act built upon the existing federal program and created new tools for shaping the course of historic preservation in the United States.

Major amendments in 1980 refined these tools and continued the evolution of the national program. Today the partnership of federal, state and local government, allied with the private sector, is firmly grounded in the legislative provisions of the Preservation Act of 1966. It is a fundamental characteristic of historic preservation in this country.

The act brought numerous innovations to the national historic preservation program, while retaining many of the administrative characteristics that developed over the preceding 60 years. Continuity in the federal program is most notable in the continuing role of the National Park Service as principal administrator of the federal government's preservation responsibilities. For the most part, the new authorities of the act were entrusted to the existing administrative apparatus, which expanded to meet the challenge. Thus, the Office of Archeology and Historic Preservation (known as OAHP) was formed within the National Park Service in 1967. Support centers, such as state and federal historic preservation offices and recently certified local governments, were added in time to create today's structure.

On the other hand, the tools introduced in the Preservation Act of 1966 represented dramatic departures from prior federal practice. An examination of the act's purposes and policies reveals both the philosophical basis and the degree of innovation in its substantive provisions.

Recognizing that the rate of loss of historic properties was on the rise, the U.S. Congress committed the federal government to accelerating its preservation programs "to give maximum encouragement to agencies and individuals undertaking preservation by private means, and to assist State and local governments . . . to expand and accelerate their historic preservation programs and activities."

Likewise the Preservation Act of 1966 reflected a more sophisticated understanding of historic preservation, the resources that make up the nation's cultural patrimony and their relation to the forces that shape modern society. This undertaking was manifested in several ways. Firstly, the act recognized a far broader range of properties as worthy of protection than had previous legislation. Similarly, concern for properties of historic and archaeological significance now included those of cultural value. Expressed more concretely in the substance of the act, this expanded scope dramatically changed the impact of the national program.

The second major change expressed in the policy and carried out by the provisions of the Preservation Act of 1966 was the introduction of a new rationale for historic preservation. Prior legislation referred to the need for federal participation in preservation to maintain historic properties in public use for the inspiration and benefit of the people. This philosophy, and the accompanying laws, limited the federal role largely to maintaining significant properties as parks, museums and monuments. The act pronounced that "the historical and cultural foundations of the Nation should be preserved as a living part of our community life and development in order to give a sense of orientation to the American people." Underlying this statement was the notion that the federal government should move beyond the traditional limits of its preservation activity and seek to ensure the continued use of historic properties as a vital and active part of contemporary society. Again, the substantive provisions of the act translated this philosophy into action and gave a major impetus to preservation in the United States.

It is worth noting that the 1966 preservation legislation was enacted during a period of a general awakening of concern for the environment in the nation. Signed into law the same day was another law, the Department of Transportation Act of 1966, establishing stringent safeguards for a wide range of natural and cultural resources. Three years later the U.S. Congress passed the National Environmental Policy Act of 1969, establishing a national policy to protect the environment. The broad approach of the Preservation Act of 1966 to conserving the wide range of historic resources reflects similar efforts to protect air and water quality, endangered species, parkland, wildlife refuges and the like. These initiatives indicated widespread concern in the 1960s and 1970s over the destruction of resources which had accompanied the unprecedented development of the postwar period. With this rising consciousness, the historic preservation movement adopted a view of the cultural environment as a living organism, requiring care and nurturing to maintain its vitality, a philosophical view that shaped the 1966 Act and transformed both the role and conduct of the federal government toward historic properties.

The federal government now assumed a role of leadership and support for the historic preservation movement. Employing the new techniques provided by the Preservation Act of 1966 and endowed with relatively substantial resources (at least in preservation terms), the federal program over the past 20 years gradually reshaped the course of historic preservation in the United States. Through incentives, standards, criteria and regulation, the federal government influenced preservation activities conducted by state and local government as well as the private sector. While most of the preservation undertaken during this period was by the private sector, the impact of the federal government was and continues to be pervasive. Examination of the current federal program reveals the extent and the nature of this influence. Its basic elements are found in the 1966 preservation and environmental legislation, with embellishments and refinements stemming from subsequent amendments.

The Federal Role Today

The Preservation Act of 1966 established a leadership role in the national historic preservation program for the federal government, organized around functions of identifying properties, establishing professional criteria and standards, providing incentives for rehabilitation and restoration, and protecting historic properties from harm. With some interpretation and legislative amplification, these responsibilities remain essential components of today's program. As the program took shape, it also significantly affected the structure of state and local government involvement in historic preservation, and it may be the most lasting and far-reaching achievement of the federal historic preservation program.

The Preservation Act of 1966 has been amended seven times since being first passed, major improvements occurring in 1976 and 1980. Five amendments dealt primarily with funding and relatively minor technical adjustments. Also, President Richard M. Nixon issued Executive Order 11593, entitled "Protection and Enhancement of the Cultural Environment," on May 13, 1971, to remedy certain shortcomings of the act, primarily pertaining to management of historic properties owned by the federal government. This important executive order was in fact incorporated in later amendments to the 1966 act.

The Federal Participants

The principal actors in the federal program today are the Secretary of the Interior, whose preservation responsibilities are carried out by the National Park Service; the Advisory Council on Historic Preservation, an independent federal agency; and the various federal agencies that own or control historic properties or undertake activities that affect historic resources outside federal ownership. Each of these players has specified responsibilities in the program, usually distinct, but occasionally overlapping and virtually always affecting the actions of nonfederal entities.

Most of the federal responsibilities are entrusted to the Secretary of the Interior. After the creation of the National Park Service in 1916, the Secretary delegated those duties to the director of the Park Service, who, in turn, created the necessary administrative apparatus. Over the years, the structure of the bureaucracy evolved as new laws were enacted and priorities shifted. While the current structure can trace its origin to 1966, there was a significant departure from this path in the late 1970s.

Interlude: The Heritage Conservation and Recreation Service

When the Carter administration took office in 1977, it brought the model of a unified program for the protection of both cultural and natural resources that had been put into place in Georgia when Jimmy Carter was governor. Department of the Interior officials attempted to reshape their responsibilities to follow the Georgia model, with two elements of the department being consolidated into a new bureau, the Heritage Conservation and Recreation Service. The responsibilities of the National Park Service for management of the external historic preservation program were assigned to the new entity, along with the personnel who had conducted these programs for the Park Service. Only the responsibility for managing the historic units of the National Park system remained as Park Service preservation duties. The second major component of the new bureau, natural area conservation and preservation, was to be built from the existing Park Service Natural Landmarks Program. The third component, outdoor recreation, was to come from the existing Bureau of Outdoor Recreation, whose duties revolved around the administration of the Land and Water Conservation Fund grants program and the development of the National Outdoor Recreation Plan. Despite its name, the Bureau of Outdoor Recreation did play a significant role in the conservation of natural areas, primarily through its grants to states for the acquisition and protection of natural areas and the encouragement of natural resource conservation as a part of recreational planning and management.

The creation of the Conservation and Recreation Service coincided with a broader effort to combine the program for the preservation of the built environment with its natural resource counterpart. Throughout the 1970s, many people in historic preservation sought just such an alliance, which they saw as the way to achieve a broad constituency. By the mid-1970s, environmental concern was reaching its apex, with significant achievements in the passage of new laws, the commitment of significant public funds for environmental protection and the development of a truly national public power base. By comparison, historic preservation was a relatively small program, growing in support, sophistication and effectiveness but lacking truly widespread recognition and public involvement.

This attempt at unification of these seemingly compatible movements was manifested in the creation of a few heritage programs at the state level; the establishment of the Heritage Conservation and Recreation Service at the national level; and a legislative initiative in the U.S. Congress to create a National Heritage Program. Sponsored by the Carter administration, this latter effort proposed bringing together the federal government's programs to protect and enhance properties of historic and natural significance into a single administrative entity. While the proposal emerged as early as 1977, no legislative enactment resulted until the end of 1980. When it did, the result was the 1980 amendments to the Preservation Act of 1966 directed solely at improving the administration of the national historic preservation program, with no mention of natural area conservation.

What went wrong? There are various explanations, among them widespread acknowledgment of a mistrust on both sides: preservationists feared being subsumed within the larger conservation movement; conservationists were wary of the more advanced regulatory systems that had by then been put in place for historic preservation. Other explanations are that the merger of interests failed simply because the effort was ineptly led and that institutional turf wars among the participants simply could not be overcome. In any case, these growing concerns, combined with opposition to extending the existing regulatory mechanisms for historic properties to natural sites, spelled the end of the legislative initiative. With the advent of the Reagan administration the following year, the Heritage Conservation and Recreation Service quietly folded into the National Park Service whose preservation bureaucracy then returned to its pre-1977 form with few changes.

This footnote to the evolution of the federal role is important because it reflects a basic aspect of the preservation movement in the nation as a

The National Register of Historic Places serves as the nation's inventory of buildings, districts, sites and places considered worthy of preservation. (Robert E. Stipe)

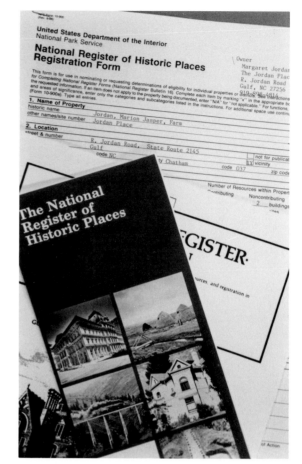

The 1912 hydroelectric powerhouse on the Ocoee River, Tennessee, is listed on the National Register of Historic Places. (Tennessee Valley Authority)

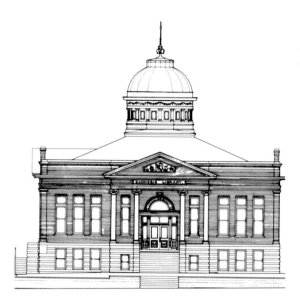

The Carnegie Library in Guthrie, Oklahoma, is one of the thousands of historic buildings recorded by the Historic American Buildings Survey. (Library of Congress)

As the result of a statewide survey of federal post offices, the state of California and the U.S. Postal Service nominated 28 post offices to the National Register of Historic Places, including the 1932–33 Town Center Station in Visalia, California. (California Department of Parks & Recreation)

The Pinch Gut Historic District in Augusta, Georgia, was rehabilitated by private investors using the federal investment tax credit. (Georgia Department of Natural Resources)

whole. After the emergence of the environmental movement as a truly national force in the early 1970s, many in preservation saw the common goals and strategies of the efforts to preserve the natural and man-made elements of the human environment. Even the Environmental Policy Act of 1969 recognized that both cultural and natural values contributed to the overall quality of the environment. However, when the realities of joining the two movements were confronted, it was soon realized that their constituencies lacked the community of interest and desire for joint action necessary for success. While both espoused the goals of conserving irreplaceable resources, the conceptual bases and practical techniques were too divergent for the movements to unify. Since 1980, the two movements advanced on their separate tracks, with occasional alliances on specific subjects of mutual interest, such as the conservation of cultural landscapes.

The National Park Service

The preservation responsibilities of the Secretary of the Interior are currently allocated to eight separate divisions within the National Park Service, reporting to the Associate Director, Cultural Resources. Firstly, the Archeological Assistance Division oversees the administration of the Archeological Resources Protection Act regulating excavation on public lands and undertaking general coordination of the federal archaeological program. The division prepares the Park Service's annual report to the U.S. Congress on the national archaeological program, provides technical assistance under the Archeological and Historic Preservation Act of 1974 and is undertaking the development of a nationwide database of federal archaeological activities.

Secondly, the History Division is responsible for the maintenance of the National Historic Landmark program. It develops themes for nominations and undertakes the preparation of nominations for consideration and designation by the Secretary of the Interior as well as in-park responsibilities. The History Division also has responsibility for the coordination of United States nominations to the World Heritage List.

Thirdly, the Historic American Buildings Survey (HABS) and the Historic American Engineering Record (HAER) are longstanding Park Service programs to document significant examples of American architecture and engineering. The HABS/HAER division conducts this program.

The Interagency Resources Division's principal responsibility is the maintenance of the National Register of Historic Places, the official inventory of historic properties worthy of preservation, as well as the provision of leadership and guidance in federal and state preservation planning. This division also carries out many of the Secretary's duties for the coordination of the statutory charges of the Preservation Act of 1966, including preparation of guidelines for the use of federal agencies in meeting their responsibilities under Section 110.

Administration of the highly successful preservation tax incentives program is entrusted to the Preservation Assistance Division, which reviews rehabilitation proposals to ensure their conformance with the *Secretary of the Interior's Standards for Rehabilitation,* a prerequisite for qualifying for the tax credits. Management of grants to states from the Historic Preservation Fund also falls within the jurisdiction of this division. Finally, it prepares technical briefs and provides assistance on a variety of preservation questions.

The last three divisions are associated most closely with operations of the many units of the Park system. These are the Park Historic Architecture, Anthropology, and Curatorial Services Divisions. The first, as its name implies, is primarily responsible for historic preservation questions involving historic buildings in the national parks. It also has responsibility for the leasing of historic buildings under Park Service jurisdiction to nonfederal parties. Curatorial Services establishes standards and policies for the Park Service's 26 million object collection, standards that are widely followed by state and local museums. Anthropology provides professional advice within the Park system on questions pertaining to anthropology and Native Americans (Indians). The National Park Service also carries out broad international responsibilities regarding national parks, natural area conservation and historic preservation.

✗ The Advisory Council on Historic Preservation

While the National Park Service is the principal agency for the administration of the federal preservation program, it shares its leadership role with the Advisory Council on Historic Preservation. This independent federal agency was created by the Preservation Act of 1966 to advise the president and the U.S. Congress on historic preservation matters and to comment on federal actions affecting historic properties. Over the past two decades its membership and functions have changed in some respects, but its basic mission remains essentially unchanged. Conceived as an advisory body operating at the highest levels of government, the Advisory Council has always included cabinet officers and nonfederal presidential appointees representative of the preservation community and the public at large, with the intention of bringing a balanced view to preservation issues confronting the federal government which may conflict with other pressing concerns. The Council's original membership of 17 has risen as high as 29 through various legislative amendments, but is currently set at 19. Federal interests are represented by the secretaries of the Interior and Agriculture, who sit ex officio, and the heads of four other federal agencies appointed by the president. Preservation interests are represented by four experts who are presidential appointees along with the chairman of the National Trust for Historic Preservation and the president of the National Conference of State Historic Preservation Officers, both ex officio. A governor and a mayor appointed by the president represent the interests of state and local government. The Architect of the Capitol and four members named by the president from the general public round out the membership. The Advisory Council's chairman is one of these appointed general public members.

The Advisory Council's statutory duties fall into the general categories of policy advice, interagency coordination, training and education, and protecting historic properties. Through periodic studies and analyses, the Advisory Council provides advice to both the administration and the U.S. Congress on historic preservation issues, such as tax policy, program improvement and pending legislative matters. By reviewing the activities of federal agencies and their state and local government counterparts, the Advisory Council often comes forward with specific recommendations to improve the effectiveness of the national historic preservation program. An increasingly important Advisory Council activity is the development and conduct of training courses for federal, state and local officials, primarily focused on the consideration of historic preservation values in project planning. The Advisory Council also has a role in the international preservation arena, being charged by statute with the coordination of U.S. participation in the International Centre for the Study of the Preservation and Restoration of Cultural Property (ICCROM) in Rome.

However, the Advisory Council's most influential role in preservation lies in its administration of the protective process established by Section 106 of the Preservation Act of 1966. Through its authority to issue regulations to implement Section 106, the Advisory Council established an administrative process that significantly shaped the way the federal government treats historic properties, as will be seen in the discussion on protecting historic resources.

In operation, the Advisory Council membership sets the general policies and priorities for its own activities at quarterly meetings. The Advisory Council staff, in the charge of an executive director, then carries out these programs, working closely with the Advisory Council chairman for policy oversight. It is important to recognize that unlike most federal agencies, such as the National Park Service, the Advisory Council has a full-time professional staff reporting to a membership which is made up of people who serve only intermittently. This has resulted in a certain isolation of the Advisory Council from the direct line of political control over the rest of the career bureaucracy and this has both benefits and drawbacks for its operations.

The historic preservation apparatus of the National Park Service and the Advisory Council essentially complement each other in the conduct of the national program. The Park Service sets the professional standards and criteria for the program and administers day-to-day maintenance of the national inventory, grants, tax incentives and technical assistance. The Advisory Council, independent of any other federal agency, conducts general oversight, makes recommendations and initiates actions to improve the efficiency of the program and resolve conflicts between historic preservation and other federal needs. Occasionally, there is overlap in the specific activities of the two but, by and large, the federal preservation establishment functions with good coordination.

Other Federal Programs

No discussion of the federal players in preservation would be complete without acknowledging the significant role of federal agencies with little or no internal preservation responsibilities. Nevertheless they shape the federal government's effect on the historic environment through the conduct of their daily programs. This influence may be positive or negative, depending upon how successfully the Park Service and the Advisory Council have done their job.

As noted above, the moving force for the passage of the Preservation Act of 1966 was public reaction to the destruction of historic resources caused by the public works projects of the 1950s and 1960s. Although tempered by the protective mechanisms of the act and by other environmental statutes, federal and federally supported projects continue to present threats to historic properties. These range from the acknowledged effects of federally aided highway construction to more subtle cases of Corps of Engineers permits or Veterans' Administration loan guarantees for private actions that threaten archaeological or historic resources. Regardless of scale, federally supported development

46

activities carry the potential to alter dramatically the historic fabric of the nation. How an agency responds to the policies and requirements of federal historic preservation laws determines whether historic values are lost or accommodated.

On the positive side, federal programs not specifically designed to promote the preservation of historic properties often provide significant resources for preservation. Some sources are apparent, such as the use of Community Development Block Grant funds to rehabilitate housing stock in historic neighborhoods or grants from the National Endowment for the Arts to enhance the visual or aesthetic qualities of the urban environment. Most, though, are far less obvious and difficult to tabulate. For example, the General Services Administration may use substantial amounts of building maintenance funds for historic properties that it manages, thereby providing an ongoing use of such structures. The Federal Highway Administration or the Corps of Engineers often provide sizeable sums of money to mitigate the loss of archaeological resources during highway or dam construction, funding good quality archaeological research that otherwise would not occur. Examples are myriad. The important conclusion is that these funds do not come from earmarked sources of preservation dollars and, in fact, far exceed appropriations for the Historic Preservation Fund in any given year. These kinds of effects, both positive and negative, make it imperative to recognize the important role of the entire federal establishment in shaping the total impact of the federal government on historic preservation.

The Federal Courts

A final note in the discussion of the federal participants in the preservation program must be reserved for the judiciary. While the U.S. Congress created the basic legislative structure of the program and the Executive Branch put it in place through regulations and program administration, it is the federal courts that have confirmed the interpretations of these laws and ensure that they are followed. For the most part, the federal judiciary is supportive of the administrative implementation, reinforcing the policies and procedures adopted by the Park Service and the Advisory Council whenever they have been tested in court. The courts have found that administrative action was not supported in law, such as when a National Historic Landmark designation was determined to be procedurally deficient and when the criminal sanctions of the Antiquities Act of 1906 were voided for being unconstitutionally vague. In both cases, subsequent legislation rectified the deficiencies. However, these cases demonstrate the role of the courts as a check on administrative action that exceeds the authorities granted by law.

A more common role for the federal courts has been the enforcement of legal requirements when the actions of federal agencies threaten historic properties. Customarily ruling on lawsuits brought by concerned citizen groups, the courts have been consistently effective in enjoining federal action until the procedural requirements of the federal preservation and environmental laws are met. This regular reinforcement of the preservation laws has ensured that federal agencies take their preservation responsibilities seriously and has contributed to the overall success of the protections in federal law.

The Federal Role as Reflected in Federal Functions

While the various federal agencies have their own defined role in the national program, in operation the dividing lines are not always clear. Accordingly, the best picture of the federal role in preservation emerges from reviewing the government's preservation functions. These include the following elements: maintenance of the national inventory of historic properties, protection of historic properties in the planning process, administration of the financial assistance program for state and local government and the private sector, and management of the federal government's historic resources. Examining each of these areas not only reveals the nature and scope of the federal role in historic preservation, but also illustrates the roles of the various federal players and the partnership that characterizes preservation in the United States.

The National Register Program

The National Historic Preservation Act of 1966 expanded the existing Registry of National Historic Landmarks, a listing of nationally significant historic properties created under the 1935 legislation, into the National Register of Historic Places. Envisioned as the nation's basic inventory of significant historic properties, the National Register is maintained by the National Park Service and currently contains more than 47,000 listings representing more than 750,000 properties deemed to be significant in American history, architecture, archaeology, engineering and culture. Administration of the National Register is indicative both of the partnership undergirding the national preservation program and also of the challenges faced by preservation in contemporary America.

Deriving their basis in the broad legislative language of the Preservation Act of 1966, the criteria for entry in the National Register as developed by the National Park Service are comprehensive:

> The quality of significance in American history, architecture, archeology, engineering, and culture is present in districts, sites, buildings, structures, and objects of state and local importance that possess integrity of location, design, setting, materials, workmanship, feeling, and association, and:
>
> • that are associated with events that have made a significant contribution to the broad patterns of our history; or
> • that are associated with the lives of persons significant in our past; or
> • that embody the distinctive characteristics of a type, period, or method of construction or that represent the work of a master, or that possess high artistic values, or that represent a significant and distinguishable entity whose components may lack individual distinction; or
> • that have yielded, or may be likely to yield, information important in prehistory or history.

The National Park Service further amplified these basic criteria with additional "Criteria Considerations." Stated as exclusions to the general criteria, they contain a subset of exclusions and are best conveyed simply by quoting them in their entirety:

Ordinarily cemeteries, birthplaces, or graves of historical figures, properties owned by religious institutions or used for religious purposes, structures that have been moved from their original locations, reconstructed historic buildings, properties primarily commemorative in nature, and properties that have achieved significance within the past 50 years shall not be considered eligible for the National Register. However, such properties will qualify if they are integral parts of districts that meet the criteria or if they fall within the following categories:

- A religious property deriving primary significance from architectural or artistic distinction or historical importance; or
- A building or structure removed from its original location but which is significant primarily for architectural value, or which is the surviving structure most importantly associated with a historic figure or event; or
- A birthplace or grave of a historical figure of outstanding importance if there is no other appropriate site or building directly associated with his productive life; or
- A cemetery which derives its primary significance from graves of persons of transcendant importance, from age, from distinctive design features, or from association with historic events; or
- A reconstructed building when accurately executed in a suitable environment and presented in a dignified manner as part of a restoration master plan, and when no other building or structure with the same association has survived; or
- A property primarily commemorative in intent if design, age, tradition, or symbolic value has invested it with its own historical significance; or
- A property achieving significance within the past 50 years if it is of exceptional importance.

It should be noted that the majority of listings in the National Register today qualify because of their significance to a particular community or state; only a small fraction, less than 10 percent, have been entered because of their significance to the nation. As a result, the criteria have provided the basis for a comprehensive inventory of the national patrimony.

The National Register today contains a broad, but by no means complete, catalogue of historic properties. It consists of nominations from state governments and, to a lesser extent, from federal and local government contributions. Of the 47,000 entries, more than 10 percent are historic or archaeological districts, comprised of numerous individual buildings or sites. Some estimate the actual number of individual properties on the National Register to be 750,000. Approximately 1,800 of the current entries are classified as National Historic Landmarks.

Although the purpose of nomination is listing in the National Register, the program has a more fundamental impact on preservation in the United States. Nomination and listing culminate an involved process to locate, document and evaluate the potential of historic properties, mainly at the state level, employing the professional expertise of the state historic preservation officers and staff. Through professional surveys of states' historic resources, and similar efforts at the local level, state offices compiled extensive inventories, which have been carried out in accordance with professional standards set by the National Park Service. Hence, there is an increasingly high degree of consistency in historic survey efforts throughout the nation.

The National Register nomination process generally requires review of the nomination by a state review board to ensure conformance to the criteria and the state's historic preservation plan. The 1980 amendments to the Preservation Act of 1966 introduced a requirement of owner notification and an opportunity for the owner to object to the nomination, in which case the property is not listed. This was stimulated by negative tax consequences of demolishing a National Register property, a provision since deleted from the tax code. The opportunity for owner objection remains, however, its effect on the National Register program is not as detrimental as many once feared.

Other nominations come from federal agencies that own historic properties, a requirement originating in Executive Order 11593 of 1971 and later embodied in the 1980 amendments. Nominations are also received from local governments that have been certified to participate in the process. The professional staff of the National Park Service reviews all nominations and, if in conformance with the criteria, the property is entered in the National Register.

While most properties found their way onto the National Register as individual nominations or as part of a larger historic district, there is a recent trend toward multiple resource and thematic nominations. Formerly, a nomination of multiple properties occurred when such properties were grouped together in a contiguous district, sharing a common link in their individual significance derived from their contribution to the historic values of the greater district. Recently the Park Service has encouraged the nomination in a single action of those historic properties that share common values even though they are not geographically linked. For example, a state may choose to nominate a group of railroad bridges, several Carnegie libraries, courthouses or National Guard armories in a single action, basing the nomination on a description of the underlying shared significant elements. Further details are set forth regarding the reason for a particular property to be included in the nomination.

This trend toward thematic nominations reflects a growing sophistication in the National Register program about the contexts of individual historic properties and the need to look at historic resources in relation to other examples of their building type. It also represents a substantial streamlining of the nomination and designation process, reducing the amount of financial and staffing resources needed to list properties in the National Register. It should prove to be a major contributing factor to the evolution of the National Register as a truly comprehensive inventory of the nation's historic resources.

Beyond providing an official, albeit incomplete, list of worthy properties, the creation and development of the National Register of Historic Places had a profound impact on the national preservation program in several ways. As noted, National Register eligibility is the basic requirement for a historic property to qualify for federal financial assistance or protection and the breadth of the eligibility criteria dramatically expanded the scope of the federal government's involvement in preservation. Secondly, the criteria established to judge eligibility significantly influenced the evaluation of historic properties throughout the nation, at all levels of government and for a variety of purposes. Thirdly, the administrative apparatus created to expand the National Register became the foundation for the current structure of federal, state and local government cooperation that is central to the national historic preservation program. Finally, the impetus of the National Register program spurred the rapid growth of skilled professional preservationists in public service.

The National Register itself was the notable innovation in the Preservation Act of 1966, designed to remedy shortcomings in the scope of federal activity up to that time. While the National Register was based on the existing National Landmarks' Registry, its criteria of eligibility introduced several new concepts that are essential to the current program. The National Register was to encompass properties possessing significance at the state and local level, as well as those of paramount national importance. This change shifted the federal government's role in the national program in a fundamental and dramatic way. Had the National Register criteria been limited to nationally significant properties, the impact of the financial incentives and protective devices contained in the act and subsequent legislation would have been severely limited. Today, nationally significant properties comprise less than 10 percent of National Register listings. The remaining 90 percent brings the preservation tools of the national program to local preservationists and, in turn, fosters grass-roots support for historic preservation that gives the program its strength and vitality.

Accompanying this expansion of the National Register criteria was another important revision. Prior federal law had defined historic resources as "sites, buildings, and objects," possessing historic or archaeological value. The Preservation Act of 1966 added districts and structures to the property categories, and cultural and architectural significance, later joined by engineering, to the definition of historic value. These terms were important to expanding the National Register and with it the scope of federal attention. The introduction of the term districts was particularly noteworthy, as it brought the concept of preserving neighborhoods and groups of historic properties to the national program, mirroring the growing concern for environmental conservation and permitting historic preservation laws to address the notion of protecting whole historic environments.

In sum, the Preservation Act of 1966 introduced a comprehensive approach to defining the range of historic resources that would be the concern of the federal government. As National Register eligibility became the prerequisite for almost any kind of federal consideration, the scope of the National Register was a primary determinant of the impact of the federal program on the nation's historic resources. Further, as the National Register criteria found wider application through the growth of federal financial assistance and protective mechanisms, states and municipalities adopted similar, and often identical, criteria for the maintenance of their own lists. This had the salutary effect of promoting consistency throughout the nation on the definition of historic properties, although there is still a long way to go in establishing uniformity.

Expanding the National Register to embrace properties of state and local significance required that the federal government find partners to aid in compiling the list, and thus state officials soon became the principal contributors of National Register nominations. Designated by the governor of each state and territory, the state historic preservation officer (SHPO) evolved into one of the principal players in the partnership of the national program. The early focus of the state offices and the primary area of contact with federal administrators were nominations to the National Register. Later with the issuance of Executive Order 11593 in 1971 and the 1980 amendments to the Preservation Act of 1966, federal property managers and local government officials joined the state offices in nominating properties. In both instances, though, the state offices retained a central role of coordination within the state and provided expert advice. It is also evident that the early success of the state historic preservation office system in providing nominations to the National Register confirmed the wisdom of the partnership and led directly to the assumption of progressively greater responsibilities by the states in the national preservation program.

While the National Register program can boast significant achievements over its 20-year lifespan, it is neither static nor without its critics. Its evolution continues, both in content and in administration. Responding in part to concerns of federal agencies that the National Register criteria are too broad and may subject potentially unworthy properties to federal legal protection, a major review was recently concluded with a decision to leave the criteria unchanged and to make any necessary clarifications or improvements through technical means.

More significant is the prospective change in the program's administration. The increasing importance of the state historic preservation office in the national program is exemplified by the National Register. The partnership concept has reached and possibly passed full maturity in this area, as the National Park Service now proposes to terminate the federal review role for nominations of properties of state and local significance, turning that responsibility over to the respective state offices. Interestingly enough, many of those who long advocated a more responsible role for the states in the national program decry this proposal as an abdication of the federal share of the partnership. It is likely, though, that the underlying cause for alarm is the fear that turning this part of the program over to states might reinforce policies currently advanced by the federal government to withdraw financial support for the states. At a slightly more abstract level, critics also argue that significant reduction of the federal role will result in the National Register no longer being a national listing, but rather a loose collection of state-maintained listings. This debate has not been concluded, but it is clear that the National Register, as with other components of the preservation program, is in an era of decentralization. Whether this is a recent phenomenon, or the continuation of a conscious policy begun by the National Park Service in 1966, is a matter of debate.

Protecting Historic Properties: The 106 Process

Prior to 1966, federal law provided limited protection to historic properties. Those provisions that did exist did not extend beyond the federal domain. This left the lion's share of the burden on the shoulders of state and local government. Before the passage of the National Preservation Act of 1966, federal stewardship of historic properties in the National Park system, a rarely invoked condemnation authority, and a permit system for archaeological excavation on federal effectively protects historic properties. At the stage of identifying eligible properties, the agency and the state office review information on potentially eligible properties and, using the National Register criteria, determine which meet these criteria. These properties then join those actually listed in the National Register as historic resources the agency is obligated to consider under Section 106. For purposes of the review process, no distinction is made between listed and eligible properties.

The next step in the process is assessment of the effects of the project on the identified properties. The agency continues its consultation with the state office, this time using criteria established by the Advisory Council to evaluate effects. The criteria broadly define effects to mean any change in the characteristics of a property that qualifies it for the National Register. However, they distinguish between those effects that are harmful and those that are not. Projects with the latter receive only cursory review. Harmful effects, known as "adverse effects" in Section 106 jargon, trigger further consultation to seek ways of avoiding or minimizing them.

The concept of adverse effect is one of the primary determinants of the scope of the Section 106 process. The Advisory Council criteria define it broadly, including almost any form of alteration or environmental intrusion that diminishes the qualities of a historic property. Clearly within the concept are direct impacts such as outright demolition or physical alterations. However, a whole range of more subtle depredations on historic properties fall within the term adverse effect. These may be visual intrusions, such as an electrical transmission line running near a rural house or incompatible new construction within a historic district; audible intrusions, such as that of a nearby highway or airport runway extension on a house or neighborhood; and alterations that change the traditional relationship between a historic property and its setting, such as a tract housing development that severs the historic association between a rural village and the surrounding landscape. Adverse effects need not be immediate or direct. Section 106 has been invoked to consider long-term indirect impacts resulting from altered traffic patterns or growth-inducing activities that may in the future change the use or character of a significant property. In sum, the Advisory Council's criteria take an environmental approach to the notion of harm, recognizing that many kinds of intrusions can degrade the significant features of historic properties over time. This broad definition has contributed to the effectiveness of the Section 106 process in protecting historic resources.

As noted, a determination that a project will have an adverse effect on a historic property launches the sponsoring federal agency into further consultation to consider alternatives that can avoid or reduce the harmful impacts. The state office is again consulted, although in complicated cases the Advisory Council staff may also be involved. At this stage, opportunities are provided for the involvement of the public and interested parties, which may include affected local governments, Indian tribes and applicants for federal assistance. The parties explore alternative locations and designs for the project and seek mitigation measures to lessen potential impacts. Usually this results in agreement among the parties, which is concurred in by the Council, completing the Section 106 process, which is then legally binding.

It is important to note that the objective of the consultation is to reach agreement on ways that the project can proceed with minimum harm to af-

The Advisory Council on Historic Preservation offers training programs on the federal historic preservation program. (Candace Clifford, Advisory Council on Historic Preservation)

Section 106 entails consultation among the Advisory Council on Historic Preservation staff, federal agency representatives, state officials and property owners. At Smith's farm in Severn, Maryland, this group discussed a proposed highway plan. (Candace Clifford, Advisory Council on Historic Preservation)

lands were essentially all the legal tools available in federal law to control threats to historic properties. There were no checks on the actions of government agencies that destroyed or damaged historic properties nor did federal law offer any constraints on private development incompatible with historic preservation values.

As noted, public reaction to the increasing loss of historic structures to urban renewal, interstate highways, dams and suburban sprawl spurred the passage of the Preservation Act of 1966. Chief among its innovative features was the creation of a seemingly modest protective system, keyed to the expanded National Register and limited to those actions having some kind of federal involvement. Over the next 20 years, this system called the "Section 106 process," named for Section 106 of the act, developed into a sophisticated federal mechanism for protecting historic properties.

The statutory basis for the Section 106 process is simple and straightforward. The Preservation Act of 1966 requires federal agencies that carry out, assist or license actions that may affect historic properties to take into account the effects of these actions on those resources and afford the Advisory Council on Historic Preservation a reasonable opportunity to comment. Through regulatory implementation, court interpretation and continued usage, this statutory charge is integrated into the daily planning processes of the federal government and of those who seek its assistance or permission for development. The creation of the Section 106 process coincided with the emergence of the broader environmental movement in the United States, which brought about a climate for the strengthening of legal protections for the cultural environment. After two decades of growth and refinement, the process now has a significant impact on the way the federal government treats historic resources. While not without its limitations and flaws, the protective system established by the act responded well to the challenges its creators saw in 1966 and those that arose subsequently.

The basic elements of the Section 106 process remained largely unchanged over the years. Essentially, the process has five steps:

- Identification of historic properties that a federal action may affect.
- Evaluation of the significance of potentially affected properties.
- Assessment of the nature of the effects.
- Consultation with preservation experts to avoid or reduce harmful effects.
- Obtaining the Advisory Council's comments and proceeding with the agreed decision.

While these principal elements have remained constant, the specifics of the process changed to meet the needs of both preservation and the federal establishment and will undoubtedly continue to do so in the future. An examination of how the Section 106 process works today reveals the extent of that development and certain trends that will shape its growth.

At the outset, it is important to note the scope of protection that Section 106 provides. First, the review process applies only when there is some federal involvement in a project. This is the primary limitation on federal legal protection for historic properties. This fundamental limitation is well grounded in

American law and politics, which traditionally assign the authority to regulate private property and undertake land use planning to state and local governments. Federal preservation requirements do not control purely private actions that threaten historic resources, with the exception of surface mining, which is subject to strict federal regulation.

The Advisory Council administers the Section 106 process and issues regulations (36 C.F.R. Part 800) that guide federal agencies in meeting their legal responsibilities. As noted, the Advisory Council is an unusual organization in the federal government. It is comprised of a 19-member board made up primarily of political appointees served by a professional staff numbering around 30. Its membership includes preservation experts as well as representatives of federal, state and local government and the general public. As its membership convenes only quarterly, the day-to-day administration of Section 106 rests primarily with the staff. The Council's regulations set forth its general duties and those of certain federal agencies, as well as those of other parties, most notably the state historic preservation office. Last amended in October 1986, the regulations continue a system that traces its primary elements to the late 1960s, but reflect many of the current trends in the national historic preservation program.

The Section 106 process commences when a federal agency determines that it has, in terms of the statute, an "undertaking" which has the potential to affect historic properties. The scope of an "undertaking" is broad; it includes direct federal construction projects (office buildings, military bases and dams), federally funded and grant-supported projects (highways, urban redevelopment) and federally licensed actions (power plants, transmission lines, construction in wetlands and waterways). Undertakings also include activities with less direct and visible federal involvement, such as federal loan guarantees for privately financed construction and other types of indirect federal financial assistance to the private sector. The critical element to bring a proposed project within the purview of Section 106 is that there be some form of federal authority that is related to the support or approval of the project. This broad definition of undertaking has made the impact of the Section 106 process a substantially greater protective device than might be expected from its limitation to federal actions.

When a federal undertaking is proposed, regulations implementing Section 106 prescribe a series of steps for the sponsoring agency to follow. First, there is the requirement that potentially affected historic properties be identified. Section 106 protection extends to all properties listed in the National Register of Historic Places and to those that meet the criteria for listing, even though they have not been formally nominated or entered in the Register. This latter category of properties was added to the scope of Section 106 by the 1976 amendments to the Preservation Act of 1966, in recognition of the fact that the effort to list all eligible properties in the United States in the Register was far from complete. Meanwhile unlisted but significant properties were being lost to federal action. Identifying listed properties requires only consulting a published list; locating eligible properties demands action by the federal agency.

The Section 106 process directs the agency to consult with the appropriate state historic preservation office to determine what efforts are necessary to identify eligible properties and to obtain information on significant but unlisted historic properties in the project area. This agency-state office consultation carries through the entire Section 106 process and is the reason the system

54

The Public Buildings Cooperative Act of 1976 encouraged the preservation of federal government buildings, such as the Old Post Office in Washington, D.C., for mixed uses, including offices, a shopping arcade and an observation tower. (Government Services Administration)

The transformation of the Lackawanna Train Station in Scranton, Pennsylvania, into a hotel and restaurant was made possible with the U.S. Housing and Urban Development's Urban Development Action Grant and Community Development Block Grant as well as the 25% investment tax credit. (Buchanan, Ricciuti & Associates)

fected historic resources. Rarely is the no-build option given serious consideration. Section 106's success lies in the fact that the participants generally enter
the process with the shared objective of accommodating preservation values with
federal project needs.

Infrequently the federal agency, the state historic preservation office and the Advisory Council may be unable to reach agreement on how a project should proceed. In that event, the case is referred to the membership of the
Advisory Council who render an advisory comment to the head of the sponsoring agency. The agency is then obliged to consider the Advisory Council's comment in reaching its final decision on the project but is not required to follow the
Advisory Council's advice. In reality the process functions to promote agreements. These occur at a lower level of bureaucracy, free of the kind of acrimony
and adverse publicity from both within and without the agency, which most federal officials seek to avoid. Also agreement among the parties is normally
reached more quickly than through the commenting process.

The Section 106 process has become well integrated into the federal planning process. In the past few years, the Advisory Council has handled
more than 2,500 cases annually and about 40,000 cases are settled on the state
level. It has raised the level of preservation consciousness throughout the federal
bureaucracy and has received strong support in the courts.

In some cases, local government and private developers have carefully avoided asking for federal support and thus evading the system and destroying historic resources. This gap is being closed as states pass Section 106-type
regulations for themselves. Sometimes, too, there are cases in which agreement
cannot be reached. Surveys have been inadequate and the eligibility of some
properties has consequently been overlooked. As a result, the Council renders
its advice which the project sponsor is free to follow or reject. The trend in recent years has been to reject. Nevertheless, increasing public awareness of Section 106 as a tool for conserving historic resources important to the community
as well as a spreading acceptance of the process by federal program officials are
positive signs for the future. Coupled with a likely continuing decrease in the
amount of federal financial assistance for development projects, it would seem
that the Section 106 process will prove adequate to challenges in the future.

Other Federal Protections

Several other statutes besides Section 106 provide a range of legal tools to prevent harm to various aspects of the historic environment. They fall into two
basic categories: those laws that are exclusively designed to protect historic values and those that deal with a broader range of environmental concerns. The
first group includes Section 110f of the Preservation Act of 1966 and the Archeological and Historic Preservation Act of 1974. Broader environmental laws that
also embrace preservation are the National Environmental Policy Act of 1969
and Section 4(f) of the Transportation Act of 1966. Each of these bears an opera-
tional relationship to the Section 106 process.

Section 110f of the Preservation Act of 1966 originated in the 1980
amendments to the act. It is designed to set a higher standard of protection for
nationally significant properties and is modeled on the provisions of Section 4(f)
of the Transportation Act of 1966. It directs that federal agencies "to the maxi-

mum extent possible, undertake such planning and actions as may be necessary to minimize harm" to National Historic Landmarks and directs the agency to seek the comments of the Advisory Council.

In its 1986 revisions to the Section 106 regulations, the Advisory Council introduced a new section to specifically deal with its responsibilities and those of federal agencies under Section 110f. The provision essentially codifies the existing practice of using the Section 106 consultation process to meet needs of this provision. As a modicum of further protection, the regulation authorizes the Advisory Council to seek advice from the Secretary of the Interior on measures to mitigate harm to landmarks, limits the ability of federal agencies to resolve cases affecting these properties without Advisory Council participation in the consultation and requires the Council to report the outcome of Section 110f reviews to the president and the U.S. Congress. These embellishments to the basic Section 106 process serve to heighten the sense of importance of dealing with National Historic Landmarks, but offer no additional restrictions on, or impediments to, federal agency action that might seriously impair or destroy such properties. The basic statutory provision simply does not authorize stronger sanctions.

In operation, it is questionable how effective this legal requirement is. Even before the enactment of Section 110f, the Advisory Council tended to put slightly more weight on the protection of National Historic Landmarks in the Section 106 process which singles out certain properties as having a higher level of significance than others. One criticism leveled at Section 110f, was that focusing attention on nationally significant properties will cause federal agencies to view properties of state or local importance as second class. So far there is no evidence to support this view.

The Archeological and Historic Preservation Act of 1974, commonly called Moss-Bennett after its legislative sponsors, does not fit into the category of preservation planning statutes in the way the previous laws do. Based on the Reservoir Salvage Act of 1960, the Archeological Act of 1974 has as its purpose the preservation of historic and archaeological data that might be lost as the result of a federal project. The 1960 legislation was limited to the recovery of archaeological data threatened by federal dam construction; the Archeological Act of 1974 extended similar provisions to historical and archaeological data that might be lost to any federal, federally assisted or federally licensed construction. It differs from the preceding preservation laws and other environmental requirements by addressing the mitigation of losses rather than requiring the consideration of alternative project designs to avoid such losses. In essence, the Archeological Act of 1974 is a mitigation statute, while Section 106 and its relatives are planning statutes.

The Archeological Act of 1974 requires a federal agency to notify the Secretary of the Interior when a project will result in the loss of significant historical or archaeological data. The act authorizes the Secretary to undertake data recovery and permits federal agencies to expend up to 1 percent of project funds for data recovery. Administered by the National Park Service, the 1974 act is most often invoked after decisions for a federal project are reached through the Section 106 process.

The Archeological Act of 1974 made two other significant contributions to federal protection of historic properties. Firstly, it allowed the National

Park Service to undertake a fairly active program of salvage archaeology in advance of federal construction. Funded by direct appropriations to the National Park Service, the program resulted in significant recovery of historical and archeological data that otherwise would have been lost. Unfortunately, it has not been funded for several years. Secondly, the National Park Service was placed in a central coordinating role for archaeological activities conducted by the federal government. To administer the program, the position of Departmental Consulting Archeologist was created, with authority to establish government standards for the conduct of archaeological research by federal agencies and their contractors. Important guidance for federal archaeological work was included as part of the *Secretary of the Interior's Standards and Guidelines for Archeology and Historic Preservation*, published in 1983.

Overall the impact of the Archeological Act of 1974 lags behind that of Section 106 and related planning laws; however, the act's provisions, offer a mechanism only for reducing damage that is scheduled to occur, rather than creating a means to avoid it. The act can do no more than ensure that retrieval is carried out in a professional manner.

While the preceding laws are specifically directed at historic properties, they are not the only federal legal tools available. As noted, a national movement to conserve the environment emerged in the 1960s and 1970s. Two significant federal environmental statutes enacted during that era extend their protections to cultural resources as well as to natural resources and both have contributed to the federal role in historic preservation.

The Environmental Policy Act of 1969 created a national policy of environmental protection, which acknowledged that the quality of the human environment rested on a combination of factors, including the preservation of "important historic, cultural, and natural aspects of our national heritage." This act ensured that historic properties would benefit from protections set forth in the legislation.

The environmental protections of the Environment Policy Act of 1969 are not markedly different from those of Section 106. Limited to those actions of the federal government that may affect the quality of the human environment, the act requires that federal agencies assess and consider the environmental consequences of their proposals. Similar to the Preservation Act of 1966, however, it provides no veto over a project that may have negative environmental effects. It requires an environmental impact statement for any major federal action that significantly affects the quality of the environment. Reaching the determination whether this threshold is passed, therefore requires a full impact statement, and the agency customarily goes through the process of preparing an environmental assessment, to identify and evaluate the full range of anticipated environmental effects.

The regulations of each agency that guide the conduct of this evaluation generally conform to government-wide regulations issued by the Council on Environmental Quality, a small agency located within the executive office of the President.

In discharging its responsibilities under the Environmental Policy Act of 1969, a federal agency completes many of the same steps it would take to meet a corresponding requirement of Section 106. The agency must establish the significance of environmental values that its action may affect, and describe and assess the impact of the project on those values. Depending on the magnitude of the project and its impact, this may be achieved through the preparation of a fairly simple environmental assessment or a more involved impact statement. However, once this information is assembled, the 1969 act and Section 106 place dramatically different obligations on the sponsoring agency.

The Environmental Policy Act of 1969 provides for public disclosure; the federal agency must fully identify the consequences of its action and permit the public an opportunity to express its concerns. Implementing regulations specify the content of the environmental documents, the public notice requirements and the timing for public review and comment. Once these procedural obligations of public disclosure are met, the agency reviews the full environmental record and reaches a final decision but without the oversight of any external body.

In comparison, the Section 106 process places an affirmative duty on the agency not only to assess and disclose the effects of its action on historic properties, but to enter into consultation with state and federal preservation agencies to seek ways to avoid or reduce the anticipated harm. The agency ultimately retains the final authority for the project decision, but in reality consultation results in negotiated solutions to conflicts. Thus the protection afforded under Section 106 is significantly greater than that under the Environmental Policy Act of 1969.

One should not conclude that the 1969 act is redundant or offers little to historic preservation. The broad scope of the act, extending to all the factors that contribute to environmental quality, has resulted in a greater awareness of its provisions by federal agencies and the public than the more narrowly defined purview of Section 106. This in turn made agencies more receptive to the integration of environmental review procedures, including those of Section 106, into their normal planning processes. The federal establishment may not welcome an overlay of rigorous environmental considerations but the broad sweep of the act does provide concerned citizens with ample opportunity to compel the thoughtful consideration of environmental factors by agencies through legal action in the courts. The history of the act is marked by aggressive litigation and supportive and expansive court decisions that made clear soon after its passage that federal agencies were not to take their environmental assessment duties lightly.

The environmental assessment procedure also serves to reinforce the Section 106 process on a practical and routine level. An agency will customarily complete the Section 106 process and then use the results to prepare an environmental impact statement. Often the preparation of those documents substantially augments the information base available for Section 106 review. In practice, the two procedures tend to be complementary rather than redundant.

There is another federal environmental law that has had an equally positive effect on the protection of historic properties although limited to the activities of a single federal department. This is Section 4(f) of the Transportation Act of 1966, signed into law the same day as the Preservation Act, October 15, 1966. It is a planning requirement governing the development of proposals for federally assisted transportation projects. The strictures of the Environmental Policy Act of 1969 and Section 106 apply to those projects subject to Section

4(f), but the latter provision adds a rigorous substantive standard that must be met when the final agency decision is reached on a project.

Section 4(f) requires the Secretary of Transportation to determine that there is "no feasible or prudent alternative" to a transportation project that uses land from environmentally sensitive areas, including historic properties. Through subsequent judicial interpretation, Section 4(f) became a formidable weapon in the arsenal of conservationists. As such, it operates in conjunction with both the Environmental Policy Act of 1969 and Section 106 reviews, but with certain noteworthy differences. Unlike the other two procedures, Section 4(f) establishes a substantive standard that the final decision on a project must be made when impacts on protected properties are considered. The courts have put a gloss on Section 4(f) that has elevated the "no feasible or prudent alternative" standard well above any duties under the other laws to reach a particular decision on the treatment of a historic property. Section 4(f) requires a clear showing that alternatives are neither technically feasible nor prudent in terms of the entire range of concerns relevant to wisdom, as one commentator has noted, before the project can use a protected resource.

It should be noted, though, that while the Section 4(f) standard is high, it has a narrow application since it applies only to projects of the Department of Transportation. Section 4(f) requires that land from a historic property or other protected resource be used which embraces a physical taking of the land and some narrowly circumscribed constructive uses.

The impact of Section 4(f) on the projects that it does cover is significant. Several major highway projects that would have had serious negative impacts on historic properties were cancelled by the Department of Transportation after 4(f) review and others were halted by judicial action. More importantly, the presence of Section 4(f) compelled federal transportation planners and their state counterparts who receive federal assistance for highways, mass transit and airports to give serious consideration to impacts on historic resources. This results from both early court decisions that set a high legal standard for the feasible and prudent alternative finding and the ensuing internal reviews that elevate the final Section 4(f) determination above the bureaucratic levels that normally are responsible for environmental decision making. Not surprisingly this regard for Section 4(f) led transportation officials to a meticulous concern for their compliance with related environmental and preservation laws, such as Section 106 and the Environmental Policy Act of 1969.

The impact of Section 4(f) on historic preservation has not always been positive, however. Stringent internal review requirements often lead transportation officials to attempt to deny that an affected property is historic, in order to avoid delay and complications. While the close oversight provided by state historic preservation offices to transportation projects prevents this tactic from working often, the effort continues and it undermines the Section 106 process as well as Section 4(f). Another problem has been the inflexible nature of Section 4(f), requiring transportation officials to go through the same process regardless of the significance of the affected historic property. Thus, an archaeological site that parties to the Section 106 process agree should be excavated and subsequently paved over so that a highway can be built is subjected to the same Section 4(f) scrutiny as the demolition of a historic building or structure of highest national importance. This inability to relate the degree of protection to the nature and value of the resource complicates the project review process and often leads to costly avoidance of a use of historic properties, even when it is unnecessary to protect the significant historic characteristics.

To sum up, the protective provisions of federal law operate surprisingly well to minimize harm to historic properties caused by federal actions. The surprise lies in the fact that none of the protective systems either compel a preservation solution or enable a preservation agency to veto or otherwise control the final decision of the project sponsor. The success of these provisions has been incremental, as procedures evolved and agency officials come to realize that they cannot take their preservation responsibilities lightly. Energetic enforcement by the preservation community, most often at the administrative level by the Advisory Council and state historic preservation offices but occasionally by citizens in the courts, has spurred this level of responsibility.

Federal Preservation Assistance: Grants-In-Aid

In the report that led directly to the drafting of the Preservation Act of 1966, the Special Committee of the U.S. Conference of Mayors recommended creation of a federal matching grants program to underwrite preservation projects and revision of the federal tax code to encourage private historic preservation. Both found their way into law, although at different times and with somewhat different consequences than were envisioned in 1966.

A fundamental concept of the Preservation Act of 1966 was the provision of direct federal financial support for the national historic preservation program. This embraced two basic categories of assistance: grants for the acquisition and development of historic properties; and grants for survey and planning. The former were designed to support brick and mortar work on historic properties, and the latter to underwrite costs of developing state historic preservation plans and nominations to the National Register. From the start, both were administered by the National Park Service. A third category was assistance to the National Trust for Historic Preservation for the conduct of its program activities. Each of these has made a significant contribution to the development of the national historic preservation program over the past 20 years.

Before examining each of these grant categories, it will be useful to review the funding history of the historic preservation grant program, the Historic Preservation Fund (HPF) starting in 1967. The historic preservation grants program was never a source of massive federal funds for historic preservation. In its peak years of 1979 and 1980, the annual appropriation barely exceeded $50 million. Appropriations for the first 10 years of the program were more frequently in the vicinity of $5-$6 million yearly. After 1981 they held steady at around $26 million. Through fiscal year 1987, the total amount appropriated for the grants program has been $459 million (of which $399 million went to the states and $60 million to the National Trust) and is less than half of one year's appropriation for the Urban Development Action Grant program. Nevertheless, these modest sums have been critical to the growth of the program nationally, and the continuing threat to terminate them is regularly the most acrimonious debate in the preservation community.

The most visible use of Historic Preservation Fund grants has been the underwriting of actual restoration and rehabilitation work on historic properties, but this probably had the least impact on the long-term vitality of the national program. The Preservation Act of 1966 authorized use of these 50 percent matching grants for the acquisition and preservation of properties listed in the National Register of Historic Places. However, since 1982 annual appropriation bills have prohibited the use of the Preservation Fund for these activities. The lone exception was a one-time appropriation in 1983 of $25 million under the Emergency Jobs Act. During the years that acquisition and development grants were available approximately $121 million was distributed and were used on a wide variety of projects, ranging from large public buildings such as courthouses, to individual privately owned houses in historic districts. For the most part they were small grants, often no more than a few thousand dollars, which served as a catalyst to further investment or fundraising. Projects originated with state and local governments, nonprofit organizations and private individuals, with the state historic preservation offices requesting the funding from the National Park Service. In return, the National Park Service was assured that the property would be preserved and maintained over the long term.

Although the amount of federal Historic Preservation Fund money going directly for bricks and mortar was never great, its impact was significant. Often these modest sums were combined with other sources of funding to make a restoration project successful. The demise of this aspect of the grants program occurred when the expanded tax incentives of 1981 became law. The rationale was that incentives would substitute for the Preservation Fund subsidies. However, while incentives have since generated many times the amount given under the Preservation Fund, not all of the properties that once received Fund support are now eligible for tax incentive relief. Archaeological sites, owner-occupied houses and properties owned by nonprofit organizations and museums are disqualified. Hence, in a major step backward, many historic properties fall outside the scope of current federal financial assistance.

In contrast, the success of the survey and planning grants probably exceeds all original expectations. These grants were originally to help support states in their surveys for nominations of properties to the National Register and to help develop state historic preservation plans. The Preservation Act of 1966 limited the federal contribution to a maximum of 50 percent until 1980, when amendments increased the federal share to 70 percent. The 1980 amendments also expanded the range of eligible activities which are elaborated in the National Park Service grants manual:

- Administration, including routine matters of office and program management.
- Local government certification/pass through, involving the certification of local governments to participate in the national historic preservation program.
- National Register, covering the full range of activities related to the evaluation and nomination of properties to the National Register.
- Planning, relating to the development of statewide and regional plans and planning processes.
- Preservation tax incentives, including the actions related to certifying properties and projects for federal tax incentives.

● Review and compliance, pertaining to SHPO participation in the Section 106 process and related environmental review systems.
● Survey, involving fieldwork and research to identify and document historic properties.

Federal support for this broad range of state preservation activity was the primary factor in the growth of the current federal-state partnership that implements provisions of the Preservation Act of 1966. While funding has not been adequate to achieve all the objectives set forth in the act, the catalyst of federal money tied to National Park Service professional standards spurred the development of competent administrative structures in each state. State legislatures generally responded favorably, appropriating the necessary matching share and often moving forward with legislation that enhanced the preservation program.

Consequently, the primary government activity carrying out the provisions of the Preservation Act of 1966 occurs at the state level. This includes the conduct of historic resource surveys, the compiling of inventories, the evaluation and nomination of historic properties for National Register listing, the development of preservation plans and systems, consultation with federal agencies on the effects of their projects on historic properties and the encouragement of local government participation in the national historic preservation program. It is clear that the successes of the program since 1966 are due in large part to the state infrastructure, developed in response to the federal incentives.

Historic Preservation Fund grants had a dramatic impact on the administrative structure for preservation at the state and local level. The National Park Service established standards governing activities conducted by states with federal funds, ranging from the composition of state preservation offices to the conduct of surveys. Through annual program audits, the National Park Service ensures that each state program conforms to these requirements. This ensures a certain level of quality in the conduct of preservation activities by states and establishes a high degree of uniformity throughout all of the states.

Another use of the Historic Preservation Fund deserves brief mention. The Preservation Act of 1966 authorized 50 percent matching grants to the National Trust for Historic Preservation, in support of the Trust's program. Since 1966, almost $60 million has been appropriated for the Trust. In recent years, the annual appropriation has stabilized at about $5 million annually, representing approximately 25 percent of the Trust's yearly budget. Federal support has been critical to the National Trust and has declined by 50 percent in the last seven years. However, the National Trust has been unable to reduce its dependence on federal funds by substituting contributions from other sources without seriously reducing its current operating capabilities.

As the Historic Preservation Fund enters its second decade, its future is uncertain. The Reagan administration has proposed termination of grants as part of its greater goal to reduce federal domestic spending. It is ironic that a program hailed as a model of federal-state partnership and that pioneered the transfer of federal responsibility to state and local government should be spurned by an administration embracing devolution. The preservation community is fortunate in having the kind of strong bipartisan support in the U.S. Congress that has continually resulted in the reinstatement of a grant to keep state programs and the National Trust funded at constant, if not luxurious, levels. It is likely that this situation will continue.

A final note on direct federal assistance is necessary before turning to the tax incentive program. The Preservation Act of 1966 authorizes a number of other financial tools to promote historic preservation, although the bulk of these have either not been implemented by the federal government or have had little impact on preservation. For example, the 1980 amendments to the act directed the Secretary of the Interior to establish a loan guarantee program to finance private rehabilitation projects which would have provided federal loan insurance for private lenders willing to finance preservation activities or National Register properties. However, this would have required major new staffing and vastly expanded fiscal obligations during a period when both are being reduced throughout the government. The U.S. Congress never appropriated funds to carry out the program. The Department of the Interior is presently advancing a proposal in the U.S. Congress to make the program discretionary with the Secretary of the Interior, which suggests a continuation of the current situation for the remainder of the Reagan administration.

The Preservation Act of 1966 also authorizes a limited program of direct grants from the Secretary of the Interior for historic preservation, using 10 percent of the annual Historic Preservation Fund appropriation and carried out independently of the normal apportionment to states. The program includes preservation of threatened National Historic Landmarks, as well as World Heritage properties, demonstration projects, development of skilled labor in trades, crafts, analysis, curatorial management, assistance to prevent small businesses from leaving historic districts and preservation of the cultural heritage of Indian tribes and minority groups. Little occurred under these authorizations. Indeed, in its recent report to the president and the U.S. Congress on the implementation of the act over 20 years, the Department of the Interior made no mention of these provisions, other than to note that funds were not available to make grants to Indian tribes.

Tax Incentives for Historic Preservation

The Preservation Act of 1966 provided for grants-in-aid, but a decade passed before revisions to the tax code were initiated. In 1976, as part of the comprehensive Tax Reform Act, the U.S. Congress amended the Internal Revenue Code to redress the imbalance between the tax treatment of new construction and rehabilitation of historic properties. Scrutiny of the tax system revealed that provisions governing investment in real estate discriminated heavily against the preservation of historic properties and encouraged the replacement of serviceable older buildings with new structures. The 1976 amendments provided some modest incentives for rehabilitating historic properties and eliminated certain tax benefits for destruction. These changes spurred an increase in preservation investment over the next few years, but it took the Economic Recovery Tax Act of 1981 to transform the economics of historic preservation. Since that time private investment in rehabilitation has surpassed all expectations, far exceeding the amount of direct preservation grant funds distributed during the 20 years of the act.

The 1976 tax changes focused on two areas, the provision of positive incentives for preservation activity and the elimination of tax benefits for actions harmful to historic properties. The first objective was achieved by allowing owners of commercial historic properties the same kind of accelerated depreciation of their rehabilitation investment that was available to investors in new construction. The use of accelerated depreciation of the annual deduction of the capital investment in a building from taxable income at a rate more rapid than the actual loss incurred by wear and tear and obsolescence was long favored as a way to stimulate investment in real estate, but was previously limited to new construction. At the same time, changes in the tax code authorized an alternative five-year write off of rehabilitation expenses.

On the disincentive side, the owner of a historic building was denied the opportunity to deduct from taxable income the cost of demolition and the undepreciated value of the building, which was usually allowed as a tax loss in the year incurred. Instead, these were added to the cost of the land on which the structure stood, resulting in a higher basis and therefore in a reduced capital gain when the property was eventually sold. As a further disincentive, the property owner was limited to straight-line depreciation on any replacement structure erected on the site of a demolished historic building. These disincentives effectively reversed the tax consequences that had previously existed when a developer tore down a historic building and put up a new structure.

The Tax Reform Act of 1976 required the Secretary of the Interior to certify properties as historically significant and their rehabilitation as compatible with their historic character in order to qualify for tax benefits. Certified historic structures included properties individually listed in the National Register and those located in, and contributing to, historic districts. They are either listed in the National Register or designated pursuant to a state statute approved by the Secretary of the Interior. For the purposes of the demolition disincentives, all properties within registered historic districts were considered to be certified historic structures unless individually decertified by the Secretary. Certified rehabilitation required conformance with the Secretary of the Interior's Standards for Rehabilitation. Further requirements were that the property be held for the production of income and that the rehabilitation be substantial; that is, exceed the adjusted basis of the building, which is the original cost of the building (less the land) with adjustments for improvements made or depreciation taken in previous years. Owners of properties were required to submit a historic preservation certification application, consisting of Part 1, verifying the eligibility of the property for federal tax incentives, and Part 2, demonstrating the appropriateness of the rehabilitation work in maintaining the historic character of the structure or district.

As with the National Register program and the Section 106 process, the primary responsibility for conducting the certification system fell to the state historic preservation offices. The law requires that the Secretary of the Interior, working through the National Park Service, certify both significance of the building and the quality of work. The state offices have the role of consulting with applicants for the tax incentives and conducting the primary review of both parts of the application but for the most part, the Park Service has accepted the decisions of the states.

An appeal process has been established for applicants to obtain review of negative decisions made by the National Park Service. Due to the often significant financial consequences of being denied the tax incentives, applicants frequently invoke the appeals process and occasionally resort to litigation to challenge a decision on certification. More often than not, however, the National Park Service's appeals officer, acting on behalf of the Secretary of the Interior, sustains the initial ruling.

In 1978, further amendments to the tax code introduced a 10 percent investment tax credit for rehabilitation, which significantly accelerated the flow of private capital into the renovation of historic renovation of historic properties. Unlike the 1976 incentives which allowed only a certain amount of the rehabilitation investment to be deducted from an owner's taxable income, new provisions permitted 10 percent of the cost of rehabilitation to be set off against the owner's tax bill. This proved substantially more attractive to developers and real estate investors. In the two years prior to the enactment of the credit, certified rehabilitations totaled $140 million. With the credit in place, that figure climbed to $300 million in 1979 and to almost $350 million the following year.

These figures, compared with funding under the Historic Preservation Fund for the same period, demonstrate the importance of tax incentives. During this four-year period, the Preservation Fund assisted approximately 3,600 historic properties with grants totaling $76.4 million. The tax incentives, while used in about a third less projects, (2,300), generated ten times that ($786 million) in private investment for the rehabilitation.

The Economic Recovery Tax Act of 1981 introduced sweeping changes to the tax treatment of investments in real estate development. A three-tiered investment tax credit (ITC) system supplanted the earlier 10 percent credit, designed to stimulate the rehabilitation of older buildings, including but not limited to historic structures. The credit for certified rehabilitation of historic buildings increased to 25 percent. Also included were tax credits equivalent to 15 percent of the investment in qualified rehabilitation expenditures for 30-year-old commercial buildings and 20 percent for those 40 years of age. The Tax Act of 1981 modified the demolition disincentives, retaining only the provision denying any deduction for demolition costs and losses. It maintained the same definitions of certified historic structure, certified rehabilitation, substantial rehabilitation and qualified rehabilitation expenditures that had been used in the earlier program. In addition, its administrative process was essentially unchanged. With the enhanced incentives, the tax program came into its own, achieving success unimagined by the preservation community only a few years earlier.

In fiscal year 1982, National Park Service figures show that 1,802 projects, representing $1.13 billion of private investment, qualified for the investment tax credit. From 1982 to the end of 1985, the National Park Service approved more than 10,000 projects for tax credits, worth $7.8 billion. In fiscal year 1985 alone, more than 3,100 projects were certified, reflecting an investment of $2.4 billion. By comparison, the Historic Preservation Fund only provided $27 million for the restoration or rehabilitation of 1,760 properties in its peak funding year of 1979.

The impact of tax credits is the dramatic evidence of the role of the federal government in the national historic preservation program. The credits have attracted financial resources at a level undreamed of by the most optimistic preservationist just a few years ago. Although there have been negative effects, the program assisted private preservation efforts to a greater extent than would have been possible under a federal grant program. With the current trend of the federal government toward the curtailment of grant programs and the preoccupation with reduction of the federal deficit, it is clear that a program of direct subsidy would be an impossibility.

Tax credit projects run the full gamut of the private development spectrum. A study prepared by the Advisory Council on Historic Preservation in 1983 found that the average project was slightly less than $500,000 and that more than 40 percent were under $100,000. However, the number of large urban redevelopment projects, such as the renovation of St. Louis Union Station or the Willard Hotel in Washington, D.C., involving massive investment in renovation of historic properties, are on the rise. Often these projects combine private investment, qualifying for the investment tax credit, with federal funds, such as Urban Development Action Grants or Community Development Block Grants. The result is a dramatic reshaping of the urban fabric across the country as old movie palaces, grand hotels, railroad stations and office buildings take on new lives. On a smaller scale, thousands of small commercial structures on the nation's main streets and residential rental properties that provide the character of individual communities underwent successful renovation. As intended by the framers of the Preservation Act of 1966, the federal tax structure was revamped to favor, not discourage, the rehabilitation of historic properties.

One positive benefit of the tax credit system is the spinoff from investment in historic preservation. The National Park Service reports that the largest number of rehabilitation projects were for the purpose of providing housing: approximately 50 percent of preservation investment tax credit projects were for housing and another 20 percent were for mixed commercial and residential uses, resulting in almost 29,000 new housing units, 7,300 created in fiscal 1986 alone. This impressive track record of the government in stimulating private investment in housing (half the units went to low and moderate-income families) is unparalleled by any other federal housing program. Further, studies at the state level show the credits' secondary impact on jobs, state and local tax bases, tourism and revitalization of decaying downtowns.

Equally unforeseen are the negative effects of the program, both on the historic properties and on the national historic preservation program. There is some concern that the introduction of the private development sector to rehabilitating historic buildings for profit has led on occasion to over-renovation, although work must meet the Secretary's standards and receive the necessary certifications. This may stem in part from requirements in the tax law itself that the rehabilitation be substantial: that is, it must exceed the value of the building undergoing renovation, but it can also be attributed to the fact that the lucrative financial benefits in the investment tax credit which may attract investors and developers whose experience with and sensitivity to renovating historic buildings are less than the optimum.

An unanticipated side effect more threatening in the long term to the vitality of the national historic preservation program was the success of the tax credits in attracting sizable private investment in historic building renovation. Since 1981, the administration has sought to eliminate the Historic Preservation Fund appropriation. Each year, the preservation constituency expends untold

The Bureau of Land Management leased South Pass City to the State of Wyoming for development and interpretation as a historic site. (Museum Division, Wyoming State Archives, Museums and Historical Department)

A result of the Section 106 process, the U.S. Soil Conservation Service preserved a historic covered bridge for foot traffic at Staats Mill in Jackson County, West Virginia. (Larry L. Sturm, U.S.D.A. Soil Conservation Service)

An archaeologist recorded the petroglyphs at Stewart Mountain Dam Site in Arizona as a result of the Section 106 mitigation of dam maintenance activities and their effects on cultural and historic resources. (Bureau of Reclamation)

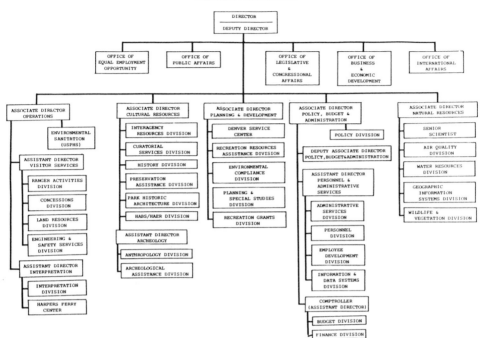

NATIONAL PARK SERVICE

DIRECTOR
DEPUTY DIRECTOR

- OFFICE OF EQUAL EMPLOYMENT OPPORTUNITY
- OFFICE OF PUBLIC AFFAIRS
- OFFICE OF LEGISLATIVE & CONGRESSIONAL AFFAIRS
- OFFICE OF BUSINESS & ECONOMIC DEVELOPMENT
- OFFICE OF INTERNATIONAL AFFAIRS

ASSOCIATE DIRECTOR OPERATIONS
- ENVIRONMENTAL SANITATION (USPHS)
- ASSISTANT DIRECTOR VISITOR SERVICES
  - RANGER ACTIVITIES DIVISION
  - CONCESSIONS DIVISION
  - LAND RESOURCES DIVISION
  - ENGINEERING & SAFETY SERVICES DIVISION
- ASSISTANT DIRECTOR INTERPRETATION
  - INTERPRETATION DIVISION
  - HARPERS FERRY CENTER

ASSOCIATE DIRECTOR CULTURAL RESOURCES
- INTERAGENCY RESOURCES DIVISION
- CURATORIAL SERVICES DIVISION
- HISTORY DIVISION
- PRESERVATION ASSISTANCE DIVISION
- PARK HISTORIC ARCHITECTURE DIVISION
- HABS/HAER DIVISION
- ASSISTANT DIRECTOR ARCHEOLOGY
  - ANTHROPOLOGY DIVISION
  - ARCHEOLOGICAL ASSISTANCE DIVISION

ASSOCIATE DIRECTOR PLANNING & DEVELOPMENT
- DENVER SERVICE CENTER
- RECREATION RESOURCES ASSISTANCE DIVISION
- ENVIRONMENTAL COMPLIANCE DIVISION
- PLANNING & SPECIAL STUDIES DIVISION
- RECREATION GRANTS DIVISION

ASSOCIATE DIRECTOR POLICY, BUDGET & ADMINISTRATION
- POLICY DIVISION
- DEPUTY ASSOCIATE DIRECTOR POLICY, BUDGET & ADMINISTRATION
- ASSISTANT DIRECTOR PERSONNEL & ADMINISTRATIVE SERVICES
  - ADMINISTRATIVE SERVICES DIVISION
  - PERSONNEL DIVISION
  - EMPLOYEE DEVELOPMENT DIVISION
  - INFORMATION & DATA SYSTEMS DIVISION
- COMPTROLLER (ASSISTANT DIRECTOR)
  - BUDGET DIVISION
  - FINANCE DIVISION

ASSOCIATE DIRECTOR NATURAL RESOURCES
- SENIOR SCIENTIST
- AIR QUALITY DIVISION
- WATER RESOURCES DIVISION
- GEOGRAPHIC INFORMATION SYSTEMS DIVISION
- WILDLIFE & VEGETATION DIVISION

An organizational chart of the National Park Service, U.S. Department of the Interior. (National Park Service)

A result of the Section 106 progress, the prehistoric settlement near the Hudson River at Fort Edward, New York, was excavated in early phases of the construction of a wastewater treatment plan funded by the Environmental Protection Agency. (Grossman & Associates)

lobbying effort to reinstate the Historic Preservation Fund despite the surge in funds resulting from tax credits.

Opponents of the Historic Preservation Fund argue that it is unnecessary because of the tax credit benefits. This argument lacks merit for two reasons. First, virtually the only funds appropriated for the Historic Preservation Fund since 1981 have been for administration at the state level and for the National Trust. Also there has been an increase in the workload on individual state historic preservation offices as a result of the investment tax credits, particularly since the National Park Service has actively sought to delegate the primary review responsibility for tax certifications and National Register nominations to state historic preservation offices.

The second problem with the argument against Historic Preservation Fund appropriations touches on a more basic shortcoming in the current federal program. Because investment tax credits are available only for income-producing properties, there is a whole universe of historic properties that currently cannot qualify for any federal financial assistance. The Historic Preservation Fund is the element which can provide financial aid, albeit small, to properties such as owner-occupied houses, buildings owned by state or local government or nonprofit organizations, and archaeological sites.

Late in 1986 the massive overhaul of the Internal Revenue Code had as one of the targets the elimination of tax credits. The preservation community faced a major challenge to preserve what had clearly become its most effective financial tool, and its nationwide lobbying effort resulted in keeping the rehabilitation credits although certain changes cast doubt on whether usage would continue at the level of the past few years.

Essentially, credits were revised from a three-tier system to two. The 25 percent investment tax credit for historic rehabilitations was reduced to 20 percent while the 15 and 20 percent credits for 30 and 40-year-old buildings were combined into a single 10 percent credit for nonhistoric buildings built before 1936. Eligibility criteria tax credits remained the same as before. Of principal concern, however, for the continued effectiveness of the investment tax credit was the introduction of the passive loss rule. Simply stated, this requires that the credit be applied to the tax on the income generated by the project. This effectively eliminates the use of the investment tax credit to shelter income from other sources, which was the primary attraction of the credit to investors under the Economic Recovery Tax Act of 1981.

Last minute changes to the passive loss rule as applied to the historic preservation tax credit softened the blow substantially and the preservation community generally views the fight to save the tax credits as a victory. However, uncertainty over the relative attractiveness of the investment tax credit to investors under the new tax law, with its reduced tax rates and other currently unforeseen twists, remains a cloud on the horizon.

One of the outgrowths of the preservation tax incentives is the development of policies and guidelines to implement the program. At the inception of the first tax incentives program in 1977, the National Park Service developed the *Secretary of the Interior's Standards for Rehabilitation*, a 10-point broad statement of policy that defined the boundaries of rehabilitation work. Rehabilitation was defined as: the "process of returning a property to a state of utility, through repair or alteration, which makes possible an efficient contemporary use while preserving those portions and features of the property which are significant to its historical, architectural, and cultural values." To further define the policy statements, the Park Service produced "Guidelines for Rehabilitating Historic Buildings," consisting of parallel practices that were recommended and those not recommended. As the Park Service gained experience, its staff identified recurrent questions of practice. In response, *Preservation Briefs* were prepared, now covering more than 60 topics. In addition, the series, *Preservation Tech Notes* was initiated to present innovative approaches to rehabilitation. These serve as a model for future publications.

Another provision of the Tax Reform Act of 1976 meets a preservation need: this is the allowance as a charitable contribution deduction of the value of an easement donated to preserve a historic property. A preservation easement is a private agreement between the property owner and a holding organization, usually a nonprofit organization or a governmental body, whereby the owner and successors are bound to preserve significant features of the historic property. Preservationists long recognized the value of easements for creating legally binding restrictions on a historic property, but questions concerning deductibility of the easement's value had often inhibited their use.

In practice, the easement provision stimulated use of this device to protect historic properties across the nation. The Advisory Council on Historic Preservation's 1983 tax study showed that only 14 percent of easements were acquired before 1976. It was also found that developers frequently used the easement provision to take a deduction for a grant of a facade easement on properties that were being rehabilitated for the historic preservation investment tax credit, providing an additional financial incentive for the developer while ensuring the long-term preservation of a property.

A recurring problem in the use of the easement deduction, however, is the question of valuation. Normally the value is defined as the difference in the fair market value of the historic property before and after the easement is granted. This assumes that a property with a preservation easement would be of less value than one without. Recently, though, the Internal Revenue Service has questioned whether this is true for historic buildings, since their value derives in part from the continued existence of their historic features. An aggressive audit policy by the investment tax credit and disallowance of the deduction, in some cases, as being overvalued cast doubt on the future of the easement deduction. At present, the debate continues.

Clearly, the federal tax incentives dramatically influenced historic preservation in the United States. It may be fittingly so, as the essence of the tax incentive program is the harnessing of the economic forces of the marketplace with the established social policy goals of preserving the national patrimony. While this alliance may have its problems at times, its successes demonstrate the resourcefulness of the preservation movement and its ability to tap the necessary sources of support for a long-term, broad-based approach to the preservation of properties that are, after all, considered in the marketplace as being essentially commodities.

As noted, not all of the financial assistance that the federal government provides for the preservation of historic properties comes from sources established for that specific purpose. Indeed, aside from the private money directed into preservation by tax incentives, most federal monetary support for historic preservation originates in programs that appear on the surface to have little or nothing to do with it. No reliable estimate exists on the full extent of this support, but some examples will serve to illustrate both its nature and magnitude.

At the outset, it is useful to identify two basic categories of support. First are those grant funds that underwrite various development at the state and local level: most often urban and community redevelopment, housing assistance, mass transit, public works and economic development. The second category embraces the use of federal project funds to mitigate unavoidable adverse effects on historic properties. Combined, the two categories produce substantial and otherwise unavailable sources of public funding to achieve preservation goals.

Most prominent in the grants category are two programs administered by the U.S. Department of Housing and Urban Development, the Urban Development Action Grants (UDAG) and Community Development Block Grants (CDBG). Both were viewed initially by the preservation community as having serious potential to destroy historic resources, the experience of urban redevelopment and renewal in the 1950s and the 1960s being still fresh in mind. However, as the focus of urban redevelopment shifted from clearance to conservation and reuse, the use of these funds proved highly compatible with local preservation goals.

The CDBG program came about in 1974 as a successor to many categorical grant programs. In lieu of categorical grants for specified urban renewal plans, block grant funds were provided to local governments for general purposes of urban revitalization, allocated at the discretion of local government. As the preservation ethic spread at the local level and priorities shifted toward the reuse of existing structures, these funds came to be committed increasingly to rehabilitation. Since these funds are federal, subject to review under Section 106 of the Preservation Act of 1966, local governments are obliged to consider carefully the potential effects on historic properties. Section 106 review in turn reinforced the efforts of local citizens to have these funds spent in a manner compatible with community preservation.

The result is increasingly widespread use of block grant funds for surveys of historic properties at the local level and then for carrying out renovation, code enforcement and public improvement projects in a manner that enhances historic values. Through sensitive planning at the outset, usually conducted and overseen by the state historic preservation office, these block grant funds often become preservation dollars.

The Urban Development Action Grant funds have a similar history. Created in 1978 to provide substantial federal grants to cities for urban revitalization projects, the UDAG program was viewed initially by preservationists with trepidation so great that it produced specific amendments to the program's legislation in 1980 that created detailed historic preservation review requirements. Changing ideas of urban revitalization, however, provided an opportunity to use these grant funds to support projects that advanced the preservation of historic properties. In fiscal year 1985, the Department of Housing and Urban Development approved 70 UDAG projects in 46 cities. Thirteen of these involved major renovation of historic buildings; none called for the demolition of significant historic resources.

Several other funding sources merit mention. While upgrading rail passenger service in the Northeast corridor, the U.S. Department of Transportation committed substantial funds to the sympathetic renovation of a number of historically or architecturally significant railroad stations. Unlike many preservation projects, this restoration effort resulted in the continued use of these buildings for their original purpose. Similar examples can be found in the use of Urban Mass Transit Administration projects to promote commuter rail and city streetcar service.

A final example that warrants mention is the Emergency Local Public Works program of 1978, conducted by the Economic Development Administration, under the U.S. Department of Commerce. Designed primarily to create jobs, the program gave preference to locally initiated projects that restored historically significant public buildings and also met the prescribed formula for generating jobs. Many projects that were originally proposed for Historic Preservation Fund assistance, but placed on hold because of the lack of funds, were revived and successfully submitted for Economic Development Administration grants. More than $300 million of Economic Development Administration grants were used for the rehabilitation of buildings listed in or eligible for the National Register.

The key to the success of this kind of funding is the increasing responsiveness of state and local government, the customary applicants for these funds, to demands of citizens and preservation organizations that government projects support, rather than work against, preservation. This, in turn, is testament to the growing sophistication of preservationists, the clear expansion of support in their community and their ability to work effectively within the political process.

The second major source of undesignated federal funds going into historic preservation is found in the dollars that agencies expend to mitigate adverse impacts of their projects on historic resources. Under the Archeological and Historic Preservation Act of 1974, agencies are authorized to use up to one percent of the total project budget to recover historical and archaeological data that would otherwise be lost. This becomes a significant figure when one considers the magnitude of a major federal construction projection, such as a dam. It has been estimated, but not substantiated, that as much as $200 million of federal project funds are expended annually to conduct archaeological data recovery in advance of construction. Were the figure even one-half of this estimate, it would represent five times what goes to support the administrative structure of the various state preservation offices each year.

Even more difficult to measure accurately are additional costs incurred by federal agencies to redesign projects to avoid or minimize harm to historic properties as required by the Section 106 process. Agencies generally consider these costs to be one more element of the project budget and often use contingency funds to cover the realignment of a highway segment or alteration of building materials to meet a preservation concern.

While the Advisory Council makes an effort to relate the cost of mitigation to the significance of the values affected, not all such decisions are made after a careful cost-preservation benefit analysis, but it would be misleading to suggest that federal agencies expend more on mitigation of impacts on historic resources than they do on other kinds of negative environmental effects. The project proceeds and preservation receives some recompense for unavoidable losses.

Finally, there are agencies that fund preservation activities as part of their primary mission, although they cannot be categorized as preservation agencies. Examples include grants from the National Endowment on the Arts to fund innovative preservation efforts as part of their broader program to advance architecture, community planning and the design arts; assistance from the National Endowment for the Humanities to support research in history, archaeology and other scholarly disciplines related to preservation; and National Science Foundation grants to conduct archaeological and anthropological research. The funding available is rarely large, most grants being measured in the thousands of dollars. However, these programs collectively make a significant contribution to the federal government's support for historic preservation, filling a gap rarely met by any other source of public support.

Collectively these federal funds greatly overshadow the modest sums directly earmarked for historic preservation. Although difficult to quantify accurately, they put the federal government clearly in the forefront of benefactors of the preservation movement.

Federal Management of Historic Properties

The preceding discussion has dealt with the federal government's role in promoting the preservation of all historic properties. There are significant legal responsibilities designed exclusively to ensure preservation of the extensive number of properties in federal ownership. These responsibilities affect properties already set aside for preservation and properties having intrinsic historic significance— on the one hand, units of the National Park system and on the other, government real estate ranging from courthouses to a virgin forest.

Tracing its origins to the establishment of Yellowstone National Park by the U.S. Congress in 1872, the National Park system today contains many of the crown jewels of the nation's patrimony. The evolution of the system includes the addition in the early 1900s of exceptional prehistoric sites in the Southwest, such as Mesa Verde, and in the 1930s the transfer of the Civil War battlefields from the War Department to National Park Service jurisdiction as major additions to the inventory of historic parks. Most others were created by the express action of the U.S. Congress, with specific legislation authorizing the creation of the park and defining its boundaries. Today, approximately 190 historical units of the 337 units of the National Park System are classed as historic parks or sites.

They illustrate American history, from events and personages of the Revolutionary War to the social, intellectual and economic currents that shaped the nation. Examples of this diversity include the Martin Luther King, Jr., National Historic Site in Atlanta, Georgia; Minuteman National Park in Lexington and Concord, Massachusetts; the Lowell National Urban Historical Park in Massachusetts; the Eugene O'Neill National Historic Site in Martinez, California; and the Chesapeake and Ohio Canal National Historical Park in Maryland.

Historic properties located within the park system are usually there for the express purpose of preservation and interpretation. Consequently, preservation is the primary mission of the managing agency, the National Park Service. The complete control exercised by the National Park Service over a property assures the highest form of long-term preservation; however, even this level of protection has its shortcomings.

Threats to these properties are both external and internal. The former present the most serious long-term problem, and current federal law provides little help. As the spread of the nation's urban centers continues to engulf more and more of the surrounding rural landscape, many heretofore isolated national parks are threatened with encroachment. Many in the National Park Service view this incessant expansion of urbanization as a primary challenge to their mission for the foreseeable future. Particularly affected are Civil War battlefields in Maryland and Virginia as well as Revolutionary War sites in Pennsylvania and New England. Few would argue that locating housing developments and shopping malls on the boundaries of the Manassas or Antietam Battlefield parks does not seriously degrade the integrity of these resources. Unfortunately, there is no current alternative to prohibitively costly acquisition of the adjoining lands to prevent these incursions.

Internal threats are more subtle, but may well be equally important over the long run. These are the actions that affect the actual fabric of the resource itself. Firstly, maintaining the integrity of a fragile historic fabric is not always consistent with meeting the visitation rights of a highly mobile American public. This threat is not unique to buildings in the park system; and indeed it is the superstar natural areas, Yellowstone and Yosemite, where this problem has been most publicized and may be most critical. Nevertheless, balancing the needs of preservation and use presents the National Park Service with its most formidable internal challenge.

The second category of internal threat is far less publicized and probably few outside the preservation establishment are even cognizant of it. Virtually all historic parks are created to commemorate, preserve and interpret a particular historical event, personage or theme. In order to best interpret the primary resource, it may be necessary to eliminate the vestiges of subsequent development unrelated to the purpose for which the park was created. Thus the 19th-century additions to a Revolutionary-period house are stripped away to allow restoration to its 1780 appearance: examples of commercial architecture spanning the period from the Civil War to the 1920s are demolished to remove incompatible intrusions on a collection of restored 18th-century buildings. An extreme example is where the only remaining authentic historic fabric of a frontier trading post, which is a ruin but rich in archaeological value, is deliberately destroyed so that a reconstruction of the structure can rise on the site. The problem also exists in the natural areas, where cultural resources, such as early tourist facilities or mining structures, may be viewed as incompatible with the primary emphasis on preservation and interpretation of natural values.

These problems are perplexing and the answers unclear. Grappling with individual cases often divides professionals whose shared goal is preservation. Most often the secondary resource is sacrificed and often this is the most appropriate solution. However, many times the loss of the lesser property is not so clearly warranted and some allege that destruction of important elements of the nation's heritage is being advanced by those who are specifically entrusted with its preservation. Few would fault the National Park Service for their commitment to the careful management of the historic properties entrusted to them. Nevertheless the situation presents a dilemma to preservation.

Much can be and is written about the National Park Service's stewardship of its park units. National Park Service properties, significant as they are, numerically speaking constitute only a small portion of the total universe of historic resources under federal jurisdiction. Due to the sheer size of the government's landholdings, federal responsibility for management of historic resources is extensive and its impact on the overall achievements of the national historic preservation program great.

Federal courthouses, post offices and office buildings were intentionally created to be symbols of the power of the federal government in cities and towns across the land. They were designed by leading architects in styles exemplifying the best of public architecture from the beginning of the republic. Often they have been maintained in relatively unaltered condition. Military and naval installations regularly contain buildings associated with significant historical events, ranging from the Revolutionary War to the development of the atomic bomb and the exploration of space. National forests and the public lands of the United States contain uncounted sites of prehistoric and historic archaeological significance, as well as structures associated with the mining and railroad industries and more recent social phenomena, such as the Civilian Conservation Corps. All but a few lighthouses built before World War I meet the National Register criteria and most of those that do are owned by the federal government.

The list goes on, embracing thousands of properties. Their most important shared feature is that, while possessing historic significance, they are still used to provide public services. They are not set aside as museums or units of the National Park System, thereby ensuring sensitive management. Rather, they are put to daily use in a variety of ways that are often inconsistent with the preservation of significant features. Section 106 and other tools of the Preservation Act of 1966 do not reach the daily property management of federal agencies. Indeed, the federal government has little knowledge of the extent of its historic property holdings.

Executive Order 11593, issued on May 13, 1971, attempted to correct this situation. First, recognizing that only a small proportion of historic properties in federal ownership were evaluated for the National Register, it directed agencies to undertake the necessary surveys which might yield further nominations to the National Register. Until these surveys were complete, the Executive Order required agencies to exercise caution when considering actions affecting potential historic properties under their jurisdiction and to seek comments of the Advisory Council on Historic Preservation when in doubt. This effectively extended the Section 106 process to federally owned properties eligible for, but not yet listed in, the National Register. A further provision of the Executive Order became the basis of an Advisory Council regulation issued in 1974, bringing all eligible properties, regardless of ownership, within the scope of this protective process.

While the establishment of the inventory requirement and the extension of the protective process were the most significant innovations of the Executive Order, other provisions also raised the level of responsibility for federal historic property managers. Chief among these was the directive to "initiate measures and procedures to provide for the maintenance, through preservation, rehabilitation or restoration, of federally owned and registered sites at professional standards prescribed by the Secretary of the Interior," thus placing an affirmative duty on federal agencies to maintain their National Register properties, and was followed by historic property management standards by the National Park Service. But it would be inaccurate to assume that all properties are being cared for as the standards dictate.

Two other provisions of the Executive Order merit discussion in the context of the federal stewardship role. One is the requirement that agencies submit records (measured drawings, photographs, and maps) of historic properties that are to be demolished or substantially altered, as a result of agency action, to the Historic American Buildings Survey of the National Park Service. The other provision directs agencies to cooperate with recipients of transferred federal historic properties to develop plans for the use of properties in a manner compatible with their historic significance.

The effect of the Executive Order has been to encourage the growth of a preservation ethic in the federal government, but dramatic changes have not been immediately forthcoming. The inventorying requirement generated a sizable number of nominations to the National Register but compliance varies widely from agency to agency. Those agencies with building inventories, such as the General Services Administration which manages the bulk of the federal government's office space and the Veterans' Administration which maintains an extensive system of medical facilities, responded with comprehensive inventories of high quality. Large land management agencies, such as the Bureau of Land Management and the U. S. Forest Service, which administer 272 million acres of public lands (plus an additional 300 million acres of federal mineral estate under state or private surface land) and 191 million acres of national forests and grasslands, are stymied by the sheer magnitude of surveying vast expanses of land primarily for archaeological sites. Budgetary considerations, as well as the consequences for land managers of the application of preservation protective systems to a large number of properties, have also hampered the effort; military installations, having a mix of large land masses and numbers of historic buildings, have a varied record of achievement in this area, ranging from excellent to nil.

Probably the most successful implementation of the Executive Order's charges occurred in the extension of the Advisory Council review process to properties not yet identified as qualifying for the National Register. It took a number of years after delineation of this requirement in the Section 106 procedures in 1974 as well as a subsequent amendment to the Preservation Act of 1966 to dispel any legal questions about the agencies' obligations before the idea of looking beyond the National Register list became second nature with agency officials. However, the duty to go the extra mile is now clearly entrenched and fully recognized by federal project planners and property managers. As noted in the earlier discussion regarding Section 106, this extension of protective provisions to the large number of properties possessing historic significance but not yet officially listed in the National Register is probably the single most important factor in bringing the protections of federal law to bear on the cultural environment.

In 1980, amendments to the Preservation Act of 1966 incorporated most of the Executive Order's federal property management requirements into the statute and are now found in Section 110 of the act. Section 110(a) directs federal agencies to "assume responsibility for the preservation of historic properties" under their ownership or control. While not specifically defining what that responsibility entails, Section 110(a) directs agencies to use existing historic properties "to the maximum extent feasible" for the purposes of carrying out their agency mission and to explore that use prior to acquiring, constructing or leasing new buildings. This provision traces its origin to the Public Buildings Cooperative Use Act of 1976, which, required the General Services Administration to give preference to historic buildings to meet federal space needs. The Advisory Council was obliged to recommend suitable buildings to the General Services Administration (GSA) and new construction could be pursued only if the GSA determined that the use of a historic building was neither "feasible or prudent," language adopted with full awareness of the stringent interpretation given the similar terms in the Transportation Act of 1966.

These provisions of the Public Buildings Cooperative Use Act of 1976 met with limited success, partially because the Advisory Council was never given sufficient funding to pursue the development of viable historic building use proposals for the General Services Administration. More important was the inherent nature of the bureaucratic and political process for determining where federal office buildings would be built. Within the GSA, it became readily apparent that confining alternative building sites to those recommended by an external agency, the Advisory Council, was an unacceptable limitation on and an unwanted intervention in the agency's internal decision making process. The good intentions of the legislation also failed to take into account that approval of new federal office buildings is often political. Congressional committees must approve prospectuses and elected representatives have a great deal of interest in the location of federal buildings within their districts. Although the law is still on the books, the process of seeking historic buildings for the GSA's use fell into disuse and only a few nonfederally owned historic buildings were ever acquired.

Section 110(a) attempted to avoid some of the pitfalls of the Cooperative Use Act of 1976 by placing the legal responsibility directly on the agency, eliminating the problem of interagency turf battles, but the required guidelines were not issued. At this writing, the legal duty remains, fraught with great potential for preservation, but hindered by the absence of any concrete direction.

One new tool for promoting the preservation of federally owned historic properties that has been successfully employed is found in Section 111 of the Preservation Act of 1966. Aided by the 1980 amendments, this provision authorizes federal agencies to lease or exchange, or enter into contracts for the management of, historic properties under their jurisdiction in order to promote preservation of such properties. Such action requires prior consultation with the Advisory Council to ensure that the preservation objectives are properly met. An important aspect of Section 111 is the authorization of the use of proceeds of these leases for the property's preservation costs. Without such an authorization, the proceeds would not be available for preservation or maintenance of the property. This provides an incentive to an agency to lease a property and obtain funds from the lease that would otherwise have to be provided out of the agency's appropriation for maintenance.

The Section 111 leasing authority has been used increasingly; an example is the leasing of obsolete lighthouses to the U.S. Coast Guard. The controls retained by the leasing agency over the property ensure its proper care and the proceeds are available to undertake repairs and upkeep as well as deferring the administrative cost of leasing the property. To date, the National Park Service has leased more than 60 properties, resulting in the private sector rehabilitation of those buildings exceeding $9 million. The potential for advancing preservation of federally owned historic properties in an era of continued budget restraint is significant.

While the foregoing discussion of federal stewardship covered legal provisions that apply to all historic properties regardless of the nature of their significance, the actual use of these tools tended to focus on historic buildings and structures. There has always been recognition in law that archaeological properties present special preservation considerations, due to the unique nature of the resource. As a result, there exists a series of federal legal protections that are written specifically for the protection of archaeological resources on government lands. Originating in the Antiquities Act of 1906, they are now embodied in the Archeological Resources Protection Act of 1979.

The basic mechanism for protecting federally owned archaeological resources is a permit system regulating the excavation of archaeological sites and criminal penalties for unauthorized excavation or vandalism. Designed to curb rampant pothunting at significant prehistoric sites in the Southwest, the Antiquities Act of 1935 created the original permit system and provided that any person "who shall appropriate, excavate, injure or destroy any historic or prehistoric ruin or monument, or any object of antiquity" on federal lands would be guilty of a misdemeanor. A judicial finding in 1977 that the term "any object of antiquity" was unconstitutionally vague led to legislative revision of the system in 1979. The resulting Archeological Resources Protection Act of 1979 solved the constitutional problem and effectively updated the 73-year old law, maintaining its essential features. The heart of updated protections for federally owned archaeological resources retains the permit system and criminal penalties.

The permit system, authorized by Section 4 of the Protection Act of 1979 is implemented through uniform regulations that were issued by the Tennessee Valley Authority and the Departments of Agriculture, Defense and Interior. Detailed definitions of archaeological resources carefully spell out requirements of the permit program, broadly covering "any remains of human life or activities which are at least 100 years of age, and which are of archaeological interest." This extends the permit requirements to those artifacts and features traditionally considered under the Antiquities Act of 1935 and also brings within the system such things as historic shipwrecks located within federal jurisdiction.

A person wishing to excavate or recover archaeological resources is required to apply to the federal land manager for a permit. To grant a permit, the land manager must determine that the applicant is qualified; that is, that the proposed work is being undertaken to further archaeological knowledge in the public interest; that the work is not inconsistent with management plans for the lands involved; and that there is an appropriate repository for the resources and records. Work then progresses in accordance with the specific conditions of the permit. Archaeological resources removed from federal lands remain the property of the federal government, unless they come from Indian lands, in which case the Indian tribe retains ownership.

Unauthorized excavation subjects the violator to the possibility of civil and criminal penalties. The civil penalties are assessed by the federal land manager and may be computed on the basis of what it would have cost to retrieve the scientific information before the violation occurred, the commercial value of the affected resources or the cost of restoration or repair. Criminal penalties can only be invoked through criminal prosecution in the federal courts, and can result in prison sentences of up to two years, assessment of fines up to $20,000 and forfeiture of equipment and vehicles used in the violation, as well as the archaeological resources themselves. Repeat offenders could be fined up to $100,000 and jailed for up to five years.

These stringent protections for archaeological resources under the government's control are the strongest form of protection afforded historic properties in federal law. Implementation of provisions of the Protection Act of 1979, however, was hampered by the delay in the issuance of the necessary federal regulations, which became effective only at the beginning of 1984. This prevented the government from using the civil sanctions for more than four years after the law's enactment. Meanwhile, criminal prosecutions were proceeding, although with some problems arising from the absence of regulations.

Even with regulations in place and an active effort underway to bring violators to justice, the task of protecting the full extent of the federal government's archaeological resources remains staggering. The sheer size of lands precludes meticulous policing of the public domain. Meanwhile, skyrocketing market values for prehistoric artifacts place even greater pressures on the protective system. Efforts at public education and exemplary prosecution and punishment remain about the only viable tools to make some inroads on pothunting and large scale commercial exploitation of these resources.

Clearly the federal stewardship role is extensive. As a result of a number of legislative enactments over the past decade, this responsibility is pursued with unprecedented vigor. The achievements in promoting the preservation of federally owned historic properties, especially since the passage of the 1980 amendments to the Preservation Act of 1966 are noteworthy and increasingly frequent. However, the realities of limited federal resources to commit to protecting and maintaining historic properties in the government's care will continue to hamper the fulfillment of the stewardship role.

Conclusion

Two decades after the passage of the Preservation Act of 1966, the partnership that is central to the structure of the national historic preservation program is firmly entrenched. The central role of the federal government in this system is evident in both the legislative framework and the administrative apparatus. With more than a century of involvement in historic preservation, it seems fitting that the current role of the federal government in the national program would be one of commitment and leadership. Indeed, most areas of federal responsibility, such

78

as the maintenance of the National Register, the establishment of national preservation standards and the conduct of the federal process for protecting historic properties reflect a high degree of refinement to meet the evolving conditions of historic preservation in the nation. As embodied in statute and administrative procedure, the federal role has probably exceeded the expectations of the framers of the Preservation Act of 1966.

However, the reality of federal participation in the national program underscores both achievements and shortcomings of historic preservation in the United States today. On the one hand, the carefully constructed partnership involving national, state and local levels of government working in concert with the private sector is uniquely suited for advancing preservation on a broad front. Successfully drawing on strong points of both the marketplace and the underlying concept of federalism, the program structure adapted well to the changing circumstances that favor or discourage the preservation of historic properties. Clearly the past two decades reflect unprecedented achievement in historic preservation, traceable in no small part to federal leadership and financial incentives.

At the same time, the forces that shape the general currents of American politics and the direction of the national government threaten to unravel this carefully knit but delicate fabric. Faltering policy leadership and retreat from financial commitment weaken the federal role in the national historic preservation program, at a time when the soundness of the program's basic concept has been proven.

Created with vision and continually adjusted to meet changing demands of society, the federal framework benefited from thoughtful and committed leadership, in the Executive Branch and the U.S. Congress, that has largely risen above partisan politics to pursue a common goal. Particularly since the passage of the Preservation Act of 1966, federal prominence in shaping the environment for preservation decision-making has been marked. Enlightened tax policy, aggressive advocacy for state and local government involvement in preservation and dedication to the establishment of effective national standards for preservation activity have characterized the federal leadership role. It is ironic that this tremendously positive program is seriously threatened now by factors that are not related to its inherent merits or achievements.

In an era of budget deficits and retreat from the concept of the federal government's role in society, the national historic preservation program finds itself in a perplexing situation. Unlike so many of the federal government's ventures into shaping social policy, its efforts in historic preservation are a successful and cost-effective catalyst for nonfederal commitments to preservation of the built environment. Whether this record of effectiveness can continue remains to be seen, as the federal commitment of financial assistance and policy leadership is an essential ingredient to the smooth functioning of the partnership.

On a more positive note, one of the current hallmarks of the national historic preservation program is its broad-based and bipartisan support. This support reflects the extent to which preservation is a part of the mainstream of American life, attracting advocates who a few short years ago did not know the meaning of the term historic preservation. While efforts are made repeatedly to cut back the federal leadership role, supporters of the partnership are articulate and persuasive, and successful more often than not in restoring funding cuts and rejecting program restrictions proposed by the current administration. This vitality bodes well for the continued success of the program and for a continued leadership role for the federal preservation establishment.

As the National Historic Preservation Act of 1966 and the program it engendered enter their third decade, challenges are clear. Clear also is the commitment of the preservation community and its allies to maintaining the system that fostered the growth of historic preservation into a major national force. Recognized as fundamental to this system is the leadership of the federal government. Under these conditions, it is possible to look at the future of the national historic preservation program and the federal government's role in it with optimism. The strength of the underlying partnership and its unique suitability to preservation in the United States foretells continued progress, despite present threats of cutback and retrenchment.

CHAPTER THREE

THE STATES: PRESERVATION IN THE MIDDLE

ELIZABETH A. LYON

THE STATES: PRESERVATION IN THE MIDDLE

ELIZABETH A. LYON

Introduction

Since 1966, the states were linked to the federal government, to each other and to local governments and organizations in a preservation partnership guided by the National Historic Preservation Act of that year. Programs that preserved and interpreted state-owned historic sites were already in place in 42 states when the act was passed. State attention was also focused on countless local efforts to preserve significant sites and districts in particular communities. From the state standpoint, the Preservation Act of 1966 provided a national, uniform framework within which more and better state and local initiatives could take place, assisted by funds made available through the new federal program.

The Preservation Act was a turning point in the development of state historic preservation programs. Spurred by the national program, and the larger environmental concerns from which it grew, states came to realize that it is not enough to own and manage a few sites of statewide importance and to mark places where significant events took place. It is not possible, through public ownership, to protect all historic properties within state boundaries, or to address the growing concern for the quality of the built environment in local communities. The Preservation Act of 1966 thus provided a framework and mechanism that encouraged the states to develop programs of preservation planning and funding assistance to the general public. Situated in the middle of a three-way partnership, the states quickly turned their attention to the broad range of prehistoric and historic resources within their borders that were a part of the nation's history, as well as their own.

Preservation in the States Before 1966

Although a detailed state-by-state preservation history for the years before the Preservation Act of 1966 remains to be written, a general outline is beginning to come into focus. State governments, often spurred to action by a local concern for a favorite site or by a strong-minded citizen or government leader, followed an uneven and sometimes haphazard course toward historic preservation. Concern for significant but usually widely scattered relics, ruins and properties constituted the earliest direct state involvement in preservation. The consequent restoration and reconstruction projects emphasized places that illustrate significant events in history or in the lives of people of state and national renown. At times state activities were affected by federal legislation or programs, such as the Antiquities Act of 1906, the establishment of the National Park Service in 1916 or the National Survey of Historic Sites and Buildings initiated in 1935. These laws resulted in federally sponsored survey, protection or acquisition activities within states. Some states took advantage of Great Depression-era programs, such as the Works Progress Administration and the Historic American Buildings Survey of the Park Service which accelerated survey and restoration work.

Early State Efforts to Study and Acquire Historic Properties

Many of the earliest state preservation efforts were initiated by individual state park organizations as a part of a general expansion of these systems following World War I. This in turn was a response to the initiatives of Stephen Mather, first director of the National Park Service, who promoted state parks as well. For example, California undertook a systematic approach to the purchase of historic properties following a park survey in 1928; Indiana established a network of scenic and historic parks between 1919 and the early 1930s; and New York purchased numerous properties to operate as museum sites during this period. Additional states, Maine, Florida, North Dakota, Wyoming and others, instituted similar surveys and acquisitions in the 1930s. The historical tie between parks and preservation was no less strong at the state level than at the federal.

State historical societies, although typically reluctant to assume continuing responsibility for property management, slowly became involved in the preservation of buildings and their associated collections of museum artifacts and papers. Pennsylvania, which established a state historical and museum commission in 1913, bought the home of a Germanic religious and communal group, Old Economy, at Ambridge in 1919, and part of the site of a colonial fort in the following year. The Ohio Historical Society acquired several properties between the 1920s and the 1940s. Wisconsin purchased its first historic house museum in 1949. Minnesota, reversing a 100-year policy, accepted the gift of a historic mansion in 1958. The movement picked up momentum in the 1950s as a number of states, among them Arkansas, Georgia and Wyoming, established historical commissions with authority to acquire historical and archaeological properties and interpret them to the public. Centennial observances in many states, especially in the 1920s and 1930s, were important catalysts for encouraging public interest in preservation. For example, Missouri's centennial celebration of 1921 resulted in its first state-owned site, Old Tavern at Arrow Rock, the spot where the Santa Fe Trail crossed the Missouri River. In 1936, Texas effectively took advantage of its centennial to focus attention on selected monuments and building projects.

State interest in preservation continued to grow. A national survey carried out in 1964 indicated that 42 states had functioning historic site management programs. The authority to conduct programs of property acquisition, restoration or reconstruction and management was provided in state laws establishing parks systems, state historical societies and commissions. They could hold property of historic and cultural significance, and preserve and administer these properties in order to promote understanding of the state's history. Thirty states were authorized to acquire property by gift or purchase; 20 of them also had authority to acquire sites by eminent domain. Operating funds came from a variety of sources: admission and concession fees, privately financed endowments and state government appropriations.

With only two exceptions, all of the states that reported programs in 1964 indicated that they also operated historic marker programs. In addition, Idaho, Maine, Washington and West Virginia, which then had no developed acquisition and management programs, did have marker programs. Some of these marker programs developed from and depended on statewide surveys. Minnesota, for example, began marking sites associated with the Sioux War as early as 1885 and, in 1960, began a survey of the state's historic sites for publication. The Texas State Historical Survey Committee, established by the legislature in 1953 and forerunner of the Texas Historical Commission, initiated an extensive marker program. By 1976, it was the largest in the country, with more than 6,500 markers. Other states with extensive marker programs were Georgia, Virginia, Pennsylvania, Kentucky, Tennessee and North Carolina; by 1976, each had more than 1,300 markers in place.

Few of the pre-1966 state highway marker or historic site acquisition programs were based on comprehensive research and survey efforts. The type of statewide survey required by the Preservation Act of 1966, comprehensive in scope and carried out according to professional standards, was rare. Missouri's historic society conducted a survey in 1925 which resulted in the marking of 350 sites. Surveys of historical and architectural sites conducted in Oklahoma in 1930, 1936–38 and 1959 became the basis for work after 1966. California's park survey of 1928, conducted by Frederick Law Olmsted, Jr., was the first statewide survey to include both historic sites and landscapes. During the 1930s, California continued to gather information on a wide variety of historic properties using the Historic American Buildings Survey (HABS).

HABS provided both an incentive and a model for future survey programs in a number of states. In Minnesota, for example, the Works Progress Administration surveyed historic sites in the 1930s. Later in Virginia, HABS served as the beginning for a student inventory of more than 3,000 structures. Pennsylvania began a historic survey in 1947–48, the goal of which was to identify all significant buildings, and historic and archaeological sites. When the Texas legislature established the Texas State Historical Survey Committee in 1953, its purpose, in addition to the marking of sites, was to study the effectiveness of historical organizations within the state and to conduct research regarding the nature and location of endangered artifacts, shrines and historical papers. From 1964–1969, the committee carried out an intensive research and survey program to place official markers covering a broad range of the state's history.

Missouri, in a pattern that became characteristic in many states, organized a statewide survey carried out by volunteers. It identified 2,400 sites, which were later published in the Missouri Historic Sites Catalog. In the late 1950s, at least two states participated in area surveys whose purpose was to identify a broad range of properties. Studies of the City of Wilmington, Delaware, and the College Hill area of Providence, Rhode Island, set a precedent for architectural surveys as the basis for comprehensive preservation planning.

By the mid-1960s, the interest of state governments in identifying and preserving a broad range of historic and archaeological properties was growing. Both Maryland and Massachusetts in the East and New Mexico in the West had proposed or initiated statewide inventories. Maryland and Massachusetts conducted this work through newly authorized historical agencies: the Maryland Historical Trust established in 1962 and the Massachusetts Historical Commission in 1963. Other state agencies, including some whose focus was not historic preservation, undertook architectural surveys. New Mexico's survey was begun in 1965 through its state planning office. During 1964 and 1965, the New York State Council on the Arts sponsored environmental surveys of architecture worth saving in several counties.

Some state preservation agencies in the West were also given responsibility for the protection of archaeological sites. Reflecting a concern that dated back to the turn of the century, a 1931 New Mexico law requires that excavation permits should be required for explorations on state land. Missouri initiated an archaeological survey and formed a state archaeological society in the 1930s. By the 1960s, Illinois, Idaho and Arkansas had also established state archaeological surveys. Arkansas through its survey was a true leader in the American public archaeological movement—in research, legislation and in promoting archaeology in the federal and other state governments. By 1966, while in 19 states there was some form of archaeological legislation, only 5 required excavation permits and only 7 provided for a state archaeologist. By and large, there was yet no state protection for archaeological resources on private land.

Early State Preservation Legislation

While the dominant preservation activity of state governments before 1966 was the management of state-owned historic and archaeological properties and the marking of places of historical interest, the states fostered preservation activity in local communities through authorizations contained in state law. Many of the laws authorized local governments and agencies to acquire and maintain historic properties and to open them to the public.

However, the most significant preservation tool given to local governments by the states was the authorization to establish historic districts and to designate landmarks. By the 1930s, the idea of preserving large areas, such as early villages and mining camps, had become part of a few state historic site programs. But the real impetus for historic district laws came from local preservationists looking for ways to protect concentrations of older buildings that they regarded as giving character to their communities.

The earliest state historic district enabling laws were addressed to specific cities or districts. The first in 1936 was the French Quarter or the Vieux Carré in New Orleans, Louisiana. Massachusetts authorized the establishment of districts in Boston's Beacon Hill, and in Nantucket and Siasconset villages on Nantucket Island in 1955. Several other states, North Carolina, Connecticut and Florida, followed suit in the 1950s and 1960s, passing laws authorizing districts in towns and cities. Few of these early laws were challenged in court. Those that were were upheld as conducive to improving the general welfare. This was notwithstanding the prevailing doctrine of the earlier period that aesthetic regulations would not be upheld on constitutional grounds. It was clear that the state courts had a special tenderness for the notion of a historic district.

The earliest historic district laws were aimed at specific places possessing obvious historical and architectural merit. In time, however, states began to pass general enabling legislation authorizing all cities, and sometimes counties, to establish historic district and landmark programs. Rhode Island was the first state to do so, in 1959. By 1963, perhaps a dozen states had passed historic district or landmark legislation in one form or another.

State Preservation Programs in the Environmental Era

In the strongly pro-environmental climate of the 1960s that would produce the Preservation Act of 1966, the states had already begun to recognize the need to assist local governments to protect their historic resources. On the eve of the passage of the national historic preservation law, many of the elements of the expanded state programs of the future were now visible.

Comprehensive and systematic statewide surveys to identify a range of historic and archaeological properties had begun in a few states. Federal programs, such as the Works Progress Administration histories and the Historic American Buildings Survey, laid the groundwork for others. In a few states, planning for the acquisition and development of historic properties or marker programs relied on statewide surveys. And, as noted earlier, several states began to survey and protect archaeological sites, especially on state-owned lands.

These years also saw the beginning of state programs of preservation assistance and encouragement for the general public. The legislation creating the Maryland Historical Trust encouraged preparation of local community preservation plans and zoning ordinances and authorized state assistance to cities, counties and the public. North Carolina established a Historic Sites Commission in 1953 to develop and administer criteria to guide state expenditure for local projects.

The principal preservation activity of state governments in the decades before the national preservation law had been one of protecting properties through acquisition and management and of encouraging interest through marking historic sites and buildings. States also gave local governments the authority to acquire and administer historic properties and, perhaps of greater importance, to establish preservation commissions and adopt historic districts. These preservation incentives, however noteworthy, were randomly scattered among states and had neither a national focus nor any interstate coordination. This would soon change dramatically.

The States Expand Their Programs, 1966–86

The Preservation Act of 1966 authorized federal assistance to the states "to expand and accelerate their historic preservation programs and activities." While it authorized federal grants to the states for comprehensive statewide surveys, plans and preservation projects, the law itself did not specifically outline the nature or extent of state participation. In the early years, the specific responsibilities of the states were developed as procedures and regulations. They were not written into the law itself until the 1980 amendments to the Preservation Act of 1966 were passed. Noting that the new law emphasized the role of state and local governments in surveys and restoration, the Secretary of the Interior in 1967 wrote to the nation's governors. He invited them to appoint a state liaison officer for historic preservation and an agency to work with the National Park Service to implement the new program.

Early Response of the States to the 1966 Act

During the early 1970s, some states authorized a historic preservation program through legislation, setting up agencies or divisions specifically to administer the new and broader range of responsibilities. Other states worked through existing commissions and agencies already in possession of the necessary authorization. A 1975 report on nationwide historic preservation, done for the National Park Service, indicated that most state preservation offices had been put in one of three places in state government. Some were an independent historical commission or similar agency; others were part of a broad historical or cultural agency, such as archives or history departments; still others were located in the state's natural resource or parks and recreation agency. To some degree, the place of the program influenced its character and the level of support given to it by different states. For example, independent state preservation agencies projected clear identities and exercised considerable programmatic flexibility, but lacked the political influence of larger state agencies. State preservation bureaus located within larger agencies, while sharing the greater resources of the parent agency, tended to project a lower-profile identity than an independent program and, thus, were less effective in dealing with other state priorities.

Archaeology programs, which had been deliberately combined with historic preservation by the National Park Service, were also administered in different ways by states. In some, universities and state museums which had begun research and salvage activities in the early period continued to handle this component of the new program. However, the well-established survey programs, of which Arkansas is a prime example, continued to maintain separate offices. In other states, Texas and Florida among them, separate divisions of archaeology within the historic preservation agency took on the new responsibilities. Others, such as North Carolina and Massachusetts, integrated archaeology with historic preservation programs. Separate programs sometimes enjoyed greater independence and political support, but they tended to be more research oriented than those that were integrated into the new preservation programs.

Although there was considerable interest among state historical agencies in beginning their new responsibilities for survey and restoration immediately following the passage of the Preservation Act of 1966, no federal funds were available until July 1968, and even then the amount was only $82,500. Considering this amount too small to be useful, many states failed to apply, leaving to those that did grants ranging from $785 to $11,745. However, one by one, each state took action to set up the new program. The number of states participating and the total allocation increased steadily. By 1970, 36 states shared $669,000 in federal funds; while in 1971, 46 states competed for a total of $4,590,000. By 1976, 50 states and 5 territories, were competing for a federal appropriation of $15,259,483. Federal funding levels increased through the 1979 fiscal year but thereafter declined. After 1981, federal funds were distributed only for survey and planning activities, with the expectation that the expanded federal tax incentives, rather than grants, would encourage the development of historic properties. Since 1979, 50 states and 7 territories have participated annually in the program.

The Preservation Act of 1966 limited federal government participation in the state programs to a maximum of 50 percent of the cost of their program. In 1976, the federal share, just for survey projects, was raised to 70%, but most states continued to contribute more than 50% of the cost of the program. This meant that considerable public and private funding support had to be available within the state itself.

The limited funding provided in the early years did not allow the states to begin building strong professional staffs, but they were encouraged to concentrate on inventory and survey work and on National Register nominations. Federal funds could also be used to fund restoration projects, and these became an important catalyst for preservation in many states. As the program developed, so did the list of responsibilities. To qualify for participation by 1980, the amendments to the Preservation Act of 1966 stipulated that states must:

- identify and research historic, architectural and archaeological properties,
- nominate to the National Register of Historic Places properties that meet the National Register criteria,
- prepare comprehensive statewide preservation plans,
- assist state and local governments with their historic preservation responsibilities through the procedures of the President's Advisory Council on Historic Preservation,
- administer grants-in-aid for survey and planning and, when funds are available, development projects and
- provide information, education, training and technical assistance.

Building a Comprehensive Inventory

Although many states were already accustomed to carrying out surveys of buildings and archaeological sites, the size and scale of the post-1966 effort posed increasingly difficult problems as the vision of history-worth-preserving expanded. In the mid-1970s, according to one veteran state survey professional, the preservation staff

> ". . . experienced a sudden explosion in [their] understanding of what was significant . . . to move from looking at individual unique or stylish buildings and then suddenly to realize that far, far more was out there that was important, the scruffy mill villages, the little tobacco barns, the ordinary farmsteads,the urban neighborhoods, the tenant houses. . . ."

Earlier surveys tended to concentrate on the oldest and the finest. But then the emerging interest in a broader human environment opened a wider vision and the Preservation Act of 1966 provided a mechanism for recording it.

The initial concept, set forth by the new law, called for the development of statewide inventories of properties of local, state and national significance which would become the basis of a state's historic preservation plan. Based on these surveys, properties were to be evaluated for listing in the National Register. The list of registered properties would, thereafter, be used to support planning to protect, restore and rehabilitate worthy historic properties by government agencies and the private sector. It was estimated that three to five years would be sufficient to complete the work or at least to provide an estimate of the scope and potential cost of the job.

When the results of the first decade of survey work were reviewed, the states were judged to be far from having a complete record. While progress had been made, the "results [were] as varied as the means," and there was great variety in coverage, numbers and types of resources from state to state. The number of properties in state inventories ranged from 135 to 25,000, with the average around 4,700. When asked to estimate the percentage of completion and target dates, states replied with estimates ranging from 10 to 95 percent and target dates from 1980 to 2040. Many states would not, or could not, provide completion dates. Approaches to survey work varied from careful research on a limited number of properties to the collection of limited information on as many properties as possible.

During the second decade, from 1976 to 1986, states and the National Park Service together developed more structured survey methods and guidelines. These were designed to accommodate a wider variety of historic and archaeological resources and to recognize the purposes for which surveys are conducted. Using terminology developed for archaeological surveys, two levels of effort were defined. The first, prescribing reconnaissance or minimum level surveys, were based on a limited amount of archival and field investigation. They were designed to provide only a general impression of the architectural, archaeological and historic properties, and values of an area. This type of survey permitted general conclusions to be drawn about property types and their distribution, but it did not produce sufficient documentation for the nomination of individual properties to the National Register. The second, more intensive level, involved systematic field and archival inspection of an area in order to document properties in sufficient detail to measure their significance against the criteria of the National Register of Historic Places.

By 1986, it was possible to summarize state survey activity in relatively consistent terms. During 1985, 281,552 properties were surveyed at a minimum level and 103,541 more intensively. The figures for the preceding two years, during which this counting system was used, were similar. This suggests that approximately 4,000,000 properties have been identified in the 20 years of the program.

How was this accomplished? By the mid-1970s, it was clear that state offices had insufficient resources to complete a comprehensive survey of the historic and archaeological resources of a state in any reasonable length of time. Partly because of this limitation, and often in response to local needs and requests, the states devised alternative approaches. In initiating programs, they relied on existing information from local surveys, marker inventories, previous HABS and National Historic Landmark and archaeological surveys. Useful information was gathered from these sources, but it proved to be uneven. Surveys required by the Preservation Act of 1966 and federal regulations to qualify for federal agency funding and planning projects, also, became an important source of information for state inventories. Most surveys, however, depended heavily upon volunteers working under the professional direction of state historic preservation office staff, regional and local planners or consultants.

Expansion of the National Register, which from 1966 was to include everything from national historic landmarks to properties of state and local significance, opened up new possibilities to the states. Even though the Secretary of the Interior, the U.S. Congress and the National Park Service could add properties to the National Register, the primary responsibility for National Register nominations was given to the states. By 1972, 61 percent of the 3,337 listings had been initiated by the states. By 1974, the total number of listings had more than doubled to 7,046 and the state's contribution had risen to 82.9 percent. Of the nearly 45,000 listings in 1986, 91 percent came from the states. Thus, the national inventory was shaped mainly by the states, both through National Register nominations and other required evaluative processes, such as environmental review and tax certification.

In conducting the statewide surveys, the states have relied heavily on local initiative and assistance in identifying and researching properties for nomination to the National Register. Once properties have been identified and evaluated and the documentation completed, they are presented to the National Register professional review committees in each state, which are intended to maintain a level of quality control over nominations. The members of these committees must, by federal regulation, include professionals in history, architectural history, architecture, archaeology and citizens with an interest in historic preservation. The committees review proposals for nominations and recommend properties to the state historic preservation officer for further action.

The National Trust for Historic Preservation drew a profile of the National Register from a sample survey of listings from 53 states and territories in 1981. Whereas earlier listings tended to recognize only the oldest structures and the properties with state or national significance, the 1981 profile revealed an increased proportion of locally significant properties and districts. In the West, where state and local preservation programs started late, there was a greater number of nationally significant and publicly owned properties, while historic districts of local significance were more prevalent in inventories from the East.

The consistent framework for nominations provided by the four broad National Register evaluation criteria allowed the addition to this national inventory of properties reflecting the distinct history and perspective of each state. A cursory sampling of nominations shows that the states used their prerogative to recognize properties representing the patterns of their own history. They include large Indian pueblo and village sites in New Mexico and Arizona, cattle ranches and Mormon tabernacles in Utah, round barns and state park lodges in Illinois, courthouses and railroad properties in Texas, simple pioneer dwellings in Idaho and Washington and downtowns and neighborhoods in virtually every state and territory.

In addition to National Register nominations, the states also add another 25 percent or more of properties or districts each year to the national inventory through "determinations of eligibility." The determination that a property is eligible for the National Register is just that: a singling out of the property to signify its eligibility, so that it can be taken into account by federally funded or licensed projects. Determinations of eligibility are made for the purpose of environmental review consideration for properties not yet listed. They were first authorized by Executive Order 11593 in May 1971 and thereafter written into the law by the 1980 amendments. Although not actually listed in the National Register, such properties are recognized officially as eligible by the Secretary of the Interior.

There are differing views about the significance of the National Register itself. Some regard listing as merely an honor. States consider that its major function is to serve as a planning tool. Communities that participated actively and extensively in the process of discovering and documenting historic district and other multiple property nominations quickly developed a clear and strong understanding of their history and development. However, what became increasingly important to their preservation and protection was the process itself which served not only as a catalyst for preservation plans and community projects, but also sometimes stimulated the formation of community preservation organizations.

One of the first states to recognize and use the National Register process for preservation planning was Rhode Island. Town-by-town surveys were organized and conducted by the state in cooperation with local planning officials, schools, and civic and preservation groups and then published. In 1979, when the statewide survey effort was only about half completed, the Rhode Island preservation office was able to report an increased awareness of the historic and architectural quality of these communities by citizens of all ages. It went on to describe case studies, building projects, educational efforts and preservation plans that had followed as a result of the publication of the town reports.

Similarly, the National Register nomination for the Nacoochee Valley Historic District in Georgia, a rural vernacular landscape of historic houses and archaeological sites, led to the formation of a citizen organization. This organization worked with the state on a survey and nomination for the adjacent historic valley and a preservation plan outlining the type of future development that could fit into the historic character of both valleys. To emphasize the importance of historic resources to the vitality of communities in northeastern Illinois, the state historic preservation office assisted one of its regional planning commissions in publishing an atlas of National Register historic districts. In 1985, Texas responded to a request to study Bosque County, which contained a historic Norwegian settlement still largely owned by descendants of the original immigrants. The study resulted in a thematic nomination of 35 individual properties and a large rural district of 14 contributing properties, all relating to the Norwegian settlement.

Archaeological properties were not used as extensively as a basis for contemporary community preservation programs; however, some notable examples were used to illustrate their potential. States are now increasing their efforts to use National Register listing for archaeological sites as a means to encourage their protection.

The proportion of archaeological sites to historic structures and districts on the Register is small—3,066 listings as of 1986 or about 7 percent of the total. This proportion has remained relatively stable over time—8 percent in 1972 and 6 percent in 1974. However, archaeological sites were not ignored by the program, but rather were identified and evaluated through the environmental review process generated by Section 106 of the Preservation Act of 1966. Specific project surveys and determinations of eligibility provided the most effective, and often the only, way to protect these sites or to retrieve some of the information they contain.

The state of Pennsylvania purchased the site of Old Economy in Ambridge, Pennsylvania, in 1919, the home of a 19th-century Germanic religious and communal group. (Pennsylvania Historical and Museum Commission)

The Old Tavern at Arrow Rock, site of the northeastern terminus of the Santa Fe Trail, was acquired by the state of Missouri on the occasion of the state's centennial celebration in 1921. (Missouri Department of Natural Resources)

The Texas Historical Commission study of the historic Norwegian settlement in Bosque County resulted in the nomination of 35 individual properties and a large rural district to the National Register of Historic Places. (Texas Historical Commission)

Through a statewide survey of historic county courthouses conducted by the Georgia state historic preservation office, the Colquitt County Courthouse in Moultrie was included in a thematic nomination to the National Register of Historic Places. (James R. Lockhart, Georgia Department of Natural Resources)

The listing of 55 miles of the 1913–22 Columbia River Highway in Oregon on the National Register of Historic Places exemplifies the emerging interest in early 20th-century transportation resources. (Jerry Robertson, Oregon Department of Transportation)

In addition to building the National Register inventory, some states have their own systems for providing recognition or protection for listed historic and archaeological properties. State registers, similar to the National Register, have been established in approximately two-thirds of the states. Often these were included in the state legislation which authorized participation in the federal preservation program, but a number of state registers pre-dated the federal law. Thus, Michigan designated properties as early as 1955 and Minnesota in 1965. In 15 states, National Register properties are automatically included on the state register. Others incorporate a wider variety of historic resources than could meet the criteria of the National Register, while still others are more restrictive. Massachusetts, under a 1982 law, established a state register composed of properties from several sources, including the National Register, Massachusetts Certified Landmarks, local designations and properties determined eligible for the National Register for federal undertakings. A few states, North Carolina among them, did away with state registers following passage of the Preservation Act of 1966, on grounds of redundancy, since the National Register contemplated inclusion of properties of statewide, as well as national, importance.

Protection and Monitoring by the States

The Preservation Act of 1966 not only called on states to identify and evaluate historic and archaeological properties for an expanded National Register but also involved them in protecting these properties against federally sponsored harm under Section 106. Some states, of course, had been protecting historic properties since the 19th century through public ownership and other protective measures under state law. Now, with the Preservation Act of 1966, they were positioned to assist the federal government in monitoring federal agency actions that might adversely affect historic and archaeological properties within their boundaries.

Notwithstanding that Section 106 called for review and comments by the Advisory Council to other federal agencies, the states were considered essential participants in the process from the beginning. In fact, the first *Procedures* published in the *Federal Register* in 1969, required federal agencies to consult the State Historic Preservation Officer (SHPO) in determining effects to properties listed in the National Register.

In this process, states were, at first, to provide any available information on historic, architectural and archaeological resources located within proposed project areas and to advise on any survey work that might be needed. However, the actual completion of such surveys has been the responsibility of the federal agency or its project applicant ever since May 1972, when Executive Order 11593 was issued. Some states made consultant services available to the agencies, and many private consulting firms added cultural resource specialists to serve this need.

The second step in the process requires consultation with the SHPO in order to determine whether or not identified properties meet the criteria for listing in the National Register. If the properties are deemed to be of National Register quality and located in the area to be affected by the project, states are expected to consult with the federal agencies or applicants on the nature of the effects to these resources. If the effects are adverse, the states work with the agencies to find either alternatives or measures to minimize the harm. States are also expected to negotiate solutions to conflicts and, when necessary, work with the Advisory Council to resolve them. Agreements are concluded by a memorandum of agreement requiring the SHPO's signature. If the SHPO determines that properties located in a project area are eligible for inclusion in the National Register, federal agencies are recommended to comply with Advisory Council procedures.

Not only is the nature of state participation in the Section 106 process extensive and time consuming, it is fraught with political dangers for the cause of preservation within the state. SHPOs, who are appointed by the governor, often find themselves in a position of having to oppose or delay other state agencies or local governments whose favorite development projects may be at stake. Local citizens and organizations are often disappointed when the SHPO, regarded by them as the highest-level preservation advocate of all in a state, cannot stop projects that they deem harmful. Nor do many local preservationists fully understand that the process is merely advisory, and that the final decision on any undertaking is left to the federal agency or its applicant.

By the end of the first decade following passage of the Preservation Act of 1966, the states were heavily involved in Section 106 review and consultation. This grew to unexpected proportions as federal funding levels increased, in the mid-to-late 1970s, for several federal programs. These included the U.S. Department of Housing and Urban Development's Urban Development Action Grants and Community Development Block Grants, the Federal Highway Administration's interstate highway and bridge replacement programs and the large water projects of the Army Corps of Engineers. Some were staggering in their complexity. For example, the state historic preservation offices in three states, Alabama, Mississippi and Tennessee, were involved in a review of the Tennessee-Tombigbee Waterway with the Advisory Council, Corps of Engineers and National Park Service. This was a large navigation and flood control project to protect hundreds of acres of land with many historic buildings and archaeological sites. The consultation lasted for three years!

This process was repeated again and again across the country in the mid-1970s for similar projects. Large highway and housing projects required a major commitment of time and effort from the states. In states with extensive federal land holdings, such as New Mexico, Wyoming and Arizona, time-consuming, often cumbersome reviews were more the rule than the exception. By 1976, 24 percent of the average state's historic preservation budget was devoted to helping federal agencies and their applicants through the process. In that year, an average of 1,439 reviews per state were conducted.

The average number of annual reviews per state by 1985 had risen to 2,831, and both the Advisory Council and states were questioning the effectiveness of the reviews for protection and preservation planning relative to the expenditure of time. Earlier, much time and effort were spent simply to ensure that federal agencies complied with procedures. However, by the late 1970s, this effort was decreasing as federal agencies came to acknowledge their responsibilities under Section 106. Environmental review responsibilities, nevertheless, continued to be a dominant part of state programs. It was not just the increasing number of reviews and the size and scope of federal undertakings that caused this workload, but also the new and complex issues they raised.

As a broader range of prehistoric and historic resources came into focus through expanded surveys and National Register programs, the issues raised by projects became more complex. The Section 106 environmental review process brought state historic preservation staff and federal agencies face to face with preservation controversies that could not be resolved by the traditional associative values of high-style architecture and the "lessons of history." For example, public housing rehabilitation projects often involved deteriorated, simple, vernacular buildings. Because they sometimes represented the history of a particular population group, previously ignored by surveys of fine architecture, this type of housing was eligible for the National Register and, thus, was subject to the review process. The powerplants, barracks and hangers of World War II airfields, once not thought to be eligible for the National Register, became National Historic Landmarks. Large-scale federal bridge replacements and rehabilitation programs forced SHPOs and transportation agencies to work out survey criteria and preservation plans for historic bridges.

By the late 1970s, the Section 106 process had become highly complicated and efforts were undertaken to reduce the workload by streamlining the procedures. The states participated in an organized effort to reduce delays caused by paperwork, an objective supported by the current national administration from the beginning. For example, methods for excluding from the review process projects, with little or no potential effect on historic resources, were put in place, and programmatic approaches covering repetitive situations were explored with the Advisory Council. Sometimes these agreements were designed to handle special programs; for example, Community Development Block Grants for facade renovation in a downtown or housing rehabilitation in a historic neighborhood. Sometimes agreements covered a single project, such as a pipeline extending through several states which might require accord among several SHPOs, the federal agency, the project company and the Advisory Council. Nationwide memoranda of agreement designed to handle recurring classes of cases, such as the automation and leasing of historic lighthouses by the Coast Guard or the management activities of the National Park Service, were negotiated on behalf of the states by the Advisory Council, the federal agency and the National Conference of State Historic Preservation Officers. However, many state historic preservation offices found these nationwide agreements less productive than those in which they worked directly with both local agencies and regional federal staff.

The Advisory Council adopted new regulations in 1986 designed to streamline and improve the review process. The revised regulations place increased reliance on the state historic preservation offices to administer most Section 106 cases. The states are given the opportunity to substitute state procedures for those prescribed by the Advisory Council. It is too soon to say how effective the changes will be.

As noted in Chapter 2, the process of review and comment set in motion by the Preservation Act of 1966 comes into play only when projects are funded, assisted or licensed by the federal government. While the volume of projects reviewed by states sometimes seems staggering, a considerable amount of development is totally unaffected by the federal review process. State and locally funded projects are not included. To counter this, some states use existing general environmental laws and develop their own legislation to address historic preservation needs. In 1975, the Advisory Council reported to the Senate Committee on Interior and Insular Affairs, that 17 states had passed state environmental policy acts patterned after the Environmental Act of 1969. These laws often included historic properties as one of several, named, environmental resources to be considered in the planning of government-sponsored projects. Some states, among them Vermont, Hawaii, Florida and California used land use planning laws as a basis for encouraging the identification and protection of historic and archaeological sites and other fragile environmental resources.

By the early 1970s, the protection of archaeological resources was a matter of growing national concern. While this national ferment produced a new federal archaeological protection act in 1974, 33 state archaeological protection laws were also passed between 1970 and 1975. These laws required permits and supervision by a state archaeologist, historical commission or similar body prior to the disturbance of archaeological remains on state-owned land. A few included public lands generally, and some required the owner's permission or consent as a prerequisite to any salvage or survey activity on private property. By 1980, virtually every state had adopted laws to protect archaeological resources.

While almost a third of the states passed environmental policy acts mentioning historic and archaeological properties between 1966 and 1976, few were vigorously or effectively used to protect the properties. During the second decade, between 1976 and 1986, states increasingly looked to their own legislatures to strengthen their legal authority for preservation. For example, in Arizona, California, New York and Oregon, laws were passed requiring state agencies to consider using historic buildings before constructing new ones. In Pennsylvania, state agency proposals to transfer or alter properties were required to be submitted to the state historic preservation office for review. Where appropriate, preservation covenants were required as a condition of transfer. The same was done in North Carolina by Executive Order.

States also began to use state registers (or the National Register) to trigger state agency reviews for both public and private actions. In Kansas and New York, for example, state agencies were required by law to explore all prudent and feasible alternatives before proceeding with development projects. Kansas extended this requirement to local government projects. Several states have laws affecting private actions. For example, permission is required from the Massachusetts Historical Commission before alterations are made to any certified landmark. In the Virgin Islands, state permits are required before alterations are made by private owners to buildings within designated historic and architectural control districts. In Illinois, the state is given up to 210 days to work with private property owners before a demolition permit must be granted. However, the practical effectiveness of such provisions is limited. Delays are possible in most states, and owner consent for landmark certification is required in Massachusetts.

By 1981, roughly half of the states had passed laws authorizing review by the state's historic preservation agency of proposed nonfederal projects that threatened archaeological or historic sites. Pennsylvania requires all state agencies to adopt procedures for considering historic resources in administering state programs. The Arizona state historic preservation office is required to submit a yearly report to the governor commenting on the preservation performance of each state agency. However, few states provide the level of consideration given to historic resources in New York and Maryland. The New York state agency review is coordinated with the Section 106 process for properties on both state and national registers. A recent law in Maryland directs state agencies to prepare preservation plans to ensure that state-assisted undertakings do not adversely affect historic resources.

Presently, efforts by state historic preservation offices and their constituencies to increase state legislative authority to protect historic resources are growing. All states whose federally mandated preservation activities had not initially specifically authorized by law were given authority for the preservation tasks of the 1980s. Several, notably Arizona, California, Oregon and Washington in the West, obtained passage of stronger and more extensive state preservation laws through specially appointed task forces. Texas contracted with the Conservation Foundation of Washington, D.C., for a study of its preservation legislation and for recommendations for the future. North Carolina for a long time made use of a special attorney general's Committee on Preservation Law Revisions to achieve substantial improvements in preservation legislation.

In addition to seeking more comprehensive historic preservation and archaeological protection laws, some states enacted laws to protect specific classes of historic resources. For example, 1968 Vermont legislation requires a 90-day notice before the destruction or removal of a covered bridge. Texas, in 1974, included special provisions to protect county courthouses. During the 1970s, 15 states passed legislation to protect their state capitols.

States also began to address special problems of building code compliance for historic buildings. Codes written primarily for new construction, using new materials and technology, discouraged reinvestment in older buildings. The problem of building codes became especially serious when, beginning in 1976, federal tax laws began to encourage the rehabilitation of historic buildings, especially commercial structures. State historic preservation offices, architects, developers, preservation organizations and others worked together to change state building codes. Some, notably Massachusetts, Connecticut and Georgia, produced state laws providing compliance alternatives for designated buildings, as well as exemptions and variances to accommodate historic buildings if a certain level of safety was achieved. Others sought changes through the Building Officials and Code Administrators International. Of 22 states polled by the Georgia Trust for Historic Preservation in 1985, 8 reported some form of state level consideration for historic buildings under building and fire codes. Eight more used national codes that included some consideration for historic buildings. Clearly the development of state historic preservation laws commanded greater attention from citizens and state legislators.

Participation in the national preservation program brought with it funds to help states carry out their new and expanded responsibilities for survey and planning. These were used for a variety of purposes. They supported professional staff to carry out the program of National Register nominations and surveys in local communities, and to prepare preservation plans and design guidelines for historic districts, historic structures reports for individual buildings and rehabilitation specifications for housing areas. Federal funds also supported handbooks, technical information booklets and special projects to address specific types of needs, such as black community resources, historic mill housing or prehistoric environments created by particular cultures. Relatively small amounts of money often served as the catalyst for increased preservation activity. For example, Arkansas provided only $2,000 in grant funds to survey the Quapaw Quarter, a neighborhood in Little Rock that later became a Neighborhood Housing Services target area for rehabilitation work. In California, $15,000 assisted the initiation of a local, low-interest rate revolving loan fund for the rehabilitation of vintage San Francisco residential buildings.

Until 1980, federal funds were also available for acquisition and preservation of properties listed in the National Register. During the early years of the program, some states used most of these funds for the restoration of state-owned historic sites. However, in time they came increasingly to be used for a wide variety of properties belonging to local governments, organizations and individuals. For example, Pennsylvania initially used funds for restoration work on state sites but later for the purchase of endangered archaeological sites.

In most states, the federal funds leveraged more than the required 50 percent matching contribution in private or local government funding and stimulated restoration and rehabilitation activity in surrounding areas. For example, in Abbeville, South Carolina, grants to key buildings, such as a hotel and courthouse, followed by grants for the restoration of individual facades, served as the catalyst for the revitalization of an entire 19th-century town square. Where buildings once stood vacant, new businesses now wait in line to locate there. By 1976, only 18 percent of the total available federal funds went to state government projects, while 22 percent went to local governments and 37 percent to private, nonprofit organizations. Individuals received 13 percent and private corporations 5 percent. Within the framework of federal requirements, each state developed its own criteria for allocating these grants. But federal funding was short from the beginning, and each year applications from states greatly exceeded the available funds. In 1977, states projected a total need of $337,106,714 or 24 times the total funding of $13,923,600 available for survey, planning and preservation work.

With the advent of a new national economic policy and philosophy of government in 1980, the U.S. Congress eliminated acquisition and development funds, except for the year 1983. That year, when the U.S. Congress responded to a substantial rise in unemployment with an emergency jobs act, historic preservation projects were included as a separate title to the bill.

Given an opportunity to demonstrate that the restoration and rehabilitation of historic properties create jobs, states responded with exemplary projects. Application figures for these grants demonstrated, once again, both the need for assistance and the availability of nonfederal matching funds greatly in excess of the available grants, $23.4 million to serve $152.8 million in requests. It is estimated that these development projects created more than 10,000 jobs, and that more than 40 percent of the projects returned vacant or underutilized buildings to active use.

The projects themselves included a great variety of building types, from meeting houses and totem poles, to barns, taverns and bridges, representing regional and often unique elements of the nation's heritage. In Rochester, New Hampshire, a city hall-opera house, closed for 20 years, was reopened as a local arts and entertainment center. A round barn in Illinois received a new roof to help preserve a singular agrarian structure, and the frame portion of Versammlungsaal, a utopian church in High Amana, Iowa, was stabilized. Even a ship, the U.S. Frigate Constellation, docked in Baltimore, Maryland, received restoration assistance. Through this one-year grant program, states effectively demonstrated that relatively small amounts of development funding stimulated significant private investment, created jobs and assisted historic properties deemed important to each state. However, it should be noted that onetime, special emergency grant programs are difficult to anticipate, since spending procedures are necessarily hurried or ad hoc. Nor do such emergency programs mesh easily with any kind of long range planning.

To fill the vacuum created by the loss of federal funds for preservation projects in 1981, a few states turned with some success to their state legislatures for historic preservation funding. Texas initiated a state funded program with $250,000 in the fall of 1983 and through fiscal year 1987 granted at least $187,271 annually to nonprofit organizations and political subdivisions in Texas. Massachusetts established a state-funded matching-grant program in 1984, which offered from $2,500 to $30,000 for research activities and between $5,000 to $100,000 for bricks and mortar preservation projects annually. State grants for preservation were, of course, not new in the 1980s. In 1969, Minnesota had awarded state funds to nine projects from a total budget of $37,000. These funds rose to over $500,000 between 1978 and 1980 and were still available in 1986 at the reduced amount of $139,000. In 1977, Maryland initiated a program which reached the $200,000–$300,000 level by the early 1980s. But some states, noting the loss of federal funds in 1980, have since reduced their own preservation appropriations.

Since 1980, there has been no nationwide program of preservation development grants available through the states, although statewide revolving funds in a few of them attempted to provide a portion of the needed funds. When states were surveyed in 1975, only 12 reported the availability of state grants-in-aid and 2 of these were only temporary. In the late 1970's, Georgia's Heritage Trust Program, which was predominantly an acquisition program, provided $100,000 for 2 years for local preservation projects. Idaho made state grants available through the state's Bicentennial Commission. Florida, which had administered a general state grant fund since 1984, took a new approach to special category projects in 1986 when applications for major restoration and renovation projects were solicited, evaluated and passed on to the state legislature for consideration as special projects. As a result, throughout the 1970s and 1980s, states continued the practice of attaching special interest appropriations to legislators' favorite projects.

State Assistance with Federal Tax Incentives

Beginning with the Tax Reform Act of 1976, tax incentives began to replace grants as the major form of federal assistance to historic properties. This tendency was strengthened following the elimination of federal grants for preservation work in 1980 and the passage of the Economic Recovery Tax Act in 1981, when tax credits for the rehabilitation of certified historic structures became increasingly important.

Following passage of the Tax Reform Act of 1976, states were given additional responsibility to help the National Park Service administer the preservation tax incentives program. The stimulus of this program, reinforced by the 1981 Economic Recovery Tax Act, produced an explosion of epic proportions in state historic preservation programs. Both the historical perspectives from which they operated and the scope of their responsibilities were changed to an extent that no one had anticipated.

States have played a key role in the tax incentive program. They were given complete responsibility for the initial review of the tax applications and asked to provide a recommendation on certification to the National Park Service. Further, since it was possible to obtain tax benefits for properties not yet listed in the National Register but preliminarily certified as eligible, states had to make a commitment to nominate the property, or the historic district in which its was located, to the National Register within a 30-month period.

In addition to this review, recommendation and nomination role, the states assumed primary responsibility for technical assistance to and education of applicants and their architectural and historical consultants. State staffs, through workshops, publications and other educational efforts explained the process and the rehabilitation standards. They helped to identify eligible properties and made site visits to work with applicants and architects in ensuring the development of certifiable project plans. States found that through this process, especially when their technical staff became involved early in project planning, they could influence the quality of work and preserve the historic character of older buildings in their communities. But they could also become embroiled in conflicts with applicants over the interpretation of the *Secretary of the Interior's Standards for the Rehabilitation of Historic Buildings*. Differences between local preservation commission review decisions and the application of the *Standards* by state and regional National Park Service staff also led to confusion. Arguments over the retention of important historic details, such as windows, doors, fireplaces, mantels and original layouts of rooms and halls led to appeals and, occasionally, into court. The blame for projects that went astray often landed on states because they were more accessible than the federal agency.

Many states also found that the increasing number of Tax Reform Act projects which produced spectacular economic development, also consumed an ever greater proportion of staff time. They drained staff resources away from properties that were not income-producing. There was a growing concern that with few financial incentives available for residential and institutional buildings, important historic properties would be lost. Further, although there were notable exceptions, the tax credits provided little or no assistance to the preservation of archaeological resources. These problems notwithstanding, in many states tax credits were successfully used to stimulate economic development. The states bent over backwards to provide technical assistance to remove potential conflicts over rehabilitation techniques and to expand public awareness. They educated a largely new group of citizens, the developers and the real estate community, to the advantages of historic preservation. Of greatest importance, they had an opportunity to influence the quality of preservation and restoration work done on a large number of historic properties.

States of the middle Atlantic and northeast regions were the most active in using tax incentives to encourage rehabilitation. In 1985, more than 50 percent of the projects were located in these states, while 26 percent of the activity was in the southeast, 16 percent in the Rocky Mountain region, and 4 percent in the far West. Among the most active states were Pennsylvania, where incentives stimulated downtown revitalization in cities such as Harrisburg; Missouri, where the historic neighborhoods that ring downtown St. Louis, led the revitalization movement; and Georgia, where the credits helped to bring investment to a deteriorated Savannah minority neighborhood without displacing its residents. The number of projects in 53 states between 1982 and 1986 ranged from 6 in Alaska to 871 in Pennsylvania. The rehabilitation investment from tax credit-assisted projects in these states ranged from $1.7 million in the Virgin Islands to $1,035,000,000 in Pennsylvania.

State Tax and Other Preservation Incentives

Federal preservation incentives clearly demonstrated that tax preferences can play an important role in determining what happens to historic properties and can influence the revitalization of whole areas. State governments also recognized this potential and state-level approaches to subsidizing preservation, as the National Trust reported in 1985, was one of the most rapidly expanding areas of preservation law. Six basic state tax methods, though not all uniformly or widely used, were available by then. These included the exemption of historical organizations from state and local property and income taxes based on their educational or charitable purposes; special or favorable treatment with respect to property tax assessment; state income tax relief to the owners of historic properties; and miscellaneous approaches, such as relief from tax on admission to historic properties, gift shop sales or special taxes on cigarettes.

As with the federal government, states have played an important role since 1966 in expanding the use of easements and relating less-than-fee real estate conveyancing techniques to historic preservation. Although the rules are changing, the appraised value of such interests in land has generally been deductible from state, federal, personal and corporate income tax when donated in perpetuity to a qualified exempt organization. Use restrictions sometimes lead to lower local property tax assessments, but the valuation of such easements remains largely an uncharted area.

In many states, there are various common law limitations on the enforceability of such restrictions. However, since 1966, these were modified or removed by laws passed at the behest of preservation or conservation interests in many jurisdictions. By 1984, seven states, Arkansas, Indiana, Nevada, Oregon, South Dakota, Texas and Wisconsin, had adopted the Uniform Conservation Easement Act proposed by the American Bar Association as their primary easement legislation. Laws in 21 other states authorized easements for both historic buildings and open space land. Forty-four states in all, including the District of Columbia, have some form of statewide easement statute. In 22 of these states, it might be noted, easements for the preservation of archaeological sites were specifically authorized.

The States as Facilitators: Education and Technical Assistance

As states increasingly took on the role of facilitator for local government and private preservation efforts after 1966, technical assistance and public information activities became important. State preservation agencies used a variety of approaches to the problem of helping citizens understand and preserve historic places in which they lived and worked. Some states went beyond buildings to explore ways to help the public appreciate the value of archaeological resources, which are often more difficult to recognize and understand.

The impact of this all-encompassing responsibility is difficult to measure, yet it is undoubtedly one of the major accomplishments of state historic preservation offices of the last two decades. The most widely used vehicles for public information and education, according to yearly reports in the late 1970s from states to the federal government, were regional and local workshops, conferences, newsletters and other publications.

States also used the media, especially the press, to reach the public. Survey guidelines and other how-to manuals for numerous program components were produced by the National Park Service and individual states. Technical preservation information, normally unavailable for general use, was developed and distributed by the same agencies. General materials produced in Washington, D.C., were sometimes augmented and adapted for statewide use in addressing the technical problems and needs of the particular area or region. For example, Illinois published the *Illinois Preservation Series*, which highlighted technical subjects, including the proper use of stucco finishes, addressed particular resources such as the prehistory of Illinois and provided guidance on documenting buildings. Maryland, as with many other states, produced a small town revitalization manual, setting forth planning and rehabilitation strategies for small towns to build economic growth based upon special historic character.

Public education to build awareness of archaeological resources is less widespread, partly because of concern for vandalism of known archaeological sites, and partly because their value is less obvious to the general public. Archaeology Week in Arizona is a notable effort to dispel the fears and misunderstandings. Armed with the governor's proclamation, the Arizona state historic preservation office, in coordination with numerous educational and preservation organizations, organized a series of statewide events and exhibitions to raise awareness of the importance of preserving the archaeological record and to demonstrate what its preservation can mean to citizens.

The States as Facilitators: Coordination Networks

The strengthened state preservation programs which arose from the Preservation Act of 1966 provided a focal point for local governments and community-based historical organizations. They contributed leadership, inspiration and, most importantly, technical and advisory services. As states discovered when they first set out to conduct statewide surveys, they did not have the resources to cope with the increasing demand for preservation assistance stimulated by the Preservation Act of 1966 and by the increasing concern for the historic environment. In response, they sought out regional and local mechanisms that could supplement state services and promote local involvement.

Several states set up regional preservation assistance systems. South Carolina, which had long supported a league of local historical societies, used existing regional planning agencies for survey and National Register nominations. Georgia built a network of them to assist local citizens, governments and organizations with surveys and National Register nominations and to provide general preservation and technical assistance. Ohio set up regional offices for both history and archaeology as part of its program. North Carolina established branch offices in its eastern and western regions. Maryland's system of county committees was perhaps unique in creating a structured system that relied heavily on volunteers. Established in 1968 to disseminate information about preservation, they have become a network of concerned and informed citizens, who in turn can provide the Annapolis-based staff with information about preservation issues statewide. Massachusetts also maintained a link with its local jurisdictions through preservation advisory commissions in each of its townships. In North Carolina the Institute of Government, School of Design and state historic preservation office collaborated on extensive training sessions for local and regional preservation planners, in addition to making use of regional councils of government for survey purposes.

Certified Local Governments

Local governments, especially those with preservation commissions and community development programs, also served as links to the states' historic preservation programs. In the 1980 amendments, a more formal structure was authorized in the Certified Local Government Program. For this new program, the established state role as enabler of local preservation and historic district commissions was important. By 1970, half of the states had enacted legislation authorizing the creation of local preservation commissions. Between 1970 and 1980, more than 20 additional statutes were passed. The majority of all these statutes authorize local governments to designate historic districts, and 24 authorize landmarks as well. The growing number of local preservation commissions established under these statutes provide an incentive to strengthen local government participation in the national program. The 1980 amendments provided the mechanism, and all states now have such authority.

According to federal law, states must require certified local governments to:

- enforce appropriate state or local legislation for the designation and protection of historic properties;

- establish an adequate and qualified historic preservation review commission by state or local legislation;
- maintain a system for survey and inventory;
- provide for adequate public participation in the local historic preservation program, including the process of recommending properties for nomination to the National Register; and
- satisfactorily perform responsibilities delegated to it under the Preservation Act of 1966.

The local government is required to review all National Register nominations which may then not be nominated if the local government objects. Certification of a local government triggers its eligibility for a share of 10 percent of the annual federal allocations in a given state, which is required by law to be passed to certified local governments.

Regulations implementing the certified local government program authorized in 1980 were long in coming, notwithstanding the efforts of the National Park Service, the National Conference of State Historic Preservation Officers and the National Alliance of Preservation Commissions. Regulations were adopted in April 1984 and, by December of that year, all 50 state certified local government procedures were submitted and approved. By February 1987, about 300 local governments were certified.

By 1986, however, the federal appropriation to states, as well as matching state appropriations, were shrinking, thereby reducing the amount available for the newly certified local governments. Nevertheless, the number of local governments participating in the program grew steadily and, even though the available funds were limited, they were useful. They were used to assist in passing and strengthening the required local ordinances and for the completion of local surveys, National Register nominations, design guidelines and educational programs.

The increased communication and coordination with state programs and the opportunities for technical assistance which it facilitated provided welcome support for both large and small communities. States that initially regarded the new program as unnecessary (most states had long worked with at least some local programs) and as just one more added responsibility with no additional resources to carry it out, now began to appreciate the potential of a structured relationship with local governments.

The U.S. Frigate Constellation docked at Baltimore, Maryland, benefited from rehabilitation funds under the Emergency Jobs Act of 1983. (Maryland Historical Trust)

The rural Norris Ranch Schoolhouse in the Texas hill country near Fredericksburg was rehabilitated by the owner using the federal investment tax credit. (Texas Historical Commission)

The Tucker Carriage House in Raleigh, North Carolina, was protected by a memorandum of agreement among the Advisory Council on Historic Preservation, the Department of Housing and Urban Development, the Raleigh Housing Authority and the North Carolina State Historic Preservation Office until an adaptive-reuse plan could be developed. (North Carolina Division of Archives and History)

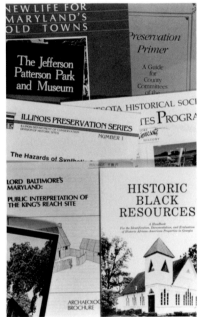

State historic preservation offices offer a variety of educational and technical publications to inform the public about historic preservation and to assist preservationists with their work at the local level. (Robert E. Stipe)

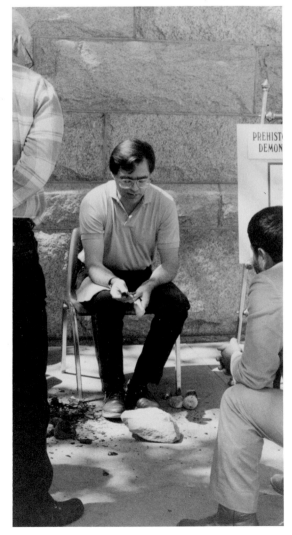

Demonstration of prehistoric tool-making methods form part of Arizona Archeological Week, a statewide effort to educate the public about the importance of archaeological resources. (Arizona State Parks)

Local and Statewide Organizations

Local preservation organizations and historical societies were the mainstay of community preservation activities from the earliest days of the preservation movement. These private nonprofit preservation organizations did much of the work of survey and National Register research, providing time and money to match federal dollars from state offices under the guidance of state staff and professional consultants. Members of these groups are often the primary participants in local preservation commissions. They become the initiators and driving force behind successful Certified Local Government programs. In addition, statewide organizations have been active in many states since before the 1960s. These statewide organizations are growing in number, now over 40, and in strength. They now have a full-time professional staff as well as growing numbers of volunteers. State historic preservation offices are successfully working with these organizations to build support for preservation in their states and to develop cooperative programs of technical and financial assistance.

One of the major contributions of nonprofit organizations is building public awareness and conducting a variety of education programs and conferences to which state historic preservation offices contribute their technical knowledge and professional expertise. In 1986, states reported impressive gains in funding and protective legislation growing out of cooperative activities with nonprofit organizations. This is a result that realized some of the hopes of the designers of the Preservation Act of 1966 by bringing together the efforts of private groups and public programs.

The States as Facilitators: Other Programs

Several related activities of state governments supplemented the federal program of preservation assistance. Most important during the first decade following the Preservation Act of 1966 was the establishment of commissions in all states to promote the nation's 1976 Bicentennial. Many Bicentennial commissions worked directly with state historic preservation offices to sponsor preservation and restoration projects, provide special grant funds, conduct architectural surveys and historical research and undertake publications programs. Although not all state Bicentennial commissions supported preservation projects directly, their activities brought about wider appreciation among the general public of their state's history, stimulating interest in the preservation of the physical reminders of that heritage.

In the decade following 1976, state planning and economic and community development agencies engaged in a variety of downtown revitalization programs which depended heavily upon the programs available in state historic preservation offices. Many of these agencies became involved in historic preservation through the National Trust's Main Street program, which instituted three year pilot programs in six states in 1980, following earlier experiments in the Midwest. Over time, 28 states carried out Main Street programs, either on their own or in coordination with the National Trust's Main Street Center. Without the technical, promotional, public education and occasional financial assistance provided by state historic preservation offices, few of these Main Street programs would have succeeded as they did.

Since 1966, states continued to own and manage historic sites and museum properties. In a few instances, even these more traditional enterprises expanded significantly as a result of state participation in the 1966 federal program. For example, the Alabama Historical Commission was created principally to carry out that state's federal program responsibilities. However, its authority expanded during the 1970s to include the preservation and interpretation of several historic houses and monuments. In a similar vein, Arizona and Maryland agencies acquired and managed important archaeological preserves for protection and interpretation.

Comprehensive Statewide Preservation Planning

It is often overlooked that participation in the federal-state partnership envisioned by the Preservation Act of 1966 required the preparation, by each state, of a comprehensive, statewide historic preservation plan, coordinated with its outdoor recreation plan. The earliest plans, prepared quickly for the purpose of getting the program underway, were designated "preliminary only." In Volume I, *The Historical Background*, each state summarized its history, including the history of its preservation efforts, analyzed preservation problems and described its intergovernmental relationships as they related to preservation. Volume II, *The Inventory*, constituted a list of cultural resources located in each state. This inventory was to be revised and expanded according to the state's own priorities and procedures, but subject to approval by the National Park Service. Volume III, *The Preservation Plan*, detailed the status of the state's current preservation program and its long range and immediate objectives. The states began to revise and add to these plans in 1972 according to a new three-volume format devised by the National Park Service. By the mid-1970s, plan revisions and reviews became part of the annual grant application process by which federal funds were apportioned to the states.

This planning approach soon proved inadequate. A moratorium on the old format was declared in 1974 at the request of the National Conference of State Historic Preservation Officers. New planning criteria were published in 1977 following a special study of planning procedures completed by the National Park Service. Having much more flexibility, these criteria outlined state historic preservation responsibilities and directed states to develop new planning documents, again organized according to their own needs. No particular form was prescribed as long as the state provided a clear rationale for each program component, evaluations of its effectiveness and future program projections. In the late 1970s, the Heritage Conservation and Recreation Service, a new National Park Service preservation agency, pushed for yet another system called "management by objectives" and greater accountability from state historic preservation programs. The annual program report itself then became the plan, a lengthy and complicated document entailing elaborate statements about objectives and performance measures. These plans had to be completed before the federal government would approve funds for the state. States objected to this new approach and sought to separate the annual grant application process from comprehensive statewide preservation planning for state programs.

The National Park Service responded to the lack of consistency among state plans and to a growing number of conflicts between states and federal agencies resulting from environmental reviews with a planning model called the Resource Protection Planning Process or, as it soon became known, RP3. This conceptual model, developed for application in the federal service by archaeologists, proposed a complex planning process based on thematic approaches to each state's history. Federal grants were awarded to several states to evaluate its feasibility, workshops were held in 1979–80 to give direction to the effort and a few states actually began a planning process according to the model. Most states got no further than the study unit framework, although many developed specific study units and a few operating plans. Many states, however, found RP3 useful as a tool to organize resource data and as a means of involving a reluctant academic community in the evaluation of the state's historic and archaeological information. Some state planners were reassured by the knowledge that historic and archaeological resources followed patterns of development that might help them in their project planning.

To date, no state has been able to develop fully the operating and management plans called for by the model. Most who used it have adapted it to better serve state program needs. In two pilot states, Massachusetts established study units using geographic and political boundaries rather than historical themes, while the Arkansas plan addressed only archaeological resources. Louisiana used cultural units to define developmental history, subdividing these into themes and dividing the state into management units. Maryland used the type of resource data framework made up of study units of sets of resources prescribed by RP3, but modified the protection portions of the model in response to professional and public input. State historic preservation offices that attempted a comprehensive preservation planning process, whether structured according to the RP3 model or a substitute, found the process useful. However, once the *Secretary of the Interior's Standards for Planning*, based on the RP3 model was published, planning became a factor in apportionment formulas and yearly program approvals, and directly affected the amount of federal funds available to the state. As a consequence, planning concepts and requirements increasingly became an issue between states and the National Park Service.

Two Decades of Achievement: 1966–86

Looking at state historic preservation programs over the 20 years since passage of the Preservation Act of 1966, certain directions and developments are clear. During the first decade, each state and territory established a state historic preservation office staffed by professionals in history, architectural history, architecture and archaeology. State legislatures and administrative departments provided funds or services to match federal funds. During the second decade, these programs were strengthened in terms of professional capability and the administrative and financial support by state governments. The state historic preservation offices quickly became the central focus for preservation assistance and technical information. The relationship between previous programs and the new federal partnership varied from state to state according to administrative location. The states, however, continued to manage and interpret historically and archaeologically significant places. Many initiated complementary programs through community development and tourism departments. They became involved in historic preservation issues through the extensive use by state and local governments of federal funds, requiring compliance with Section 106 of the Preservation Act of 1966. The most important recent development, with profound implications for the future is the Certified Local Government Program.

The basic components of the program initiated by the 1966 federal law are now firmly established as functions of state government, even in states that did not have strong preservation programs before that time. The states accepted the responsibility to identify properties of historic, architectural and archaeological importance, to evaluate their significance and to develop and maintain state and National Register inventories. They provide review and consultation for all federally funded and licensed undertakings and, in a growing number of states, the review of state actions as well. They administer federal and state assistance programs, such as grants and tax incentives. In addition, they cooperate with a variety of statewide and local agencies and organizations to facilitate the preservation of their historic resources and they provide a wide variety of preservation services to their citizens.

Current Issues

The preservation issues that brought the states together in 1969 to form the National Conference of State Historic Preservation Officers remain relatively constant. Federal funding levels and the formulas by which they are distributed were controversial topics at the first meetings in Alabama and Georgia and have remained so ever since. The states, through their own senators and representatives and through cooperation with the National Trust for Historic Preservation, Preservation Action and the National Alliance of Preservation Commissions, succeeded in obtaining and maintaining federal funds for the program even when successive administrations proposed to cut or eliminate them. In support of these efforts, the states collected and analyzed project and cost figures to demonstrate the amount of professional work carried out by states under federal law. They emphasized their contribution of more than 50 percent and argued that federal funds were, after all, reimbursement for 50 percent of the costs of a national program. Indeed, when the concept of The New Federalism was elaborated on by the new Reagan administration in 1980, a task force study of the national historic preservation program asserted the financial advantage to the federal government of the existing arrangement with the states.

A second issue discussed by the states with the National Park Service from the beginning is the administration of the program. The need for the National Park Service to provide timely and meaningful opportunities for comment on regulations, standards and guidelines has been a refrain at meetings of the National Conference of State Historic Preservation Officers for many years. In 1977, the Conference noted the proliferation of rules and regulations and established a Rules and Regulations Committee to work with the National Park Service and the Advisory Council. Subsequently, a succession of program committees dealt with a host of specific federal standards and regulations in an effort to make them responsive to state needs.

In recent years, the program review process, whereby the National Park Service regional offices conduct periodic on-site program audits in the state offices, became a critical issue. The dilemma is how to achieve accountability on the part of states without destroying state program flexibility, and without requiring the submission of excessive statistics and reports. Programs such as the tax incentives and the Jobs Act produced good coordination and some creative solutions to preservation problems. Now there is concern that increasing and meaningless paperwork can subvert the program's goals to preserve and use the nation's heritage for enriching the community's life and development.

Another recent administrative issue between the states and the federal preservation agencies grew from differing views of the nature and purpose of the Certified Local Government Program. The National Park Service and the Advisory Council, focusing attention on the National Register and protective provisions of the Preservation Act of 1966, appeared to envisage local programs as mini state programs. Responsibilities of state programs would be delegated to local governments. States, on the other hand, believed that local government programs should be based on distinct local initiatives but within the legal framework in each state. They emphasized the established local historic zoning and design review authority in some states, and planning and education programs in others. From this perspective, local programs are viewed as a complement rather than a substitute for established state programs.

The number of such programs grew rapidly during 1985 and 1986 and in 1987 numbered more than 350 nationwide. This growth, together with increasing focus by states and the National Park Service on local needs and issues, suggests the potential of this program for community preservation in the context of the national program.

A third component of the national program, which has raised issues of long standing, is the interaction between states and government agencies at all levels arising from Section 106. As early as 1972, the National Park Service urged states to study the new Advisory Council procedures carefully and to provide comprehensible comments to federal agencies. By 1976, when the southeastern region held the first regional state historic preservation officers meeting, the states' sensitive and often difficult middle position between agencies seeking to use federal funds or licenses, and their responsibilities under the Advisory Council's procedures, became a major component of three days of discussions. Some of these issues were solved by revised Advisory Council procedures in 1978, but the states' responsibility under Section 106 often brought them into conflict with other state agencies, especially with departments of transportation and community affairs. There were also conflicts with local governments seeking to use federal funds for community development. State preservation officials, offering their opinion on National Register eligibility as required by environmental review procedures, forced local governments to consider historic buildings and districts and this, in turn, delayed projects and forced changes. The significance of historic buildings was often not apparent to local officials who wanted to show signs of progress through new buildings in deteriorated downtowns.

Inherent in the review structure, however, was a gap between the federal sponsoring agency and the complex bureaucratic framework at the regional and local levels that actually carried out review and compliance activities. For example, the U.S. Department of Housing and Urban Development encouraged the use of community development block grant funds for the rehabilitation of historic buildings. This policy, however, was often not conveyed to or recognized by the staff of local government community development departments. As a result, states were accused of standing in the way of progress when reviewing proposals to demolish blocks of buildings in historic districts for office buildings or new housing.

Since 1978, a growing emphasis by the Advisory Council on programmatic approaches to the broad array of federal undertakings and the use of categorical exclusions for projects of little or no potential impact on historic resources reduced some of the conflict. States found the use of programmatic memoranda of agreement tailored to specific state and local situations, such as housing rehabilitation programs for particular historic districts, to be effective. On the other hand, nationwide memoranda were not useful because they are a part of general plans that do not address specific situations. The revised Advisory Council Regulations of 1986, which offer states the opportunity to substitute their own state laws and regulations for the federal process, may address these and other review-and-compliance issues.

The way in which federal funding and economic assistance shaped the direction of state programs became a matter of serious concern. So long as federal or state grant-in-aid funds were available for restoration and rehabilitation projects, it was possible to respond to the preservation needs of all types of historic properties. Public or privately owned museum buildings and eventually residential neighborhoods had received the bulk of the available grant funds. Federal tax incentives provide assistance only for income-producing properties; therefore, an emphasis on the economic benefits of historic preservation grew and became a driving force of downtown revitalization programs in most states and also fostered a substantial amount of neighborhood revitalization. By the second decade, fears were voiced that the profit motive was distorting the program. Those who successfully used the tax incentives to foster historic preservation, countered that the new constituencies which had developed could be used to gain support for a much broader range of projects.

Changing concepts of historic and archaeological significance became an issue not anticipated by the program's framers. They seemed to envisage an easily and neatly defined program of survey, National Register listing and protection for properties and sites. Increasingly complex questions were raised by the recognition of broad historic patterns and the cultural diversity of the states. In addition, planning and treatment issues are complicated by the need to balance the information and research values of archaeological sites against functional, visual and environmental values of historic buildings and districts. Concepts of preservation planning reflecting the issues also changed and developed as states endeavored to understand and better serve the particular needs of their constituents and to cope with the proliferation of preservation activities and issues in which they found themselves embroiled. These changes produced philosophical differences and administrative conflict between the federal and state partners which raised questions about the future direction of the system created by the Preservation Act of 1966.

Looking to the Future

Will the present system survive a period of federal budget deficits, changes in federal environmental philosophy and other changes in governmental policy? This was the major issue on the 20th anniversary of the Preservation Act of 1966, at least from the perspective of states. As a long-time preservationist put it: "Will the apparatus set up to implement the act continue to serve as a delivery system for a national program?"

Many questions were raised about the role of the states in a national program. Both the National Park Service and the National Conference of State Historic Preservation Officers proposed that greater authority for actions, such as National Register listing and tax certification, be transferred to the states. The Advisory Council's regulations already provide a considerable degree of such authority. Some wonder whether this can be accomplished without losing the national framework which has been the strength of the program.

Comprehensive planning conflicts brought to the fore confusion over the functions of the state programs. Are the states simply to serve as a repository of resource and technical information and regulator of federal undertakings? Or are they to provide a full range of preservation services to their citizens and to local governments? How much flexibility is to be allowed the states in developing comprehensive statewide preservation plans? Should a specific planning model be imposed? Could the needs of both archaeological, and historic and architectural resources, with their often differing preservation goals, be met by one historic preservation program and integrated into one plan? Is the purpose of the plan to serve the requirements of federal agencies or the goal of the Preservation Act of 1966, to preserve and use historic resources as a living part of community life and development?

The enormously successful historic preservation tax program demonstrated conclusively that historic preservation can be profitable, but its success in using historic preservation as a tool for economic development raised questions. Some states share the concerns expressed by architectural historians, historians and many preservationists, that the growing emphasis on preservation-for-profit is endangering those buildings and archaeological sites which cannot be used for development. They also question whether the objectivity of the cultural record represented by the National Register and the character of the preserved environment will be distorted by concentrating on income-producing properties. Others see an opportunity to build public awareness and generate wider support for all properties of significance as the link between economic development and historic preservation.

One of the most troublesome issues is the level of public funding. Since 1980 when the Reagan administration first omitted historic preservation funds from its proposed budget, the U.S. Congress put them back, albeit at ever-reduced levels. Some states increased their support of state preservation offices well beyond the minimum required to match federal funds. However, many states now struggle to maintain even a minimal program and, the federal government cavalierly maintains that since it is in the best interest of states to continue a program, it is not necessary for the federal government to contribute money. That, in the words of one state historic preservation officer, requires a 100 percent grant of the program's cost by states to the federal government. It is doubtful that many states would be willing to do that.

Does it really matter who pays for a national public historic preservation program in states? The federal government through the Preservation Act of 1966 declared historic preservation to be a national policy, and many states have followed this imperative. States believe that the basic concept of a federal-state-local partnership needs to be expressed through financial support by each government level.

The history of the National Conference of State Historic Preservation Officers provides evidence that the tension between the states and the federal government can be used creatively to produce results. The 14 years between the Preservation Act of 1966 and its 1980 amendments produced an administrative framework dependent upon states but guided and encouraged by federal policies and actions. In the early period, the states, working with the National Park Service and the Advisory Council, addressed both administrative and substantive issues in a remarkably effective and efficient manner, and in an atmosphere of reasonableness and mutual respect.

Changes in this relationship, brought on by the change of administration in 1980, became evident from 1980 onwards. As the issues came into focus, on the 20th anniversary of the Preservation Act of 1966, the network of public agencies and private nonprofit organizations that the law had nurtured, and in which the states now were leaders, turned their attention to the survival and improvement of the national program.

It is clear that this national tension must be used to solve the administrative issues so that states may turn their attention to the many preservation needs that remain. The Certified Local Government Program must be used in ways that will bring local governments more fully into the partnership envisaged by the creators of the Preservation Act of 1966. Local design review and many other planning tools, coordinated with and supported by statewide planning, can make preservation an effective mechanism to manage growth and accommodate change. Wider recognition of the contribution historic preservation can make to economic and community development provides an unprecedented opportunity to achieve truly integrated community planning.

Today's state historic preservation programs and their legislative framework still depend heavily upon local preservation efforts. Yet it is difficult to imagine the local activities and programs of today continuing or flourishing without the framework of planning, technical and educational services now provided by state historic preservation offices nationwide. These services were largely a product of the Preservation Act of 1966. The federal government thus served as a catalyst to the states' expansion of their programs from site management and interpretation to public assistance programs which attempt to meet varied needs and multiple constituencies. The system of states working within a national framework that includes local governments must survive if Americans are to preserve and respect the cultural diversity of the nation.

CHAPTER FOUR

Where the Action is: Preservation and Local Governments

J. Myrick Howard

WHERE THE ACTION IS: PRESERVATION AND LOCAL GOVERNMENTS

J. MYRICK HOWARD

Introduction

Historic buildings are saved locally. Local preservation programs may depend heavily on state laws for authorization and on federal programs for financial support, but if local preservationists fail to rally when needed, state and federal programs, in and of themselves, are of little value. Relatively few of America's historic landmarks are of truly national significance. Most mark people, places and events of essentially local interest. It follows that preservation actions to save them can almost always be undertaken best through local government action. The real action in preservation is at the local level, as it should be.

Even though some local governments have long been actively involved in historic preservation, the widespread embracing of it by America's cities and counties is a relatively recent phenomenon; witness the exponential growth of preservation commissions during the late 1970s and early 1980s.

The success of historic preservation at the local level, however, has not always been consistent. Preservation is a movement heavily dependent on volunteer leadership and individual initiative. Each preservationist has highly personal reasons for involvement, ranging from interests in genealogy to urban design, from artistic recognition of high craftsmanship to concern for downtown revitalization. As a result, communities with similar physical resources and economic circumstances may take widely divergent paths of redevelopment because of the abilities of preservation leaders to understand and communicate their own ethics.

Successful preservation efforts also vary according to the economic well-being of the community; often the best-preserved are those experiencing long periods of economic stagnation during which it was infeasible to tear down and replace historic resources.

Preservation Prior to 1966

Preservation in the United States had a slow start, partly because of the perception of the nation as a new land without a deep history. Most early local efforts were spearheaded by a few individuals or a private historical organization rallying around landmarks of great significance. Except in their roles as owners and administrators of public buildings, such as courthouses, city halls or, occasionally, museums, local governments were seldom involved.

One of the first local governments to become active in historic preservation was Charleston, South Carolina. There, interest in preservation was sparked by a 1917 publication, *The Dwelling Houses of Charleston*. After the end of World War I, the city, which had developed a way of its own due to its distance and inaccessibility from other urban centers, was invaded by prosperity for the first time since the firing on Fort Sumter and the start of the Civil War in 1861. The popularity of the automobile, the appearance of new commercial establishments and the extension of the business district resulted in more parking lots, service stations and widened roads. The community was also invaded by museum directors and collectors who sought to remove paneling, ironwork and antiques, even bricks, from Charleston houses. In 1928, community leaders developed a campaign, among other things, to consider the use of zoning in Charleston. For the next three years, local citizens worked with professional planners to develop a zoning ordinance in creating the first historic district in the nation.

Today's preservationist would be unnerved by Charleston's decisive action. The historic district designation in the zoning ordinance had no legal precedent, and no enabling legislation existed for it. The city adapted a relatively new and controversial legal tool to meet its needs, which would make a city attorney of today blanch. Under the zoning ordinance, a Board of Architectural Review was established to review plans for exterior alteration or new construction within the district. If a proposed alteration or construction project was approved by the board, a certificate of appropriateness would be issued.

The Old and Historic Charleston District became a prototype to be reproduced by many other local governments. In 1936, by Constitutional amendment, the Louisiana legislature authorized the creation of the Vieux Carré Commission by the City of New Orleans for the preservation of buildings such "as shall be deemed to have architectural or historical value." Authorization included architectural controls and tax exemptions. The creation of other historic districts followed (San Antonio, Texas, in 1939; Alexandria in 1946 and Williamsburg in 1947 both in Virginia; Winston-Salem, North Carolina, in 1948; Georgetown in Washington, D.C., in 1950; and Natchez, Mississippi, and Annapolis, Maryland, in 1951), primarily in the South and West, sometimes with legislative authority and sometimes not.

Concern about the destruction of historic resources abated during the early 1940s as the nation focused its attention on World War II. During that period civilian construction slowed to a halt, and historic resources gained a reprieve.

The Flight to the Suburbs

The late 1940s and 1950s were tragic years for the nation's heritage as two decades of pent-up consumer desires were unleashed without restraint. During the Great Depression and war years, dreams of new homes and automobiles were postponed. However, the prosperous post-war years brought a wave of suburban growth and highway development, destroying in its path thousands of older structures and neighborhoods.

Moving to the suburbs was nothing new in American social history. Preceding generations moved to new suburban developments taking advantage of current transportation improvements. What was different after World War II was that government programs and the affordable automobile were making it possible for an entire generation of middle class families to fulfill the dream of moving to the suburbs. Mortgage assistance was provided to returning soldiers, thereby stimulating unprecedented suburban construction, and the new highways (unlike the streetcar lines of the previous generation which were paid for by private companies) were built by federal and state governments.

Preservationists, few in number at the beginning, saw entire sections of cities destroyed for commuting highways to serve the suburbs, while downtown business districts lost favor to suburban shopping centers. Older neighborhoods, left behind by the affluent and repopulated by poor tenants, declined into slums. The federal government, first through the Title I, Property Improvement Loan Program administered by the U.S. Department of Housing and Urban Development (HUD) and later through its urban renewal program, provided subsidies making it possible to demolish block after block of historic properties. By 1966, almost half of the structures listed in the Historic American Buildings Survey had been destroyed. (This is a deceptive statistic because one of the reasons for a Historic American Buildings Survey recording is to document a building before its scheduled demolition. Nevertheless, this statistic became a rallying point for new federal legislation in 1966.)

The Early Broadening of the Movement

During the 1950s and early 1960s, as a result of this massive destruction, the nation began to awaken to the value of historic preservation. Starting with Beacon Hill in Boston in the early 1950s, interest in creating historic districts began to grow in all regions of the country, not just the South and West. The Philadelphia Historical Commission became, in 1956, the first historical agency to have jurisdiction over an entire area of a major American city; earlier commissions had operated within a geographically limited district. The Philadelphia commission, however, had control over all alterations proposed for any historic building throughout the city, thereby becoming a predecessor for the many landmarks commissions to be established.

Successful preservationists learned in the 1950s to take nonpreservation programs and put them to work to preserve rather than to destroy the built heritage. In those relatively few places where local preservation leaders worked cooperatively with local planning authorities, successful coalitions were forged with the very agencies that elsewhere were viewed as culprits.

HUD Programs and Historic Preservation

Many preservationists viewed HUD, and especially its urban renewal program, as an enemy rather than as an ally. And yet, here and there, some local preservationists were able to turn the financial resources of the department to preservation purposes and in time historic preservation became an element, albeit a minor one, in HUD's overall program. Local preservationists had to prevail on their local governments to initiate projects using these federal programs for historic preservation; preservation was not generally promoted by the department itself.

The Urban Renewal Program of 1954 could be used for rehabilitation (as well as clearance) of older neighborhoods, if so desired by the local government or its redevelopment or housing authority. Intended to carry out projects for slum prevention as well as the redevelopment of blighted, deteriorated urban areas, urban renewal was based on plans that were developed locally. Federal funds could be used for planning activities related to historic preservation, such as surveys, rehabilitation feasibility studies, educational materials and professional services for property owners.

In New Orleans, despite the work of the Vieux Carré Commission, the proximity of the French Quarter to commercial Canal Street and the rapidly growing downtown business district threatened historic structures near the edges of the Vieux Carré district. Parking lots, service stations and motels intruded in the area. A debate raged over the location and design of an eight-lane expressway, which would radically change the character of the district and its relationship with the waterfront of the Mississippi River. Here HUD's Urban Renewal Administration financed a demonstration study to develop a preservation plan for the Vieux Carré, including an inventory of approximately 4,000 properties in the district along with highway studies. The urban renewal program eventually helped save the French Quarter from a devastating road construction project.

A similar demonstration project was conducted in the 1960s in Providence, Rhode Island, where urban renewal funds were used to conduct an extensive inventory of the College Hill area and to develop a preservation plan. The plan became a prototype for numerous others in the next decade.

The Boston Redevelopment Authority carried out an extensive rehabilitation program in the early 1970s as part of an urban renewal project in Charlestown, an old area of Boston which was burned to the ground by the British in 1775. A study of the history and architecture of Charlestown was published, emphasizing the importance of preserving the character of the buildings and containing guidelines for appropriate rehabilitation and landscaping. More than $8 million was invested in the area in rehabilitation loans and grants as more than 1,000 buildings were rehabilitated.

Urban renewal funds could also be used for acquisition and restoration of historic properties, area beautification, open space and the relocation of historic structures. The Redevelopment Agency of Sacramento, California, preserved more than 40 buildings dating from 1849 to 1870 in an urban renewal project in the Old Sacramento Historic District. Most were preserved on their original sites, although some were moved from the path of freeway construction. Buildings were sold for private use with deed restrictions requiring purchasers to preserve historic features. The agency, as the local match for HUD funds, installed an underground utility system, wooden sidewalks, cobblestone alleys and gas lights.

The preservation failures of the urban renewal program typically resulted from a failure of local preservationists to get involved until after the urban renewal plan was completed and work had begun. Under the program, a completed plan for an entire project area was required before funds were allocated to carry out the project. Redevelopment agencies, anxious to show results, were reluctant to change plans long in the development and approval processes.

Since the urban renewal program was based on a locally developed plan, in many cities the redevelopment authority came to be viewed as the nemesis of historic preservation, typically operating an urban redevelopment program that razed older areas. However, where preservationists were involved in the development of urban renewal plans, they became allies. Thus, in Philadelphia, the Redevelopment Authority and the Historical Commission developed a close partnership which worked to restore the Society Hill area. This joint effort helped to persuade the community of the financial value of good restoration.

Another HUD program to be used for historic preservation was popularly known as the 701 program after the authorizing provision of the Housing Act of 1954. Comprehensive planning and management grants were made to state and local governments for a broad range of activities. Historic preservation planning was eligible for assistance when undertaken as part of a comprehensive planning program. Eligible preservation activities included the establishment of criteria for evaluating properties, historic and architectural surveys, preparation of historic district legislation, rehabilitation cost estimates and the development of a historic preservation program for local government.

About 1966, the Housing Authority of Savannah, Georgia, developed its Historic Preservation Plan under HUD's 701 program, which included design guidelines for new development in the historic district. It identified 16 aspects of a building's exterior details that were to be compared with neighboring buildings and evaluated by the historic district commission to determine the appropriateness of the new construction. The Savannah Plan was adopted with variations, as a model by many historic districts throughout the nation. A historical survey of Natchez, Mississippi, describing each structure in the area, was also prepared as an adjunct to the city's comprehensive plan under the 701 program.

The Housing Act of 1961 provided for open space and urban beautification programs, with grants of up to 50 percent of project costs. The act was amended in 1966 to provide grants specifically for historic preservation. Unlike many HUD programs, the beautification projects did not have to be in a designated urban renewal area.

Section 312 of the Housing Act of 1964 made grants and loans available for repair and rehabilitation of properties within the boundaries of federally assisted urban renewal, neighborhood development or housing code enforcement projects. Similar to the urban renewal program, the financial incentives from HUD were administered through local public agencies, requiring that preservationists develop support for preservation activities at the local level. Interest rates of 3 percent on loans for rehabilitation stimulated widespread interest in older neighborhoods as word spread of the program's use.

Where Things Stood in 1966

Historic preservation, by 1966, was a widely accepted activity for local governments in the United States. Local preservation leaders could now initiate projects and obtain funding for them. Historic district zoning was becoming common: By 1964 the American Society of Planning Officials listed 14 states with enabling legislation for historic districts. Further, several court decisions had upheld the validity of historic district regulations. By the time major preservation schemes came before the courts a solid legal framework for validation was laid in litigation involving more refined zoning questions.

Landmarks commissions, dealing with individual landmarks instead of districts, were beginning to be created as well. In 1965, New York City adopted its Landmarks Preservation Law, which authorized the designation of both historic districts and landmarks.

But, in 1966, the historic resources of a community that had not developed political support for preservation were still extremely vulnerable to destructive governmental actions, frequently by the same state or federal agencies that were accomplishing preservation work elsewhere. By this time, historic preservation was no longer the exclusive domain of purely private, civic-minded individuals and groups; it had begun to go public. However, preservation activities were still essentially local endeavors, notwithstanding that they sometimes required the use of state or federal help and money.

The Expanding, Changing Role for Local Governments after 1966

The 89th U.S. Congress, which became known as the "Preservation Congress," adopted a number of laws in 1966, affecting historic preservation. These laws brought greater legitimacy to the increasingly public role in historic preservation and changed many roles of local government in preservation.

The 1966 legislation locked local governments into a more active role in historic preservation. Before then a local government had to take the initiative to be involved in historic preservation. Tools and funding existed, if the local government saw fit to avail itself of them. But after 1966, a local government could not totally ignore historic preservation, because destruction of the built heritage could result in the loss of funds and projects. Among other laws passed in 1966 with historic preservation components were the Department of Transportation Act of 1966, the Demonstration Cities and Metropolitan Development Act of 1966 and the National Historic Preservation Act of 1966.

Section 4(f) of the Transportation Act of 1966 prohibits the Secretary of Transportation from approving a program or project that would require use of land from a historic site of national, state or local significance (as well as publicly owned park, recreation areas or wildlife refuges) "unless there is no feasible and prudent alternative" to the use of the land and the project included "all possible planning to minimize harm" to the land. This special review procedure applied to any significant historic site, regardless of ownership or actual designation. Historic significance is determined by appropriate federal, state and local officials and in the absence of a finding of insignificance, sites are assumed to be significant.

The impact of Section 4(f) on highway projects in urban areas is significant, since highway planners are often tempted to route their roads through older areas or parks because of lower right-of-way acquisition costs. Parks offer large parcels of land, already in public ownership, which do not require condemnation. Typically, older areas were less expensive to acquire and had less political influence.

Section 4(f) is also procedurally significant to local governments in several ways. If the local government has a preservation commission, the commission's involvement is laid out by statute in the review process for new transportation projects with federal funding. If the commission determines that a property has historic significance, the 4(f) review process is triggered and alternatives are considered. Additionally, if the local preservation community objects to a highway (or other transportation) project that would damage historic resources, it has an additional way to register its objections other than at a local government public hearing. If the local government chooses to ignore the preservationists' concerns, the Department of Transportation (DOT) is required by law to consider them. In effect for the first time, the preservation community could go over the heads of local government in transportation planning matters, when federal funds were involved, if the local government was not responsive. Thus the threat of delay or loss of funding forced local governments to heed the concerns of preservationists.

Under the Demonstration Cities and Metropolitan Development Act of 1966, HUD was authorized to provide grants to municipalities and counties for two-thirds of the cost of surveys of historic structures and sites. Each survey is to be carried out in an area determined by appropriate local authorities to be of historic or architectural value. The Development Act of 1966 also amended urban renewal law to include specifically historic and archaeological preservation within the definitions of urban renewal plans and project activities; furthermore, local expenditures for historic preservation are counted as a match for federal urban renewal funds. In 1966, HUD published *Preserving Historic America*, a report showing by example how HUD programs could be used to assist preservation.

Because of the tremendous financial resources of the agency, this direct legislative involvement of HUD in historic preservation cheered the spirits of preservationists. And yet, the timing of the move was, in some ways, too late. Social, rather than physical, solutions to the problems of the urban poor were becoming a higher program priority for HUD in the late 1960s. Within a few years, the Community Development Block Grant program and revenue sharing replaced categorical programs, providing funding for locally determined and administered programs that no longer must fall into a programmatic category. Decisions about the expenditure of these new block grant funds became a local political issue, and the fiscal requests of the preservation community for preservation and the amenities were quickly outweighed by the need of the urban poor and minorities for housing, social services, and similar requirements.

The National Historic Preservation Act of 1966
and Local Government

The most significant legislative development for historic preservation was the National Historic Preservation Act of 1966 (NHPA). The act created the National Register of Historic Places, authorized a grants program for surveys and planning as well as property acquisition and development; and established an environmental review process for historic sites and an independent federal agency to conduct the reviews. Unlike previous federal historic preservation programs, the National Register includes properties of local and state significance as well as those of national significance.

The designation of a State Historic Preservation Officer (SHPO) to serve as liaison officer between the states and the federal government resulted in local officials working more frequently with state officials than federal ones on matters relating to historic preservation, even though the laws governing the relationship were federal. Through the survey and planning grants-in-aid program created under the Preservation Act of 1966, the SHPO could work with local governments to identify and evaluate historic properties and nominate them for listing in the National Register.

The 1966 Act's acquisition and development grants-in-aid program consisted of matching grants to the states for purchasing and restoring historic properties. These funds could, in turn, be passed along by the states to public or private recipients. Local governments could thereby obtain funding for historic preservation projects.

The creation of an environmental review process for historic properties through Section 106 of the Preservation Act of 1966 required local governments to consider the effect on historic resources of any proposed project using federal funds or authority, regardless of whether the project was a new highway or a housing project. As described in Chapter 2, where a federal agency is involved in funding or licensing a project, Section 106 requires the federal agency to consult with the SHPO and the Advisory Council on Historic Preservation to determine whether there is an adverse effect on a historic property of the proposed project.

The immediate impact of the Preservation Act of 1966 on local governments was substantial. No longer could a local government obtain, without any reflection, federal funds for a highway or an urban renewal project that would destroy historic resources, as demonstrated in the decision of the U.S. Court of Appeals for the Second Circuit in *WATCH v. Harris*. The case arose out of an urban renewal project in Waterbury, Connecticut, for which HUD signed a Loan and Grant Contract with the Waterbury Urban Renewal Agency in 1973. At that time, and in 1977 when HUD completed its environmental clearance for the project, no properties within the project area were included in or nominated to the National Register. However, HUD had not consulted with the SHPO or the Advisory Council on Historic Preservation as required under Section 106, nor had it prepared an environmental impact statement. In 1979, the Court of Appeals held that HUD must comply with Section 106 and its regulations even after the signing of the Loan and Grant Contract, as long as decision points requiring agency approval remain. This litigation, which stalled the local urban renewal agency's actions for years and eventually required compliance with the Preservation Act of 1966, also effected 365 other urban renewal projects. Local governments were required to heed the protective laws for historic properties or face long delays. These new historic protection laws made the success of an unsympathetic project less likely, if for no reason other than that the federal agency preferred not to have to go through the review process.

The impact of the Preservation Act of 1966 was subsequently to be felt in numerous other ways. A property's National Register status, initially determined to protect it from actions of the federal government itself, was to become the trigger for federal tax incentives and numerous state and local regulatory, funding and planning programs. For example, even though National Register listing initially imposed no limitation on a private property owner's demolition or alteration of a property so long as no federal funds or licensing were involved, the 1976 Tax Reform Act created a financial disincentive through the tax codes for the demolition or improper rehabilitation of a National Register structure, as well as an incentive for its proper rehabilitation. This substantially changed the financial impact of designation. The Preservation Act of 1966 was reinforced in 1969 by the passage of the National Environmental Policy Act, which reconfirmed historic resources as an important part of the nation's environment to be protected.

The Return from the Suburbs

Historic preservation expanded greatly at the local level during the late 1960s and early 1970s, especially in large cities. Planners were beginning to replace historians as historic preservation professionals. Cities that had experienced tremendous declines during the previous two decades saw historic preservation as a potential tool for drawing both investment and people back into old areas. Printed materials on historic preservation touted improved or stabilized property values, increased tax bases for cities and a return of middle class people from the suburbs.

Just as preservation was given a devastating blow in the late 1940s and early 1950s by consumer dynamics created by the Great Depression and World War II, it was given a lift by different trends of the late 1960s and early 1970s. Numerous demographic and economic factors coincided to stimulate a rebirth of downtown neighborhoods and business areas. As the baby boom generation started to reach adulthood, older buildings in depressed urban real estate markets provided inexpensive first homes. Increased energy costs made it more economically attractive to live downtown and to renovate rather than build anew. Aesthetically, older buildings had features and charm not found in look-alike suburbs. Many large cities attracted young homosexual men and women seeking to embrace the freedom advocated by the Gay Liberation movement of the late 1960s and early 1970s. With two incomes in many households (more money to spend on housing) and no children (less concern about security and schools), both homosexuals and young couples established their own homes in old urban areas.

By 1971, New York City's Landmarks Preservation Commission (established in 1965) had designated 18 historic districts, containing more than 6,000 properties. According to its chairman in 1971, "The popularity of [the historic districts] has exceeded all expectations. More people than anyone had ever imagined really enjoy living and working in neighborhoods that are characterized by the harmonious qualities of good urban design and by a sense of continuity with the past. The joint effort to preserve their qualities has raised community morale, and the designation of historic districts has, in fact, proven to be a surprisingly potent force for social stabilization." Good news, indeed, for a city on the edge of default. Other cities were getting the same message, as demonstrated by the growth of historic district zoning. While only a dozen historic district commissions were created between 1931 and the mid-1950s, more than 120 were established between the mid-1950s and 1972. By 1986, almost 2,000 historic districts had been designated by local governments.

The 1976 Bicentennial of the signing of the Declaration of Independence did much to stimulate interest in historic preservation. America's history became the focus of local events and publications, as well as commercial advertising and television programming. The Bicentennial had the effect of emphasizing that the United States, although a relatively young country, had a rich and powerful history. Throughout the country, historical societies and preservation commissions erected plaques, distributed maps of historic resources, created history exhibits and undertook preservation and restoration projects to commemorate the Bicentennial.

An unexpected boon for the historic preservation movement was the oil embargo of 1973 and its impact on building materials. Because building materials and new construction are energy-intensive, their prices increased greatly in the wake of the oil crisis, resulting in a relative economic advantage for rehabilitation. The impact of rising energy costs was examined by the Advisory Council on Historic Preservation in a 1978 study. It found, for example, that the Grand Central Arcade in Seattle was rehabilitated at a cost of 17 billion BTU's and that a new building of comparable size would have required 109 billion BTU's (85 billion for materials and 24 billion for construction).

Rehabilitation, in spite of its uncertainties, became much more competitive in price with new construction. In this post-1973 era, preservationists could at last talk to developers about the economic sense of historic preservation. Case studies presented in 1975 demonstrated that the cost of rehabilitating old structures generally runs 25–33 percent less than comparable new construction. In those cases where the costs were equivalent, rehabilitation frequently provided advantages, such as time saved in construction, more space in either height or volume, better community relations, fewer delays, higher occupancy rates and rents and better location. In the late 1960s and early 1970s, these factors attracted investors as well as new residents to older neighborhoods. Both groups realized tremendous appreciation in property values, as inner-city areas became more popular. For example, in the Castro district in San Francisco, in 1976, old Victorian houses were fetching five times their value in 1973.

Passage of the Tax Reform Act of 1976, which finally removed the disincentives for rehabilitation and the incentives for demolition from the tax code and replaced them with incentives for historic rehabilitation, provided the icing on the financial cake. The estimated dollar value of investments in rehabilitation work using the tax incentives increased from a combined total of $140 million for fiscal years 1977 and 1978 to more than $2.1 billion in fiscal year 1983. In 1983, for the first time in the nation's history, rehabilitation expenditures exceeded those for new construction. The rehabilitation incentives also added significantly to the nation's rental housing supply, which had reached a crisis stage in 1979. During fiscal years 1977 through 1982, the number of rental housing units increased from 5,451 to 25,948 under the rehabilitation tax incentives program.

All of these changes meant that the message of the local preservationist was changing and indeed, in many cases, their stereotype of the preservationist was changing, too. Preservationists were now armed with talk of grants, loans, tax incentives, rehabilitation estimates and an enhanced tax base. If the local officials did not hear those messages, the preservationist could also talk about environmental impact statements, Section 106 reviews and legal standing to sue. The young professional, sometimes a developer, frequently replaced "the little old lady in tennis shoes" as the advocate for preserving the local heritage. The tools of local historic preservation were also advancing, becoming increasingly sophisticated, moving into the realm of the real estate and planning professional.

New and More Complex Local Regulatory Tools

These moves toward increasing complexity are nowhere more evident than in the evolution of tools used by historic district or landmark commissions. Since the establishment of the first district in Charleston in 1931, the primary tools for historic districts have been design review of exterior changes and the demolition delay or prohibition.

In the decade following 1966, many new tools were added to the arsenal, especially in larger cities, such as New York City which, in 1968, became the first to permit the transfer of a landmark's development rights in order to preserve it. Briefly, a transfer of development rights permits a developer to take development rights foregone by preserving a historic building which is smaller than the zoning code would otherwise allow, to transfer those development rights to another site, and there build a bigger or taller building than zoning would otherwise permit.

In 1973, New York City passed legislation expanding the power of the Landmarks Preservation Commission to protect publicly and privately owned interiors generally accessible to the public. Several other cities, notably Boston and Seattle, also now have active programs to identify, designate and protect significant interiors. Protection of interior features represents a broadened application of the police power in regulating for historic preservation, since the protection of interiors must generally be based on aesthetics rather than on traditional public welfare arguments.

Another broadening of preservation ordinances involves the addition of minimum maintenance and anti-neglect requirements. Many local preservation ordinances require that landmarks be maintained in accordance with local building and housing codes. Minimum maintenance ordinances have generally been upheld in court on a case-by-case basis when the public interest involved was found to outweigh the economic burden on the owner. As found in the 1975 case of *Maher v. City of New Orleans*, "Once it has been determined that the purpose of the Vieux Carré [historic district] legislation is a proper one, upkeep of buildings appears reasonably necessary to the accomplishment of the goals of the ordinance." The most difficult issue in this area is a practical rather than a legal one—the necessity to prove that the owner neglected the building. To convince a judge or jury that the owner deliberately failed to repair a leaking roof or purposely allowed a foundation to rot is a much more difficult task than proving affirmative acts of vandalism.

New Orleans and other communities went further to include anti-neglect (or affirmative maintenance) requirements, specifying a list of structural defects that must be repaired on a continuing basis. Anti-neglect requirements, which prevent an owner from effectively demolishing a structure by not maintaining it, raise a variety of additional legal questions, such as how inspections of properties for structural defects are to be made and who pays for the necessary repairs.

Some local governments in some states obtained authority, through enabling legislation, to use the power of eminent domain to acquire designated landmarks threatened with demolition. Historic preservation is statutorily defined as a public purpose and a public use, which are prerequisites for the exercise of eminent domain. Under North Carolina law, for example, if a property owner makes application to demolish a designated landmark, the local government can acquire the property through eminent domain if it chooses, and then dispose of it to a sympathetic purchaser with the added protection of restrictive covenants insuring its preservation. The political hurdles of using this authority would be great, since the local government would likely face litigation on the valuation of the property.

Other evidences of the evolution of local historic preservation from an activity for volunteers to a largely professional one can be seen in recent years. In 1974, Seattle, Washington, became the first city to appoint a City Conservator to be responsible for directing all municipal preservation activity. More and more cities across the country began hiring professionals to direct their historic preservation programs. Indicative of the new legal complexity of the tools of the historic preservation movement, the National Trust for Historic Preservation established a legal services program for urban landmark and historic district commissions in 1975.

Revenue Sharing and Community Development Block Grants: Transferring Authority to the Local Level

The State and Local Fiscal Assistance Act of 1972 administered by HUD marked the beginning of a trend toward replacing categorical federal programs with broader assistance programs for local governments. The Assistance Act of 1972 created a revenue sharing program, which allocated funds to local governments for eight broad categories of programs. The local government was charged with determining the use of the revenue sharing funds, and local public hearings became forums for financial decisions. Historic preservation was included in two of the eight broad categories of funding—environmental protection and recreation.

Two years later, the Housing and Community Development Act of 1974 consolidated existing HUD categorical grant programs into a new program called Community Development Block Grants. While the act contained a number of preservation-oriented measures, the responsibility for decisions about whether to use its federal block grant money for local preservation projects was clearly placed on local elected officials. Responsibility for environmental review

Weak local preservation programs lead to the demolition of significant examples of historic architecture, such as this building in Grand Rapids, Michigan. (National Trust for Historic Preservation)

Landmark buildings are also destroyed by fire, such as the one that destroyed the Crown & Eagle Mill in North Uxbridge, Massachusetts, in 1975. The fire was a suspected arson. (Worcester Telegram & Gazette, copyright 1975)

The National Trust's Main Street demonstration projects served as models for many locally inspired downtown revitalization projects. In South Dakota, Hot Spring's restored sandstone buildings house profitable commercial enterprises. (James L. Ballard, National Trust for Historic Preservation)

CHAPEL HILL HISTORIC DISTRICT
Guidelines Handbook

The enforcement of local government controls over additions and alterations to historic districts is assisted by design guidelines manuals, such as this handbook for the Chapel Hill, North Carolina, historic district. (Robert E. Stipe) under the Preservation Act of 1966 and the National Environmental Policy Act of 1969 was increasingly transferred to the local government.

Shifting the authority for the use of revenue sharing and community development funds to the local level proved to be a disadvantage for preservationists. They found themselves competing for the same dollars as advocates for street paving, water treatment and sewer facilities, housing programs and assistance for the homeless. Preservation frequently did not receive a high priority when compared to urgent infrastructure or housing needs.

A new HUD program established by Congress in 1977, Urban Development Action Grants (UDAG), harkened back to the days of urban renewal and categorical programs. Designed to stimulate economic development, create new jobs and reclaim deteriorated neighborhoods in distressed communities through public and private development partnerships, the grant program also delegated environmental review to the city applicant. Early case studies of UDAG projects in Charleston, South Carolina; Louisville, Kentucky; New Orleans, Louisiana; and Pittsfield, Massachusetts, presented a pattern of large scale, expensive and highly political downtown renewal projects. They steamrolled opposition from citizen and historic preservation organizations alike, as well as environmental-review defense mechanisms, raising alarm among preservationists. As with earlier HUD programs, whether a UDAG project was beneficial to historic preservation depended on the success of local preservationists in the political arena. However, the grant program was to be short-lived, dying along with many other domestic programs during the Reagan administration.

Cooperative Programs

The years after passage of the Preservation Act of 1966 were also marked by increasing efforts to coordinate preservation efforts with those related to planning, community development, public works and private-sector activities. In 1974, HUD and the Federal Home Loan Bank Board established the Urban Reinvestment Task Force to develop Neighborhood Housing Services. (In 1978, the Neighborhood Reinvestment Corporation, the successor to the task force, was created as an independent agency.) Local Neighborhood Housing Services involved older neighborhoods and local thrift institutions in a partnership to encourage rehabilitation and new construction lending in areas that were previously considered poor risks. Although not specifically a preservation program, Neighborhood Housing Services became a strong preservation ally where local governments provided protection and enhancement for historic resources through preservation ordinances or through sympathetic capital improvement projects.

The National Trust's Main Street project represented a partnership between preservationists and local business communities. Developed in 1976 in the Midwest as an experiment to assist small towns with revitalization of older commercial areas, the Main Street program focused on using design qualities of the downtowns in communities of 50,000 and less to attract new businesses and jobs. The program encouraged joint participation and action between private individuals and local governments. These programs included street and sidewalk improvement projects, improved facade design and window displays supplemented by marketing events such as parades and street fairs. The experimental program was highly successful in the three pilot communities. Sales tax revenues increased by 25 percent in Hot Springs, South Dakota (population 5,000); the downtown occupancy rate rose to 95 percent in Galesburg, Illinois (population 38,000) and six new businesses opened in Madison, Indiana (population 13,000). Based on the success of the pilot program, the National Main Street Center was created by the National Trust in 1980 in cooperation with the International Downtown Executive Association with funding through an interagency agreement coordinated by HUD. Preservationists involved in the Main Street program were clearly moving into the main stream of their communities.

The HUD urban homesteading program, exemplified a partnership between federal and local governments to revitalize destitute inner-city neighborhoods through historic preservation. Initiated in 1973 in Wilmington, Delaware, urban homesteading permitted buyers to purchase tax-foreclosed properties for $1 on the condition that they be rehabilitated to local code standards within specified deadlines and be owner-occupied. The local government would forego past taxes and penalties due on the properties in the hope of building a future tax base. HUD, through a variety of programs, assisted with loans and other funding for homesteaders. Just as the original homesteading program in the American West during the 19th century captured the public's imagination, the urban homesteading program generated tremendous interest in older deteriorated inner-city neighborhoods. It was such a success in Baltimore, Maryland, that the city expanded the concept in 1977 to create shopsteading. Tax-foreclosed commercial structures could be purchased for $1 with requirements for rehabilitation and use.

Rural Preservation Concerns

Rural preservation also became increasingly a concern of preservationists. In the 1970s demographic statistics clearly indicated urban decline and rural gains, as unprecedented numbers of Americans migrated into rural areas. During the 1970s the population of rural areas increased 40 percent faster than that of urban centers. Various ways of preserving rural structures and landscapes in light of these changes were proposed, with a recognition of the important role of local government in planning for and protecting rural resources. Many of the same tools used in urban preservation could be applied by local governments to preserve rural areas, such as tax incentives, historic designation, capital improvements, development rights transfers or acquisitions and zoning tools. For example, Suffolk County, Long Island, New York, approved a $55 million plan in 1975 to purchase development rights on 12,000–15,000 acres of farmland. In the first phases of the plan, farmland owners could voluntarily sell the development rights for their acreage to the county. Under the final phase, the county would use its power of eminent domain to acquire rights to parcels needed to fill out blank spaces in and around acquired parcels. But these rural tools have not yet been widely used. As Robert E. Stipe put it in the 1980 publication, *New Directions in Rural Preservation,* " . . . until rural preservation can be recognized as a much more important aspect of local community life and thereby command more attention and respect as an appropriate subject for local political concern, little that is done in state or national capitals will be of much real benefit."

Ironically, the issue of rural preservation was to be turned around in the 1980s by a rural crisis of a different nature. A severely depressed farm economy and a tightening of farm credit abruptly reversed the migration patterns and the escalating farm property values of the 1970s. Whereas in 1975 rural areas gained 1.6 million people, in 1984 they lost 351,000. With the attention of policy-makers focused on the deepening economic crisis of farmers, the preservation of rural areas and farmland continued to receive a low priority at the local level.

Local Governments as Funding Sources

During the years after the Preservation Act of 1966 many local governments themselves funded historic preservation activities. Sometimes the funding was directly for historic preservation. The grants made under the provisions of the Preservation Act of 1966 required recipients to match federal funds; HUD programs and many state appropriations for historic preservation also required local contributions to projects. Often, the funding was indirect. Cities completed expensive capital improvements or arranged financial incentives in an effort to stimulate further private historic preservation activity. Working with a consortium of private banks and using its own tax-exempt status, Charlotte, North Carolina, arranged for early purchasers in its downtown Fourth Ward district to receive long-term financing at a substantially reduced interest rate. The city, after rectifying zoning and through-traffic problems, also committed itself to making major capital improvements in the area, such as pocket parks, pole-mounted street lighting, street medians, landscaping and brick sidewalks. The district evolved from a largely vacant and blighted urban renewal area to a dense, trendy neighborhood for young professionals in less than a decade, thereby greatly enhancing the tax base and adding to downtown revitalization.

Sometimes local government financial support for preservation came in the form of funding for the restoration of its own buildings. Restoration of the Old City Hall in Baltimore, Maryland and the Marshall County Courthouse, Iowa, where voters had repeatedly rejected bond issues for replacement of the courthouse but approved one for its restoration, are but two examples of a common trend toward refurbishing historic governmental structures that would have been discarded two decades earlier. Frequently, where local governments built new facilities and vacated historic city halls or courthouses, those buildings were turned over to nonprofit groups for historical or cultural uses.

Many preservation-minded local governments also provided funding to local nonprofit organizations for preservation programs or assisted them with free office space, supplies and other benefits. Sometimes indirect funding is used: Raleigh, North Carolina, sold a parcel of land to the local historical society at a considerably reduced price in order to assist its revolving fund work, and a neighboring town, Cary, purchased an endangered historic landmark and leased it to a nonprofit group for rehabilitation as a community center for $1 a year for 25 years.

Local governments also provided funds through revenue losses created by local tax incentives for historic preservation. Established by state legislation, these incentives might benefit all landmark owners or only those who undertake specific preservation activities, such as rehabilitation or easement donation.

128

The New Mexico Cultural Properties Act of 1969 exempted designated properties from local city, county and school property taxes to the extent of approved restoration, preservation and maintenance expenses each year. This act required the property owner to take some action to enhance the landmark before the local government provided its subsidy. Local governments in Illinois provided a reduced tax assessment for designated properties. Any reduction in property value resulting from landmark designation would be deducted from valuation for tax purposes. In Oregon, properties with preservation easements were assessed at true cash value, thereby taking into account the reduction in value created by the easement. Prince George's County, Maryland, offered local tax credits for the preservation of open space.

Some local governments subsidized properties where their regulation created hardships for the owner. In New York City, in order to get a demolition permit, the owner of a locally designated landmark must show that earning a reasonable economic return with the property is impossible. When the owner establishes this, the burden is then placed upon the landmarks commission to devise a plan, which may include, but is not limited to, a grant of partial or complete tax exemption, remission of taxes and authorization of alteration, construction or reconstruction.

Protection Against the Hand of Man: Local Regulatory Programs

Just as the protection of historic buildings against the hand of time usually requires restorative measures after the damage is done, protection against the hand of man is essentially a matter of preventing damage to the building or its setting in the first place. As in other countries, this is accomplished by uncompensated regulations that seek to prevent the owner from damaging or changing the physical fabric of the building in inappropriate ways, moving or demolishing it or constructing inappropriate buildings in the immediate vicinity. These regulations are typically called historic district or landmark ordinances.

The source of the authority for the creation of historic districts or the designation of landmarks is, of course, the state. Having no autonomous authority, local governments must be specifically authorized by the state in which they are located to do just about anything. Authorization to adopt historic district and landmarks ordinances is customarily part of a state package for historic preservation. These enabling acts also typically provide the city or county with authority to acquire, own, manage and support historic sites as public facilities, facilitate the preservation of privately owned landmarks, make grants and loans to private individuals, acquire and maintain properties, issue bonds, levy taxes and perform other relevant preservation tasks.

Historic District Ordinances

Historic district ordinances regulate all properties within locally designated districts, whether or not the properties are individually significant. The basic assumption is that the value of the district as a whole is greater than the sum of its parts. The legal foundation for historic district designation is the health, safety and welfare components of the police power (the use of state authority to regulate private actions). The use of the police power for historic district zoning was justified because a district strengthens the local economy, enhances property values, affirms historic and community values and promotes tourism. Until recently, aesthetics was only a secondary legal justification for historic district regulation.

State enabling legislation for historic districts falls generally into two categories. The statute may be general and broadly worded, such as New Mexico's Historic District Act, which simply authorizes counties and municipalities to enact and enforce zoning ordinances, to expend public funds and acquire property by eminent domain and otherwise accomplish preservation objectives. A statute such as this gives the local government a wide latitude in developing procedures for designation and regulation of historic districts. The local government, of course, is still bound by state and federal constitutional constraints on its actions.

On the other hand, the enabling statute may confer carefully defined authority and powers, including detailed procedures for designation for historic districts. Although more restrictive of the local government's options, this type of statute gives less sophisticated local governments specific instructions on how to create local historic districts and it assures greater consistency of regulation among the state's historic districts.

Both the district boundaries and the regulations imposed on property owners inside them are established by the local governing body, such as the city council, board of aldermen or county commissioners, typically as part of the zoning regulations. A historic district commission is established by an ordinance, with members to be appointed by the governing body or mayor. Before a property owner within the district can make alterations to the exterior of an existing structure or build a new one, a certificate of appropriateness must be obtained from the historic district commission. It reviews the proposed exterior plans and decides whether they are supportive of the historic aspects of the district. If they are not, the property owner is denied permission to proceed and other needed permits are not issued. The degree of control experienced over private property depends on the grant of power in the state's enabling legislation and whether the local government is willing (or politically able) to exercise the full powers permitted thereunder. In many districts the exterior paint colors are regulated by the commission. Landscaping has been added in some states to the list of appurtenant features that may be regulated.

The historic district commission is usually also authorized to delay or prohibit demolition within the district. Again, state enabling legislation determines whether the demolition control is in the form of a delay or a prohibition. The demolition regulations apply to all structures within the district, not just to the historically significant ones. The historic district commission is authorized to permit the demolition to proceed when it believes that demolition is not harmful to the character of the district.

Landmarks Ordinances

Individually significant historic landmarks, usually located outside of historic districts, are controlled by a landmarks ordinance. This typically requires landmark designation by the local governing body and imposes restrictions on altering or demolishing the landmark without the approval of a landmarks or historic properties commission.

The regulation of individual historic landmarks has a somewhat different legal basis than that for historic districts, although the two usually share similar mechanisms (the certificate of appropriateness for alterations and delay or prohibition of demolition) and are frequently administered by the same commission. Whereas historic district designation is typically based on the health, safety and welfare components of the police power (the use of state authority to regulate private actions), the best legal justification for landmarks protection under the police power is aesthetics. Because they stand in isolation rather than as a collection within a district, a different approach is necessary. Unlike districts, landmark buildings cannot easily be protected through zoning. They do not necessarily contribute to the economic and social well being of the community through area revitalization and tourism. Indeed, under traditional zoning, landmark protection could in theory constitute the illegal practice of spot zoning, the singling out of one parcel for treatment different from that accorded to surrounding parcels.

Landmarks protection, however, can be based on aesthetics. When Philadelphia adopted its wide-reaching ordinance in 1956, few state supreme courts considered aesthetics alone to be a sufficient basis for the exercise of the police power. Two years earlier, Supreme Court Justice William O. Douglas in *Berman v. Parker*, a case involving a redevelopment plan to eliminate substandard housing conditions in Washington, D.C., had written: "It is within the power of the legislature to determine that the community should be beautiful as well as healthy, spacious as well as clean, well balanced as well as carefully patrolled. . . . If those who govern the District of Columbia decide that the Nation's Capital should be beautiful as well as sanitary, there is nothing in the Fifth Amendment that stands in the way." Although Justice Douglas' comments about aesthetics were not central to the decision in the case, they were enormously influential in state courts as, one by one, they accepted aesthetics alone as a sufficient basis for the exercise of the police power. By the 1980s a substantial majority of state courts had so ruled.

The Operation of Historic District and Landmarks Commissions

Since historic district and landmark commissions are the primary regulatory tools of local government and since the regulations involved cut deeply into the traditional private property rights of owners, the activities of these commissions are the subject of much judicial review, creating a highly structured system for regulation. The requirements for establishing a historic district or landmarks commission are usually established in state enabling legislation.

The status of a commission within the local governmental hierarchy and the nature of its membership and staffing have a direct impact upon its orientation and effectiveness. Many commissions are administratively placed in municipal or county departments dealing with zoning, planning or land use and are staffed by planners, thereby providing some integration of preservation with other land use functions affecting historic resources. Other commissions are associated with housing or redevelopment authorities, where preservation has become the basis for revitalization projects and an emphasis is placed on public improvements and subsidy programs. Yet another alignment for preservation commissions is with cultural affairs departments, with the unfortunate consequence that preservation is viewed as an arts activity, with staff dominated by historians and architectural historians. Some preservation commissions are independent, with their orientation determined by local perspectives. However, all too often, independent status for a preservation commission results in political isolation or programmatic ineffectiveness, because the commission is not integrated into other municipal functions that have an impact on the preservation of historic resources.

The orientation and effectiveness of a commission is also shaped by its membership and its leadership. Preservation ordinances in larger cities and counties commonly specify the occupational makeup of a commission. The local ordinance might establish, for example, that the commission have, among its membership, a specified number of architects, landscape architects, realtors, lawyers, neighborhood residents, property owners or historical or preservation organization representatives. Commissions in smaller towns are less likely to have representation from as many professions because of the smaller population base from which to draw. Whether appointments to a commission are largely political or based on real preservation interests will affect the commission's effectiveness. Having a commission in which preservation professionals are well represented can be of significance to a court in the event that a decision of the commission is appealed, since a judge may be less likely to substitute his opinion for those of recognized experts in the field. It is interesting to note that preservation commissions are composed of volunteers rather than paid professionals, and these volunteers exercise considerable regulatory authority. Unlike many countries that place such authority in the hands of professional design staff, the American long-standing mistrust of professionals in public office has created a complex regulatory system that is basically administered by appointed laymen.

Whether a county or municipality chooses to combine its districts and landmarks commissions into one body affects the community's preservation dynamics. Since local preservation leadership is a critical criterion of effectiveness, the value or the detriment of having separate commissions depends largely on local personalities. Either multiple preservation commissions may divide the loyalties of preservationists or they may work in concert and provide strong advocates for historic preservation.

One of the first tasks of a historic district or landmarks commission is a survey of historic and architectural resources within the commission's jurisdiction. A survey provides the commission with detailed information about the buildings and sites with which it may be dealing, thereby allowing it to make better informed decisions. The survey can also educate the public about the values to be preserved, especially if it is published. A thorough survey will also aid in the event of a judicial challenge to a commission's decision by helping to establish that the commission's action is part of a comprehensive preservation program, and that decisions about individual buildings are not arbitrary or capricious.

One of the most difficult tasks in establishing a historic district is determining its boundaries. Care must be taken to include the bulk of significant structures and sites, but it is also important that the district's fringe areas be included in order to protect the most significant areas from environmental deterioration. For some of the same reasons, a landmarks commission has a complex task in selecting properties to recommend for designation. The orientation of the commission and its local governing body will determine whether the commission's priorities are the most architecturally and historically significant structures, the most endangered structures, the most culturally representative structures or the structures likely to have the greatest educational impact. Such priorities will do much to shape the public's perception of the commission and its role.

Practice varies among the states as to how the process of actually designating a landmark or putting historic district regulations into effect is accomplished. In most states, the actual designation is done by passage of an ordinance to that effect by the local governing board. Typically, this follows the submission of a special report describing and attesting to the significance of the property or the district. In other states, the act of designation is executed by a resolution of the commission itself, which must follow standards of eligibility prescribed in the state law or local ordinance. This approach may create special problems, as it can easily lead to an unconstitutional delegation of legislative authority to a nonlegislative body unless strict standards are followed. In all those cases, a public hearing is required, and this always reveals a strong and outspoken political dimension to the act of designation. This, in turn, is closely linked to the support, or objection, of the property owners or neighborhood residents.

Historic district and landmarks commissions share the task of reviewing applications for alterations, additions, new construction or demolition. Because the owner's property rights are directly affected by this review, the procedural aspects of the commission's decision- making process becomes equally as important as the substantive aspects. The correctness of the design decisions matter little in a court challenge if the property owner's due process rights have been trampled, because an American court will strive always to protect the owner's rights. Therefore, a procedurally complex system was developed for the process of reviewing applications. This mechanism typically includes deadlines and specifications for applications,legal public notice to interested parties, a formal hearing on the application (in some states, complete with the swearing in of witnesses, rebuttal opportunities, findings of fact and tape recordings of the proceedings) and detailed minutes of the process.

A preservation commission develops design standards to guide it in its deliberations, so that decisions will not be made arbitrarily or in a discriminatory manner and to aid property owners in developing their proposals. The design standards indicate the criteria to be considered in reviewing an application for an alteration, addition or demolition. For example, for the review of a proposal for an addition, standards may specify that the commission is to consider building materials, height, scale, color, fenestration, building form, architectural detailing and means of attaching the addition to the existing structure. The commission must then review the addition in the light of these design guidelines only, so that the property owner knows what to expect in the process, thus guaranteeing the property owner's right to due process of law.

Design guidelines will vary from district to district, even within one city or town, because the features to be protected vary. Some commissions have adopted the *Secretary of the Interior's Standards for Rehabilitation* and its accompanying guidelines. Since these standards were developed for one purpose—professional evaluation of rehabilitation projects under the federal tax incentive program—and are being used for another purpose—design review by a local, typically volunteer, commission—sometimes the fit is problematic. Property owners applying for the federal tax credits occasionally get caught between conflicting opinions of the National Park Service and the local commission. The National Park Service focuses on how the specific historic structure under consideration was rehabilitated, whereas most district commissions look at how alterations to existing structures and new construction fit into the context of the local district. Understandably, the concepts of streetscape and townscape do not pervade the Secretary's Standards, and yet they should be paramount in district regulation.

Many landmarks commissions, especially in smaller towns and counties, began as owners and managers of historic properties owned by the local government. Often, when a local government purchased a historic property in order to ensure its preservation, it turned the property into a museum or other cultural facility under jurisdiction of the landmarks commission. Museum efforts played an important role in raising the public awareness about preservation and history, but they are expensive to maintain without public subsidy, earned income or endowment. As a result, commissions are turning to the revolving fund as a tool for preserving significant properties without the public expense of maintenance. Now, unless a property is of the highest significance, a commission would be more likely to sell the property with strict deed restrictions to a new owner for private use, and use the proceeds to acquire another landmark. The Charlotte-Mecklenburg, North Carolina, Historic Properties Commission established an Endangered Properties Fund to acquire endangered designated properties for resale to private parties.

Legal and Political Challenges

As preservationists developed increasingly sophisticated, complex and extensive regulatory measures to protect historic resources, legal and political challenges to these measures were laid down. Challenges to both the constitutionality and the application of historic district and landmark regulations occurred in numerous courts.

In the early development of preservation law in the United States, local regulations were challenged on substantive grounds but generally were upheld. In 1941, the Louisiana Supreme Court upheld the validity of historic district regulation in *City of New Orleans v. Pergament*, affirming the principle that all buildings in a historic district could be regulated, whether or not individually significant, since the value of the district, the tout ensemble, is greater than the sum of its parts.

The Massachusetts Supreme Court provided an advisory opinion to the state senate when the enabling legislation for historic districts in Nantucket and Boston was being considered. Answering the argument that the proposed law was unconstitutionally vague, the court upheld the validity of design and demolition controls in historic districts, saying that the proposed act was not "too indefinite or lacking in sufficient standards."

In 1964, in *Santa Fe v. Gamble-Skogmo, Inc.*, the Supreme Court of New Mexico held that a general enactment authorizing New Mexico cities to make regulations and restrictions in accordance with a comprehensive plan to promote public health and general welfare was sufficiently specific to authorize historic district regulation by Santa Fe. In that case, a challenge was made to a regulation limiting the size of window panes in the Santa Fe historic districts to no more than 30 square inches. Since New Mexico did not then have enabling legislation specifically for historic districts, Santa Fe had relied on the general zoning enabling authority.

Challenges presented in the 1970s focused on more specific issues relating to local preservation regulation. The authority of a city to draw historic districts boundaries to include nonhistoric fringe areas was upheld in 1973 by a California appellate court in *Bohannan v. City of San Diego*. Affirmative maintenance requirements imposed on the owners of landmark buildings were upheld by the Fifth Circuit Court of Appeals in 1975 in *Maher v. City of New Orleans*. The case of *Figarsky v. Historic District of the City of Norwich* in Connecticut in 1976, although technically not applicable in other states, underscored the importance of a local preservation commission's compiling an extensive record, following prescribed procedures, and giving specific reasons for its decision.

The Landmark Penn Central Decision

The U.S. Supreme Court's opinion in the landmark case, *Penn Central Transportation Co. v. New York City*, in 1978 provided the touchstone for local preservation regulatory programs. This decision settled a number of legal issues that had previously haunted preservationists, since the validity of preservation regulations were never reviewed by the U.S. Supreme Court. The *Penn Central* case, in addition to answering major constitutional questions, provided guidance on many fronts for local preservationists.

In 1956, New York became the first state to authorize its municipalities to enact landmark ordinances to protect individual structures. Nine years later, New York City became the first major city to adopt a landmarks ordinance that provided significant protection for designated landmarks. Under the ordinance, the Landmarks Preservation Commission was established to designate structures of historic or architectural significance as landmarks and to regulate their restoration, alteration and demolition. If an inappropriate modification of a landmark was proposed, the commission was authorized to disallow the change unless mitigation was required to avoid economic hardship to the owners.

One of the first landmark designations was the highly significant Grand Central Terminal. The building's owner, Penn Central Transportation Company, objected to the designation, but did not appeal the city's action. In 1968, Penn Central entered into a lease with a company that proposed to construct a 55-story office building atop the terminal. The construction would have placed a tower approximately 500 feet high on top of the terminal and required the destruction of a portion of the interior concourse. In 1969, the commission denied the applications for new construction and alteration on the grounds that the proposed changes would be highly inappropriate. Shortly thereafter, Penn Central filed a lawsuit against the city. It charged that the effect of the commission's denial of the building permit was so burdensome as to amount to a taking of its property without just compensation.

The 5th Amendment to the U.S. Constitution, which is applied to state and local governments through the 14th Amendment, provides that property shall not be taken by the government without the payment of just compensation. In the late 19th and early 20th centuries, courts began to apply the taking clause to government regulation where the economic burden imposed on a landowner was too great. The most important zoning cases of the early 20th century turned on whether zoning ordinances that resulted in reduced property values for certain parcels amounted to an unconstitutional taking. The U.S. Supreme Court in *Village of Euclid v. Ambler Realty Co.* decided this issue, holding that the burden imposed on a property owner by limiting the use of his property was permissible without compensation because the same burden was imposed on all other nearby property owners and because the benefits of the limitations also applied to all owners. If the burdens created by the zoning were nondiscriminatory and reasonable, then the regulation would not be considered to be a taking.

After litigation in the state courts, Penn Central appealed an unfavorable decision of New York State's highest court to the U.S. Supreme Court. The stakes for preservationists were high. It would be the first review of landmark preservation regulations by the Supreme Court, and one of the few land-use cases to be decided by it since *Euclid* in 1926. Before the Supreme Court, Penn Central argued that the commission's rejection of a permit to build a tower atop the terminal amounted to an unconstitutional taking of its property. It also argued that the landmark designation was unconstitutionally discriminatory because it singled out one property for special unfavorable treatment.

The Supreme Court's opinion in the case was a major victory for preservationists. The court upheld the action of the New York Landmarks Preservation Commission. The court determined that where state courts or legislatures so provide, aesthetic considerations alone are not an improper basis for the use of the police power; "states and cities may enact land use restrictions or controls to enhance the quality of life by preserving the character and desirable aesthetic features of a city. . . ." In addition, the court rejected Penn Central's taking claim by applying the same concepts that had been used in earlier zoning cases, thereby making clear that, when it comes to economic impact, local historic preservation controls are to be viewed as yet another form of land-use regulation.

The court also explicitly rejected Penn Central's claim that the landmark designation was discriminatory, at least where a city has designated a substantial number of landmarks. This rejection made it clear that local governments could designate landmarks as well as establish historic districts. District regulation had previously been viewed as more clearly permissible because of its similarities to zoning.

The *Penn Central* case gave the preservation community much insight for further reference. One of the reasons that the court was able to avoid a finding that the designation was discriminatory is that New York City had adopted a comprehensive preservation program. Carefully drafted preservation ordinances had been adopted, many city landmarks and districts had been designated after careful surveys, and the commission's activities had been generally coordinated with land use and zoning.

A form of economic assistance to landmark owners was provided in the New York City ordinance. The court was impressed by the fact that the city had established a scheme to mitigate financial burdens on owners of landmarks. Even if a landmark owner was not able to use the designated property for its most lucrative use, at least a reasonable economic return on the property was assured. New York City had developed a system of transferable development rights that permitted owners of landmarks to sell the air rights over their buildings to developers of other parcels. According to the court, "While these [transferable development] rights may well not have constituted 'just compensation' if a 'taking' had occurred, the rights nevertheless undoubtedly mitigate whatever financial burdens the law has imposed on appellants and for that reason, are to be taken into account in considering the impact of regulation."

The Issue of Owner Consent

In the *Penn Central* case, the court upheld the terminal's designation and regulation even though its owner objected to designation. Shortly thereafter, owner consent to National Register designation raised its head as a political issue in a different forum.

In 1966, when the National Register program was established, Register designation was considered to be primarily an honorary matter for the private property owner, since the program's protective mechanism was triggered only by federal funds or licenses. Placing property on the National Register did not require the owner's consent. Since the Register was to be a listing of properties that met objective criteria, the owner's opinion had no bearing on whether the property met those criteria, and the listing did not restrict a private owner's use of his property in any way. However, National Register listing increasingly came to be a mechanism for triggering reviews, incentives and penalties by state and local governments, as well as by federal programs. After passage of the Tax Reform Act of 1976, owners of National Register properties received tax benefits for the proper rehabilitation of properties for income-producing purposes and suffered tax penalties for their demolition. Yet, the owner had no voice in the matter. Some property owners objected to having demolition disincentives placed on their properties without their consent. In 1979, the Procter & Gamble Company of Cincinnati, Ohio, upset by the designation of its Ivorydale plant, built in 1837 in St. Bernard, Ohio, lobbied aggressively to add an owner consent requirement for landmarks of an industrial nature.

At the same time, many preservationists sought additional protection for properties listed in the National Register. When in 1980 preservationists worked to persuade the U.S. Congress to enact an ambitious preservation agenda, Congress was not willing to accept the added restrictions being advocated for National Register properties. In amending the National Historic Preservation Act of 1966, Congress continued the process of decentralizing the nation's historic program and returning it to the local level. At the center of the debate was whether property owners and local elected officials should have any input into whether properties are listed in the National Register.

The 1980 amendments to the Preservation Act of 1966 added an owner consent provision requiring in effect that the property owner or owners must be given an opportunity to concur in or object to the designation. If the owner, or in a district a majority of owners, objects, then the property may not be included in the National Register.

Local government officials also had no voice in the National Register listing process, and local projects using federal funds were being reviewed, and delayed, because of the impact of the projects on historic resources. So, in 1980, when mayors sought a veto over National Register designations within their jurisdictions, the U.S. Congress responded by giving local governments the power to veto register listing if both the mayor and the landmarks commission objected to the nomination. This veto injects local politics into the process of nominating structures to the National Register.

The National Register owner-consent requirement set an unfortunate precedent for local landmark or district designation, making local governments more likely than before to require owner consent for local landmark or historic district designation, even though the U.S. Supreme Court clearly did not make owner consent a legal requirement for designation. Because the designation of historic properties under federal law now requires the consent of property owners and governing bodies, the educational, informational and political roles of local preservationists have become more important than ever.

Certified Local Governments

Another decentralizing feature of the 1980 amendments to the Preservation Act of 1966 was the creation of the certified local government program, which had the effect of providing more involvement for local governments in the National Register listing process. Once a local government is certified by the State Historic Preservation Officer (SHPO) as having a historic preservation commission and a program that meets federal and state standards, the local government becomes eligible to participate in nominating properties within its jurisdiction to the National Register and to apply for especially earmarked grants. At least 10 percent of a state's funding from the National Historic Preservation Fund must be passed along to certified local governments. The funding may be used for surveys and inventories of historic or archaeological resources, preparation of National Register nominations, comprehensive planning activities and public education programs. Although the certified local government program has tended to strengthen local preservation commissions, especially in small towns, by requiring that their ordinances and programs meet certain standards, the program was weakened considerably by the fact that funding from the Historic Preservation Fund was slashed in 1980, the same year that the certified local government program was established. Many large cities have not become certified local governments because the financial incentive to do so has been so diminished.

The 1980 amendments and the election of President Ronald Reagan, who pledged to cut deeply into the federal government's spending for domestic programs, decentralized the federal historic preservation program. Although guided into many historic preservation programs by the federal government, local governments are assuming more responsibility for National Register nominations, environmental reviews, and funding for many historic preservation activities that were previously the responsibility of the federal government.

Religious Landmarking

In the 1980s, conflict between preservationists and the religious community over the local landmark designations of houses of worship heated up, as it became clear that landmark designation would restrict an urban congregation from demolishing its architecturally significant church located on valuable real estate. Unlike a private developer, a religious body may not be able to use its structure for other economically viable uses. In addition, the religious group does not benefit from preservation tax incentives since it is typically exempt from such taxation.

The issue of religious landmarking is nowhere more visible than in New York City. In 1981, the rector and vestry of St. Bartholomew's proposed a $110 million tower which would rise 59 stories over part of the domed Byzantine-style church. The tower would provide the Episcopal church with an annual rental income of approximately $9.5 million, which it would use to defray its deficit and for new charities. In a bitter debate with the New York City preservation community, the church claimed that the development would serve its religious purposes, while opponents accused the vestry and rector of simple real estate speculation. The New York City Landmarks Commission tied up the proposal indefinitely by denying the application for the new construction. Claiming that the religious community is the greatest preservation force in history and that landmarks designation interferes with the internal decision-making of congregations by forcing them to maintain old buildings and divert money from religious ministry, the Interfaith Commission, a coalition of churches and synagogues, promoted a bill in 1983 in the New York state legislature that would exempt certain religious properties from local landmark laws. The bill failed, but the issue remains hot in New York City; Independence, Missouri; Salt Lake City, Utah; and elsewhere.

Unresolved Issues for the Future

The two decades since passage of the Preservation Act of 1966 have been years of phenomenal growth for the historic preservation movement. With developers occasionally being heard as advocates for historic preservation because of tax advantages and local governments supporting historic preservation because of central city revitalization achievements, the preservation movement finds itself moving into the main stream of American life. But as the rapidly growing adolescent matures into the calming assurance of adulthood, the preservation movement must also deal with the responsibilities that accompany success. Instead of continued rapid growth, preservationists now face a time of refinement and consolidation.

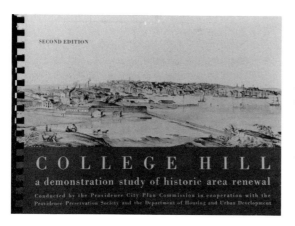

SECOND EDITION

COLLEGE HILL
a demonstration study of historic area renewal

Conducted by the Providence City Plan Commission in cooperation with the
Providence Preservation Society and the Department of Housing and Urban Development

In the 1960s, federal government urban renewal funds supported a survey of the College Hill area in Providence, Rhode Island. This demonstration project served as the prototype for many other local preservation studies. (Robert E. Stipe)

The adaptive use of historic properties is a common result of a strong local preservation program. In San Francisco, California, this bank building now serves as a radio studio. (Carleton Knight III, National Trust for Historic Preservation)

Grand Central Station in New York City served as the subject of the landmark court case, Penn Central Transportation Co. v. New York City, and the U.S. Supreme Court opinion that validated state and local controls to preserve historic buildings. (National Trust for Historic Preservation)

What to Preserve?

In a short period of time, the focus of the preservation movement evolved from individual landmarks and museum houses to historic districts, to downtown revitalization and neighborhood conservation and to broad community appearance and landscape/townscape conservation concerns. But the preservation movement did not bring the public along in this process. For example, preservationists comfortably discuss among themselves vernacular architecture and the importance of preserving examples of roadside architecture of the mid-20th century. But the public at large has not digested the broadening of the preservation ethic to include structures that they view as embarrassing eyesores. "Why is that considered historic?" is a common question skeptically put to preservationists.

Preservationists in most communities failed to educate the public and instill a preservation ethic that assumes that older structures are worthy of preservation unless proven otherwise. Just the reverse is true—the burden of proof is still on the preservation community. The education and public relations processes must be initiated at the local level, though with the assistance from state and federal preservation entities. Currently, education is not a high programmatic priority of either the National Park Service or the National Trust. If there is a glaring weakness in the preservation movement as a whole in the United States, it lies in the area of public education.

As the preservation movement matures, decisions as to what is worthy of preservation, and why, they will need to be more clearly articulated to the public at large; and that, in turn, will require preservationists to think through their own decisions more thoroughly. The reasons based in history? Are they aesthetic? Are they based on cultural considerations? For example, why should a southern city save its last shotgun houses? Who should pay for their preservation? How will they be used? What will be achieved through their preservation? The general public needs to know, if its support is needed, now and in the future.

The Local Planning Process

Preservation needs to be better integrated into the local land use planning and development mechanism. The future preservation of buildings and landscapes will depend greatly on land use decisions which in point of time come before preservation decisions. Preservationists must be more actively involved in the comprehensive planning process, integrating preservation concerns into that process. Integration of preservation with other city hall functions, such as building inspections, public works, school administration and housing authorities, are critical to preservationists in the long run. Developing a comprehensive program requires that preservationists look beyond simple building preservation.

Nowhere is the impact of land use planning on existing structures and neighborhoods more evident than in a consideration of infill development. In many communities, preservation succeeded in making downtown business and residential districts attractive places to live and work. Because of this success, developers of new buildings are looking hungrily at older areas they would have avoided a decade ago. Developers are constructing new buildings to the full extent permitted by local land use controls. As a result, peaceful restored neighborhoods are now finding themselves assaulted by an invasion of condominiums placed cheek-by-jowl on crowded lots. Downtown areas in many communities are attracting new construction for the first time in decades. Small older buildings, in some cases restored under the 1976 tax incentives, are demolished to make way for large post-Modern buildings. Preservationists must look carefully at the existing land use controls in older areas that they have succeeded in making viable to ensure that zoning densities, floor area ratios and height allowances do not undo past preservation successes.

Forces driven by the private real estate market will direct future preservation decisions, just as urban renewal and highway programs did in the 1950s and 1960s. Significant early 20th-century suburban estates will be doomed to condominium development if zoning and land use pressures so dictate. Addressing preservation concerns in the early stages before the current owners move on and before the building permit is sought may succeed; last-ditch confrontation surely will not.

When older buildings cannot be feasibly or sympathetically renovated because of unsympathetic building codes or building code officials, preservation successes will be severely limited. Code problems should also be systematically addressed at the local level to reduce impediments to feasible rehabilitation. Street tree maintenance and planting programs will do much to enhance the desirability of older residential and commercial areas, as will public works programs dealing with other street amenities, such as street lighting, sidewalks, street paving and street furniture. If schools in older neighborhoods are inferior, families with children will be discouraged from living there. Subsidized housing that is poorly sited or maintained will hinder the revitalization of older neighborhoods. Work with housing authorities to improve the quality of public housing in older areas and to encourage the use of rehabilitation instead of new construction for housing is needed for a comprehensive and successful preservation program.

As local governments explore partnerships with private developers in real estate ventures, preservationists must encourage the active involvement of local government in solving preservation problems. Acquisition of major endangered historic properties by local government for private redevelopment with public equity involvement is a realistic possibility, enhancing the public tax base and encouraging additional private reinvestment.

Local Politics

Many of these measures to establish a comprehensive preservation program at the local level require, as a priority, developing local political support for preservation. A full program requires adequate staffing and broad volunteer assistance. It also requires that the preservation community be well represented on the many local boards and commissions that do not have preservation as their function.

Candidates with a preservation ethic should be solicited for locally elected offices and state representation. Local preservationists should require candidates for public office to clearly state their stands on preservation matters. Only through the political process will the preservation community make preservation a priority for local government.

Funding for Historic Preservation

Funding for historic preservation activities will be increasingly borne by local governments as a result of federal cutbacks and the requirement that the states pick up programs terminated by the federal government. Local funding will require local political support, but this in turn also requires greater innovation and accountability on the part of the preservation community. Larger segments of the public will need to be served by projects supported with public dollars. Preservation projects must be more accessible to the public. Public support for house museums rarely opened to the public or those lacking outreach activities will be more difficult to justify. Architectural or historical significance alone will no longer be a sufficient justification for the use of public funds; utilization of properties for educational activities, business and public events will be required. This kind of varied usage will also be necessary to maintain the private and volunteer support of new generations.

The funding dilemma faced by the federal preservation program will also result in new and changing relationships between local preservationists and state and federal agencies and organizations. The decentralization of the national preservation program and the growth of statewide private nonprofit organizations will require that local preservationists turn increasingly to their state capitals rather than to Washington for technical assistance and information. Preservation networks between local governments and nonprofit organizations and among themselves will take on increased importance. Increased accountability from state historic preservation offices to their local constituents will be demanded.

Displacement and Minority Issues

Innovative ways of dealing with difficult preservation social issues, such as gentrification or the forced displacement of lower-income residents by wealthier newcomers to the neighborhood, should be explored. Although preservationists alone cannot solve the problem of housing for the poor or be unconcerned about the displacement of the elderly or poor from older housing stock, preservationists should be actively involved in finding solutions. An apparent lack of concern by the preservation movement for these problems brands preservation as elitist and will inevitably result in a political backlash.

Preservationists have generally failed to involve racial and ethnic minorities. The desire for knowledge about roots runs deep for all people regardless of race, color, or creed. As long as preservationists view preservation as a way of transmitting community values rather than simply a way of saving buildings, the preservation movement needs to embrace all people and recognize the diversity of human interests.

Other Significant Issues

Local governments will need to look more closely at their own historic resources for the development of preservation standards. The preservation issues yet to be litigated will be more and more technical, since many of the basic constitutional issues are resolved. If the federal preservation standards do not provide a tight fit with the local needs but are adopted through convenience as local standards, the local preservation community will be tempted to stray from the standards. New standards reflecting local needs will be preferable to charges of due process violations where a property owner claims that the adopted standards are not appropriately applied.

The preservation of rural historic resources will be one of the most difficult preservation tasks as long as the farm economy remains depressed. People who invest money in historic preservation in areas where there is outmigration and a depressed economy are most likely to be those with other sources of income and aesthetic or emotional reasons for living in a rural setting. The market for second homes and retirement properties will be the best hope for rural properties until farm economies strengthen.

Tourism will be both a blessing and a curse for historic preservation. Since tourism is about to become one of the nation's top industries, preservationists will increasingly point to the economic value of tourism as a justification for historic preservation. Studies from state after state point out that historic sites and cultural events are the major reasons why many people choose destinations and stay there. But without strict and vigilant control, precisely those resources that attract people will be lost as pressures mount for excessive or inappropriate adaptive use, convention facilities and larger hotels. Phony historic sites will spring up to take advantage of history's lure. Residents of historic houses will find themselves greatly inconvenienced by tourists who crowd their streets, litter their yards and walk uninvited into their houses. The attractions of tourism, a quiet and clean industry in modest doses, can be overturned by too much success.

The regulation of church-owned property will continue to raise difficult constitutional and emotional issues. Since churches are not infrequently architectural and community landmarks, their preservation will be critical to any comprehensive preservation program. But as a church grows or declines and as its social priorities evolve, preservation of its physical facilities may not be part of its religious priorities and indeed may run counter to them. And, churches frequently carry significant political clout. The preservation community needs to be able to develop satisfactory alternatives for congregations unwilling to preserve their physical plants or else be willing to take on ferocious political battles over church preservation.

In Conclusion

A final unresolved issue for local preservation will be to develop future leaders who have a clear understanding of the movement and a clear vision of what the movement can and cannot do. The scope of the preservation movement broadened so much in the last two decades that its own roots may be clouded. Should history be put back into historic preservation? Or is aesthetics alone a sufficient justification for preservation? Is there a healthy balance between history and aesthetic concerns? In each community, strong continuing leadership is needed. Training future leaders must be a constant priority for preservationists, because the field is heavily peopled by volunteers who in time move on to other concerns. The leadership must truly be able to lead the preservation community and constantly attract the support of other communities, especially the business and development communities.

Since local preservation succeeds or fails more on the basis of leadership than on the basis of the actual historic resources, the preservation community must demand real leadership from national and state agencies and organizations and be satisfied with nothing less. The networks of preservation created by these more centralized institutions give strength and guidance to local leadership, which in turn actually makes the critical difference as to whether or not the built resources will survive for the enjoyment and edification of future generations.

CHAPTER FIVE

What Do We Preserve and Why?

W. BROWN MORTON III

WHAT DO WE PRESERVE AND WHY?

W. BROWN MORTON III

One thing hastens into being, another hastens out of it. Even while a thing is in the act of coming into existence, some part of it has already ceased to be. Flux and change are forever renewing the fabric of the universe, just as the ceaseless sweep of time is forever renewing the face of eternity. In such a running river, where there is no firm foothold, what is there for a man to value among all the many things that are racing past him? (Marcus Aurelius, Meditations, *6:15)*

Introduction

Historic preservation is an autobiographical undertaking. A person, a community, a society or a nation paints its own portrait by what it chooses to save. The motivations that move human beings to preserve some remains of the past but not others are as complex as the human spirit itself. The results of these choices are passed on to future generations, but the impulses that stirred the vanished hearts, minds and hands are not as readily available for inspection.

Written documents provide the raw material for discerning preservation motivations: public statements, impassioned speeches, preambles to legislation and the private correspondence of preservation leaders. The reasons that appear in official minutes only hint at the complex spectrum of spoken and unspoken factors that give flesh to decisions. For a deeper understanding, it is not necessary to look any further than ourselves.

The tesserae of the American preservation mosaic resembles the pieces in a kaleidoscope. Some familiar fragments remain visible although they may change in relationship to one another, while new fragments from an ever-expanding national vision continually replace others that no longer transmit the light. There is, unfortunately, no obvious place to begin to understand the motivations that have shaped historic preservation in the United States.

Only in far off Eden was there ever a true beginning. The rest has been adaptation. We take some of what survived from the past into the present and preserve it for the future, but not all of it. What do we keep? We keep what we need. We keep what we need to feel safe. We keep what we need to feel authentic. We keep what we need to survive. Historic preservation is a dynamic element of change. We are never at square one.

The deeds, myths and legends that constitute the living memory of most families and communities cover a time period of approximately six generations at the outer limit. Great-grandparents tell stories about their great-grandparents to their great-grandchildren. After that, the chain of personal witness is broken, the tracks grow cold and we must rely on the formal tools of history to touch a more distant past. It is as if we drag a scythe behind us through time at a maximum distance of approximately 125 years. Just now the last ripples of the American Civil War as a current event are vanishing. The war is becoming an icon of history that is read about but no longer quite remembered.

The Universality of Preservation

A review of the world's cultural heritage reveals that the monuments or sites most likely to survive through time are those associated with religion and worship. This is not accidental. It testifies to the tremendous motivation people felt down through the ages to construct and preserve permanent expressions of their quest for harmony with the Divine. This is clearly evident in American prehistory.

Many groups of Native Americans (Indians) have a highly developed sense of preservation, much of it related to religion. Rich traditions of oral myth and legend have survived in communities such as the Hopi Indians of the American Southwest. These traditions speak of an integration of man and his environment and a respect for specific sites that represent the meeting place of mankind and the holy. Evidence from the study of pictographs, petroglyphs and archaeological analysis of preconquest settlements testifies to the use and reuse of certain sites for religious and ceremonial purposes representing the most basic preservation motivation of all, the preservation of holy places.

Such a place is a series of large boulders between the Hopi mesas and the Grand Canyon, in the Painted Desert of New Mexico. Jake Page, co-author of the recent book *Hopi*, comments, "These boulders are found beside a salt trail that for countless generations has been plied by Hopi priests every four years in order to obtain supplies of sacred salt needed for various ceremonies. The boulders bear the marks of these generations of priests, each clan making its own marks, by way of honoring the past, present, and future use of the trail. Indeed, among the Hopi, there is no real difference in past and present tense."

Old Cultures Adapt to the New World

One of the earliest pieces of the American mosaic to be found in the preservation kaleidoscope, following the European conquest of North America, is the compelling motivation to establish and maintain political and social legitimacy. Spanish, French, Dutch and English, as well as all the other first contact groups that dared to cross the Atlantic Ocean or the Bering Straits, brought their past with them and established old cultures in new worlds. Subsequent waves of immigrants did the same thing, although by the 19th century other groups had gone before them and the slate was not so clean.

Among the first things to be preserved by Europeans in America were names of people and places from the Old World. This satisfied a need to transfer political and social legitimacy to the New World through the preservation and continued use of the familiar. Large sections of the continent were named New France, New Spain and New England. Twelve of the 13 original colonies preserved names of European people or places. One colony did it twice! New Amsterdam became New York City. Cities, towns and villages were christened New Bedford, New London, New Bern and New Orleans.

The explorers and settlers brought Europe with them to America in more than names. They brought it also in their language, their religion, their law, their cultural and social patterns and, of course, their architecture. This transfer provided continuity and a semblance of stability. Preserving the past by repeating its forms in a new context was not new to the American colonists. This phenomenon can be seen at work across the sweep of human history linking, for example, Classical Greece with Imperial Rome, Rome with Renaissance Europe and Europe with the New World. Preserving the forms of the past in a new context satisfied the need for stability and continuity and helped things to seem like home, in time to become home and to make the new settlers feel they belonged. Human beings refer, rather poignantly, to the things they carry with them when they move from place to place as their "belongings."

Thus we are never without our past or our need for our past. We cannot leave history behind. Sir Francis Drake brought the full beauty of Thomas Cranmer's *Book of Common Prayer* ashore in California in 1579, just as John Smith and his companions brought attitudes and expectations of the Stuart court to the mosquito-infested swamps of Tidewater Virginia in 1607. The occupants of the Mayflower brought the stern lessons of the Protestant Reformation intact to the sandy coast of Massachusetts in 1621.

The pattern of permanent settlement in America brought many Europeans into contact with Indian communities of impermanent structures. Colonists who came to the Atlantic Coast did not encounter an architectural tradition to be assimilated or modified by European example. Had the opposite been the case, had the climate and the indigenous culture of Virginia and Massachusetts supported buildings of the sophistication of the cliff dwelling of Mesa Verde, Colorado, or the complexity of Pueblo Bonito in Chaco Canyon, New Mexico, the development of architecture in the United States might have been quite different.

As it was, the architectural development of eastern America moved from first generation impermanent structures to permanent construction along fairly standard European lines modified to the demands of the climate and available building materials. In New England, the colonists moved from impermanent to permanent construction within the first decades of settlement, whereas in Maryland and Virginia impermanent structures were the predominant building type well into the 18th century. As a result, fewer than a half dozen 17th-century structures survive in Maryland and Virginia.

The Need for Antiquity in the New Nation

One of the earliest recorded comments mourning the impending loss of an American building was that of architect Benjamin Henry Latrobe concerning the demolition of Green Spring, the 17th-century home of Governor William Berkeley in James City County, Virginia. In 1796, Latrobe commented in his diary, "The antiquity of the old house . . . ought to plead in [behalf of] the project, but its inconvenience and deformity are more powerful advocates of its destruction. In it the oldest inhabited house in America will disappear." Latrobe's concern about the destruction was motivated by the structure's age and the need for antiquity in the new nation. Inconvenience and deformity did it in.

Latrobe was in America only a few months when he put his finger on this conflict of values that has characterized American preservation ever since: the inconvenience of history and permanence versus the convenience of efficiency and change. Hiding just out of sight, unwritten and unexpressed in his diary, were no doubt other motivations that had led Latrobe to be the architect in charge of the demolition of Green Spring in the first place. Perhaps his written comments helped to quiet his highly developed antiquarian conscience? After all, this was the same man who had carved his name in Greek, on the stone portico he designed in the archaic Doric style at Hammerwood Park, Sussex, his last major country house commission before leaving England forever.

The need for antiquity in the new nation is also seen in the work of Thomas Jefferson, especially his efforts to bring the Roman past to Virginia. Jefferson retired to his hilltop at Monticello near Charlottesville, Virginia, in 1809, having completed his term as the third president of the United States. Throughout his life, he was a passionate student of architecture. During his years in Paris from 1785 to 1789, where he served as Minister to the Court of Louis XVI from the newly independent United States, Jefferson immersed himself in the rising tide of neoclassicism that was sweeping Europe. He became a serious student of the monuments of ancient Rome.

Jefferson believed that the architectural forms of ancient Rome were appropriate to express the democratic ideals of the new republic. His design for the Virginia State Capitol in Richmond was inspired by his visit to the Roman Maison Carrée in Nîmes. In 1817, he began to put into final form his ideas and designs for an academical village for the University of Virginia at Charlottesville. Jefferson wished to have individual buildings of the composition be copies, insofar as possible, of the classical orders of specific Roman prototypes. For example, the Ionic portico of Pavilion II is taken from the Temple of Fortuna Virilis. The main building of the complex, the Rotunda, is an adaptation of the Pantheon. This was a deliberate attempt to bring an old culture into the New World. It also demonstrates an intellectual attitude toward cultural preservation in the United States during its infancy that was a precursor of formal historic preservation as it is known today. Jefferson was preserving a past more distant than the visible past outside his door and making it available to students in the mountains of Virginia who would probably never have the opportunity to appreciate the Roman original.

Early Efforts to Preserve America's Past

Americans exhibited the first signs of real interest in preserving their past early in the 19th century. With the death of George Washington in 1799 and John Adams and Thomas Jefferson in 1826, giants of the American Revolution moved from reality into myth and the fascinating process of apotheosis began.

American preservation was dominated by motivations of patriotism and worshipful respect for the nation's founders. This phenomenon is not unique to the United States. It can be seen around the world in many nations, especially those in the first decades of nationhood. It is a part of establishing and validating political and social legitimacy.

There are several inherent dangers in patriotic preservation motivations. There is the tendency to focus only on the sites and buildings of transcendent national historical importance. Those sites and buildings, because of their associations with the life of one person or one outstanding event, are often stripped of all traces of later history. The emotional and patriotic investment of preservers in the preserved can disrupt thoughtful scholarship. The attempt to bend history, to over-restore and to over-furnish, is almost irresistible. In short, the urge to create a flattering past all too often overwhelmed historical accuracy, so that when one gazes into the looking glass of time, the truth of the past is not seen but only the shine of over-polished brass and our reflections in fancy dress.

In 1813, the City of Philadelphia performed one of the first acts in preserving America's heritage by purchasing Independence Hall, then known as the Old State House, from the State of Pennsylvania. The city intended to sell the aging structure and subdivide the ground into building lots. Those who rose to save the building stressed its continued utility but backed up that argument with an appeal to historical associations. "The spot . . . is hallowed . . . by many strong and impressive recollections." It was not the architecture but the associative historical values that saved Independence Hall. Those same associative values were again the justification for including Independence Hall on the World Heritage List in 1979. Independence Hall is the second most frequently imitated building in the United States after Mount Vernon.

In addition, George Washington, revered as the father of his country, commander-in-chief of the Revolutionary forces and first president of the new nation, came to represent all that was to be admired, respected and imitated by succeeding generations of patriotic Americans. Around his person and legend grew a mystique and a reverence that was religious in intensity and tone. Historic sites associated with Washington and other heroes of the early American republic became places of pilgrimage and were repeatedly referred to as shrines or meccas. The clear inference was that every citizen had the patriotic duty to make a visit. This choice of attitudes and a vocabulary borrowed from religion was without question an authentic and spontaneous impulse.

The power of the memory of George Washington can be seen in the life of his step-grandson, George Washington Parke Custis, the builder of Arlington House, who grew up at Mount Vernon. Custis took to Arlington House many objects associated with George Washington, including campaign tents from the Revolution. On special occasions, Custis would set up the campaign tents at the house and preside with great feeling and dignity over the Washington relics, keenly aware that he was a major part of the exhibit. The Washington association imbued Arlington House with a depth of historical feeling that blended perfectly with its dramatic, larger-than-life, Greek Doric architecture and superb natural setting facing the nation's capital across the Potomac. Robert E. Lee, who married Custis's daughter in 1831 and came to live at Arlington, sensed this special quality and referred to the house as "Old Arlington," even though most of it was younger than he.

George Washington's association with properties both within and outside his home state of Virginia constituted powerful reasons for preserving them. The associations ranged from ones of long duration, such as Revolutionary War headquarters, to places that he merely visited for a brief span of time. For example, Hasbrouck House in Newburgh, New York, served as Washington's headquarters during the last two years of the Revolutionary War. In 1850, the State of New York purchased the property, goaded by the argument that it was nearly the last physical remain in the state associated with Washington. With the building and surrounding lands preserved, the property became the first historic house museum in the country, and served as a prelude to the country's most illustrious preservation project, Mount Vernon.

Washington's home, Mount Vernon, served a dual role as home and tomb of the father of the country. These connections gave it a symbolic importance unequalled by any other historic property associated with him. Both the house and the tomb are visible from the river. It became a tradition for boats passing Mount Vernon to toll their bell in respect. The setting of the house, placed at a slight angle to the river with its cupola and expansive porch crowning a broad meadow sweeping up from the river bank, and the lachrymose Gothic Revival tomb further down toward the water were made to order for anyone wishing to immerse themselves in the picturesque.

As early as 1846, in response to the deteriorating condition of Mount Vernon, a petition was presented to the U.S. Congress for *The Proposed Purchase of Mount Vernon by the Citizens of the United States, in Order that They May at All Times Have a Legal and Indisputable Right to Visit the Grounds, Mansion, and Tomb of Washington.* The petition failed, but it raised the curtain on a national preservation effort that shaped American attitudes toward preservation for the next century.

Before its ultimate rescue, there was continued interest in having the home and tomb of Washington acquired by the federal government or by the State of Virginia. A stumbling block was the $200,000 price asked by John Augustine Washington, a great nephew of the president. This price seemed exorbitant to elected officials for a house in need of repair with 200 acres. A recurring theme in America is that all but the rare politician has been reluctant to expend public funds to purchase historic sites from private individuals when the price reflected something other than what a practical use could justify. In 1851, the U.S. Army considered the purchase of Mount Vernon for an asylum. In 1853, the governor of Virginia appealed to the state legislature to purchase Mount Vernon and put forward various justifications, such as using it as an agricultural school. All to no avail. The price was too high for the ostensibly intended uses.

In the end, it was a private citizen who won the day for the preservation of Mount Vernon. A South Carolina native, Ann Pamela Cunningham, did it by making an unabashed appeal to patriotic sentiment and by recognizing the tremendous organizational abilities and capacity for hard work that lay, largely untapped, among women of means raised in the gentility of mid-19th century America. Mount Vernon's rescuer was inspired by a letter she had received from her mother deploring the shabby state of Mount Vernon as seen from the deck of a tolling steamer. As a result she decided to appeal to the "Ladies of the South" to save Mount Vernon "with all its sacred associations."

From this appeal grew the Mount Vernon Ladies' Association of the Union, a private organization of women with representatives from each state. The association grew slowly at first and with much opposition but, finally, in 1858 the State of Virginia granted the association a charter to hold title to and manage Mount Vernon. John Washington agreed to sell the property to the association, even though he had earlier hoped to see it become the property of the State of Virginia.

The Mount Vernon Ladies' Association became a model for private initiative in historic preservation. Efforts to copy its success were made on behalf of many other historic properties elsewhere in the country. Some of the variations on the basic Mount Vernon theme were successful, such as the Kenmore Association, which preserves the home of George Washington's sister in Fredericksburg, Virginia. Another was the Robert E. Lee Memorial Association, which protects Stratford Hall, the colonial Virginia home of three signers of the Declaration of Independence and the birthplace of General Lee, the commander of the Confederate forces during the Civil War. Other efforts to form a national association of women to protect a single historic property were less successful, often due to the remote location of the property in a preautomobile age and to the simple fact that there was only one George Washington and one Mount Vernon.

Later projects benefited from financial support from their respective states. In 1856, the Hermitage, home of President Andrew Jackson, was purchased by the State of Tennessee. The Jackson descendants were permitted to remain in residence, which was just as well since they continued to own the original Jackson furnishings. The motivation for the purchase was described in the bill as being "good policy . . . to inculcate sentiments of veneration for those departed heroes who have rendered important services to their country in times of danger." Thirty years later in 1888, some members of the legislature tried unsuccessfully to pass a bill to sell the property. This alarmed the incumbent Mrs. Jackson who sought the advice of the Mount Vernon Ladies' Association. The result was the formation in 1889 of the Ladies' Hermitage Association which was given permission by the State of Tennessee to operate the house and 25 acres as a museum. The new association succeeded in its goal to preserve the Hermitage and eventually much of its original furnishings. However, the association was never able to muster significant national support for its project and it remained largely a local effort.

Other national women's organizations followed the pioneering efforts of Mount Vernon to the field of historic preservation. Patriotic organizations, such as the National Society of the Colonial Dames and the Daughters of the American Revolution, were founded in the early 1890's. They made significant contributions to the preservation of America's heritage, especially by encouraging local projects which focused on sites and buildings associated with the American Revolution or with colonial history.

The idea of creating a private organization to preserve historic sites and buildings on a statewide or regional basis did not take place in the United

States until the late 19th century. The first such effort was the formation of the Association for the Preservation of Virginia Antiquities in 1888. Its membership included both men and women and, unlike the Colonial Dames and the Daughters of the American Revolution, membership was not based on genealogy. The object of the Association for the Preservation of Virginia Antiquities was to "restore and preserve the ancient historic buildings and tombs in the State of Virginia, and acquire by purchase or gift the sites of such buildings and tombs with a view to their perpetuation and preservation." The focus of the association was clearly on colonial history. Its early projects were the purchase and protection of the site of the first permanent English settlement of 1607 at Jamestown Island, the Powder Magazine at the colonial capital of Williamsburg and the home of George Washington's mother in Fredericksburg.

Preserving the Historical Environment

Just after the turn of the century, far to the north of Virginia, a man of energy, vision and, happily, a private income, took the concept of the statewide preservation organization one step further to create a regional preservation advocacy group. In 1910, William Sumner Appleton of Boston, Massachusetts, founded the Society for the Preservation of New England Antiquities. For the history of American preservation, a new day had dawned.

Appleton's vision moved preservation in a new direction. His society advocated preserving interesting early buildings, wherever they might be found in New England. They did not have to be the homes of Revolutionary patriots or former presidents. They could be fine examples of architecture or even simple buildings that reflected the past in some special way. They did not have to be all of one period; the passage of time was permissible and indeed valued. Nor did they have to be museums open to the public. Appleton encouraged leasing of the society properties to maintain traditional uses in neighborhoods and to keep buildings occupied with a minimum of fuss and bother. He was a pioneer in preservation economics and clearly recognized that financial strategies far beyond the model of the historic house museum needed to be developed if the rank and file of historic American buildings were to be preserved. In 1911, the society purchased its first property, the late 17th-century Swett-Isley House in Newburg, Massachusetts. By 1916, five properties were purchased, including the first Harrison Gray Otis house in Boston, which served as society headquarters.

Appleton was the first American to study European preservation methods seriously and he advocated the anti-scrape philosophy of John Ruskin and William Morris while avoiding the doing-the-past-a-favor excesses of Viollet-le-Duc. Appleton was an early believer that preservation in the United States was best achieved by the private sector rather than by government. He and the society he created to carry out his vision mark a watershed in American preservation motivations because he made the act of preservation not merely a route to a political or social objective, but an educational and moral end in itself.

Mount Vernon, George Washington's house in Virginia, became a model for private initiative in historic preservation. Granted a charter in 1858, the Mount Vernon Ladies' Association under the leadership of Ann Pamela Cunningham, tapped the organizational abilities and capacity for hard work in women of means in mid-19th century America. (Mount Vernon Ladies' Association)

Yellowstone National Park in Wyoming was established in 1872, the first such park in the world. (National Park Service)

The Casa Grande Ruin in Arizona was the first structure in the United States to receive federal government protection. A shelter was built in order to conserve the ruin. (National Park Service)

The outstanding historic architecture of Charleston, South Carolina was protected in 1931 by the nation's first local historic district ordinance. (National Trust for Historic Preservation)

The restoration of the colonial capital of Williamsburg, Virginia, funded by the philanthropist John D. Rockefeller, Jr., was the first time in America that there was an intentional effort to achieve living history through restoration and reconstruction. (Colonial Williamsburg Foundation)

America's Colonial Past Rediscovered

As the Society for the Preservation of New England Antiquities was developing in the first quarter of the present century, the American public also rediscovered its own colonial past. The rediscovery represented a trend that was rooted in the 1876 Centennial Exhibition in Philadelphia and gained increasing popular favor in periodicals and books. By the turn of the century, the colonial style was firmly established in the minds of the general public. Perhaps this was an inevitable reaction to nearly a century of stylistic revivals that imitated European and Asian architecture of every type and description. Perhaps it was a reaction to the opulent architectural excesses of the industrial revolution's robber barons. Perhaps it was a spontaneous home-grown response to the whiter-than-white neoclassical fun of the 1893 World's Columbian Exposition in Chicago. Whatever the reasons, the red brick, white clapboards and green shutters of neocolonial architecture became, and remain to this day, America's favorite style.

This renewal of interest in America's own architecture was also reflected in early 20th-century preservation. In 1901-02, the McMillan Commission developed a neoclassical plan for the monumental city center of Washington, D.C. It recaptured the original spirit of the L'Enfant plan, and refocused the eye on the city's major historic buildings. The commission spurred the first of many restorations of the White House, this one by the architectural firm of McKim, Mead and White, pioneers of the neocolonial style.

Also in the early years of the 20th century, during Charles F. McKim's tenure as its president, the American Institute of Architects acquired The Octagon, in Washington, D.C., as its national headquarters. McKim justified the purchase of this historic house, designed at the end of the 18th century by William Thornton for the Tayloe family, in terms of the institute practicing preservation, a philosophy that it preached. "It is a cause for rejoicing that the institute which has urged upon governments . . . the duty of preserving historic monuments, has itself secured possession of one of the historic houses of America."

With the turn of the 20th century, American architecture began to be valued. For inspiration American architects began to study buildings of their nation as well as ones from Europe. An indication of this interest was the publication of the *White Pine Series* beginning in 1915. It was distributed by the White Pine Bureau to encourage the use of white pine in new buildings. A typical issue contained photographs of an early American building of some architectural distinction and several pages of measured drawings of details from that building that architects might wish to incorporate into their work.

As the 20th century progressed, Americans looked back nostalgically to their colonial roots. In 1907, the Essex Institute in Salem, Massachusetts, under the leadership of George F. Dow, became the first museum to take historic or period rooms from existing buildings and reerect them as exhibits in museum galleries. Dow went on in 1909 to imitate the Swedish model of Skansen, the first outdoor museum of historic buildings reassembled on a new site. He moved the late 17th-century John Ward house to the grounds of the Essex Institute from its original location. Dow's example was soon followed across the country.

In 1914, a colonial village of houses from New England reappeared at the Public Museum in Milwaukee, Wisconsin. Two years later, the Metropolitan Museum of Art in New York City purchased the paneled drawing room from Marmion, an early 18th-century farm house in King George County, Virginia. In the case of Marmion, there was no threat of demolition. Indeed, the house retained a rare and complete set of 18th-century dependencies and outbuildings and all of its fine Georgian interiors. It was simply a matter of a willing buyer and a willing seller, in this case a direct descendent of the original builder. The space vacated by the drawing room became a plain but useful ground floor bedroom and more importantly, an indoor bathroom. The house remained open to visitors with the new bedroom door shut and photographs of the drawing room, as recreated in New York City, hung on the wall in the entrance hall.

Scenic Preservation and the Evolution of the National Park System

As Americans awakened to their architectural heritage, they also developed a growing appreciation of the nation's natural and scenic beauty, wildlife and prehistoric sites. The threat posed by rapid settlement and urbanization to wilderness areas, to archaeological sites and to native American culture was recognized as early as 1832 by the American painter and ethnologist George Catlin. On a trip to the Dakotas in that year, he articulated the concept of the national park. He wrote that he hoped that these vanishing resources might be "by some great protecting policy of the government preserved . . . in a magnificent park. . . .A nation's park, containing man and beast, in all the wildness and freshness of their nature's beauty." Catlin's ideal was to protect Indians and their culture in an unspoiled natural setting. He commented, "What a beautiful and thrilling specimen for America to preserve and hold up to the view of her refined citizens and the world, in future age!"

Read in a certain light, one might infer from Catlin's comments that he viewed Indians as totally apart from the national mainstream, human curiosities to be preserved in innocence, an exotic side-show in a federally designated Eden. George Catlin seems a true visionary: Not only did he conceive the idea of a national park, he also recognized the inseparable link that exists between traditional societies, their cultural resources and the natural setting in which they "live and move and have their being." Catlin's observations did not bear immediate fruit, but they formed part of a rising chorus in favor of federal government protection of outstanding scenic and natural resources.

After several government-sponsored expeditions to inspect the wonders of Yellowstone, the world's first national park was established by an act of the U.S. Congress on March 1, 1872. Two million acres of public land, in what is now Wyoming and Montana, were set aside to protect them from settlement or development "as a public park or pleasuring-ground for the benefit and enjoyment of the people."

Yellowstone National Park was followed in the 1890s by similar national parks for Sequoia, Yosemite and portions of the Sierra Nevada in California. At the turn of the century, Mount Ranier National Park in Washington state

155

was added, to the nation's park inventory, as was Crater Lake National Park in Oregon. In 1906, Mesa Verde National Park in Colorado was established. It was the first to protect specifically, through designation, a prehistoric site. At Mesa Verde this included the spectacular cliff ruins occupied by a succession of Indian cultures from the time of Christ to 1300 A.D.

Throughout this early period in the development of national parks, the U.S. Congress charged the U.S. Army with maintaining and making accessible most of the properties, although ultimate responsibility for them was vested with the Secretary of the Interior. In 1916, after years of urging by the U.S. Department of the Interior, the National Park Service was created to promote and regulate the use of the growing number of national parks, monuments and reservations "to conserve the scenery and the natural and historic objects and the wildlife therein and to provide for the enjoyment of the same in such a manner and by such means as will leave them unimpaired for the enjoyment of future generations." A separate bureau was thus created to administer the national parks. Over the years, its professional expertise in natural and historic sites made it the suitable focus for the historic preservation program of the federal government.

While many of the nation's first national parks were in the western states, the rapid industrialization of the Northeast led to efforts to preserve scenic areas in the midst of dense settlement. In 1890, Charles Eliot, a young landscape architect from Cambridge, Massachusetts, and son of the president of Harvard University, recognized that the scenic splendor of his state was threatened by long-range industrial development and urban growth. He believed that "several bits of scenery . . . of unusual refreshing power" should be held in trust for the public benefit and protected forever. In the following year, the Trustees of Reservations was chartered under his leadership. The primary objective was the protection and preservation of threatened areas of exceptional scenic beauty. This organization became a model for the formation of the National Trust for Places of Historic Interest or Natural Beauty in England in 1895. In that same year, the example set by the Trustees of Reservations in Massachusetts also stimulated the formation of the Trustees of Scenic and Historic Places and Objects in New York state. In 1901, the latter expanded its vision to include the nation as a whole and was renamed the American Scenic and Historic Preservation Society. For various legal and bureaucratic reasons, success with its programs beyond the borders of New York state did not ensue. But the importance of the far-reaching vision of the American Scenic and Historic Preservation Society to combine scenic and historic preservation efforts in a single comprehensive organization as early as 1895 should not be overlooked. In the end, the vision first became a national reality, not as a private sector initiative, but as program of the federal government.

Protecting Antiquities

In the 1780s Thomas Jefferson set a model for early archaeology in the United States when he excavated and studied a prehistoric burial mound in Virginia. He conducted what was probably the first scientific excavation of an aboriginal site in a search for information about burial practices of the prehistoric Indian. His interest in prehistoric Indian mounds was shared by others of European background. They encountered mounds frequently as exploration spread west from the Atlantic coastline. Curiosity, vivid imagination and fairly sturdy ignorance gave rise to theories that the mounds existed because the Indians were buried standing up or that the mounds were evidence of a vanished civilization and a pre-Indian golden age of mound builders.

Even though prehistory in the New World, in the strict sense of the term, was still a current event as explorers made contact daily with aboriginal cultures, archaeology in 19th-century America was more closely linked with scientific, geological and ethnological expeditions or exploration than it was with an interest in the cultural heritage per se. Archaeology prior to the Civil War did not exist as an organized, disciplined profession in the United States. Much of the information from that period comes from written descriptions of travelers and explorers and haphazard excavation that bordered on poking around.

In 1879, Major John Wesley Powell was placed in charge of the newly created U.S. Bureau of Ethnology under the Smithsonian Institution. A decade earlier, this one-armed Civil War veteran had led thrilling scientific expeditions down the Green and Colorado Rivers, in what was the first expedition to make it successfully all the way through the Grand Canyon. During his expeditions, he developed an interest in the Indians and urged the creation of a government bureau devoted to their study. In his new job, he sponsored archaeological work at southwestern Indian pueblos and prehistoric ruins, such as Casa Grande in Arizona (c.1350). These studies led to greater scientific and public interest in contemporary natives and the physical remains left by their predecessors.

Following these pioneering ventures, interest began to develop in protecting the antiquities of the American Southwest: prehistoric archaeological sites, cliff dwellings, pueblos and Spanish colonial structures, many of which were located on public lands. These often remote sites were, and are, special prey to vandals and pot hunters. The first site to receive special attention was the Casa Grande Ruin. In 1892, President Benjamin Harrison, authorized by the U.S. Congress to protect the site from development, created the Casa Grande Ruin Reservation. It was not until 1904, however, that the first formal survey of antiquities on federal land was commenced by Dr. Edgar Lee Hewett, whose work contributed directly to the passage of the Antiquities Act of 1906.

The act had three major provisions. It gave the government the power to fine or imprison "any person who shall appropriate, excavate, injure or destroy any historic or prehistoric ruin or monument, or any object of antiquity, situated on lands owned or controlled by the Government." It authorized the president, "in his discretion, to declare by public proclamation historic landmarks, historic or prehistoric structures, and other objects of historic or scientific interest that are situated upon the lands owned or controlled by the Government of the United States to be national monuments." The act also authorized federal department heads to issue permits "for the examination of ruins, the excavation of archaeological sites, and the gathering of objects of antiquity upon the lands under their respective jurisdictions."

In 1906, the first national monument to be proclaimed under the act, by President Theodore Roosevelt, was Devils Tower, Wyoming, a stone formation nearly twice the height of the Washington Monument, an ancient landmark to both Indian and settler. In 1908, the Spanish mission at Tumacacori, Arizona, became the first structure dating from the European conquest to be made a national monument.

The act marks an important advancement in American preservation thinking. It was the first piece of federal legislation to protect specifically cultural and archaeological resources as a matter of policy, rather than as a response to a specific crisis at a specific property. The act also gave the president the opportunity to protect both prehistoric and historic sites, as well as objects of both historic and scientific interest. With this act, American preservation moved to embrace preceding cultures and beyond its earlier ethnocentric focus on icons of the colonial and early federal eras. It also placed into legislation the legitimate intellectual claim of both science and history upon cultural resources owned or controlled by the federal government.

Colonial Williamsburg

The preservation focus of the federal government was national, but its far-flung activities were in remote areas and had little immediate effect on public tastes or on preservation needs at the state and local levels. It was the combined efforts of an Episcopal priest and a millionaire that transformed the taste of the nation and changed the direction of American historic preservation. The place was Williamsburg, Virginia, the seat of government of the colony of Virginia from 1699 until 1780 when the capital was moved to Richmond. From that time onward Williamsburg suffered a severe decline. Although a significant number of buildings from the colonial period survived into the 20th century, others, including the Capitol and the Governor's Palace, were lost to fire and neglect.

The restoration of the colonial capital of Williamsburg was the single most influential historic preservation project in the history of the United States. In 1903, the project first stirred the mind of Rev. W.A.R. Goodwin, the rector of the colonial Bruton Parish Church in Williamsburg. In that year, Goodwin commenced the restoration of his church. By the time the work was completed in 1907, his vision had moved far beyond the churchyard to encompass the town that surrounded it. Goodwin wished to recapture the spirit, the history and the genius of 18th-century Williamsburg through the restoration of the entire historic area. Published in 1907, his book, *Bruton Parish Church Restored and Its Historic Environment*, announced his vision of historic preservation to encompass the church and its larger historic surroundings. It would take another half century for the rest of the country to fully understand the far-reaching importance of his thinking.

After an absence from Williamsburg of 16 years, Goodwin returned in 1923. In the following year, he told his ideas to John D. Rockefeller, Jr. By 1926, Rockefeller was fired with patriotic passion, convinced of the immense educational opportunities a restored Williamsburg could provide the American public. Quietly, and at first anonymously, he began what matured into a major philanthropic undertaking—underwriting the costs of purchasing the required real estate, retaining the Boston architectural firm of Perry, Shaw and Hepburn to plan the restoration and reconstruction work and supporting the necessary scholarly research to insure an acceptable level of historical authenticity. The Williamsburg project was the first time in America that there had been an intentional effort to achieve living history through restoration and reconstruction. It was an attempt to make, in the present, a reality of the past. Rockefeller's commitment is all the more remarkable given his simultaneous involvement in the 1930s in the purchase of lands to create the Great Smoky Mountains National Park.

At Williamsburg, a new kind of archaeology tried its wings, historical archaeology. The National Park Service also used it at Jamestown and other historic sites. The idea was new in the 1930s and those archaeologists who abandoned prehistorical pursuits to sift for broken saucers from the relatively recent past were viewed by mainline archaeologists with some disdain. However, at Williamsburg, prior to World War II, historical archaeology played second fiddle to architectural research. The information provided by archaeology, when heeded, was largely corroborative.

The excellence of the work at Williamsburg captured the imagination and respect of the traveling public, now set free to see historic sites for themselves by the advent of the automobile. The Williamsburg staff was deluged with requests for information about all aspects of the restoration, from house plans to recipes for beaten biscuits. Americans adopted the look and taste of Colonial Williamsburg as a national style. For a few decades in the 1940s and 1950s, Williamsburg so dominated American taste that many people confused the process with the product. They believed that if a restored building did not look like Williamsburg, it could not have been properly done. Such are the burdens of success.

Early Historic Districts and Areas

Charleston, South Carolina, is to America what Venice is to Italy. Born from the water, it is dense, beautiful and fragile. It remained remote from the forces of modernization for much of the post-Civil War period and its antebellum buildings mellowed over the years. During the early 20th century, with the introduction of the automobile, the city could no longer remain aloof from the onslaught of development, commercialization and change. Gradually, parking lots, gas stations and widened roads gnawed away at the city's fabric. Even more alarming was the stream of collectors and museum officials who prize loose building elements for use or display elsewhere.

The Charleston City Council created a temporary planning and zoning commission in 1929 and a permanent Board of Architectural Review in 1931. Except for preserved museum villages, there was no precedent for the preservation of whole sections of cities still in active and productive use. However, zoning controls were recently introduced in communities in order to separate residential areas from commercial and industrial ones. It required only another step to apply zoning powers to the protection of historic areas. The purpose of the Review Board was to review and approve or disapprove plans for any exterior alterations and additions to buildings in the Old and Historic Charleston District. In doing so, the city embraced the right of the larger community to assert an interest in the use of private property and the maintenance and survival of its buildings. Preservation in the United States had broken important new ground.

The Charleston example provided a model for other cities with threatened historic areas. In 1936, the Louisiana constitution was amended to increase the powers of the Vieux Carré Commission in New Orleans. A decade later, the city of Alexandria, Virginia, adopted its own Charleston Ordinance. Today, historic districts and architectural review boards (seated by local ordinances) are common in communities across the country. The wisdom of the people of Charleston, enlivened by their sure and early grasp of the need to protect a total environment, prepared the way for the next generation of preservation thinking.

The Spirit of Early Landscape Preservation

Gardens and other designed landscapes played an important role in historic preservation. However, exacting scholarly study of historic gardens and designed landscapes, as cultural resources in their own right, only recently gained general acceptance. Until the 1960s, historic gardens were viewed more as beautiful settings for the historic buildings they surrounded than as historic objects themselves. Strict application of evidence gained from garden archaeology and research of early plant species was rare. The urge to make pretty or to have a garden based on a fashionable historical stereotype became accepted practice. Even at Colonial Williamsburg, a maze was constructed in the garden at the Governor's Palace. Its creation was not based on archaeological evidence. Relatively inexpensive to plant and similar to the one at Hampton Court, England, it would be popular with the public. Throughout the 1930s, boxwood hedges, brick walls, geometric herb gardens and orangeries found their way into the gardens of East Coast historic properties with scant evidence to justify their presence. On the West Coast at the Mission La Purisima Conception restoration project, a deliberately pseudo historic garden was installed because "the bare dusty area [of history] will be of little interest to the majority of visitors."

There are several factors that combined to create this situation. Historic garden and landscape features are highly vulnerable to neglect and to changes in ownership, property size, land use and economics. Remnants of early features are quickly covered by later work, and plant material, unlike building material, is never static. Since serious garden archaeology is painstaking and expensive, it is easier and less restrictive to start from scratch. A final factor that contributed to permissive standards for early garden and landscape restoration is the simple fact that glorious gardens are glorious money makers, whatever their degree of authenticity. In 1929, the Garden Club of Virginia undertook the restoration of the 18th-century garden at Kenmore, in Fredericksburg. In order to raise money for this project, the club developed the idea of Historic Garden Week, an organized tour of private historic gardens around the state. This met with immediate success. In a modified version, the idea became the nucleus for the famous annual Garden Pilgrimage in Natchez, Mississippi.

It is easy to criticize in hindsight. Although garden and landscape restoration in its infancy fell short of present-day standards of scholarship, it was a major component in the years between the wars in the fostering of public awareness of historic preservation as a national undertaking.

Forging a Nationwide System of Historic Places

Advances in preservation attitudes come in waves. The decade from 1925 to 1935 was such a wave. As the renaissance at Williamsburg unfolded and historic districts elsewhere struggled to life, Americans discovered the relationship that historic sites have with one another across geography and time. The country moved toward a national preservation awareness.

This awareness showed itself in several ways. First, the National Park Service accelerated its acquisition of historic properties, particularly on the East Coast. In 1926, it assumed the management of the House Where Lincoln Died on 10th Street in Washington, D.C. Then, in 1930, stimulated by preparations for the sesquicentennial of the victory at Yorktown in 1931 and the bicentennial of George Washington's birth in 1932, the National Park Service acquired the George Washington Birthplace National Monument, Westmoreland County, and Colonial National Monument comprising much of Jamestown Island and Yorktown, all in Virginia.

The triumph of the automobile and the increase in leisure time resulting from the 40-hour work week forged an important link between historic preservation and recreation. A major benefit of this partnership was the development of the scenic parkway, often linking major historic sites. Many scenic parkways were financed, designed and constructed as part of federal make-work projects during the Great Depression. In 1929, the George Washington Memorial Parkway was begun. It was designed to follow both banks of the Potomac River above and below Washington, D.C., and to connect the capital city with Mount Vernon. Early designs, later abandoned, called for it to follow the south bank of the Potomac to Washington's Birthplace in Westmoreland County. The present, shorter, parkway preserved several miles of the Potomac Palisades. It also protected from dense development the approaches to Washington, D.C., by two major airports. In 1933, the Colonial Parkway, connecting Jamestown, Williamsburg and Yorktown was created. It preserved a wide band of scenic and natural beauty across the entire peninsula from the James River to the York River. The far-reaching benefits of these projects are only now, a half-century later, being fully appreciated.

In 1931, the National Park Service hired its first historian to stimulate the expansion of the Service's historic areas and to assemble a trained professional staff to develop and manage them. This signaled a dramatic change in the attitude of the federal government regarding historic properties. Historic archaeology and historic preservation began to be viewed as legitimate scholarly undertakings. Historic sites were deemed worthy of interpretation and management by professionals.

The year 1933 brought the National Park Service fully into the business of preservation in the eastern half of the nation. In March, the U.S. Congress established the Morristown National Historic Park in New Jersey; later in the summer, the parks and public buildings in Washington, D.C., and the battlefields, monuments and national cemeteries of the Departments of War and Agriculture were transferred to the U.S. Department of the Interior by order of President Franklin D. Roosevelt. In time, the National Park Service came to have more historic areas under its management than natural areas.

Prince Street, near the waterfront in Old Town, Alexandria, Virginia, has been protected by a historic district ordinance since 1946. (Library of Congress)

Jackson Square, the center of the Vieux Carré, in New Orleans, Louisiana, has been protected by a local historic district ordinance since 1936. (Library of Congress)

The gardens at Oatlands, a property of the National Trust for Historic Preservation, in Loudoun County, Virginia, are an essential component in the interpretation and appreciation of the house. (National Trust for Historic Preservation)

The urban renewal programs of the 1950s and 1960s encouraged the destruction of many buildings in historic urban areas and their replacement by new structures. (Robert E. Stipe)

Mystic Seaport in Connecticut provides education in maritime history and in traditional boatbuilding skills. (National Trust for Historic Preservation)

Federal government transportation, housing and tax policies of the post-World War II era encouraged the creation of dispersed, low-density residential development, exemplified by Levittown, New York. (National Trust for Historic Preservation)

Great Depression-Era Preservation Programs

When President Roosevelt took office in March 1933, the country was in the slough of the Great Depression. His New Deal brought into government a rainbow of make-work programs with confusing initials: The PWA (Public Works Administration), the WPA (Works Progress Administration) and the CCC (Civilian Conservation Corps). The National Park Service was quick to seize upon the opportunities these programs provided, and the effect on historic preservation was dramatic. Significant amounts of labor and skill were directed toward public works projects, including the construction of scenic parkways, planning and development of natural and historical parks and the documentation of American historic architecture.

In November 1933, National Park Service officials saw an opportunity to use New Deal funds to provide work for unemployed architects to make measured drawings of historic buildings across the nation. The initial idea was contained in the crushingly bureaucratic title, "The Relief Employment Under the Civil Works Administration of a Substantial Number of the Architectural Profession in a Program recording Interesting and Significant Specimens of American Architecture." One month later, a much better name for the fledgling program emerged, the Historic American Buildings Survey. Originally intended to provide 10 weeks of work for unemployed architects and draftsmen, it grew to become the first national survey of historic architecture in the history of the country.

This new program clearly grasped the crisis that faced American cultural resources. "Our architectural heritage of buildings from the last four centuries diminishes daily at an alarming rate. The ravages of fire and the natural elements together with the demolition and alterations caused by real estate 'improvements' form an inexorable tide of destruction destined to wipe out a great majority of buildings which knew the beginning and first flourish of the nation. It is the responsibility of the American people that if one great number of our antique buildings must disappear through economic causes, they could not pass into unrecorded oblivion."

The wave of historic preservation innovation that began in 1926 with the decision to restore Colonial Williamsburg and included the development of historic districts and the Historic American Buildings Survey, crested in 1935 with the passage of the Historic Sites Act of 1935. The act declared "That it is a national policy to preserve for public use historic sites, buildings, and objects of national significance for the inspiration and benefit of the people of the United States." A combination of disparate factors brought the act into being. They included the success of the Williamsburg experiment, the growth of tourism due to the automobile and a growing sense of the threat to historic resources from development. The economic shock of the Great Depression and the New Deal employment opportunities for architects, historians and archaeologists also contributed to a climate ripe for the act. In Washington, the transfer of federally owned historic sites and monuments to the Department of the Interior, bold leadership in the National Park Service and President Roosevelt's personal interest in historic preservation all coalesced with other national forces that made the time right for legislation authorizing a comprehensive national historic preservation program.

The Historic Sites Act of 1935 created the legislative framework for the federal government to conduct a national survey of historic resources through the conduct of serious scholarly research and investigation. The act also facilitated the development of criteria for acquiring and preserving property. In order to carry out these new responsibilities, the National Park Service sought the advice of leaders and experts outside the federal government and the cooperation of state and local governments in preserving resources not under agency control.

In testifying before the U.S. House of Representatives Land Committee a few months before the passage of the Historic Sites Act of 1935, Secretary of the Interior Harold L. Ickes made it plain that his intention was to achieve a national preservation program. He testified that the goal of the legislation was "to lay a broad legal foundation for a national program of preservation and rehabilitation." His primary focus was on expediting the preservation programs of the National Park Service, but it is clear from his testimony that he understood that a national program on the federal level must also be closely integrated with state and local programs. His testimony regarding the proposed national survey demonstrates this. Ickes urged "a thorough survey of all historic sites in the country . . . such a survey would make it possible to call to the attention of the states, municipalities, and local historical organizations, the presence of historic sites in their particular region which the National Government cannot preserve, but which need attention and rehabilitation."

Following the passage of the Historic Sites Act of 1935, the National Survey of Historic Sites and Buildings, commonly referred to as the Historic Sites Survey, commenced in July 1936. The process developed by the Branch of Historic Sites and Buildings divided American history into themes. Each theme was then studied to identify historic buildings and sites to determine national, state or local significance to the development of the theme. The final step of the process was to develop a national preservation plan.

The Historic Sites Survey was originally motivated by the thought that properties designated nationally significant would become units of the National Park Service. To reduce real estate speculation and the fears of private owners that their property might be taken by the government, determinations of national significance were at first kept secret. The Interior Department also needed to protect itself from intense congressional and public pressure to take second-rate properties into the federal government's system for perpetual care. As early as 1933, criteria was developed to evaluate historical sites for potential inclusion in the National Park system. The criteria included such "sites as are naturally the points or bases from which the broad aspects of prehistoric and historic American life can be best presented . . . sites as are associated with the life of some great American, and which may not necessarily have any other outstanding qualities than association . . . and sites as are associated with some sudden or dramatic incident in American history."

The World War II and Post-War Era

The entrance of the United States into World War II on December 1941 brought national preservation efforts to a standstill. In the early years of the war, President Roosevelt informed Secretary Ickes: "While I favor the preservation for public use of historic sites, buildings and objects of national significance . . . it seems inappropriate, when the nation is at war, to utilize the time of Government employees in conducting investigations looking to the designation of such sites. I believe that such employees could be assigned duties more closely related to the war effort."

A fortnight later, the president's wartime directive was implemented. Visitation to the national parks plummeted from 21 million in 1941 to six million in 1942. The National Park Service appropriation dropped from $21 million in 1940 to $5 million in 1943.

When the war was finally over America entered a period of unashamed self-indulgence; peacetime was upon the nation and the baby boom could be heard throughout the land. This was the disposable era. Oil was cheap, cars were big and self-confidence reigned supreme. Millions of acres of open space were plowed under for prefabricated housing development. Historic resources were under seige as never before. In the private sector, much of the energy for preservation was still devoted to historic house museums. Society matrons, immortalized by Helen Hokinson's cartoons in *The New Yorker*, were the butt of jokes about "blue-rinsed ladies in tennis shoes." The humor heralded an unmistakable truth about American historic preservation at this time. The great majority of preservation work was being carried out at the state and local level by private groups as an undertaking, identified with the upper-class.

A characteristic of historic house museum preservation in the 1940s and 1950s was the tendency to improve upon the past. Lines between historic accuracy, antique collecting and interior decoration often blurred and many historic houses became theater sets for the decorative arts. The distinction was not always honored between what was and what might have been. Furnishing committees frequently ignored inconvenient or disappointing information found in historic inventories. The resulting impression in many houses was that the historical occupants had been on a first-name basis with the great cabinetmakers of London and Philadelphia and that every yard of silk brocade manufactured in the 18th century was exported to the colonies. Social position, money and personality too often influenced decisions at the cost of dispassionate scholarship. The committee system of many historic house museums encouraged personal fiefs that sometimes thwarted truly interdisciplinary management.

After the war, there was a renewed interest in creating outdoor museums for cultural resources. One of the most interesting was Mystic Seaport, created by the Marine Historical Association, in Mystic, Connecticut. The association had undertaken the preservation of the whaling ship Charles W. Morgan just before Pearl Harbor. Now, in peacetime, the association expanded its vision to an outdoor museum of early vessels and maritime buildings. Interest in maritime preservation gained ground slowly over the next 25 years. It then completely captured the nation's interest at the time of the Bicentennial celebration with OPSAIL 76, a parade of tall ships through New York City harbor.

In the public sector, the first decade of the post-war era was devoted to restoring federal programs to their pre-war vitality. It soon became apparent that it was neither politically nor administratively feasible for the federal government to own, manage and interpret more than a tiny fraction of the nation's historical and cultural resources. The National Park Service did not have sufficient budget or staff to fully develop the properties already under its mandate. The U.S. Congress was unwilling to authorize or appropriate funds necessary to expand the system greatly.

Officials of the National Park Service believed that the time had come to consider more efficient mechanisms for managing historic preservation in America. Their position was shared by several others of influence, experience and judgment. A group of concerned preservationists gathered at the National Gallery of Art in February 1947, and planned a larger meeting in April to organize a National Council for Historic Sites and Buildings. The council's program was to build public awareness of preservation issues and to develop and disseminate practical preservation information. The council was also charged with research and survey work. The National Council for Historic Sites and Buildings was organized on April 15, 1947. Its bylaws committed the council to the formation of a national trust to acquire and manage historic properties.

Enthusiasm for an American National Trust was stimulated by two principal forces. One was the successful model of the National Trust for Places of Historic Interest or Natural Beauty in England, which a few Americans had the opportunity to view first hand during the war. The second was the clear understanding, both within government and without, that the National Park Service was unable by itself to address adequately all preservation issues around the country. The private sector needed to be focused and coordinated by a national preservation organization. In November 1948 at the council's annual meeting, a charter was unveiled for members' comment and approval. The council perceived the overall need for historic preservation in political, educational and patriotic terms.

In summer and autumn 1949, Public Law 81-408, establishing the National Trust proceeded through the U.S. Congress and was signed by President Harry S. Truman on October 26. The act stated that the National Trust for Historic Preservation was created as a "charitable, educational, and nonprofit corporation" and would "facilitate public participation in the preservation of sites, buildings, and objects of national significance and interest." For a few years, the new National Trust coexisted with the National Council for Historic Sites and Buildings. In 1953 the National Trust absorbed the National Council.

With the creation of the National Trust in 1949, the National Park Service at last had a partner to share the challenges and burdens of a national preservation program. With the Trust ready to devote its energies to the private sector, the Park Service was free to concentrate more fully on its own congressionally mandated properties and programs. However, the situation was not encouraging. Post-war visitation rose from 22 million in 1948 to 54 million in 1954, while funding from the U.S. Congress failed to keep pace. Park Service properties had deteriorated from years of deferred maintenance because of the war. In 1956, Director Conrad Wirth proposed to the U.S. Congress a bold plan, called Mission '66, to launch a decade of development in anticipation of the 50th anniversary of the National Park Service in 1966. Part of this effort was to resurrect the Historic American Buildings Survey and restructure the National Survey of Historic Sites and Buildings as regularly funded programs. Throughout the National Park system, plans were developed and implemented for the improvement of existing units of the system and studies made for further expansion.

Urban Renewal, Highway Construction and Water Impoundment

At this time in American urban history, the older commercial residential neighborhoods of cities and towns were in a marked state of decline as the attractions of suburbia lured young families and retail businesses away from downtown. The government response was the urban renewal program that provided federal funds for cities all over the United States to rebuild their decaying central cities. The Housing Act of 1949 permitted the use of federal funds for the purchase and clearance of deteriorated urban neighborhoods and the later resale of the vacant land to private developers for new construction. Whole sections of cities vanished as block after block of run-down buildings, many of them in old and historic neighborhoods, were felled by the wrecking ball. What remained was wasteland, punctuated later with modern, often high-rise buildings or left vacant, sometimes for years, as private developers failed to step forward. The Housing Act of 1954, however, allowed federal funds to be used for the rehabilitation of existing old houses in urban renewal areas and for limited preservation planning. Some cities took advantage of this change to save old neighborhoods not already lost.

In 1956, President Dwight D. Eisenhower signed the Federal Aid Highway Act that initiated construction of the interstate highway system. The radical redevelopment unleashed in cities by urban renewal was brought to the countryside by interstate highway construction. Tens of thousands of limited access highways paved thousands of acres of ground and made the nation's cities more accessible to each other and to the surrounding countryside.

Many historic and archaeological resources that survived urban renewal and the interstate highway system suffered inundation in the third federally financed initiative, that of water impoundment, which flooded thousands of square miles through dam and reservoir construction. The hundreds of prehistoric and historic sites in the Little Tennessee River valley, submerged by the completion of the construction of the Tellico Reservoir in 1979, represented one such example.

Reaction to the Forces of Destruction

The destructive edge of post-war prosperity finally reaped an inevitable reaction. The death rattle of so much of the nation's heritage served to renew public interest in local history and in the sights, sounds and tastes of the past. A sign of that interest could be seen in the 1950s, in historic neighborhoods such as Georgetown in the District of Columbia, Beacon Hill in Boston, Massachusetts, and College Hill in Providence, Rhode Island. Concerned residents began exploring the possibilities of creating historic districts, such as the one pioneered in Charleston, South Carolina, before the war. They were motivated by a strong desire to protect the character and integrity of their neighborhoods from an epidemic of indiscriminate change.

Three factors common to the creation of many historic districts were a genuine appreciation of history, a concern for aesthetics and urban design and a wish to control institutional and commercial expansion. The work required to survey and define a historic district often stimulated renewed community pride and sense of place. A veteran of preservation efforts in Rhode Island speaks of survey work in Newport during this time as "giving houses a history and a name." Architectural review boards also gave local morale a boost by providing people a measure of control over the visual destiny of their cities. The creation of historic districts by many smaller communities awaited the enactment of state enabling legislation permitting local initiative.

By the 1960s, growing numbers of young American families discovered the joys and headaches of rehabilitating old houses. Prior to the war, such activity was limited to the artistic and rich. The rising generation, critical of the traditional values of older preservationists, were not attracted as much to Fourth of July patriotism or the selective elegance of a vanished age, as they were to the amenities of character, scale and community that life in a historic neighborhood could provide. Historic preservation was becoming a quality-of-life issue.

Historic Preservation as a Global Reality

The influence of television and jet travel contributed significantly to a growing understanding in the United States that environmental and preservation issues were global issues. World conditions were brought directly into living rooms on the evening news and jets carried Americans in record numbers to the four corners of the earth in a few hours. United States participation in international intergovernmental organizations, such as the United Nations Educational, Scientific and Cultural Organization (UNESCO), expanded professional awareness that American culture was not an isolated phenomenon but an integral part of an interdependent worldwide reality. UNESCO, founded in 1945 from the ashes of World War II, asserted in its constitution that ignorance of other cultures is a root cause of armed conflict. The organization, of which the United States was a founding member, provided a forum for an exchange of views on preservation philosophy and practice and for the development and dissemination of international recommendations and conventions on specific cultural heritage matters.

The work of UNESCO in developing conventions dealing with a variety of subjects important to preservationists around the world provided Americans with an attitude toward preservation missing from their own practice. The Europeans were much more concerned with preservation doctrine; Americans had been used to pragmatic approaches. As American preservationists became familiar with European preservation methods, they too began to develop their own principles somewhat akin to national standards. These standards were articulated in the meetings and studies that preceded the National Historic Preservation Act of 1966 and gained currency in the 20 years since then in the form of policies, criteria, standards and guidelines. By the 1970s, the United States took a leadership position in the initiation of international conventions, such as the Convention for the Protection of World Cultural and Natural Heritage; in participation in nongovernmental organizations, such as the International Council on Monuments and Sites (ICOMOS); and in intergovernmental organizations, such as the International Centre for the Study of the Preservation and the Restoration of Cultural Property (ICCROM).

The exact impact on American preservation of these international organizations is difficult to quantify. Material from abroad received limited circulation to the preservation rank and file; however, individual Americans in key policy positions in government and universities often participated in the deliberations of these international organizations and made their experience available to other preservation leaders. Even though there is a natural reluctance in the United States, shared no doubt by other nations, to swallow whole any specific international preservation practice, useful concepts and ideas came home in the briefcases of important Americans and worked their way slowly into the American mainstream. Above all else, it became clear that cultural heritage has no edges, no breaks, no borders. It is woven of one piece out of many strands, whole and seamless.

The 1966 National Historic Preservation Act

In 1964, as UNESCO celebrated International Monuments Year, the United States observed the American Landmarks Celebration. In anticipation of this commemoration, the National Trust and Colonial Williamsburg sponsored a preservation conference in 1963. The conference's *Report on Principles and Guidelines for Historic Preservation in the United States* was presented to the National Trust membership at its 1964 annual meeting. Full proceedings were published in 1966 as *Historic Preservation Today*. The proceedings contained a full range of suggestions for integrating preservation awareness, preservation policy and preservation planning with all levels of American life.

Simultaneously, President Lyndon B. Johnson organized a Task Force on the Preservation of Natural Beauty and followed up with a White House Conference on Natural Beauty in May 1965. Both the task force and the conference issued strong statements that caught the president's attention, calling for major improvements in the national preservation program. This prompted Secretary of the Interior Stewart L. Udall and National Park Service Director George B. Hartzog, Jr., to put together a legislative package of their own.

In October 1965, the U.S. Conference of Mayors organized a Special Committee on Historic Preservation under the chairmanship of U.S. Representative Albert Rains of Alabama. The committee traveled to Europe to study national preservation practices in eight different countries and returned home to prepare a report for the second session of the 89th U.S. Congress. Their report, which included a foreword by Lady Bird Johnson, essays by preservation leaders and scholars, findings and recommendations for congressional action, was published under the title *With Heritage So Rich*. In the preface Rains and Laurance Henderson, director of the Joint Council on Housing and Urban Development, commented: "We do not use bombs and powder kegs to destroy irreplaceable structures related to the story of America's civilization. We use the corrosion of neglect or the thrust of bulldozers. . . . Connections between successive generations of Americans . . . are broken by demolition. Sources of memory cease to exist. Why then are we surprised when surveys tell us that many Americans . . . lack even a rudimentary knowledge of the national past? We ourselves create the blank spaces."

The conclusions of the report stirringly articulated a new understanding of the place of preservation in American life: "If the preservation movement is to be successful, it must go beyond saving bricks and mortar. It must go beyond saving occasional historic houses and opening museums. It must be more than a cult of antiquarians. It must do more than revere a few precious national shrines. It must attempt to give a sense of orientation to our society, using structures and objects of the past to establish values of time and place. . . . In sum, if we wish to have a future with greater meaning, we must concern ourselves not only with the historic highlights, but we must be concerned with the total heritage of the nation and all that is worth preserving from our past as a living part of the present." It was a vision and a call to action that was to dominate preservation for the next generation.

The 89th U.S. Congress went to work to consider a wide range of bills that focused on important environmental issues. On October 15, 1966, President Johnson signed seven pieces of legislation to conserve the natural and cultural heritage of the United States. One of them was Public Law 89-665, the National Historic Preservation Act of 1966. With pen in hand, President Johnson commented: "I am . . . signing today the Endangered Species Preservation Act and the National Historic Preservation Act. Both of these will help us to preserve for our children the heritage of this great land we call America that our forefathers first saw."

The Preservation Act of 1966 is a cultural document in its own right. It demonstrated an enormous shift in attitude since the 1930s. The Historic Sites Act of 1935 justified federal involvement in preservation primarily for educational purposes. Historic resources were viewed then as things set apart, curiosities to go to look at, in short, yesterday in a bell jar. The preamble to the Preservation Act of 1966 presents the refreshing argument that historic and cultural resources are dynamic, not static, but woven into the fabric of our daily lives and not separate from it. It is appropriate for the federal government to assist state and local governments and individuals in preserving the common heritage.

In the Preservation Act of 1966, the concept of significance was broadened to include architecture and culture. However, the category of science found in the Antiquities Act of 1906 was dropped. The addition of the category of architecture reflected a growing appreciation of the genius of American design and construction. It also marks a shift away from the earlier view of historic resources as a theatrical backdrop for history. In addition, the inclusion of architecture as a category of significance provided a rationale for recognizing historic religious structures.

Adding culture to the list of categories of significance mirrored the growing interest in ethnic groups, folklore and indigenous building practices that was to typify the Bicentennial era that followed. The Preservation Act of 1966 also added two new categories of eligible properties, districts and structures. The addition of districts demonstrated the expanding horizons of preservation to in-

The main commercial thoroughfare in Corning, New York, served as the setting for the first experiment in the main street revitalization effort. (National Trust for Historic Preservation)

The listing of Dulles International Airport in Chantilly, Virginia, designed by Eero Saarinen and completed in 1962 represents an effort by the preservation system to recognize and protect outstanding landmarks of recent vintage. (U.S. Department of Transportation)

The original MacDonalds in Des Plaines, Illinois, has won many adherents in the preservation field, particularly those concerned with commercial archaeology. (National Trust for Historic Preservation)

The 1940 Greyhound Bus Station in Washington, D.C., recently was designated a historic landmark, reflecting interest in the architecture of the recent past. (National Trust for Historic Preservation)

The preservation of surviving gunmounts and personnel shelters at Dutch Harbor Naval Operating Base in Alaska, undertaken by the Corps of Engineers, responded to strong interests in the historic resources of the World War II era. (Jim Stuhler, U.S. Army Corps of Engineers)

clude not only whole neighborhoods of cities and towns, but also entire rural villages and their unspoiled settings. American preservation was thinking well beyond buildings. The inclusion of structures reflected the growing interest in industrial archaeology, civil engineering and complex networks such as transportation systems.

The Preservation Act of 1966 expanded the National Register of Historic Places to include properties of less than national significance. This expansion to include properties of state and local significance in a national register was the most forward-looking contribution of the act. For the first time it enabled comprehensive preservation planning on a national scale. It also greatly reinforced the concept of cultural heritage as an integral part of communities across the nation. Each community possesses unique historical attributes that are also tied to the broader history of a region, state and nation.

The Bicentennial Era

In 1966, coincident with the passage of major preservation legislation, the United States anticipated its 200th birthday. In February 1967, the American Revolution Bicentennial Commission was established by President Lyndon B. Johnson to develop and recommend plans for the occasion. The Commission issued its report in 1970. In 1974, it was given a new name, the American Revolution Bicentennial Administration, and a new task, that of coordinating and approving all official Bicentennial activities. The decade between the implementation of the Preservation Act of 1966 and July 4, 1976, can properly be called the Bicentennial era.

The Bicentennial celebration focused unprecedented public attention on the history, culture and traditions of the nation. In this era, historic preservation burst into full bloom as a national not-for-profit undertaking. It had the new tools and financial support provided by the Preservation Act of 1966 and the national network of state historic preservation offices to facilitate growth and change. Responding to the expansion of the National Register, new historic districts were created across the country. The availability to owners of National Register properties of matching federal bricks-and-mortar grants through the state offices encouraged a surge of preservation work on buildings of all levels of significance. Projects long postponed by local historical societies and preservation groups were initiated because of access to matching funds. Preservation easements, required by federal regulation of grant recipients, gained greater public acceptance. Increasingly they were used by the National Trust and state and local organizations to acquire less-than-fee interest in historic properties for their protection.

In this decade, there was a proliferation of initiatives focused on special interests in historic preservation. New organizations to study and appreciate the warp and the woof of the built environment sprang up everywhere. The names of organizations reflected this diversity of interests. The Victorian Society in America sought respectability for Victorian architecture, decorative arts and culture. The Friends of Cast Iron Architecture grew out of an appreciation of the cast-iron front buildings in the SoHo area of New York City and expanded to encompass cast-iron facades and structural elements throughout the nation. The

Association for Preservation Technology drew membership from preservationists concerned with historic building materials and preservation methods. The Society for Commercial Archeology focused on the appreciation of commercial and roadside architecture, particularly from the 20th century. The separation of special-interest groups into separate membership organizations represented an expansion of the field, but also its increasing fragmentation into splinter groups that had little in common with one another.

In discovering its diversity, America was discovering that it was an old culture. Everyone got into the act: folklorists, urban geographers, cultural geographers, cooks, musicians and semioticians (those who study signs). A shining example of this growing interest can be found in the Appalachian Mountains. In 1966, Eliot Wiggenton, a high school teacher in Rabun Gap, Georgia, recognized that a great body of valuable cultural history and folklore was vanishing unrecorded into silent graves of older people whose lives bridged a period of astonishing change. To stimulate his students' interest in their own history and folkways, he encouraged them to publish a magazine containing articles they would write about the vanishing world and people around them. The nationally acclaimed *Foxfire* and the *Foxfire Books* that followed contained irresistible lore about "hog dressing, log cabin building, mountain crafts and foods, planting by the signs, snake lore, hunting tales, faith healing, moonshining, and other affairs of plain living."

Foxfire epitomized the growing appreciation for "intangible cultural resources." Eliot Wiggenton commented in the first *Foxfire* book, "Daily our grandparents are moving out of our lives, taking with them, irreparably, the kind of information contained in this book . . . when they're gone, the magnificent hunting tales . . . the eloquent and haunting stories of suffering and sharing and building and healing and planting and harvesting—all these go with them, and what a loss." *Foxfire* encouraged local history activities in schools across the country. The enthusiastic response to the 1976 *Roots* written by Alex Haley led to the study, *Cultural Conservation: The Protection of Cultural Heritage in the United States*, sponsored by the American Folklife Center of the Library of Congress in cooperation with the National Park Service.

Many mainline preservationists were brought to a new appreciation and understanding of vernacular architecture by the publication in 1968 of cultural geographer Henry Glassie's *Patterns in the Material Folk Culture of the Eastern United States*. It marked the entry of American folklorists into vernacular architecture studies by providing a theoretical base and a visual catalogue of traditional artifacts against which subsequent field workers have measured their findings. In 1979, a vernacular architecture symposium held at George Washington University in Washington, D.C., stimulated a *Vernacular Architecture* newsletter, followed shortly by the organization of the Vernacular Architecture Forum. The establishment of this organization represented another special-interest group within a larger field. It also provided a forum for exploring the architecture and landscapes produced in the ordinary course of life by the common man.

Growing interest in vernacular architecture had a strong influence on American preservation. An example of this was a thorough reevaluation of 17th and 18th-century material culture in the Chesapeake Bay region of Delaware, Maryland and Virginia. Recent studies confirmed that the preponderance of buildings in the colonial period in this region were impermanent structures.

They were not constructed on masonry foundations but were wood-frame buildings with vertical posts set directly in the ground. Few of these structures remain. They are known to us through artifacts and the archaeological stains they left behind. A common interest in these resources among archaeologists, architects, cultural historians and folklorists dramatized and enriched the interdisciplinary approach to preservation.

As American preservation developed a growing appreciation for ordinary things, it simultaneously developed a growing appreciation for the role of ordinary people in the midst of great national events. Encouraged by the work of historical archaeologists, such as Ivor Noel Hume at Colonial Williamsburg, the preservation profession gained more precise information about the material culture of everyday life than had ever been known. In the 1960s and 1970s, myths were shattered across the whole spectrum of American history, architecture and the decorative arts. A thorough reevaluation of previous restoration work commenced. Historic house museums, even reconstructed ones such as the Governor's Palace at Williamsburg, were reinterpreted in the light of new knowledge and a new attitude toward the past. Scientific advances, such as the use of dendrochronology to identify the date of wooden timbers, also helped to uncover and correct past errors of judgment and wishful thinking.

The popularity of vernacular architecture studies and the increasing demand for the authenticity of historical context also contributed to a widening concern for the cultural heritage of minorities. One of the results of the civil rights achievements of the Bicentennial era was an increased interest in historic sites associated with black history. As late as 1971, there were few National Park Service properties directly associated with black history. The birthplace of George Washington Carver in Missouri was brought into the system in 1943; Booker T. Washington's birthplace in Virginia in 1956; and the Frederick Douglass home in Washington was added in 1962.

In order to address this deficiency, the National Park Service obtained funds from the U.S. Congress, in the fiscal 1973 budget, to contract with the Afro-American Bicentennial Corporation to carry out a study. The research covered three subthemes: the development of the English colonies from 1700 to 1750, major American wars, and society and social conscience. In 1974, the first National Historic Landmarks were designated as a result of this study. By 1986, there were 85. They included the Harriet Tubman Home for the Aged in Auburn, New York; the Dexter Avenue Baptist Church in Montgomery, Alabama, and the Maggie L. Walker House in Richmond, Virginia.

The displacement of elderly, low-income or minority families from changing urban neighborhoods emerged as an issue during the mid-1970s. Although displacement is caused by a complex array of urban forces, many preservationists and neighborhood residents cited historic preservation as the culprit. It is unlikely that preservation efforts, survey, historic district designation and property rehabilitation alone cause displacement. Preservationists, however, bear a responsibility to address this perception. Several communities, using federal, state and local programs, successfully encouraged long-time residents to improve properties and stabilize neighborhoods. However, this repair proved more difficult to achieve in areas characterized by absentee owners and large numbers of abandoned units.

Probing the Outer Limits of Historic Preservation

The increasing diversity of special interests embraced by preservation led to areas of concern that generated debate as to whether they properly belonged within the field. Questions were also raised regarding the appropriateness of existing preservation tools in addressing these topics.

Landscape preservation is one of these concerns. The historic formal, designed landscapes of urban parks as well as the natural landscapes of national parks, such as Yellowstone, Yosemite and Mount Ranier, represented types of resources readily addressed by the preservation field. Less understood were the ordinary landscapes of urban and rural America, the land formations created by ordinary people in the normal course of life. The patterns of farmland division and cultivation in the Shenandoah Valley of Virginia, the suburban subdivisions of the 1910s and 1920s that developed along rail lines and the ordinary streetscapes of small town America all serve as indicators of the hand of man. Preservation of these common landscapes may lie more in the retention of normal activities that keep land and buildings in productive use than in any concerted effort to designate and regulate.

The establishment of historic districts around collections of historic buildings and landholdings is a major and commonly used tool to ensure protection of these places for future generations. But are such measures appropriate for all older areas, especially those possessing marginal historic or architectural merit? Preservationists have collaborated with local planning officials to explore other kinds of designations, such as conservation areas, special improvement districts or appearance districts. Rather than protecting these areas by regulation, alternative types of designations trigger municipal actions, such as street cleaning, building code enforcement, tree planting and upgrading of sidewalks.

Finally, there is the question of the age that properties must reach before they are considered worthy of preservation. The 50-year limit for properties is taken as a gauge for the National Register and numerous local preservation programs. Exceptions are properties of extraordinary significance, such as Eero Saarinen's Dulles Airport near Washington, D.C., and Frank Lloyd Wright's Guggenheim Museum in New York City. The 50-year mark is justified on the basis that a distance of time is necessary for the objective evaluation of buildings and places and that preservation efforts must be based on more than current taste. However, the onrush of development is rapidly eradicating important buildings and places of the World War II and post-war periods, causing many preservationists to take a more flexible position on contemporary resources, especially of local significance. In doing so, preservationists must also step up educational efforts on behalf of the recent past to counter the reluctance of many members of the public to support the preservation of buildings constructed within their own lifetimes.

Historic Preservation Enters the Marketplace

By the late 1970s the deterioration of America's main streets reached crisis proportions. Row upon row of handsome two and three-story Italianate commercial buildings stood empty or nearly empty. Vacant store fronts, plywood in upper windows and rusting metal cornices announced a stark reality. The popularity of suburban shopping centers and regional shopping malls emptied traditional downtown commercial districts of both customers and merchants.

As the urban renewal programs wound down, downtowns across the country tried a variety of approaches to stem the tide of decay. These efforts ranged from remodeling shop fronts to look like shopping centers to blocking-off entire streets to make downtown into a pseudo mall, complete with street furniture, pedestrian plazas and playground equipment. These cosmetic changes did little to alter the fortunes of downtowns.

In Corning, New York, in the early 1970s Market Street, the community's downtown, was a typical example of the problem. However, it served as the setting for a new approach. The Corning Glass Works, which had its world headquarters there, noticed reluctance on the part of executives and their families to settle in the area. Spouses of prospective employees were reported to have cried when first driven down Market Street. In 1974, the Market Street Restoration Agency was created to improve the appearance of Corning and to stabilize the downtown commercial area, treating the existing buildings as assets rather than liabilities.

The Corning example and the National Trust pilot projects in Galena, Illinois; Madison, Indiana, and Hot Springs, South Dakota, led to a national Main Street program aimed at central business districts, headquartered at the National Trust. The essence of the program was to develop a systematic approach to economic revitalization that included preservation of existing buildings. Radically new approaches to marketing provided communities with something in their old downtowns that could not be found in the malls. From the three demonstration towns in 1977, the Main Street program spread throughout the nation to the enthusiastic welcome of downtown merchants and their customers.

At the same time that the Main Street project was getting started, the federal government initiated its most successful program to encourage the rehabilitation of historic structures. The Tax Reform Act of 1976 provided initial tax benefits for the preservation of certain historic structures. These benefits were enhanced with the passage of the Economic Recovery Tax Act of 1981. Since inception, tax incentives dominated the American preservation scene; although, they proved to be a stick with two ends. On the one hand, they promoted unprecedented private sector preservation activity. Many American downtowns are shining once again after generations of neglect. Complex resources, such as redundant industrial facilities and obsolete hotels in the grand style, were given a second life through imaginative mixed use strategies. On a scale never achieved before, America reclaimed its old buildings.

On the other hand, the investment tax credit program had some negative effects on American preservation. The lure of the tax credits made false friends for historic resources who viewed buildings as objects to be exploited for profit rather than treasures to be preserved. The *Secretary of the Interior's Standards for Rehabilitation,* the first national standard for preservation to be included in the Code of Federal Regulations, proved to be a bulwark against overly intrusive rehabilitation.

Because tax benefits apply only to certified historic structures rehabilitated for a business-related purpose, the program also encourages the conversion of single family, owner-occupied residences into multi-unit rental proper-

174

ties. This can cause significant demographic change in the urban geography of traditional single family, owner-occupied neighborhoods. Installing multiple rental units in what were formerly owner-occupied houses greatly increases the number of non-family households, reduces the number of children and the length of family tenure in a neighborhood. It also encourages loss of open space as yards are sacrificed to the need for increased off-street parking. The success of the investment tax credit program also tends to overwhelm the energies of federal and state preservation agencies responsible for its administration. This has been at the cost of other, much-needed initiatives, such as aggressively continued state and local surveys and archaeological salvage.

In the 1980s, many people and institutions came to regard historic preservation as a business rather than a vocation. Conferences and seminars where program topics focused on fundraising, deal-making and equity partnerships, were attended by investment counselors. Preservation consultants became a visible sector of the professional community of preservationists. Business and corporate leaders were invited to positions on preservation organization boards. Developers made clear that they undertook preservation projects in order to make money, not because they liked old buildings. Balancing economic benefit with responsible preservation policy is not an easy task.

1986

1986 marked three important anniversaries: the 10th anniversary of the Tax Reform Act of 1976, the 20th anniversary of the passage of the National Historic Preservation Act of 1966, and the 100th birthday of the Statue of Liberty. Several organizations, such as the Mary Washington College Center for Historic Preservation, used the occasion to bring people together to contemplate the achievements and failures of the past decade in order to develop a future vision for American preservation.

For a less contemplative event, nearly everybody in the nation got involved in wishing Miss Liberty many happy returns of the day. *Newsweek* magazine crisply captured the importance of the event:

> Somehow it all came off without a hitch—a four day extravaganza of patriotic cheer whose gargantuan gaudiness seemed, in the end, incontestably American. There were fireworks, laser beams, tall ships, small boats and millions of happy gawkers . . . And there was the Statue of Liberty, triumphantly restored for her centennial—the focal point, a symbol and pretext for a Fourth of July that celebrated America's currently contented mood no less than its immigrant past.

The celebration epitomized the present place of preservation in America and demonstrated how far we have all come from the moonlighted deck of a lonely steamer tolling its bell for a decrepit Mount Vernon more than a century before.

The Call Beyond 1986

An examination of what Americans have preserved and why, reveals historic preservation to be fractal, something growing and expanding that carries into the future the structures and attitudes of the past. Preservation, which sprang from a concern for preserving single, nationally significant monuments and commemorating specific historic people and events, multiplied to embrace a concern for the care of the entire natural and built environment and the understanding and appreciation of all people and all events. The American experience closely resembles that of other countries in this regard. As the preservation fractal continues to develop, ideas and concepts from the past will exist with new ones to create a new reality. The future will reveal both the unknown and the familiar. American preservation appears to be growing most vigorously in four areas: land use planning, design, institutional change and education.

Photographs of the earth taken by American astronauts from the moon showed our planet to be small, finite and fragile. Recent advances in environmental research and technological development made us all more aware than ever of the interdependence of our global life support systems. Thomas Jefferson wrote, "The earth belongs in usufruct to the living." Usufruct means "the right of using and enjoying the fruits or profits of an estate or other thing belonging to another, without impairing the substance." We must come to understand that individual historic properties taken together constitute the cultural heritage of the nation, and form, therefore, a common trust. Until the spirit of usufruct is second nature in the United States, the rule of the bulldozer will continue unabated.

In our fast-changing world, recognition is growing that there is benefit in preserving long-term relationships between people and their historic places. There is something of value about a community or a family and a historic neighborhood or property that have shaped each other over centuries and are still together today. The concept of highest and best use may be rethought in terms of people rather than dollars, as the interactive historical relationship between people and their places is understood and appreciated better. It is hoped that historic preservation may have succeeded so well in infusing some of its values into a wider world, that the word "preservation" is now obsolete. James Marston Fitch's phrase "curatorial management of the built world" is moving closer to the truth.

Our concept of what is historic and what should be preserved, and for whom, widens daily. We are beginning to understand, also, that historic preservation has more to do with the present and the future than with the past. Our job is not to decide what from the past we want to keep, but what from the present. This, then, calls into the question arbitrary cut-off dates, such as the 50-year guideline for the National Register. Things are moving too fast for cut-off dates.

Historic preservation is truly a quality-of-life issue. When all else is said and done, it grows out of a universal human need to establish networks of family and community that have some chance of taking root and thriving. With this in mind, taking responsibility for the cultural heritage should not come as a surprise. It should be a value learned from earliest childhood taught at all levels of our educational system and reinforced by sound government policy.

Historic preservation is an autobiographical undertaking. In our own generation, we are painting a portrait of a society that is increasingly respectful of the diversity of human experience and mindful of its fragile traces on the land. In what we preserve and why, we are proclaiming our own commitment to a pledge as old as the U.S. Constitution and as new as tomorrow "to form a more perfect union."

CHAPTER SIX

Discovering Old Cultures in the New World: The Role of Ethnicity

ANTOINETTE J. LEE

DISCOVERING OLD CULTURES IN THE NEW WORLD: THE ROLE OF ETHNICITY

ANTOINETTE J. LEE

Introduction

W hat is preserved is a function of what society thinks is important to it now and to future generations. Historical knowledge, interest in architectural styles and construction methods and perceptions about threats to the environment all contribute to what is studied and valued in the built environment. Decisions about significance are also a result of the kinds of individuals participating in the preservation process. Family background, professional training and personal interests influence judgments about what is important. Access to financial resources and to the political process are also important factors in what is ultimately saved. The factors that influence society's decisions about what is saved are not static, but change over time in response to forces both within and without the preservation movement.

A road map to historic preservation projects of the pre-1966 era led to fewer destinations than those of today. In that earlier period, the destinations emphasized aspects of the American past that affected the nation as a whole or pointed to historic resources of interest to a national audience. The most valued buildings and artifacts of that period were houses associated with national leaders and the best examples of architecture from the colonial or federal periods. By 1986, many new destinations had been added. They now include buildings and places of state, regional and local importance and interest, as well as those of national significance. The scope of the preservation movement expanded to embrace, among others, engineering structures; buildings of the Great Depression, World War II and the postwar era; and sites of no particular architectural distinction but with close ties to ethnic groups.

The differences in the preservation road maps reflect, in part, the major concerns of the history profession. Before the mid-1960s, historians tended to be preoccupied with national figures and events that influenced the nation. The focus on national significance was codified in federal preservation legislation. In addition, pioneering 20th-century preservation efforts focused on high-style architecture, the importance of which was agreed upon generally. Local research was pursued by historical societies and antiquarians, but the results were not typically influential in academic circles or in the mainstream of historic preservation activities.

Today, the history field is more diverse and the divisions between the academic, public and local historians, preservationists and antiquarians are blurred. Subjects of local interest, with important lessons for a larger audience, are now prime topics of historical research. The revolution in the profession was fed by the social upheavals of the 1960s and the efforts of historians to reflect on the changes in the nation. The localization of preservation efforts, within a national framework, also spurred the demand for historical skills applied to locally important events, individuals, groups of people and building methods. Once the papers of great men formed the keystones of historical research. Now historians are consulting building permits, census records, wills, diaries, land transfer records and old newspapers. They also pursue information not found in written records such as oral interviews and the material culture of everyday life. These pursuits have resulted in the designation and protection of thousands of local sites and produced the road map to the many preservation destinations of 1986.

The elements of American society that participate most actively in preservation activities have also changed in the last two decades. If a person visited preservationists from the earlier period, he would observe older, more affluent citizens of a community. Today, the preservation community covers a broader spectrum. Its members are found in preservation organizations and agencies, as well as in urban revitalization organizations, ethnic and minority cultural establishments and neighborhood development organizations. The participation of a larger number of economic groups and nationalities is a result of the broadened field and the expanded definition of historic and significant. It is, also, a result of broader-based educational opportunities in society at large. Today, the past is a commodity that is claimed by a large number of cultural groups whose forefathers once lived, visited or were associated with historic buildings and places. A greater variety of cultural groups are also involved because they are currently occupying historic buildings and places and are in a position to help determine their future.

Cultural Influences on the American Landscape

When Columbus discovered America, Native Americans (Indians) were distributed across the continent, with many tribes living close to rivers and lakes. The clustering of subsequent cultural groups in the United States is the result of many factors, but transportation was an important one. The earliest English, Dutch and Swedish settlers arrived by boat and clustered along the East Coast in the original 13 colonies. Spanish explored the Gulf Coast and the coast of what later became California. French moved into the American Midwest from the North, away from French Canada and down the Mississippi River. Africans were brought to the continent against their will and were sold into slavery primarily in the Southern States. The first Asians settled in the far West in the California goldfields and the farms and ranches of Hawaii.

After the Civil War and Reconstruction, many blacks migrated to the industrial cities of the North in search of jobs and a better life. With the emergence of a national railroad system in the 19th century, immigrants from

Scandinavia and Germany settled on the Great Plains of the upper Midwest, situating their towns along the rail lines. In our own era, Puerto Ricans alighted in New York City from airplanes, Cuban immigrants settled in Florida and the boat people of Southeast Asia arrived in the United States by airplane, settling mainly in large cities in the southern half of the nation where the climate is milder.

The great mobility of the American population in the 20th century diffused many of the geographically limited settlements of immigrant groups. Nonetheless, the concentrated nature of their early settlement patterns left tangible remains of their history. Many of their descendants remained in place on the land, testimony to the achievements of immigrants in settling the continent.

In time, land was subdivided and adapted to local conditions, resulting in distinctive land settlement patterns. Land development also reflected the attempt to create an environment in which arrivals could feel at home in a new setting. For example, in New England, farms were usually small, placed close to one another and situated near the highway to improve accessibility in time of heavy snow. The carving up of the land into cities and towns reflected the attitudes of the nation toward land ownership and notions about ideal urban life. In 1682 in Philadelphia, Pennsylvania, William Penn used a rectangular gridiron plan, with equally spaced green squares in each quadrant of the original city. In 1695 in Annapolis, Maryland, Francis Nicholson drew up a Baroque scheme with diagonal boulevards connecting major public buildings. In the southern states, the scattered plantations served as self-sufficient economic units, making market towns unnecessary. Instead, towns developed around rural courthouses, an indication that the primary purpose of the town was to participate in local government.

Not all immigrant groups had an opportunity to express their heritage and aspirations for a new life in new buildings. Many groups settled in existing developed areas and altered existing buildings to suit their needs and tastes. Commercial signs on restaurants, bakeries and laundries provided tangible evidence of the immigrant presence. Because of the challenge of making their way in a new country, urban immigrant groups tended to live in concentrated clusters with others from the same country, creating Little Italys, Chinatowns and Little Havanas. With rising economic fortunes, the second and third generations dispersed into outlying areas, away from strong ethnic bonds. The process played over and over again as old city neighborhoods continued to attract new arrivals.

Outside urban centers, the character of the cultural landscape was shaped by farming methods brought from the Old World and adapted to the New. These methods determined the configurations and methods of dividing fields, the appearance of buildings that support agricultural operations and the pattern of buildings and structures on the land. Other economic activities also molded the land outside the cities and towns. Rural industries, such as mineral extraction and timber processing plants, left their imprint on the landscape. Religious communities, such as those formed by the Shakers, Hutterites and Mormons, and utopian communities such as New Harmony and the Amana colonies, endowed the landscape with tangible reminders of their community life, religions, belief systems and social theories.

In New Harmony, the town plan and buildings initially were developed in 1814 by the Harmonists, a religious group from Germany that lived a co-operative life, in substantial prosperity in what was then a pioneer outpost. The town was laid out in the shape of a square filled with dormitories, breweries, churches, shops, factories and granaries. A decade later, Harmonists sold the town to Welsh-Scot Robert Owen and moved to Economy, Pennsylvania. Owen adapted the town to his vision of a community of equality through cooperation and rational education. In a few years, the social experiment splintered into smaller groups, each going its own way. Today, New Harmony stands as a testament to the ideals of those early groups in the adaptation of old buildings to modern uses, enhanced by the construction of the Roofless Church, designed by Philip Johnson, and the establishment of the Paul Tillich Park, named in honor of the world-famous theologian.

Lands and buildings associated with specific groups of settlers represent not only their own practices, but also those of later immigrants who refashioned the natural and cultural resources to suit themselves. Building materials and climatic conditions shaped the built environment. In addition, settlers borrowed Old World memories, often in an impure or idealized form. This combination of old, new and borrowed architectural ideas provided much of the force of innovation in American architecture.

Presently, the preservation movement is working to identify features of the built environment most directly and meaningfully associated with individual cultural groups. This effort is driven by the search for a better understanding of the evolution of the American townscape and landscape, and the means to determine which elements are worthy of protection for future generations. This research effort is immediately related to and builds upon the local historical surveys sponsored by federal, state and local historic preservation programs.

The individuality of countless American cities and towns is reflected in localized building traditions. Just as with large cities, small settlements also frequently possess unappreciated special buildings and traditions, tangible and intangible, that deserve to be kept and maintained. A key challenge to the preservation movement is educating the present occupants, frequently two or three generations removed from the original settlers, to the importance of their local heritage.

Cultural Unity Versus Cultural Pluralism

The expanded historic preservation program of the past two decades drew on and abetted the changing view of the adaptation of cultural groups to America. Prior to the 1960s, the accepted hypothesis was that immigrants settled in the New World and strove to adapt to American ways. Names were Americanized, immigrant children were sent to public schools, which were viewed as great centers of Americanization, family members took up American habits and tastes, and the family climbed up the American economic ladder. This search for a unified national culture was based on the then-popular perception of the United States as a melting pot, where diverse cultural groups would in time blend together and form a new culture known as American.

The process of fitting many cultural groups into a single mold is no longer a singular expectation of American society. To the melting pot image was added widespread acceptance of cultural pluralism as an ideal. In actuality, some

New Harmony:
A Peaceable Kingdom

New Harmony, Indiana, has been the site of three experiments in community life. It was settled in 1814 by a group of Lutheran separatists, who worked to produce a utopian society. Despite the Harmonists' success in achieving a cosmopolitan and efficient community, New Harmony was sold in 1825 to British industrialist Robert Owen who sought to establish a community based on education and science. Owen's invitation to join his "halfway house between new and old" attracted scholars, primarily educators and naturalists. In the 1960s and 1970s, New Harmony underwent its third experiment, led by Jane Blaffer Owen and the Robert Lee Blaffer Trust, to create a dynamic community of the future amid the surroundings and inspiration of the past. Historic buildings were preserved, some adapted for new uses and others maintained to interpret the past. Major public improvements were also made to strengthen the town. New Harmony has become again an intellectual center, the site of educational courses, theater and national and international meetings. There is also a renewed spiritual aspect, symbolized by the Roofless Church and a park honoring 20th-century theologian Paul Tillich. In 1982, New Harmony received the American Institute of Architects Medal for "Blending the original Harmonist constructions, lovingly preserved, with the work of contemporary architects, New Harmony is a peaceable kingdom: a continuum of past and present that gives new meaning and added luster to its name."

(left)
Main Street, 1912, exemplifies the traditional small-town character of New Harmony, Indiana. (Historic New Harmony, Inc.)

(right)
The New Harmony Inn echoes the Harmonist building style while providing accommodations for visitors from around the world. (George Cserna)

(above)
The West Street Log Cabins were erected to re-establish the character of the Harmonist streetscape (1814–1819), part of the effort to maintain the continuum in New Harmony. (Historic New Harmony, Inc.)

(right)
The Roofless Church (Philip Johnson, 1960) was inspired by the 19th-century writer George Sand who said that only one roof, the sky, is vast enough to embrace all worshipping humanity. The shape repeats the Harmonist symbol of the Golden Rose. (Robert E. Stipe)

(left)
The small-town character has been maintained and renewed through the efforts of the community, insuring a useful future for the buildings of Robert Owen's era in the world of tomorrow. (Historic New Harmony, Inc.)

immigrant groups sought to preserve their traditions and lifestyles well beyond the period of adjustment to the New World, going so far as to shield their offspring from aspects of American life that they considered undesirable. A few, for example the Amish and Mennonites, maintained their special identity for generations. Some groups also undertook conscious efforts to perpetuate their heritage, customs and values, seeking to reinforce their differentness and coalescing around their own social groups in order to share experiences that only members of their group could fully comprehend. The vision of the American as a homogenized whole is an ideal that still has adherents. Much of American society, however, now accepts the notion that not all immigrant groups must adopt the tenets of any one cultural standard. America will always to some extent be a nation of many subcultures, coexisting within a dominant culture, but comprising in the aggregate an American society.

One result of the acceptance of cultural diversity is the hyphenated American. The terms Afro-American, Asian-American, Arab-American, and Mexican-American, raise other images of distinctive experiences, lifestyles and traditions. Few hyphenated Americans are pure examples of their ethnic origins, but their association with an ethnic group endures well beyond that of Americans of European origin. Some hyphenated Americans also tend to fall into the category of minority groups within the dominant culture, particularly those who at some time in history have been denied equal access to housing, and economic and social opportunities. The terms are useful in evaluating the significance of buildings and places. A single building or place may serve as one part of a large network of sites associated with a particular group. In addition, in the full development of a thematic study, the terms help interpret the importance of a site to the general public.

Settling the American Landscape

The development of the American landscape began when man first set foot in the western hemisphere. However, the pace of physical change accelerated after the early 19th century. A greater number of immigrant influences placed their mark on the land and new technological methods for taming the land and constructing buildings speeded up the process of development.

The occupation of North America began about 10,000 years ago. The first settlers came from Asia across the Bering Strait by a land bridge during the last ice age. When subsequent climatic changes warmed the earth, raised the water level of the oceans and severed this route, the population that occupied the New World evolved in a different way from their Asian relatives. Over the years, the New World population separated into many subgroups. By 1492, when Christopher Columbus landed in the New World, at least 2,000 different languages were spoken.

Pre-Columbian peoples of the western hemisphere evolved according to climatic conditions that ranged from the Arctic north to the southern tip of South America. These widely varying conditions and the relative isolation of each group provided ideal conditions for the development of cultures ranging from simple hunters and gatherers, to stable, agriculture-based settlements to complex urban centers. The remains of the pre-Columbian cultures can be seen in camp sites along rivers and estuaries. In them can be found remains of a rich material culture including buildings that were once part of city or village settlements. The many cultures that developed separately were also concerned with the relationship of man with the gods. Their beliefs were given physical form in temples, tombs and petroglyphs, many surviving to this day on the American landscape.

The occupation of the hemisphere by the first Americans remained virtually free from contact with the Old World until 1492, when Christopher Columbus landed in the Caribbean on October 12, 1492. From this first foothold, the European countries sent navigators to explore land previously unknown to them. The earliest explorations were conducted by the Spanish, who investigated the new land from Florida to California and throughout Central and South America. Here the Spanish established elaborate baroque churches and missions; while they brought with them traditional ideas of religious architecture, the realities of available materials and labor produced a notable fusion of European and indigenous ideas.

The first successful English colony was established in 1607 at Jamestown, Virginia. Harsh conditions caused the settlers to be more concerned with survival than with building permanent structures, so the settlement was formed of simple mud huts and log structures. Other English settlements were soon established along the East Coast, bringing security to earlier outposts. Time and hard work brought prosperity and the luxury of imported goods and ideas from Europe, particulary England. During the late 17th and early 18th centuries, America could boast buildings of brick, stone and wood which were based in part on available pattern books of the period. Never exact copies, the English-inspired buildings formed an architectural imagery that is encapsulated in the American colonial style. The popularity of this style endured through the 18th century, was largely eclipsed in the 19th century and then was rediscovered in the 20th century. Through many permutations, this style remains the most popular style for residential construction.

As with the Indians, Spanish and English, the architectural concepts of later settlers from other countries are revealed in the floor plans, framing systems, roof form and construction, and materials of their buildings. They are also reflected in the spatial relationships among groups of buildings, distinctive building types and the location of structures on the landscape. Dutch colonial architecture of the 17th century consisted of a framing system made up of horizontal anchorbeams that ran from the front to the back of the buildings, wide overhanging eaves and gambrel roofs. Another of the earliest distinctive buildings in America was the shotgun house, a narrow house several rooms deep with a front porch, associated primarily with black settlers in the southeastern states. This building type, responding to the hot and humid weather of the region, combined Caribbean, European and African influences.

French-Canadian settlers in Louisiana built structures with unique pavilion roofs. German and Swiss houses on the East Coast were notable for their framing systems and use of rubble stone. On farms built by Irish settlers, buildings were placed on the landscape in a linear configuration. Belgian log buildings were covered by brick veneer. Czechs built log structures with filled chink walls. Finns introduced horizontal cross-timber log construction to the continent. German-Russians used puddled clay in their buildings.

Traditional Shinto architecture is evident in the Japanese-influenced modern architecture of the 20th century, particularly in the work of Frank Lloyd Wright and his Prairie School followers. Midwestern German buildings are notable for their half-timber walls constructed of stone, brick and earth. Norwegian farm complexes were patterned after Old World examples, with the farm houses on the upper slope of a hill and the barn on the down slope. The interior of Ukrainian churches in North America was divided into three spaces, porch, nave and sanctuary. The exterior was adorned with a bell tower, dome or cupola. German breweries and family homes were frequently fashioned after similar structures in the old country.

Many successful urban architects of the 19th century were of immediate European origin. Among them were John L. Smithmeyer, one of the architects of the Library of Congress building in the nation's capital, and Adolph Cluss, who designed many notable public buildings in Washington, D.C. Other German-trained architects settled in Chicago and contributed to its development both before and after the great Chicago fire of 1871. For example, Louis Sullivan's partner, Dankmar Adler, designed urban structures which were reminiscent of buildings in Germany. Trained in the Government School of Design in Dublin, Ireland, Jeremiah O'Rourke became a noted architect in the late-19th century in New Jersey and during a brief period, 1893–94, served as Supervising Architect of the U.S. Treasury Department. By the mid-20th century, Finnish-born and trained architect, Eliel Saarinen enjoyed a successful practice in the United States and bequeathed many cities with examples of his moderate modernism derived from Scandinavian and German influences. Today, the field of architecture is filled with foreign-born and trained practitioners who continue to infuse American architecture with ideas from all of the continents.

The segregation of certain ethnic groups from the mainstream of American society produced its own unique material culture. As much as some may wish today to forget that racial segregation was an accepted way of life during much of American history, others seek the preservation of related buildings and places as object lessons for future generations. Studies are being conducted of black schools, black theaters, black hotels, areas that were ringed with iron fences to keep out blacks and black settlements with road systems that do not connect to the larger surrounding area.

The relocation of Americans of Japanese descent during World War II represents another dark page in American history. The federal government relocation effort moved thousands of Japanese-Americans away from their homes on the West Coast to camps in California, Arizona, Idaho, Wyoming, Colorado and Arkansas. For the duration of the war, the internees lived within communities of barracks, common baths, laundries and mess halls, surrounded by barbed wire and patrolled by military police. Today, camp vestiges are evident in building foundations, guard stations, cemeteries and rock gardens. Camp sites are important to the internees, their descendants and those who recognize the need to exercise constant vigilance in the protection of human rights.

While many cultural groups are associated with buildings constructed for or by them, other groups adapted existing structures to serve new purposes. The development of Chinatowns in the late-19th and 20th centuries occurred in older, low-rent areas. Because many newly arrived Chinese had difficulties with the English language and suffered from discrimination, they were able to make a living only by engaging in trades and businesses for which there was little competition, and for which a command of the English language was not essential, such as restaurants and laundries. These businesses clustered together in low-rent areas. Chinatowns, like other ethnic settlements, served as way stations for successive waves of immigrants, with the second and third generations moving into the mainstream of American life through education and acculturation. Chinatowns also acquired a special physical presence through commercial signs and decorative features that advertised the services provided inside.

The phenomenon of the ethnic neighborhoods continues to the present. Older, low-rent areas are occupied by Hispanics, Japanese, Vietnamese, Portuguese, Italians and Greeks in such concentrations that they take on a special character. This is a result of the types of commercial establishments located there and the remodeling of existing buildings to advertise goods and services.

The wide availability of mass-produced building materials, however, tended to mute these distinctive contributions to American architecture. Few of the special elements of American ethnic architecture survive in modern building practice. Exceptions include the pervasiveness of colonial revival architecture based on English models and evident in numerous permutations in American residential and commercial architecture. Other exceptions include the continued popularity of Spanish colonial architecture in cities throughout the nation and of Japanese elements, especially on the West Coast and Hawaii and throughout the Pacific region.

In the rural landscape, mechanization of the family farm and the consolidation of family farms into corporate farms changed the appearance of the countryside forever. New irrigation systems and machinery altered the shape and geometry of the land. Buildings associated with farming were replaced with prefabricated barns, silos and related buildings. Even the traditional white clapboard family farmhouse is being abandoned and replaced with suburban style split-level or mobile homes. Rural areas within a 100-mile radius of major urban areas are swept up into a more densely developed exurbia, complete with shopping malls, subdivisions and industrial parks. The rural cultural landscape, shaped by descendants of the first settlers, could become as homogenized and predictable as many urban centers.

The surviving examples of ethnic architecture constitute some of the richest materials for historic preservation research. Federal preservation planning and rehabilitation standards emphasize historical research before National Register nominations and architectural plans are prepared. Because much of this research is directed at buildings of primarily local interest, reading the ordinary landscape through research and documentation has become an integral part of the preservation movement.

The Evolution of the Historic Preservation Movement, Pre-1966

The status of historic preservation prior to 1966 contributed to the image of the single American cultural norm. Historic properties associated with the nation's founding fathers, military heroes and early European settlers served as beacons of inspiration to arrivals, no matter what their country of origin. These properties reflected the nation's history and its struggles to carve out a life of taste and culture in a new land.

The focus on national figures and events reflected the interests of historians, and the emphasis on national significance enunciated in federal legislation. Although many cultural groups contributed to the building of the nation, few preservation projects of the early period reflected this dimension of the national experience. Large estates built by the country's national figures were valued for their historic associations and tastes that copied those of the Old World. The everyday lives of servants and slaves were subjects that were virtually untouched.

The interests of ethnic and immigrant groups constituted a small and barely visible part of the preservation movement before 1966. However, the groundwork was laid for the legal and programmatic framework that would facilitate the study and protection of these interests in the years after 1966. The non-profit governing body that administers Mount Vernon was adapted by preservationists concerned with sites associated with ethnic groups. Historic building surveys constituted the first step in the creation of the Charleston, South Carolina, historic district in 1931 and served as a model for all subsequent preservation initiatives, including those in ethnic and minority communities. Even established preservation projects, such as Colonial Williamsburg, Virginia, and Greenfield Village, Michigan, were reexamined in recent years for their relationship to the life of the common man, the disenfranchised and the newly arrived immigrants. By 1966, the framework for historic preservation was coalescing into a national program of identification, registration and protection. It was simply a matter of time before forces behind ethnic history would make their mark on the field.

In retrospect, the vision of the pre-1966 preservationists might be characterized by some as narrow. However, in an era when historic preservation was viewed as a highly esoteric activity, those involved in the process were pioneers. The early preservationists laid the groundwork for a broader movement by developing a methodology for documenting and preserving buildings. Rudiments of local protection legislation were formulated during this period. While many protected historic buildings were used as house museums, many others were maintained by private individuals for residential and commercial purposes.

In an era with few government incentives or assistance, the character of historic preservation in this period was shaped by individuals and organizations with the financial resources to come to the rescue of historic resources. Preservation was dominated by the white, female, upper-class and elite elements of society. Historic preservation as a full-time, salaried pursuit was virtually unknown, except for a small number of architects who fashioned their careers around the restoration of colonial buildings.

A New Era for the Past, 1966–86

By 1966, the historic preservation map of the United States was dotted by restoration projects and protected historic districts in cities and towns across the country. The overwhelming number of them were associated with the nation's English traditions. But seeds of change were in the wind.

The post-World War II era witnessed many drastic urban renewal projects that wiped away whole sections of many American cities and towns. These projects were well-intentioned, but, nonetheless, were highly destructive efforts to rid old cities of slums and blight that resulted from many factors, including the flight of the middle class to the suburbs and the occupation of inner city neighborhoods by low-income residents. The retreat from central city was abetted by the automobile and the federally subsidized roads that were constructed to accommodate it. The disruptive effects of massive urban renewal and highway construction projects in turn provoked a reaction; the seeds of the environmental movement were sown. This movement, originating in the 1950s, served as the basis for much of the environmental protection legislation of the 1960s and 1970s and provided an expanded constituency for historic preservation.

The civil rights movement was another important postwar development that affected the character of the historic preservation movement. Beginning as an effort to increase voter participation among the nation's black citizens, to desegregate public facilities and to end discrimination at work and in housing, the movement ultimately altered the nation's perception of itself. Black citizens not only sought equal opportunity in the political and economic life of the nation, but also national recognition of their contributions to the country's development.

Although black citizens stood at the forefront of the civil rights movement, their efforts also spread benefits to other minority groups. Asian-Americans and Hispanic-Americans asserted their rights as citizens and sought recognition for the contributions of their forebears in the nation's development. Ethnic pride and identity spread to other nationalities, including those of European origin. By the time of the 1976 American Bicentennial, the immigrant experience was a transcendent theme. "A Nation of Nations," the name of a major exhibition at the Smithsonian Institution's National Museum of American History, reflected the importance of this story. The United States began to draw strength from its diverse character.

The National Historic Preservation Act of 1966 set the stage for greater appreciation and recognition of historic resources of state and local significance. The mandate for broader historic preservation interests, especially at the local level, coincided with a broadening of the scope of historic research, the emergence of the civil rights movement and the involvement by more nationalities in heritage projects. The convergence of these trends changed the movement from a concern of small groups scattered around the country to a truly national audience that embraced a range of historical resources unimaginable two decades earlier.

One of the parties to this transformation was the history profession. Caught up in social upheavals of the 1960s, both ivory-tower academic historians and those associated with historical societies and museums sought rele-

Promises of greater economic opportunities and religious freedom drew many newcomers to the western states via the Overland Trail in Wyoming. (Carbon County Museum)

The Santa Barbara Mission in California reflects the important role of Spanish religious orders on the architecture of the western states. (National Trust for Historic Preservation)

The town of Locke in Sacramento County, California, represents a unique surviving Chinese immigrant community. (Jet Lowe, Historic American Buildings Survey/Library of Congress)

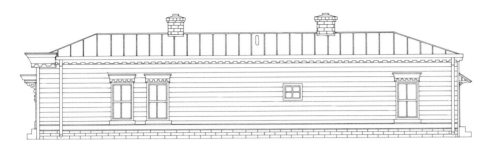

The form of shotgun houses in Louisville, Kentucky, is derived from Caribbean, European and African influences. (Preservation Alliance of Louisville & Jefferson County, Inc.)

The open chinks and corner notches of this double-crib log barn in Kawaunee County, Wisconsin, are indicators of the Czech American influences on rural architecture. (William H. Tischler, University of Wisconsin)

vancy in writing the history of identifiable ethnic groups, in neighborhood development studies and the pursuit of family histories. Dubbed the new social history, many lines of inquiry delved into areas that had not been scratched earlier by the profession. Historians turned their attention away from the details of great national events and toward the actions and lifestyles of the common people who witnessed and lived through these events. Today, much research is conducted on family histories, the behavior patterns of large population blocks and how disenfranchised groups lived an everyday existence within the limitations imposed by American society.

The growing interest in the everyday life of the common citizen permeated large-scale preservation projects, such as Colonial Williamsburg. There the lessons of history, rendered in street theater as well as in restored buildings, cover not only the great national events that happened in the town, but also the lives of ordinary men and women caught up in a time of revolution. Outside the confines of the museum village, historians conducting surveys as part of the preservation process are seeking to uncover the footprints of cultural groups important to the history of communities. They look at residential locations, social institutions and places of business of everyday life. Through this process, formerly invisible parts of the community can be reinstated as part of a comprehensive narrative of American history as seen through preserved sites, buildings and places.

Publications that emerged from this effort detailed the struggles of groups that did not enjoy equal access to the American dream. Thus, the preservation and interpretation of the history of the struggles of minority groups served as inspiration to them and as lessons from the past with meaning for the entire population.

Federal programs charged with historic preservation, such as the National Park Service, as well as state and local agencies and organizations, encouraged studies of historic resources that related to ethnic and vernacular history. Private preservation organizations at all levels sought to include these resources in their funding, technical assistance and educational programs. The publicity surrounding governmental and private initiatives influenced the subject of studies undertaken by individual historians and specialists, both inside and outside academe.

Early Minority Preservation Projects

The rise of a national historic preservation constituency coupled with the civil rights movement resulted in initiatives that would have been unthinkable in the pre-World War II era. Federal, state and local studies and surveys of historic buildings and places yielded heretofore unrecognized resources associated with minority groups. Of those resources identified, the most significant were preserved and opened to the public. Other buildings were protected through historic district zoning or through the participation of community groups in determining the future development of their respective neighborhoods. Many of these projects received a positive response from government historic preservation agencies and private foundations.

One of the earliest minority preservation projects to receive national attention was Project Weeksville, which began in 1968 in the Bedford-Stuyvesant section of Brooklyn, New York. Here an urban renewal project uncovered the remains of an affluent 19th-century black community called Weeksville. Archaeological investigations of this area yielded many artifacts, photographs, household objects and records of businesses and benevolent organizations. This discovery spurred the creation of a Society for the Preservation of Weeksville and Bedford-Stuyvesant History to preserve the physical remains of the historic neighborhood. The purpose of the project was to provide a sense of continuity of culture to those who lived in the immediate neighborhood and to acquaint black people with the richness of their heritage even beyond Weeksville.

It is difficult to recapture the electrifying effect of the Weeksville Project when it was publicized in the early 1970s. Here was a historic black settlement that had been discovered by leaders of the local community and valued for its historical lessons. The charming tintype photograph of The Lady of Weeksville served as a powerful symbol, recalling the affluence of some black citizens more than a century earlier. The society president became a spokesman not only for the Weeksville Project but also for the value of the preservation of black historic sites throughout the nation. Beyond the actual physical remains of Weeksville was the significance of the idea it represented. Nearly every community possessed historic resources that were created or modified by black or other minority groups. The challenge was to find historic resources in local records and to examine old buildings first hand.

The involvement of minority groups in historic preservation in the late 1960s and early 1970s extended to areas that were recently occupied by them. It was common for inner city neighborhoods to be successively inhabited and later abandoned as immigrant occupants moved away to escape the hazards of the buildings themselves and the congestion of older cities. By the mid-20th century, many central city neighborhoods were home to black Americans. These areas also held the greatest concentration of historic resources.

The Mt. Auburn neighborhood in Cincinnati, Ohio, is a community steeped in the history of early suburban villas occupied by the city's leading 19th-century families. By the 1960s, it was a predominantly black community ringed by major medical institutions and bordered by the University of Cincinnati. In another era and place, Mt. Auburn might have become a prime candidate for a urban renewal efforts formulated by city planners and housing specialists. By the 1960s, however, there were many examples of failed urban renewal projects in the nation's cities and a new approach was gaining attention. In Cincinnati, a task force of the Model Cities Physical Planning Program organized the Mt. Auburn Community Council to "bring about improved housing and a new neighborhood spirit through decision making by its own residents." The Community Council and its housing arm, the Mt. Auburn Good Housing Foundation, undertook the improvement of housing through the purchase and management of buildings in the area and the designation of the area as a historic district. As described in a national publication, "the Mt. Auburn effort is strictly of, by, and for the neighborhood." Displacement of residents by affluent newcomers was not an important factor in the efforts of the Community Council, although the gradual expansion of surrounding institutions was perceived as a threat. This project was a good example of how historic preservation concerns could be related to basic bread-and-butter issues of housing, education and health care. It proved irresistible to preservationists throughout the country.

Since the historic buildings of the Mt. Auburn area were primarily created by the affluent members of the dominant culture in the 19th century, they could not be viewed as associated with a minority or ethnic population until the mid-20th century. However, the buildings came to be embraced by the community as part of its own heritage and constituted important anchors in a community searching for footholds of neighborhood pride, stability and commitment.

Following national public recognition of the Weeksville and Mt. Auburn projects, others emerged. For example, the Soulard neighborhood in St. Louis was studied and designated as a historic district for its history as home to successive waves of German, eastern European and black immigrant groups.

In time, the importance of acknowledging the contributions of minorities and ethnic groups to building American cities was recognized, even embraced, by historians, planners, architects and archaeologists. As statewide preservation programs developed in response to the Preservation Act of 1966, efforts to preserve the cultural resources of Hawaiians, Puerto Ricans and Indians became an important part of the American preservation movement.

The Role of the National Park Service in Minority Preservation

The role of the National Park Service in historic preservation includes the ownership and management of several hundred natural and historic parks of national significance and the conduct of a variety of survey and recording efforts. The National Historic Landmarks program recognizes sites of national significance; the National Register program, in cooperation with state and local governments, officially recognizes those of state and local significance as well. By the mid to late-1970s, the National Park Service had responded to the rising tide of interest in ethnic history. The Park Service actively sought opportunities to bring properties of ethnic and minority interest into all of the programs. Much significant work is underway in this field, which is a relatively new area for intensive work.

National Park Service Units

The National Park Service owns and manages a number of the nation's most important historic sites associated with black history. Many of the Civil War battlefield properties that came into the National Park Service system related to the black experience. However, the major message of these sites revolved around battles between Union and Confederate armies in a war fought over the slavery issue. The role of blacks in such sites was a secondary, albeit important, theme.

The first property to enter the National Park Service system specifically for its primary relationship to black history was the George Washington Carver National Monument in Diamond, Missouri, which was added in 1943. The site includes a birthplace cabin site, a statue of Carver as a boy and the Carver family cemetery, all related to the early years of Carver who became the renowned agricultural scientist at Tuskegee Institute. In 1956, the Booker T. Washington National Monument in Hardy, Virginia, was added to the bureau's system to commemorate the achievements of the famous black educator. The Carver and Washington monuments are significant early examples in the recognition of black historic sites.

The first major urban black site to enter the National Park Service system was the Frederick Douglass Home in Washington, D.C., which was acquired in 1962. Since the death of the 19th-century civil rights leader, orator and advisor to President Lincoln, the home was maintained by the Frederick Douglass Memorial and Historical Association, an organization founded by his widow. The acquisition of the site by the National Park Service gave national prominence to the property, provided an infusion of funds toward its restoration and offered the National Park Service a pioneering opportunity to educate the public about black history. The property served as a focal point for the study of the surrounding Anacostia Historic District, listed in the National Register in 1978.

In subsequent years, the National Park Service bestowed its highest designations on and assumed management responsibilities for other black historic sites. In 1974, part of the campus of Tuskegee Institute in Tuskegee, Alabama, was declared a National Historic Site. Founded in 1881, Tuskegee Institute was the nation's first black normal school. Its first principal, Booker T. Washington, was a proponent of teaching trades to black students. Instead of producing future teachers, the school provided training in masonry, blacksmithing and architecture, in addition to academic subjects. As a result, many of the campus buildings were designed and built by faculty and students. The same congressional legislation that created the Tuskegee National Historic Site authorized restoration funds for The Oaks, home of Booker T. Washington; the George Washington Carver Museum; a Historic Campus District; and Grey Columns, a large antebellum house on the campus. Because of the national recognition given to the site and the major investment of federal government funds in the project, an architecture professor at Tuskegee characterized the effort as "a giant step toward bringing black contributions into the mainstream of the nation's preservation movement."

Other black historic sites embraced by the National Park Service system include the Martin Luther King, Jr., National Historic Site in Atlanta, Georgia, managed jointly with the Martin Luther King, Jr., Center for Non-violent Change; the Maggie Walker Home in Richmond, Virginia; Storer College at Harpers Ferry, West Virginia; and portions of forts that housed black soldiers in the post-Civil War frontier in the Midwest and the West. Other sites are maintained by the National Park Service on an affiliated basis, where an independent private organization manages the daily activities. They include the Boston African-American National Historic Site in Boston, Massachusetts, and the Bethune Museum-Archives National Historic Site in Washington, D.C.

In 1972, the National Park Service funded a survey of black historic sites carried out under auspices of the Afro-American Bicentennial Corporation. The purpose of the survey was to increase the number of National Historic Landmarks directly related to black history beyond the handful identified up to that time. Out of this and subsequent projects, important black historic sites were added to the list of designated National Historic Landmarks. These included Dexter Avenue Baptist Church in Montgomery, Alabama, center of Martin Luther King, Jr.'s civil rights activities from 1954 to 1959; Mother Bethel AME Church in Philadelphia, Pennsylvania, the first in the line of African Methodist Episcopal churches in the country; and the Battle of Rhode Island site in Portsmouth, Rhode Island, where the all-black First Rhode Island Regiment participated in the Revolutionary War. Today, approximately 85 properties significant in black history have been designated National Historic Landmarks. This list includes residences associated with or built by black Americans, schools, commercial areas, neighborhoods and communities populated by blacks.

American colonial history, including English, Spanish, French, Dutch, Swedish and Russian contributions, were surveyed early in the history of the National Historic Landmark program. Later immigration was not examined at the same level of intensity. In order to increase the recognition of other unrepresented nationalities and minority groups, the National Park Service contracted in 1979 with the American Association for State and Local History to prepare studies of several dozen ethnic communities that could be used as the basis for National Historic Landmark nominations. These embraced a diverse and rich collection of historic resources, including Chinatowns, Swedish and German settlements in the Midwest and the Irish community of Boston. For administrative reasons, these studies were not processed. The National Park Service is now, however, turning its attention to these studies which will serve as the building blocks of a broader and more representative ethnic heritage list.

As part of the War in the Pacific thematic study, the National Park Service conducted a study of Japanese-American internment camps. In 1985, the bureau designated the Manzanar War Relocation Center in Lone Pine, California, as a National Historic Landmark. Of the 10 internment camps, Manzanar was the first to be built. It educational value for future generations was greater than the other 9 camps because it was located close to the large population center of Los Angeles. This assessment was confirmed by annual pilgrimages to the site made by former internees, their descendants and other interested persons since 1969 to recall the sacrifice of the Japanese-Americans. At the dedication, National Park Service officials spoke of the importance of acknowledging the racial prejudice, mistrust and fear that resulted in the creation of the internment camps. They said recognition of the site would serve as a reminder that a "democratic nation must constantly guard and honor the concept of freedom and the rights of its citizens."

Historic American Buildings Survey

In 1979, the Historic American Buildings Survey (HABS) sponsored a study of Washington, D.C., buildings, designed by black architects. Six buildings important for their role in the black community were selected for documentation according to HABS standards, as were examples of the best work of black architects. The buildings surveyed include Founders' Library at Howard University, designed by Albert I. Cassell, and the Anthony Bowen YMCA, designed by W. Sidney Pittman. The inclusion of architectural resources by black architects in a permanent research record inspired the search for buildings, elsewhere in the nation, created by black and minority design professionals.

Another model ethnic heritage project carried out according to HABS standards was the study of the site of Nicodemus, Kansas. Known as the oldest and best-known black town in the Midwest, Nicodemus was settled during Reconstruction in the 1870s by a group of black emigrants from the upper southern states. The settlement of Nicodemus was an episode in a massive immigration of blacks out of the South in search of greater opportunities. When the town was bypassed by the railroad in the 1880s, it withered and by the mid-20th century only a small group of buildings remained. In 1976, Nicodemus was designated a National Historic Landmark. Unfortunately, the designation did not affect the rate of deterioration and, by the early 1980s, the National Park Service began to plan for the permanent recording of the endangered site. During 1985–86, the town was documented according to HABS standards. The resulting publication, *Promised Land on the Solomon: Black Settlement at Nicodemus, Kansas,* is an important contribution to the literature of the black experience in the United States. The publication also serves as a model in documenting a historic ethnic settlement that may well evolve into an archaeological site.

National Register Program

Over the two decades since the establishment of the expanded listing program in 1966, 47,000 entries were placed in the National Register. These entries include single buildings, historical and archaeological districts, structures and sites. Of this total, 1,260 entries were listed for their significance to an ethnic or minority group. The small number of entries reflects the relatively low level of effort in this area as well as the difficulty in relating buildings and places to an identifiable ethnic or minority group.

In order to encourage a greater effort in this area, several state historic preservation offices have, in recent years, developed technical information on how to identify and conduct research on the subject. The publication, *Historic Black Resources: A Handbook for the Identification, Documentation, and Evaluation of Historic African-American Properties in Georgia,* produced by the Georgia state historic preservation office, is one example. Other states sponsored survey projects that address ethnic history, which can serve as models for future projects under state sponsorship or by localities and individuals.

The development of new preservation planning models for the National Register program may also spur a wider interest in finding and evaluating the large number and variety of environments created by immigrant groups. As the most recent guide to completing National Register nominations states, the

*Japanese influence on architecture
in the Pacific region is evidenced in
this church in Honolulu, Hawaii.*
(National Trust for Historic
Preservation)

*The Annala Round Barn and
Milkhouse in Iron County,
Wisconsin, are representative of the
agricultural structures built by
Finnish settlers in the Upper
Midwest region of the country in
the early-20th century.* (State
Historical Society of Wisconsin)

With its congregation in the foreground, the Ukranian church in Gorham, North Dakota, reflects the adaptation of Old World forms to a New World setting. (The Ukranian Museum collection, courtesy of The Ukranian Cultural Institute, N.D.)

Designed by German-born architect Adolph Cluss, the 1872 Sumner School was the first substantial school building constructed in Washington, D.C., for black students. (Sumner School Archives)

focus of the program has shifted to localities. "Here the most difficult decisions about significance are encountered . . . critical analyses and interpretations, from a historian, archaeologist, or anthropologist's point of view, of the pivotal, outstanding, representative, commonplace or unique events and resources in the locality's history and development are more difficult to formulate."

The development of historic contexts, the first step in the Resource Protection Planning Process (RP3) for properties, is essential to the understanding of "vernacular resources, isolated local events or persons, properties of recent age, commonplace and ubiquitous resources, and resources of questionable integrity." This historic context consists of three elements: theme, place and time, such as the Norwegian Settlement in Bosque County, Texas, 1860 to 1885. As a method for organizing information and as a means of enhancing the opportunities for the study of ethnic history, the new preservation planning system also holds the potential for adapting survey work to the research methods of cultural geographers, folklorists, landscape architects and others.

New Ways to Teach History

An inevitable effect of the recasting of history and historic preservation was in the teaching of history, particularly at the elementary and secondary levels. Where at one time, teaching state or local history consisted of instruction in governmental systems, today history lessons encompass family and neighborhood history, histories of ethnic and minority groups that make up a community and the linkages between these local topics to the larger city, region, state and nation. Groups of students now conduct surveys of historic buildings in order to read their date, style and building materials; study old newspapers to discern how much their community has changed; interview their grandparents and elderly neighbors to gather information on everyday life in the past and inspect historic maps of areas familiar to them to determine how their community developed. Preservationists view the teaching of local history in this way as an investment in the preservation constituency of the future.

In less formal settings, students learn about the foods, holidays and customs of their fellow students. In urban public school systems that serve minorities and recent immigrants, it is common for each classroom to include students whose primary language is not English and whose knowledge about ethnic lifestyles is firsthand. On public education television, ethnic groups are portrayed in a more realistic light, rather than as comic stereotypes, enhancing the public's appreciation of the mosaic of customs and outlook on its doorstep.

At college and graduate levels, the teaching of history was revolutionized by the proliferation of majors and degree programs in Afro-American history, historic preservation, public history and applied history as well as specializations in American studies and history departments that emphasize American material culture, oral history, historical archaeology and urban history. These new academic programs developed first in the late 1960s and responded to student interest in alternatives to traditional history. The growth of historic preservation, archival and museum fields also spurred the establishment of these new academic offerings.

The new ways of teaching history at all levels of the formal education system necessitated new textbooks and teaching materials. Academic and nonacademic historians, cultural geographers and folklorists produced many books on Afro-American history, the history of ethnic groups and urban history. In the area of methodology, the American Association for State and Local history led the way with its journal, newsletters and technical leaflets series. In the 1980s, the Association published several standard texts on the subject, including *Nearby History: Exploring the Past Around You* (1982), *Using Local History in the Classroom* (1983) and *Ordinary People and Everyday Life* (1983). New professional associations sprang up to represent the interests of non-traditional history and provided their own publications that address subject matter and methodology. In school districts around the country, curriculum guides were written to direct history classes in the area of local, ethnic and minority history. Teachers pursued continuing education classes in the use of the new materials. These educational efforts promise to yield a larger and more supportive preservation community a generation from now, a flowering of published ethnic and minority historical studies, and an increase in preserved buildings and sites across the nation.

Preservation of the Intangible Cultural Heritage

While the study, protection and interpretation of minority historic sites gave national visibility to the contributions of minority groups to the development of the country, it was the book *Roots* written in 1976 by Alex Haley and subsequent television series that captured the imagination of the general public. The appeal of this story of one black man's family through five generations rested on the ability of viewers, both black and white, to identify some part of their own family history through the book. *Roots* was grounded in the author's meticulous research effort through sources already well-known to genealogists and on oral histories. The *Roots* phenomenon demonstrated the wide appeal of the family life of the common man. It perhaps did more to inspire black pride and identity than any single preservation project.

The popular success of *Roots*, the importance of the Bicentennial celebration in advancing the cause of local history, the role of the *Foxfire* books in encouraging student recordings of folklife and folkways and the enlightening force of public education television in portraying ethnic groups in America promoted a national review of the status of cultural conservation in the United States. In the 1980 Amendments of the Preservation Act of 1966, the Secretary of the Interior and the American Folklife Center of the Library of Congress were directed to report on the preservation and conservation of the intangible elements of our cultural heritage, such as arts, skills, folklife and folkways. The study team and its consultants reviewed the current system of laws, programs and organizations that related to the study, protection and encouragement of the nation's heritage, including the historic preservation programs. The group also noted that many other countries recognized the importance of intangible properties. However, in the United States, it was often the case that while a historic property was protected, the cultural context from which it took its significance was not.

The resulting report, *Cultural Conservation: The Protection of the Cultural Heritage of the United States,* published in 1983, reviewed the independent efforts at cultural conservation on the federal, state and local levels to illustrate the broad range of activities already underway. In order to strengthen the support system for cultural conservation, the report recommended a closer tie between state historic preservation offices and state folklife offices. It also recommended the development of a standing memorandum of agreement between the National Park Service and the American Folklife Center "to delineate and coordinate their efforts in cultural conservation." The report outlined ways in which many existing organizations at all levels could expand their roles in cultural conservation.

The response to the *Cultural Conservation* report reflected the genuine desire of established preservation agencies and organizations to apply their programs to the designation of people and intangible resources. Questions arose over the relative significance of intangible resources, the effects of designation on the conduct of the lifeway and the possibility that the resource would change over time in unpredictable ways. A coordinating effort was recommended in order to draw together federal and private programs to implement the report's recommendations, an effort thought to hold the potential for improving the conduct of environmental planning overall.

Institutionalization of Minority Heritage Concerns

While established agencies and organizations were expanding their efforts over the past 20 years to reflect more fully the varied cultural sources and nature of American life, many participants in these efforts thought that the cause could be advanced by the creation of new organizations, the sole purpose of which would be ethnic and minority history. At the local level, the Society for the Preservation of Weeksville and Bedford-Stuyvesant History, and the Afro-American Bicentennial Corporation were only two of the new organizations to emerge from this period. Afro-American historical museums, study centers and institutes were formed in many American cities, many of which are represented in the membership of the African American Museums Association. Other organizations such as the Beach Institute Historic Neighborhood Association in Savannah, Georgia, took up the cause of protecting the city's black commercial and residential areas through brokering leases, purchase of real estate and limited partnerships.

For four consecutive years between 1979 and 1982, the Conference on Historic Preservation and the Minority Community met in major American cities. Topics for discussion included the preservation of black churches, economic development, housing strategies, rehabilitation techniques, oral history and grantsmanship. Although many of the subjects were covered in the annual meetings of other preservation organizations, such as the National Trust for Historic Preservation, the discussion was focused around minority and ethnic historic resources within the universe of minority neighborhoods and professionals. Although this conference has not been held since 1982, its record serves as a document of the status of minority preservation issues at that time.

The Displacement Dilemma

The great mobility of the population and the resultant quick turnover of neighborhood populations is part of American urban life. In the past, the frontiers of the country always seemed infinite. Americans were quick to conquer new ground and set down new roots every few years. Climbing the economic ladder also encouraged Americans to seek out new housing commensurate with their new status.

The mobility of the urban population consigned those occupying the lower rungs of the economic ladder to the least desirable housing choices. In the mid-20th century, the older, historic sections of cities were considered undesirable by the middle classes, who moved to the suburbs. In recent years, other factors made the inner city attractive again: a desire to live close to the city's cultural attractions, the availability of lower-cost starter housing and the lingering effects of the energy crisis.

Displacement of the poor and elderly as a result of this new interest in the inner city was quickly perceived as a threat by residents, by many preservationists and by others. The threat was not seen as one based on urban dynamics but on historic preservation itself. Well-publicized examples of residential turnover from low-income minority to affluent majority were seen in the Georgetown and Capitol Hill areas of Washington, D.C.; Alexandria, Virginia; in various sections of New York City's Manhattan and Brooklyn; and the Church Hill district of Richmond, Virginia. Displacement and gentrification became rallying cries for residents of older neighborhoods.

Despite the conviction held by some that historic designation and preservation cause displacement, many examples can also be cited of preservation efforts that resulted in little or no displacement. For example, community leaders in the Le Droit Park neighborhood in Washington, D.C., sought to have their neighborhood designated as a historic district in 1977 in order to fight the expansion of nearby Howard University. While the university's expansion was held at bay, little new investment occurred to bring back deteriorated and abandoned housing within the historic district. On the other side of the coin, displacement and gentrification of the older housing stock occurred in some areas, even in the absence of historic district designations. Thus, displacement must be viewed more as a result of a complex array of urban forces than a single phenomenon, such as historic preservation.

Although it can be shown that preservation efforts alone are not likely to cause displacement, low-income and minority residents of older neighborhoods perceive that one action is a function of the other. When this perception is widespread, residents organize to oppose historic preservation. Ironically, this is a situation that places preservationists in the same position as the urban renewal proponents of the 1950s. This situation is one that is exploited by real estate interests and politicians who chafe at landmark and historic district restrictions. Valid or not, the mere perception of preservation as a cause of displacement is one that must be faced by both preservationists and neighborhood residents.

The merging of historic preservation and neighborhood concerns in recent years has resulted in programs of neighborhood conservation or urban conservation. This new approach requires that preservationists become as concerned about protecting rights of residents to be secure in their neighborhoods as they are about saving old buildings. Neighborhood conservation also implies that other needs, such as housing, schools, public works, protective services, and neighborhood appearance and character, must also become preservation priorities.

One of the pioneering efforts in neighborhood conservation dates from the late 1960s in the Mexican War Streets and Manchester neighborhoods of Pittsburgh, Pennsylvania. Here preservationists, in cooperation with a consortium of financial institutions and the city government, created a low-interest loan pool available to homeowners to rehabilitate their houses. This cooperative effort was required to overcome the practice of redlining by which banks and other financial institutions refuse to make loans in low-income neighborhoods, even if the potential borrower meets conventional loan standards.

The Pittsburgh approach to rehabilitation was such a success that it attracted the attention of the Federal Home Loan Bank Board. With the assistance of the Ford Foundation, prototypes of the Pittsburgh program spread throughout the nation in the form of Neighborhood Housing Service (NHS) organizations. The Neighborhood Housing Service programs offer rehabilitation counseling, analysis of home repair needs and rehabilitation monitoring services. They also administer special revolving funds for residents who do not meet normal credit standards. For their part, city governments provide a higher level of municipal services and enforced building codes in target neighborhoods. Today, more than 250 Neighborhood Housing Service programs operate in 135 cities across the country and have made substantial and lasting contributions to the sensitive rehabilitation of older building and the stability of neighborhoods.

Yet another approach to preserving both historic buildings and neighborhood values is represented in the Savannah Landmark Rehabilitation Project in Georgia. Created to preserve the city's Victorian District, Savannah Landmark made effective and coordinated use of a number of publicly supported grant and loan programs and private foundation grants to rehabilitate and restore buildings. The coordinated use of public and private subsidies together permitted rent levels to be held at affordable levels for the resident population, thus preventing wholesale displacement. In the early 1980s, Savannah Landmark used both the federal preservation tax credits and Department of Housing and Urban Development block grants to undertake additional building purchases and rehabilitations in the Victorian District. Throughout the process, the city's housing programs assisted with rental subsidies, public works improvements and the installation or improvement of public spaces and walkways. Although Savannah Landmark was not able to prevent displacement completely, it made a significant contribution to solving the problem.

The Savannah Landmark project demonstrated that a creative use of both public and private programs could successfully result in simultaneously promoting historic preservation and neighborhood protection. Publicity accorded the project spread its lessons to all urban centers of the United States and to locations abroad. Requests for guidance in initiating similar projects elsewhere resulted in the preparation of the report, *Preservation for People in Savannah,* which recounts the history of the project and provides advice on property acquisition, financing, rehabilitation and management. The report concluded that while the preservation of the Victorian District was an important goal, the organization's primary goal was to "continue to provide decent housing for the poor."

Other ventures into historic preservation and neighborhood conservation included the creation of the Parkside Development Company in Philadelphia by a young black entrepreneur who used landmark designation to "raise capital through facade easements, tax incentives and accelerated write-offs." Led by a Marist nun, the Greenlaw neighborhood in Memphis, Tennessee, was designated as a historic district. Its housing was upgraded for neighborhood residents through a sweat equity program in which the residents themselves undertook some of the actual rehabilitation work. They were assisted by the Department of Housing and Urban Development grants and loans, Comprehensive Employment Training Act grants and other public subsidies. In Rhode Island, the Providence Preservation Society created a low-interest revolving loan fund for rehabilitation and resold properties at cost to property owners in the Armory District. These and the many other projects that have sprung up across the country give heart to preservationists who want to share the benefits of historic preservation with all segments of society.

National Trust Financial Assistance Programs

To address displacement problems in historic neighborhoods and to involve more minority groups in historic preservation, the National Trust for Historic Preservation created the Inner-City Ventures Fund in 1981. Initial seed money for the Fund came from the National Park Service and the National Trust. Today, corporations and foundations support the $2.5 million fund, which provides grant and low-interest loans for a period of five years to community organizations undertaking rehabilitation projects in historic districts associated with low or moderate-income residents. The National Trust gives priority to projects administered by or directed at large minority populations. In most cases, the fund grants and loans constitute a portion of a larger financial package that includes municipal and state grants and loans, bank loans, syndication investors, Community Development Block grants, private foundation grants and loans and seller loans.

With support of the Inner-City Ventures Fund, the Chinese Community Housing Corporation in San Francisco rehabilitated a residential hotel in the Chinatown Historic District occupied by single, elderly Orientals. In the Bronx section of New York City, the Longwood Historic District Community Association acquired, rehabilitated and sold brownstone row houses as moderate-income housing units in a predominantly Hispanic and black neighborhood. The American Indian Center of Omaha, Inc., in Nebraska rehabilitated several older apartment houses for occupancy by Indians and other minority groups. In the Over-the-Rhine Historic District of Cincinnati, Ohio, the Owning the Realty organization rehabilitated low and moderate-income apartment units for the residents of the black neighborhood.

Another National Trust financial assistance program, the Critical Issues Fund, was not established specifically to address minority preservation concerns. However, since its inauguration in 1980, the fund has supported several research and model projects of national interest that relate to minority concerns. For example, a grant was awarded to 1,000 Friends of Kauai, Hawaii, to

A familiar sight in many American cities, Chinese laundries reflected the limited employment opportunities for Asian-American immigrants. This Chinese laundry stood on the site of the present Social Security Building in Washington, D.C. (National Archives)

The unidentified Lady of Weeksville, derived from a late-19th century tintype uncovered in a 1968–69 archaeological excavation, became the symbol of the Weeksville preservation project in Brooklyn, New York. (Society for the Preservation of Weeksville & Bedford-Stuyvesant History)

The Pleasant Hill Historic District in Macon, Georgia, is an example of a traditionally black neighborhood placed on the National Register of Historic Places in recognition of its special architectural character and place in local history. (James E. Lockhart, Georgia Department of Natural Resources)

Neighborhood leaders transformed the Mt. Auburn neighborhood of Cincinnati, Ohio, into a model historic preservation project and one that addressed housing, education and social services. (Carleton Knight III, National Trust for Historic Preservation)

The Savannah Landmark Rehabilitation Project, Georgia, tapped public and private funding sources for the rehabilitation of houses in the Victorian District while enabling the low-income residents to remain. (Savannah Landmark Rehabilitation Project, Inc.)

develop a cultural resources management plan to keep in productive use the historic taro farms, rice mills and irrigation system that make up the cultural landscape of the island. Preservation of these landscape features is a challenge, given the redevelopment of the Hawaiian Islands to appeal to tourists. In another example, the New Mexico Community Foundation received a $40,000 matching grant to develop preservation plans for eight communities with adobe churches. These churches constitute some of the most significant Hispanic contributions to American architecture.

Beyond 1986: Some Unresolved Issues
Problems in the Identification of Ethnic Historic Sites

American architectural history tends to focus on the substantial buildings designed by architects of recognized stature. Increasingly, small contingents of architectural historians undertake studies of buildings for which there was no architect. These new studies of vernacular architecture are concerned with the shape, form and distribution of buildings over the landscape. Despite the growth of interest in vernacular architecture, architectural historians are still regarded as being riveted to matters of style, the architect, date and a technical analysis of the details of substantial buildings. This is beginning to change.

The influence of ethnic groups in the development of American architecture is less visible than that of established architects who undertook the larger and more expensive projects. The small fraction of American buildings designed by architects influenced much or most of the building stock of the country. Lower-income ethnic groups were rarely in a position to commission or design buildings, and properties associated with ethnic history are thus often without architectural distinction. In other cases, the structures were not substantial enough to have survived the passage of time.

Historians of black and other ethnic historic sites criticized the architectural history and preservation professionals for their unwillingness to designate sites with little pure architectural integrity or with no physical remains whatsoever. They argue that such sites cannot be evaluated on the same basis as sites associated with the dominant culture. In their eyes, historical associations are having to play second fiddle to unreasonable standards of architectural or structural integrity. Historians of vernacular architecture naturally agree with this position, arguing that the rank-and-file architectural historians and preservationists have ignored vernacular buildings and those associated with ethnic groups and therefore do not understand them.

The national historic preservation program as it has evolved during the 20th century emphasized the need for places, tangible remains of history. It was with considerable concern then that the National Park Service added to the National Historic Landmarks the William E. B. DuBois Boyhood Birthsite in Great Barrington, Massachusetts, because it contains no remains associated with the historical figure. Some National Park Service staff members also had misgivings about accepting one of the boundary stones of the District of Columbia as the site to recognize the contributions of black surveyor Benjamin Banneker. Some National Park Service staff members thought that these additions damaged the integrity of the National Historic Landmark program.

Many preservationists are also concerned about designating historic sites based on their association primarily with an ethnic or minority individual. They consider that to link the significance of a site with an individual of a given ethnic background might then be extended to designating sites solely because they are identified with an Anglo-American or with other nationalities identified with the dominant culture. Would a property designed by an architect of English origin therefore be identified as being of importance to Anglo-Americans? Many preservationists are uncomfortable with designating properties on ethnic or cultural grounds because of the perceived disservice to the concept of national homogeneity. Recognizing sites associated with ethnic institutions and communities presents less of a problem because of their significance to an entire group, rather than to a single individual. Such sites may also be treated nationally as a thematic study.

This disagreement between preservation agencies that prize historical and structural integrity on the one hand and historians interested in vernacular and ethnic history on the other, will likely continue for years to come. The difference in these points of view underscores the importance of encouraging scholarly studies of ethnic history and associated sites. The situation also argues strongly for the development of ways in which the preservation field can recognize, document and protect the intangible cultural heritage.

Who Owns the Past?

Inherent in the dilemma over displacement and the paucity of scholarship in ethnic history is the basic question of who should determine the future for the past. The preservation professionals? The descendants of those who created the past? Or the current owners or occupants?

Who can lay claim to the past is a complex question that needs to be carefully analyzed before any steps toward preservation are taken. Conflicts between the claimants to historic resources resulted in a mediation process that recognizes an objective known as cultural equity. This goal was defined initially by archaeologists and anthropologists who advanced the notion that preservationists are duty bound to ensure that the interests of small, isolated, non-English speaking, powerless and otherwise non-mainstream groups are taken into account in any historic preservation effort. Negotiations with Indians and other native groups, for example, have either halted federally sponsored projects or resulted in their redesign in order to take into account views and values of the affected groups. Although negotiating efforts do not always satisfy all the parties, proponents of the process view regard it as "preferable to ignoring those values, more realistic than trying to stop the process altogether, and more likely to have a truly positive outcome than . . . litigation."

Ethnic Participation in the Preservation Profession

The number of ethnic and minority individuals serving on boards of private historic preservation organizations and on advisory commissions of state and local historic preservation agencies increased significantly after 1966. Their presence provided a range of opinion and experiences that contribute to the effectiveness of the programs. They also enhance the ability of the organization or agency to reach a greater cross section of the nation, state, city, town or county. For public commissions, their participation also is a reflection of the presence of ethnic or minority populations in the community.

Although ethnic participants can be found everywhere in the preservation movement, their numbers in the professional league are minuscule. If all employees of preservation agencies and organizations at every level were gathered together in a single location, only a few would be identified as belonging to a minority group. Why is this the case, given the important role of professionals in the preservation movement and the growing awareness of the importance of ethnicity in historic resources and preservation efforts?

The selection of a profession is often a matter of role models. The dominance of European-Americans in the preservation profession can be ascribed to the awareness that relatives or friends were active in the field or that a preservation field existed. Preservation work is also associated with education and affluence. Preservation as a profession usually is considered after an individual reaches that economic status which permits the luxury of engaging in cultural pursuits.

Many minority and recent immigrant groups have been primarily concerned with earning a living. They tend to orient their offspring towards professions for which there is a predictable route to success, such as medicine, business, law or engineering. A lack of facility with the English language is a reason why many recent immigrant groups, particularly from Asian countries, pursue careers in mathematics and science. Fields like art history, architecture and museum work require advanced language skills and are widely viewed as impractical—surefire routes to lifelong economic struggles.

It is no wonder, therefore, that the preservation profession is nearly devoid of minorities and recent immigrants. Preservation organizations, making concerted efforts to provide equal employment opportunities and to increase the number of minority professionals on their staffs, consequently can draw from only a small pool of qualified minority applicants. This lack of professional representation will likely hinder the ability of the preservation community to address ethnic historical sites, to engage in cultural equity negotiations or to touch all segments of American society.

What ought to be done to encourage more ethnic and minority groups to enter the preservation profession? The few who are involved could encourage predominantly black college and universities and other educational institutions to offer training in historic preservation, or at least include it in career counseling. Colleges and universities already offering training in historic preservation might make special efforts to recruit students from ethnic and minority groups. Preservation organizations can develop preservation programs for elementary and secondary schools to make young people aware that the field exists. Minority professionals advancing the cause of ethnic historic sites should also work in the mainstream of historic preservation; it does little to advance the cause if they are viewed primarily as tokens or as a noisy special interest group within the field.

The Evolving American Mosaic

Like the varied complexion of the individuals active in historic preservation today, the historic resources protected for future generations can be read as a book
on the history of immigrant groups in the New World. Where in an earlier period, the history book focused on national leaders associated with the dominant
culture, the history represented in preservation projects today offers many insights into the imprint of many cultural groups on the American landscape.
These projects range from the adaptation of existing buildings in a major city
into an Asian-American enclave to the patterns of farmland development in the
Pennsylvania Dutch country of southeastern Pennsylvania. The earliest settlements or alterations to the landscape contain the essence of local history and define the uniqueness of communities, towns and cities.

      The mosaic created by American immigrant groups is in a state of
constant change as upheavals around the world bring new groups of hopefuls to
the North American continent. The continuous stream of new immigrants promises to have profound effects on the political leadership of the nation as well as
bringing about a redefinition of the dominant culture. Because the evolution of
historic preservation concerns mirrors the changes in American society as a
whole, the rise of the second, third and succeeding generations of ethnic Americans to positions of financial and political leadership will transform the content
of the preservation movement. These groups will redefine what is old, what is
historic and what is significant. Just as cultural groups that populated the nation
in the 18th and 19th centuries, the 20th-century immigrants will also leave their
marks on the American landscape. They, too, will want to protect important
physical reminders of the road they traveled.

CHAPTER SEVEN

HISTORIC PRESERVATION IN THE PRIVATE SECTOR

GREGORY E. ANDREWS

Historic Preservation in the Private Sector

GREGORY E. ANDREWS

Introduction

The period 1966–86 was one of tremendous growth and change in private sector involvement in historic preservation. The number and the breadth of groups concerned with preserving the nation's historic building stock multiplied almost geometrically during this period, causing the preservation community to move from a cause with a small following to a major nationwide concern.

Many factors underlie this dramatic transformation, none more significant than the reinterpretation and expanded meaning of historic preservation. Historic house museums, the traditional focus, are now one of many related aspects of and methods for preserving old buildings. The range of tools grew impressively in number and sophistication, making it increasingly possible for the private sector to implement preservation projects effectively. Federal tax incentives vastly increased the economic feasibility of saving old buildings and drew scores of developers to the process. Professionals, in fields as diverse as structural engineering and the decorative arts, now share related roles and a common goal in this broad endeavor.

All of these remarkable changes also created problems and issues. The historic preservation community, while loosely united around a common ideal and continuing to achieve extraordinary success, occasionally finds itself split and its troops engaged in controversy. Without doubt, the private sector's role in historic preservation will remain substantial, but its impact will likely be more varied and controversial as the preservation community speaks with more and more voices.

Pre-1966: Setting the Stage

The world of historic preservation before 1966 was more narrow than it is today. Its focus was on buildings, sites and artifacts associated with individuals who had a transcendent influence on the nation's early history. With few exceptions, it was generally understood that only nationally important figures from the first

208

quarter of the 19th century or earlier deserved this recognition. Within this sphere, the American Revolution and its legendary players occupied center stage. Buildings with some direct connection to those times and figures were preserved, although typically more as repositories for historical collections than for their own intrinsic qualities, whether historic or architectural. The best-known private historical organizations of the time, such as the Daughters of the American Revolution, the Society of Colonial Dames and the Society for the Preservation of New England Antiquities, owned and operated historic houses or museums of collected buildings.

A multitude of historical groups existed solely to administer as museums, the houses of notable early Americans. The archetype of such an organization is the Mount Vernon Ladies' Association of the Union, which owns George Washington's house in Virginia. Many states and communities also had well-established state and local historical societies whose involvement and interest in old buildings were limited primarily to their use as museums. The National Trust for Historic Preservation and a few other organizations, including Historic Annapolis, Inc., in Maryland, and the San Antonio Conservation Society, in Texas, began to expand their programs in order to emphasize the importance of preserving buildings of varied architectural styles and types. Efforts of this sort, however, were the exception and not the rule. Not surprisingly, the community of people connected in some way to these historic preservation activities was small. Museum administrators and interested volunteers, typically drawn from families of the establishment, composed the bulk of active participants; their interests and backgrounds gave historic preservation an elitist image.

Efforts to restore or rehabilitate historic structures were relatively scarce prior to 1966. Most restorations were undertaken by historical groups needing space to display their collections. The relatively small balance was done by devotees of early America who acquired deteriorated 18th-century central-chimney houses and restored them for their own residences. Restorations for any other purpose, including adaptive use, were almost unknown.

Negative, or at best neutral, public perceptions about the merits of old buildings in general had a direct impact on public policies and laws, which offered little support for their preservation. Real estate tax statutes encouraged the preservation of only those old buildings owned by nonprofit historic and patriotic organizations by exempting them from local property tax. In many other respects, the tax laws discriminated against old buildings. Tax deductions were available for the expenses incurred in their demolition; tax depreciation rules were more beneficial for new structures than for existing ones. The now widely used device known as a historic preservation easement was of doubtful legality under the laws of many states and its favorable tax implications were also still somewhat unclear. Public funding, other than to maintain publicly owned historic buildings and sites, was nonexistent.

1966–1976: Laying the Groundwork

The events that occurred from 1966 to 1976 are the most important in the entire story of private historic preservation initiatives in America. The most crucial was the broadened meaning that historic preservation acquired, making it possible for the cause to arouse support from a much larger segment of the population than ever before. Historic preservation became popular to an extent previously unimaginable as Americans discovered their trove of architecturally significant buildings of many different styles and began to fight to preserve them. Spurring on their efforts were new or evolving tools, such as the National Register of Historic Places and preservation easements. Private preservation groups, primarily at the national and local levels, were largely responsible for and beneficiaries of these changes. The decade witnessed the emergence of the National Trust for Historic Preservation and Preservation Action as the leading national organizations, while local groups in virtually every state became a vital grassroots force.

This new concept of historic preservation had two major aspects. First, it accepted that buildings and sites ranging widely in age, design and use are historically or architecturally significant and deserve appreciation and preservation. Furthermore, their significance can be national, state or local in nature. This new idea had wide implications. A late 19th-century warehouse conceivably could be more important than a 17th-century structure. Buildings from many different periods and backgrounds became worthy of scholarly attention and understanding. Second, the idea emerged that a significant structure could and should be preserved and utilized for its original purpose. If this is not possible, another use compatible with its design and layout should be found, rather than saving the structure only for museum purposes. This second concept, even more than the first, had far-reaching implications resulting in the integration of old buildings into modern American life.

The small community of long-time historic preservation advocates can claim much of the credit for this change, although events considerably abetted their efforts. The questioning of conventional wisdom by a younger generation during the 1960s and early 1970s brought a tide of new supporters. The environmental ethic was a major new force that emerged from this thinking. A natural component of its aesthetic concerns was a heightened awareness of the built environment. The awful cost of urban renewal became clear. The result was the destruction of many American downtowns and the massive and wrenching dislocations of urban poor and ethnic communities. The public found it increasingly difficult to relate to the size, scale and design of newly constructed buildings. In retrospect, the smaller, more human scale and often elaborate architectural detailing of the demolished older structures had been appealing. With the coming of the Bicentennial celebration, a new-found nostalgia for the past reinforced these feelings.

Economics also played a part. The recession and skyrocketing inflation of the 1970s affected real estate decisions of business and individuals alike. The climbing cost of new construction made rehabilitation of often undervalued, old buildings, either for office or home, a financially competitive proposition. For example, once elegant rowhouses in deteriorating urban neighborhoods could be bought for a fraction of the price of houses in desirable areas. Latter-day urban pioneers repaired these structures, displaying their beauty and suitability for new tenants. Rehabilitation gained momentum, particularly among young professionals who were priced out of housing elsewhere or rejected a suburban life which they perceived as sterile.

Historic preservation advocates, like their brothers and sisters in the environmental movement, became activists with a missionary zeal. Agitation over the demolition of well-known national landmarks, such as Pennsylvania Station in New York City, triggered similar responses to a variety of buildings that had been lost elsewhere. These losses fortunately gave rise to many private historic preservation groups, such as the Hartford Architecture Conservancy in Connecticut, that are now well-established. The losses prompted people to question the accepted notion that demolition is progress.

The breadth of programs and tools developed during this period contributed greatly to the preservation initiatives of the private sector. Both public and private mechanisms became part of the foundation of the nationwide preservation program. They included the National Register of Historic Places and were the first steps in an evolutionary process of programmatic expansion and sophistication that continues today. By providing the impetus for greater visibility, more effective activism and organizational development, they stimulated a wave of public appreciation and support.

The Effects of Federal Government Programs

The National Historic Preservation Act of 1966, the groundbreaking legislation that created the federal and state-level public preservation program, had a powerful and positive effect on private efforts, particularly at the local level. Perhaps more than any other event prior to 1976, this statute equipped preservation advocates in the private sector with mechanisms to achieve their goals. Its provisions became the stimulus for the creation of innumerable preservation groups and the transformation of many others. It created, for example, the National Register program and authorized the historic and architectural resources surveys that have become a basic method for local preservation groups to document their important buildings and give them public recognition. The new Historic Preservation Fund offered organizations financial assistance to restore endangered historic buildings. Many local organizations were formed in order to conduct municipal architectural surveys, to initiate nominations of properties to the National Register or to purchase and save deteriorating buildings. These activities remain key programmatic elements for virtually all organizations around the country, whether large or small.

The Preservation Act of 1966, provisions in the National Environmental Policy Act of 1969 and other federal laws armed preservationists with perhaps their most potent weapon: legal recourse to delay or halt proposed actions that might be harmful to significant structures and areas. For the first time, grounds existed to argue in court against threats to buildings that were not protected by local landmark ordinances. The impact of these laws was enormous. Private preservation groups fought countless legal battles using the federal statutes and saved many buildings or at least delayed and perhaps mitigated the effect of their loss. The resulting publicity also greatly expanded public awareness. Time and again, private preservation groups are the standard bearers for the entire preservation movement, ensuring that the intent of these laws is carried out.

A number of new federal programs during this period designed to pump money into depressed and deteriorating urban areas also played a role in furthering early private preservation efforts. Preservation groups, working in tandem with municipal agencies, soon found it possible to use these programs to accomplish the twin goals of urban revitalization and historic preservation. Starting in 1966, with the Model Cities program under the Department of Housing and Urban Development (HUD), federal funds were used, typically, in conjunction with matching private money, to prepare feasibility studies for rehabilitating run-down, inner-city buildings for residential use. Subsidized housing programs of the U.S. Department of Housing and Urban Development (HUD) were also used to rehabilitate historic buildings, often to support public and private partnerships either directly or indirectly involving preservation groups.

The HUD Community Development Block Grants initiative in 1974 was one of the early federal housing assistance programs to include specifically historic preservation as a stated policy objective. As a result, preservation groups found it possible to tap these funds for a greater number and variety of preservation projects than ever before. Block grants became a principal funding source nationwide for architectural and historical survey programs. HUD's Urban Development Action Grants were also useful in urban public and private development projects typically involving specific historic buildings or larger projects in which they were a component. These HUD programs were used for preservation efforts, as well as in development projects that destroyed historic buildings. In many cases, the role of the private preservation group was a central one. In the early years of these programs, preservationists fought to bring endangered buildings and historic urban areas to the attention of government officials for funding consideration. As attitudes toward historic preservation changed and urban revitalization became a policy goal, preservation organizations gained public respect and played a larger and more direct role. Today they often take the lead in urban revitalization efforts by packaging a project. This involves bringing together municipal officials, developers and funds from public and private sources in a partnership to accomplish a specific preservation or revitalization project. Without the involvement of preservation organizations at this stage, many projects would never get started.

Preservation Easements

Nonstatutory and nongovernmental methods and techniques to achieve preservation ends evolved and gained considerable momentum during the period 1966–76. The first to emerge was the historic preservation easement. Easements traditionally constituted "the right in the owner of one parcel of land . . . to use the land of another for a special purpose not inconsistent" with the rights of the other owner. Historically, easements existed for a variety of purposes, including such mundane reasons as to give a landlocked parcel a means of access to a public road. One of the recognized features of easements was that the privileges always benefited the adjoining property to the one burdened by obligations, hence they were described traditionally as easements appurtenant. Another feature was that easements could run for many years, binding successive owners.

Preservation easements were developed as a way to protect the important architectural and scenic aspects of a property having architectural or historic significance. As with many historic preservation initiatives, easements grew out of parallel efforts of other private groups for preserving the natural environment. The successful use of easements by environmental groups to restrict the alteration of important natural areas, such as a wildlife refuge, aroused the interest of preservationists because of their similarity in purpose and regulation. Preservation easements offered an effective means for a preservation organization to accomplish its goals in a lasting and nonconfrontational way.

During the 1960s, organizations such as the National Trust for Historic Preservation and Historic Annapolis, Inc., began to negotiate with owners of historic properties, particularly those faced with some threat, for the donation or purchase of historic preservation easements. By the mid-1970s, these organizations had acquired easements covering, respectively, large portions of the Georgetown area in Washington, D.C., and of the center of Annapolis, Maryland, both of which have important concentrations of 18th and early 19th-century structures. Several of the best-known plantations of the Virginia tidewater near Williamsburg, including Westover, also became subject to preservation easements at a relatively early date by donations to the Virginia Conservation Foundation.

Under the organization's terms, the owners of the burdened historic properties typically agreed to obtain the approval of the benefited preservation organizations prior to making any changes to exterior architectural features of significant buildings on their land or to the land itself. These agreements, therefore, controlled any alterations, modifications, erections or demolitions to the property or its improvements. Unlike public regulations, easements could also be placed inside the property to save valuable interiors and could be specifically tailored to the special features of each property. The easement document also usually stated that it would remain in effect indefinitely unless revoked by the preservation organization. In effect, easements are similar in many respects to the restrictions that accompany designation as a local historic landmark. The main difference is that an easement is a private agreement between two parties, while landmark designation is a public act granting rights to the municipality. In addition, public regulations usually do not address interiors or result in specific guidelines for each designated property.

The attraction of preservation easements to owners of significant properties was twofold: aesthetic and financial. Both they and the grantee preservation group were assured of the preservation of an important building and its grounds. This benefit carried great weight with those families who had owned a property for several generations and did not trust the permanence of regulatory schemes. There were also monetary benefits. While the purchase price of an easement was generally a matter of negotiation, its logical starting point was the cost to the owner of imposing this set of restrictions on future use and disposition of the property. In the case of either a large urban house or estate, the cost might be great. A donation by the owner might also carry a tax advantage because changes to the federal tax code made in 1969 gave donors grounds for claiming a tax deduction for the full value of the easement. A comparison of the value of the burdened property before and after the imposition of the easement, as required by federal tax regulations, again offered the potential of a high value for the gift of an easement to a preservation agency or organization.

Doubt about the validity of easements in common law was an obstacle that prevented them from being used more widely during this period. Many preservation organizations, therefore, either shied away from their use or were unaware of their availability because they did not receive widespread publicity. In virtually all cases, the crux of the problem was that the benefited preservation group was not the owner of the property adjacent to the encumbered property. The easement consequently did not qualify as a traditional easement appurtenant, which could be enforced, but rather as an easement in gross, which could not be enforced. Historically, this form of easement was considered personal and did not survive the original parties to the agreement, thus defeating the intent that the easement be indefinite in duration. A movement began, both in legislatures and in courts, to improve this uncertain state of affairs. States began to enact laws specifically recognizing the validity of easements in gross and, in particular, conservation easements for either natural or historic preservation purposes. The U.S. Tax Court began to issue decisions upholding their deductibility for tax purposes. As this occurred, preservation organizations set up easement acquisition programs.

Revolving Fund Programs

Revolving funds are another important innovative mechanism that developed during this period, although in 1976 they were still in their infancy and utilized by relatively few private sector organizations. The publication, *Revolving Funds for Historic Preservation: A Manual of Practice,* is generally credited with introducing this concept to the preservation audience. The appeal of revolving funds to preservation groups lay in their potential for achieving a tremendous bang for the buck. The limited resources of virtually every preservation organization in the nation made this proposition extremely attractive. A revolving fund is a pool of money that is used to acquire endangered historic buildings, either through direct purchases or by means of loans to other parties and often requires the use of creative financing. Typically the investment is short-term, lasting only as long as is necessary to stabilize a structure and ensure its preservation through, for example, the imposition of a preservation easement and resale. In the case of a loan, it would be written to mature upon sale or within a specified short time. The reclaimed funds then return to the fund and revolve, in other words used again to buy another property. The major goals of the revolving fund technique are to preserve buildings and to improve entire neighborhoods. By investing in individual buildings in key locations, snowballing of rehabilitation and restoration commences and then affects an entire area.

The National Trust's National Historic Preservation Fund and the revolving funds established by a few other leading preservation organizations, among them the Historic Charleston Foundation, Inc., in South Carolina; Historic Savannah, Inc., in Georgia; and the Pittsburgh History and Landmarks Foundation, in Pennsylvania, pioneered this technique. The National Historic Preservation Fund offers financial assistance to National Trust member organizations to assist in setting up their own revolving funds. Early recipients included Historic Harrisville, Inc., a New Hampshire organization that revitalized an early 19th-century mill village, and the Lafayette Square Restoration Foundation, St. Louis, Missouri, which rehabilitated 19th-century rowhouses in that historic neighborhood.

The Historic Charleston Foundation launched its revolving fund in 1957. This is ancient history in the context of most preservation developments but was the first of its kind. The initial $100,000 principal paid for the acquisition of more than 50 buildings in the deteriorating Ansonborough residential neighborhood. With the exception of a few facade or interior restorations, Historic

Charleston resold these unrestored structures with deed covenants or easements requiring the new owners to restore the exteriors, sometimes according to specific standards, and to maintain them for 75 years. The foundation's efforts in this neighborhood led to the private restoration of another 50 residences by 1973.

Historic Savannah's revolving fund grew out of the initiative of individual members who were buying endangered properties and then revolving their investments into other structures. After documenting the economic benefits of tourism that would result from restoring the city's huge stock of old buildings and completing an inventory of the two-and-one-half square mile downtown, Historic Savannah raised $200,000 for its fund. This money allowed the organization to buy 54 buildings in the Pulaski Square-West Jones Street redevelopment area, following which Historic Savannah spent $1.5 million on their restoration prior to resale. Of great importance to their early efforts was a revolving line of credit with local banks which made it possible to act quickly, when necessary. Historic Savannah also became adept at arranging creative financing terms for its purchasers including extended-term purchase money mortgages.

The goal of the Pittsburgh Restoration Fund from its creation in 1966 was to revitalize urban, often low-income, neighborhoods of historic or architectural distinction, without removing the inhabitants. Its success made it a national model for enlightened and sensitive intervention. Grants from local foundations provided it with $200,000 initially, which grew to $500,000 by 1973. Its strategy was to purchase a key building of particular historic or architectural importance, restore it and have it serve as a magnet to attract reinvestment in adjacent buildings. The fund had restored both residential and commercial structures in the Mexican War streets and Manchester neighborhoods within five years of its inception. The investment of $350,000 had generated an additional $1,830,000 in private reinvestment. While the fund lost money and has not recovered its full investment, it achieved significant gains in historic preservation and urban beautification.

Transferable Development Rights

Transferable development rights (TDRs) are another real estate technique of value to historic preservation that came to the fore between 1966–76. Introduced to the general public in "The Chicago Plan: Incentive Zoning and the Preservation of Urban Landmarks," a 1972 *Harvard Law Review* article, the concept suggested that unused development rights of a parcel containing a historic building could be transferred to another site. Following the transfer, the landmark parcel would be barred from future intensive use, thereby protecting the existing building from development pressures. TDRs mitigated the burden of local landmark designation, with its attendant architectural controls, by compensating the owner with development rights that he could use elsewhere or sell. The owner of the receiving site also gained the right to develop the property to a higher density than its zoning might otherwise allow. TDRs offered the greatest preservation potential in urban centers where growth pressures threatened the survival of historic structures and therefore created the most demand for unused development rights.

New York was the first major city to enact a transferable development rights ordinance for preservation purposes. This 1968 law provided that the

Lyndhurst, in Tarrytown, New York, is administered by the National Trust for Historic Preservation as a historic house museum. Most administrators rely on admission fees, private donations, as well as available public funds to maintain historic properties. (Jack E. Boucher, Historic American Buildings Survey)

The financial burdens of historic house museums during the 1970s, resulted in many owners developing profit-making enterprises to help properties pay for themselves. An example of this is the Deerpark Restaurant, in a renovated calf barn, on the grounds of Biltmore House, constructed in the 1890s for George W. Vanderbilt in Asheville, North Carolina. (Biltmore Estate)

This gothic confection, Roseland Cottage in Woodstock, Connecticut, is protected by a preservation easement held by the Society for the Protection of New England Antiquities. (J. David Bohl, SPNEA)

These second empire town houses in the Lafayette Square neighborhood of St. Louis were rehabilitated with a revolving fund loan from the Lafayette Square Restoration Committee, Inc. (Barbara Elliott Martin)

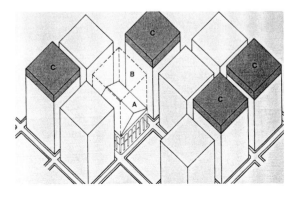

The transfer of development rights allows for unused development rights over low-rise landmark buildings to be allocated to neighboring buildings within a transfer district. (*Space Adrift.* John J. Costonis, University of Illinois Press)

unused development rights of a municipally designated landmark could be transferred to nearby, similarly zoned parcels but the building floor area of a transferred lot could increase by no more than 20 percent. These limitations were intended to ensure that the impact of the TDRs on density, traffic and public services would be as benign as possible. The full transferable potential of a lot, on the other hand, could be divided among one or more recipient lots. The landmark owner also had to agree to a program of continuing maintenance to preserve the designated property.

TDRs failed to gain widespread use as a preservation tool either in New York City or elsewhere. By the end of 1986, the owners of approximately a dozen New York City landmarks had sold their development rights, representing less than 2 percent of the city's designated landmarks. The New York City experience has offered several lessons about their use: the limited sphere of nearby properties to which development rights might be transferred restricted their applicability. Developers were able to achieve the benefits of purchasing TDRs, for example greater height and bulk in new buildings, through other means such as zoning variances, allowable bonuses for public amenities and lot mergers. The value of unused development rights to designated landmarks, therefore, lessened in part, by a lack of demand. Concern also remains widespread in New York City and elsewhere that the use of transferable development rights, unless carefully controlled, may have harmful effects on urban density and the adequacy of municipal services.

Within the past few years a few other cities, including Denver, Colorado, in 1980, and San Francisco, California, in 1985, have enacted transferable development rights ordinances in their downtowns. In San Francisco the ordinance is too new to judge its impact and in Denver only a small number of landmarks have been the subject of development rights transfer. The weakness of the real estate market and the availability of other zoning techniques diminished the value of transferable development rights as a weapon in the preservation arsenal.

Historic House Museums

A more difficult problem facing many preservation groups was the financial burden posed by their historic house museum properties, but new solutions were not long in coming. The heavy maintenance costs associated with historic buildings went through the roof because of high inflation during the 1970s. Preservation groups found themselves forced to adopt a pay-as-you-go attitude toward their properties. What emerged in response was the community preservation-center concept of making museum properties available for community and commercial activities. The idea was that both the public at large and the organizational owner would benefit.

Merchandizing historic house museums became the order of the day. Virtually every museum opened a shop, offering souvenirs and gifts. Renting museums for social functions became a favorite technique that successfully exploited their attractive settings and prestige value. Historic Charleston, Inc., followed by the National Trust and many other organizations, sponsored a collection of furniture reproduced from pieces in its properties. The National Trust developed an equestrian center at Oatlands near Leesburg, Virginia, and made its properties available as backdrops for television programs and movies.

Another result of the financial situation was the greater care taken in the acquisition and ownership of new properties. Organizations now generally require the donor to establish an endowment that would support at least the museum's annual maintenance costs. In the case of the Cooper-Molera Adobe in Monterey, California, the National Trust lessened the burden of accepting this property by arranging to lease it to the California Department of Parks and Recreation. The National Trust also pioneered the creation of property councils to assume the day-to-day responsibility for running a property.

Private Preservation Organizations: The National Trust for Historic Preservation

These developments were accompanied by dramatic growth in the private sector preservation community. Leading the way at the national level was the National Trust for Historic Preservation. Its gains in membership and budget between 1966 and 1973 indicate the scope of the national trend. Membership rose almost 400 percent from 10,668 to 40,720, paralleled by a budget increase of $784,310 to $3.1 million. The groundswell of state and local efforts is indicated by the almost threefold increase during that same period in the number of preservation organizations that were National Trust members. The increasingly diverse audience that these numbers represented is equally impressive. Preservationists now counted among their number supporters ranging from professionals in architecture and real estate to inexperienced homeowners attempting to repair their own old houses. The half-humorous, half-derisive label of preservationists as little old ladies in tennis shoes was fast becoming obsolete.

Preservation groups nurtured the expanding acceptance of the preservation ethic by focusing their programs in several key areas. Education, technical advice and assistance, and activism were almost universal core-elements of each organization's efforts. Within this framework, the most far-reaching and ambitious program thrusts during this decade were those of the National Trust, whose position of national leadership imposed on it responsibility to address the needs of the entire private preservation community. To this end, it focused its attention on improving its own outreach programs and creating a network of state and local preservation groups to join it in spreading the message.

The National Trust's initiatives between 1966–76 illustrate the scope of its programs: to improve its educational outreach, *Preservation News* and *Historic Preservation,* its monthly and quarterly publications, expanded in size, scope and depth; its publication office was reorganized as the Preservation Press; and its books sought to satisfy both general educational needs and specific, often technical themes. A series of *Information* pamphlets, begun in 1976, instructed the preservation community in some detail on topics such as how to rehabilitate old houses and the legal steps in setting up a historic preservation organizations. A much-expanded public relations effort included advertisements promoting historic preservation; a major film, *How Will We Know It's Us,* in 1967; and the initiation in 1973 of National Historic Preservation Week as an annual countrywide celebration.

A program of seminars, workshops and conferences was begun by the National Trust to spread the message and increase the competence of local groups and preservationists. The diversity of topics was a measure of the community's new breadth. Community Preservation Workshops gathered local activists from around the country to solve specific problems in the host community. The National Trust organized conferences which addressed preservation issues of particular geographic regions, problems of local preservation commissions and training seminars for their house museum staffs.

Greatly expanded forms of technical and financial assistance within the National Trust also served the twin goals of outreach and organizational stimulus. A preservation services office, created in 1968, offered advice and counsel from a staff with expertise in many disciplines. Beginning on the West Coast in 1971, the National Trust opened regional offices that took staff to all 50 states, Puerto Rico and the Virgin Islands. The creation of a preservation law program in 1971 anticipated the escalation of the legal complexities of preservation efforts.

New forms of financial assistance enabled the National Trust to assist local organizations in more substantial and permanent ways with grants and loans from the National Historic Preservation Fund to spurring the creation and expansion of revolving funds throughout the country. The Consultant Services Grant program offered matching grants to help private preservation groups and municipalities hire professionals for specific pressing needs. The $20,400 distributed in the program's first year (1970), for example, helped pay for a feasibility study of the rehabilitation of the St. Louis, Missouri, Old Post Office. The fund also helped pay for expert testimony in the legal controversy surrounding Memphis' Overton Park in Tennessee. By operating on a matching grant basis, the National Trust effectively leveraged its assistance and focused its help on those groups demonstrating initiative and some degree of organization.

Other Private Preservation Organizations

Rivaling in importance the developments at the National Trust was the emergence in 1974 of Preservation Action, a national preservation lobbying group based in Washington, D.C. This event, as much as any other, symbolized the maturity and sophistication of the preservation movement. By the early 1970s, preservation leaders realized that achieving their goals required substantial increases in federal support. This included especially appropriations for the federal-state preservation program, changes in laws and regulations and an understanding in the U.S. Congress and the federal government of the benefits of historic preservation. Experience had shown that the preservation community must become an active player in the political process for this to happen.

Many now-prominent local organizations owe their existence to the threats to or the loss of a significant building. Community preservation groups organized most quickly in those parts of the country with the oldest building stock and most active urban renewal programs. Large metropolitan areas were an especially fertile ground, and by 1970 most major cities had a landmarks conservancy or preservation society. Their names often indicated the immediacy of the threat and described a specific goal. Examples are: Save the Courthouse Committee in White Plains, New York; the Association for the Preservation of the Las Vegas Mormon Fort in Nevada; and Don't Tear It Down in Washington, D.C. (now the D.C. Preservation League). Several statewide organizations, such as the Association for the Preservation of Virginia Antiquities, were organized prior to 1966 but during the period 1966–76, many others, including the Preservation League of New York State, were formed.

In contrast, local historical societies, the traditional home of historical programs and interests, generally did not become involved in this new concern for historic architecture and preservation. The new and old groups coexisted, occasionally with some disdain among the latter about the activism of the former, and their memberships often had considerable overlap. Exceptions to this general rule, of course, existed and some historical societies eagerly responded to the times. The Princeton Historical Society in New Jersey is a case in point. In 1974, the group bought a c.1840 Greek Revival house, relocated and rehabilitated it, and then sold it with restrictive covenants using the proceeds to establish a restoration fund.

In some cases, the local preservation initiative found enthusiastic supporters within a sympathetic professional or community group. The Chicago Chapter of the American Institute of Architects played a key role in the lamentably unsuccessful 1970–71 efforts to save the Chicago Stock Exchange. The Washington, D.C., chapter of the Junior League gave crucial early support to the activities of the city's Don't Tear It Down.

The emphasis in most preservation groups, especially the newer ones, was on a combination of activism and education. Threats to important buildings continued unabated, necessitating a readiness to exert whatever leverage the preservation group could muster in response. "Manning the barricades" by picketing a demolition site was a favorite immediate action that grabbed headlines and often generated considerable public sympathy. Taking a leaf from the tactics manual of the more sophisticated environmental groups, preservationists became adept at going to court. Many proposed projects affecting historic sites involved an expenditure of federal funds or some other action triggering the applicability of federal preservation and environmental laws. Procedural flaws by federal agencies in their implementation were common. Preservation groups around the country successfully challenged federally related undertakings on this basis and established important legal precedents benefiting historic preservation in the process. For example, while only temporarily delaying the demolition of the Westchester County Courthouse in New York, the Save the Courthouse Committee's 1975 legal action in federal court broadened the protection afforded historic buildings. The suit by Hawaii's Stop H-3 Association in 1976, in turn, clarified the Department of Transportation's historic preservation responsibilities in planning highway projects.

Education was the long-term solution and the other major focus. The public typically was apathetic about historic preservation, viewing demolition and new construction as progress. Municipal officials, building owners and developers assumed, with some justification, that rehabilitation was both more expensive and more complex than erecting a new building. Building codes and tax laws, furthermore, discriminated against old buildings. Preservation organizations had to demonstrate clearly the effectiveness, in dollars and use, of saving their beautiful white elephants.

Local preservation organizations developed a range of programs to change public perceptions generally and to meet specific problems. An architectural survey of a community's entire building stock, funded with the assistance of federal preservation dollars, was almost always an important first step. It served a two-fold purpose: to identify the number and quality of old buildings for the public at large and to help a preservation group establish its priorities about buildings and neighborhoods. Often the survey was published. Other key elements of a preservation education program included public lectures, tours of significant areas, rehabilitated structures, adaptive use projects and the nomination of buildings and districts to the National Register. To establish credibility with the business community and developers, preservation groups often commissioned economic feasibility studies to buttress their arguments against demolition. The early projects of Maine's Greater Portland Landmarks are instructive in this regard. In 1972, it published an illustrated architectural history of the city and followed with walking tour brochures; publication of a bimonthly newsletter, *Landmarks Observed,* began the same year and the organization created an annual businessmen's conference on historic preservation issues in 1973.

Preservation groups around the country are generally similar to one another in their organizational frameworks. Like most nonprofits, their operations are run by a small staff that is accountable to a board of directors and is assisted by a phalanx (as large as possible) of interested volunteers. Beyond these common features, preservation groups are tremendously varied, depending on a multitude of factors such as the size of the community, the quantity and quality of its old buildings and the level of popular concern about historic preservation. The staff size often is 3 to 10 people, headed by an executive director. In many organizations, some or all of the employees are part-time and it is not at all uncommon at the local level for the executive director to be the only full-time staff. The backgrounds of staff are tremendously varied and include training in related professional fields such as architecture and planning, experience working for another nonprofit organization, not necessarily related to historic preservation, and an exposure to preservation through volunteer activities. Over time, the percentage of professionals in the field that have preservation-related educational degrees or career experience grew sharply.

The make-up of boards of directors evolved greatly over time. In many organizations, boards consisted largely of public-spirited individuals, some, but not all, with related backgrounds. Commitment to historic preservation and an ability to give time to the organization were typically the essential prerequisites. Members often included emigrés from local historical societies whose interests had broadened, urban pioneers and architects. Board memberships have changed a great deal as preservation groups have matured and their programs grew more complex. To broaden their community support and influence, organizations recruited representatives from business and government. Increasing lawsuits and lobbying to save endangered buildings made it essential to include at least one lawyer. As is the case with virtually all nonprofits, preservation organizations came to recognize that board members must have one or more of these attributes: time, influence, money.

Volunteers are essential to the operation and budget of nearly every preservation organization. Financial constraints make it impossible to function without them in the future. Their presence is particularly crucial in tours, fundraising programs and special events. The Historic Landmark Foundation of Indiana's school tours are run almost exclusively by volunteers, as are the "Niosita" fiesta celebrations that the San Antonio Conservation Society relies on for much of its budget. Organizations with historic properties often use volunteer guides and interested members also assist freely in routine daily administrative tasks.

Private preservation groups also typically lead the effort to create municipal historic preservation programs. Effective partnerships between these private and public entities often are the result. A municipal program usually involves the enactment of an ordinance allowing the community to designate landmarks and create historic districts that would be subject to protective architectural restrictions. The commissions created to supervise these designated properties themselves serve a variety of other important functions such as being a voice for preservation concerns in city policy and funding decisions. The importance of private groups remains undiminished because of their independence and flexibility in action and position on issues. In cities such as Hartford, where preservation ordinances have not been politically acceptable, the private organization remains both voice of and vehicle for preservation concern.

1976–86: Coming of Age

Over the past 10 years, the historic preservation community has experienced unparalleled growth and change. Its size, measured in number of organizations directly or indirectly involved in related activities and their membership, mushroomed almost beyond expectation. The qualitative changes, too, are remarkable with its influence and public support much more substantial than before. This is in part a result of the greater sophistication and effectiveness of its programs. Key elements in the success of the movement have been its ability to shed its elitist image and to become a player in the process. It is now a recognized, legitimate participant in both public and private decision-making. Generous federal tax incentives for historic rehabilitation projects went far in accomplishing the movement's goal to preserve significant older buildings and they immeasurably changed public attitudes. The nation's real estate developers and financiers jumped on the bandwagon of this attractive opportunity, and historic preservation became a big and profitable business. A rapidly expanding community of preservation professionals, embracing several disciplines, also emerged during these years.

A seemingly greater complexity of issues and conflict both within and without the preservation community not surprisingly also occurred during this period. "Facadectomy" and "bits and pieces preservation" are popular terms for an aesthetic issue that remains divisive and unresolved. An even more fundamental difference of opinion regarding the goals and future direction of preservation activities arose. In many respects, then, the future of historic preservation remains as much a challenge as did its past.

A key product of this explosive growth is the development of a framework of private preservation organizations at the national, state and local levels and a division of roles and responsibilities among them. The national groups, namely the National Trust and Preservation Action, consolidated their positions as the leaders of the entire private historic preservation community. These two organizations occupy the central position in formulating policy and in generating new ideas and programs. Statewide groups, which grew in number from 14 in 1976 to more than 42 today, generally coordinate activities within their states, assist local bodies and fill in the gaps although their roles vary depending on the strength of local efforts. Municipal and regional preservation organizations continue to be the most involved in day-to-day local preservation problems and generally they are broader in scope than the other groups in order to meet the demands placed upon them. Narrowly focused groups, however, such as easement-holding organizations and revolving funds, are found in greatest number at the local level.

Outside of this framework is a wider set of organizations whose interests overlap those of preservationists. The best-known from the standpoint of preservationists is the American Institute of Architects. Its involvement in historic preservation is longstanding and substantial. In 1966, the Institute established a network of state preservation coordinators. Its efforts, highlighted by an annual award for meritorious preservation design, transformed the attitude of the architectural profession toward preservation. Other groups range widely from environmental organizations, such as the Sierra Club, to real estate trade organizations, such as the National Association of Home Builders. At the local level, these organizations include chambers of commerce and neighborhood improvement and housing associations. Over time, the preservation community has worked with an ever-widening circle of interest groups. Drawing these diverse groups and the preservation community together is the growing awareness that old buildings and neighborhoods can offer many benefits to American life.

Funding Historic Preservation

An overriding concern among all preservation organizations during these recent years is finance. Preservation leaders increasingly came to see economics as the key to sustaining the movement's growth in impact and influence. Despite impressive past successes, the preservation community found it difficult to ensure its future growth or, in many cases, even maintain existing activities because of unpredictable support. Assuring the financial stability of preservation organizations, therefore, became perhaps the major objective. Because of human and financial limitations in dealing with the ever-expanding threat to old buildings, it became clear that a much larger set of individuals and groups must become involved.

Concern over money and people resulted in a series of policy and program decisions that have had a fundamental impact on the direction of historic preservation up to the present day. A heavy emphasis on fundraising and cost-effectiveness of programs and staffing became the order of the day. Making historic preservation economically beneficial to a wider community, such as by providing financial incentives for rehabilitating historic structures and educating the public, developed into another essential strategy. The preservation community also devoted much attention to marketing a positive image of its purposes and programs to achieve these desired ends.

The precarious state of preservation funding is largely attributable to the uncertainty and limitations of government support. Following passage of the Preservation Act of 1966, the federal government became the chief financial backer of historic preservation nationwide, both private and public. Its annual appropriations reached $60 million in the mid-1970s, but this was reversed at the beginning of the Reagan administration in 1980. The proposed federal budget for fiscal year 1988 is the eighth in succession in which no funds were earmarked for National Park Service preservation programs. Although the U.S.Congress has blocked these efforts at zero funding every year, current annual appropriations fell greatly from $60 million in 1979 to $25 million. Funding levels for other federal programs that had proven helpful to historic preservation, such as the HUD Community Development Block Grants, Urban Development Action Grants and Section 8 Housing Assistance Payments, also fell off or dried up completely. Implications for private preservation organizations are great. Federal dollars paid the lion's share of the architectural survey and National Register nomination components of their programs.

Preservation groups also worked to develop a firm base of support from other sectors. Membership typically remains the single most important source of funds, although costs associated with servicing members reduces its impact. Corporations and private foundations are the other prime sources of money. Corporate generosity, as most recipients found, can range from feast to famine, depending in part on the economic health of the company and its priorities for giving. During the Reagan administration and the accompanying cutback in social programs, many formerly reliable donors to the preservation cause cut back their gifts substantially in order to assist more pressing community needs, and private foundations generally did likewise. Another major problem is the reluctance of many donors, particularly foundations, to fund program operating costs; hence, worthwhile projects and programs, begun with foundation or corporate backing, failed because of the sponsoring organization's inability to pay for operating expenses.

Fundraising strategies and image-marketing now are at the core of most preservation groups, and the sophistication with which preservation organizations solicit contributions now matches that of most other nonprofits. The earlier genteel reluctance and sense of propriety that obstructed hard-nosed efforts to raise money for preservation has largely disappeared. Direct mail appeals for memberships and donations are the order of the day, highlighted by special mailings targeted to specific groups and organized around particular programs and emergencies. Corporate memberships skyrocketed. Thus the National Trust now has American Express, Exxon, Sohio and Atlantic Richfield among its major backers.

The preservation community has shown considerable skill in utilizing the breadth of its programs to attract support and gain income. Many groups, such as the Landmarks Association of St. Louis, Missouri, now provide consulting services for a fee, including National Register documentation, design advice and investment tax credit assistance. Lining up individual and corporate members to bear the entire expense of specific programs or events has proven successful and, in some cases, a program is shaped to suit a targeted donor. Among the best examples of this phenomenon is the Yankee Internship Program, which is supported by *Yankee* magazine and places student interns with preservation organizations.

The larger organizations created extensive tour programs. In a city where tourism is the second largest industry, Historic Savannah Foundation, in Georgia, earns up to 70 percent of its annual budget from guided tours. Those with historic properties exploit their commercial potential more effectively than before, ranging from setting up inns to housing summer Shakespeare. Other or-

Ghiradelli Square in San Francisco, California, is one of the earliest nationally publicized adaptive use projects in the nation. An old chocolate factory serves as a centerpiece of a new shopping precinct, tied to nearby old and new buildings with plazas and walkways. (Courtesy of Ghiradelli Square)

Artists' studios, lofts and galleries have been carved out of old warehouse buildings in the historic Lowertown district of St. Paul, Minnesota, through a partnership of the city, a private development corporation, artists and public agencies. (City of St. Paul Planning & Economic Development Department)

The successful conversion of Faneuil Hall in Boston into a popular shopping arcade served as a model for the reuse of historic buildings in other cities throughout the country. (National Trust for Historic Preservation)

The conversion of Old City Hall in Boston into commercial office space demonstrates the ready adaptation of surplus public buildings for private uses. This building provides tenants with prestigious office space. (Notter, Finegold & Alexander, Inc.)

The 2000 Pennsylvania Avenue project, also known as Red Lion Row, in Washington, D.C., is a facade preservation project. The front section of the row of townhouses was preserved and separated from the new highrise office structure to the rear by an atrium. (George Washington University)

ganizations allow the use of their properties for advertising and media back-drops. Theme-related fundraising events have had marked financial success, none more than the San Antonio Conservation Society's Niositas. Based on the Society's annual Night in Old San Antonio (NIOSA), a citywide celebration of its Spanish heritage, these smaller versions are staged profitably up to eight times a year for the city's large convention traffic and as with many commercial ventures by nonprofits, they rely on volunteer participation.

Perhaps the most visible commercialization of nonprofit historic preservation activities occurred with the commencement of advertising in major preservation publications. These advertisements offer wares running the gamut from period lighting fixtures to oak toilet seats and describe investment opportunities in historic rehabilitation syndications. Historic Hawaii Foundation raises approximately 25 percent of its monthly newsletter costs from paid advertising.

New Preservation Programs

Efforts to reshape the image of historic preservation through emphasis on its concrete financial and quantitative societal benefits broadened its appeal and resulted in the establishment of many new programs. Preservationists succeeded in establishing the legitimacy of their activities in the public mind and, in many places, shed their elitist image. For example, the preservation community demonstrated that historic preservation contributes to urban revitalization, energy conservation and job formation. The success with which preservationists achieved the enactment of financial incentives for preservation projects at all levels of government made it possible to justify many of these claims. These incentives engaged the vast resources of the real estate development industries in the preservation movement.

A multitude of programs were created or reshaped to achieve these ends. The Main Street program of the National Trust for revitalizing small urban centers and efforts by many local preservation groups to rehabilitate historic properties for low and moderate-income housing, established the commercial and housing potential of preservation work. The joint sponsorship of the Main Street Program by the U. S. Conference of Mayors and the U. S. Chamber of Commerce illustrates the preservation community's ability to spread its message beyond its own borders. Many reports show the energy conservation resulting from the reuse of historic structures: Over 2 million gallons of gasoline, for example, would be required to demolish and replace the landmark Pension Building in Washington, D.C., which fortunately now has been adapted to house the National Building Museum. The National Trust makes effective use of the annual National Historic Preservation Week to publicize such manifold benefits while conferences and publications hammer home the same messages.

Lobbying

Lobbying has been a tremendously effective tool in achieving preservation goals. Because of the joint work of Preservation Action and the National Trust, backed by the National Conference of State Historic Preservation Officers and a nation-wide network of preservationists, the community became a respected player in the halls of the U.S. Congress. Preservation has powerful allies in both the U.S.

Senate and the House of Representatives because of its demonstrated social and economic benefits. The measure of preservation's success is the ability to maintain funding for the national preservation program. The greatest achievement, however, was saving most of the investment tax credit for rehabilitating historic structures, the only significant real estate tax shelter that survived in the Tax Reform Act of 1986.

State and local lobbying initiatives fared equally well or better. Preservationists in most states learned the ropes of the legislative process and gained passage of an impressive breadth of worthwhile statutes and ordinances. In a few states, lobbying organizations now exist for this purpose. One of the oldest is Connecticut Preservation Action, founded in 1979 to overturn a newly enacted law that would have crippled the state's National Register program. By setting up a strong board and hiring a lobbyist, the organization has scored one or more legislative successes each year. Its credits include the creation of a $1 million statewide revolving fund, the Endangered Properties Fund, administered by the Connecticut Trust for Historic Preservation; a law enabling localities to designate individual historic properties for architectural protection; protection for National Register properties from unreasonable destruction; and beneficial revisions to the state building code.

Measuring Success

The past 10 years witnessed a proliferation and refinement of programs, the net result being a much greater sophistication of effort and effectiveness than ever before. Programs of an educational nature demonstrate this diversity. As awareness grew that there are many different aspects to preservation, conferences and seminars addressed many different topics. Preservation groups, from the National Trust down to the local level, now hold conferences on issues such as historic sailing vessels, tourism and historic sites and the preservation or replacement of windows in historic structures. Neither are issues being ignored that sometimes divide preservationists: A March 1987 seminar in Connecticut addressed the pros and cons of dismantling and moving historic structures, marketing architectural ornamentation and removing period rooms from old buildings.

While walking tours, lectures and other educational activities remain a staple of the programs of most preservation groups, a more realistic attitude, borne of economic realism, now governs their breadth and extent. Educational programs are the most vulnerable to attack in a financial crunch and those with depth, requiring a continuing commitment of resources, are the most threatened. The National Trust's donation of its library to the University of Maryland, perhaps the finest collection of preservation materials in the country, is the best-known example of this phenomenon. It illustrates the inability of many preservation organizations to maintain permanent educational resources or support non-paying scholarly or professional endeavors.

Publications issued in the nonprofit sector have flourished in recent times. Their strength represents both their overriding importance as a basic means of communication and their growing economic hardiness. Virtually every preservation organization publishes a newsletter or newspaper as the key benefit for its membership. These publications have also come to exhibit an impressive variety of topics as special-issue groups, such as the Friends of Cast Iron Architecture and the Victorian Society of America, have emerged within the preservation community.

Technical advice and assistance remains a cornerstone activity of preservation groups at all levels of operation and sophistication. However, the form it takes varies greatly and is primarily a function of the group's position in the preservation hierarchy. Local organizations tackled an array of basic problems cutting across all social, economic and structural lines. Design and building repair assistance to homeowners in deteriorated neighborhoods or commercial core areas is now equal in importance to advice regarding appropriate period paint colors and detailing. However, statewide organizations typically focus on broader issues, even though their resources are already stretched to cover local problems in states, mainly in the West, where fewer local groups exist. Statewide organizations have made a contribution in helping to write state building, health and safety codes which are sensitive to historic buildings and in addressing problems of large geographical scope, such as downtowns encroaching on surrounding old residential neighborhoods.

Preservation Organizations in the Development Process

Direct real estate investments by preservation groups grew dramatically in number, extent and sophistication after 1977, but not without considerable risk and mixed success. Most organizations took the plunge and stepped in to save an endangered building. The desire to take concrete action was irresistible and often unavoidable. As groups grew in size and expertise, many created easement acquisition programs and revolving funds. Their success with easements varied greatly depending on local circumstances and the vagaries of the federal tax laws. Revolving funds, however, became effective tools and generally scored impressive successes. Many preservation groups attacked broader housing and urban revitalization issues by rehabilitating deteriorated residential and commercial properties. Some ventured into long-term investments yielding significant social and financial benefits, and a few became successful practitioners of the art of project packaging.

Easement programs failed to reach their full potential because of a number of problems concerning their definition and valuation. The U.S. Congress explicitly recognized the deductibility of preservation and scenic easements of 30 years' duration in the Tax Reform Act of 1976. However, 1977 and 1980 changes in the law required them to apply in perpetuity and established strict standards for their terms. The restrictions and responsibilities imposed by the law on donors and recipients somewhat limited their appeal. The expectations of public access and the ban on any uses that would interfere with conservation purposes are not acceptable to some property owners. The endowment fee that most recipient organizations charge the donor to cover future enforcement expenses is another barrier.

Challenges by the Internal Revenue Service to the values assigned to these easements for tax deduction purposes have aroused considerable controversy and affected their impact. During the mid-1980s, the Internal Revenue Service took the position that preservation easements in several cities across the country, including Washington, D.C., and New Orleans, Louisiana, did not result in decreases in property value. Their blanket rejection of tax deductions was

226

successfully challenged, but a chilling effect remains, since tax considerations are at the heart of many easement donations.

Most revolving funds achieve success by carefully targeting their efforts, usually geographically or by building type, sometimes by financing technique. Focusing on a particular residential neighborhood, the model established by the early funds, continued to be the favored route. The Galveston Historical Foundation in Texas, facing a serious decline in its downtown core known as The Strand, pioneered in adapting this tool to a commercial setting. The Historic Preservation Fund of North Carolina, established in 1976 as the first statewide revolving fund, focused its efforts on saving endangered buildings in small towns and rural areas. In the beginning, funds concentrated on turning over properties quickly in order to revolve their investment; with time, the real estate tools expanded to include options, leases, long-term loans and partnerships.

Revolving funds were quick to address new issues and meet changing needs. As concerns about gentrification became widespread in the preservation community, revolving funds rehabilitated architecturally significant housing for low and moderate-income residents. One by-product was the development of expertise in packaging the funding for such projects. Savannah was a leader with its Savannah Landmark Rehabilitation Project. Begun in 1974, this program has been carried out in Savannah's Victorian District, an area of dilapidated 19th-century housing; rehabilitated, they were re-rented to their former tenants. Many funds were organized expressly for such housing goals as the 19th Ward Community Association in Rochester, New York, which sells its renovated housing to low or moderate-income families. To make its projects work, this group combined public and private money from a United Way Fund and a HUD Neighborhood Self-Help Development Grant.

Project packaging yielded significant financial rewards for some organizations. The preservation group typically earns a fee for bringing together, up front, all components of a historic rehabilitation project, including the financing, governmental subsidies where applicable, in some cases, title to the property and a developer. As part of this technique, the preservation group may also handle the certification process to obtain the investment tax credit. The Hartford Architecture Conservancy achieved success with this tool by acting as the facilitator for better commercial and residential rehabilitation projects.

Some preservation groups ventured into more extensive and longer-term real estate investments to achieve their social and financial goals. One of the largest projects of this kind is Station Square in Pittsburgh, Pennsylvania. The Pittsburgh Historic and Landmarks Foundation is an equity partner in the $200 million-plus adaptive use and expansion of a former railroad terminal for a combination of commercial and residential uses. Many groups rehabilitated large old buildings for their own offices and earn income from rentals on the remaining space. The old Allegheny Post Office in Pittsburgh now houses the Foundation's headquarters, while the rehabilitated Cummins School in Cincinnati, Ohio, is large enough to contain the offices of its owner, the Walnut Hills Redevelopment Foundation, Inc., and those of commercial tenants and a local social services agency.

The Profit Sector

The emergence of a huge private, profit-making preservation business community in the 1970s is primarily the result of the happy coincidence of certain basic economic and social factors. Preservationists played an essential role in the enactment of the watershed rehabilitation tax incentives by the U.S. Congress and these are the single most important cause. However, external and larger forces at work in American society were the key to transforming historic preservation into the broad-based and widely accepted force it is today.

The energy crisis of the mid-1970s, double-digit inflation, growth of the service sector of the economy and changing demographics of the American population had a crucial impact in spurring public policy and informed opinion to encourage the revitalization of American urban areas. Uncontrolled suburban sprawl came to be seen as a luxury in transportation and energy costs that America could no longer afford, to say nothing of its increasingly apparent damage to the environment. During the 1970s, the service sector supplanted the manufacturing sector as the largest employment component in the economy. Service-related companies, unlike those in manufacturing, favored central city locations. Smaller families and the tremendous increase in single households gave rise to a new segment of the population that found central city living to be a popular option. Government policy-makers at all levels were quick to recognize these trends and public policy and funds began to be targeted at urban revitalization efforts. The celebration in 1976 of the Bicentennial reawakened the nation's sense of patriotism and history and in so doing, it considerably accelerated the growing popular commitment to historic preservation.

Arguments for the rehabilitation of urban buildings were strengthened by these same forces. Studies demonstrated convincingly that rehabilitation was more energy efficient and more cost effective than new construction. The energy costs alone associated with clearing a site for new construction are a forceful statement; besides, older buildings are less expensive to heat than new ones. Escalating inflation made financing for new construction virtually impossible to obtain in many sections of the country in the mid-1970s and the related cost of servicing debt and materials was becoming almost prohibitive. In contrast, less time is needed to complete a rehabilitation project and materials cost less. Being more labor intensive than new construction, rehabilitation had considerable appeal to public officials and the labor movement. Under these conditions, American cities facing shortages of downtown office space, which for example reached critical proportions in Boston in the 1970s, found rehabilitation to be the only sensible answer to their problems.

Within the real estate and financial communities themselves, new economic realities gradually overcame a long-standing skepticism about rehabilitation. Professionals in the field saw a host of problems associated with rehabilitation including a large measure of understandable uncertainty about its market behavior. Work on old buildings, depending on the extent of the planned renovation, might involve substantial and sometimes unforeseeable upfront costs in evaluating the structure's condition and dealing with its deficiencies. Obtaining the requisite municipal permits and approvals could be a drawn-out process, and bringing the building up to current code standards could entail widespread and expensive modifications. Existing tenants had to be dealt with and removed and this raised the prospect of litigation. Some of these problems were real, and they helped confirm the real estate community's preference for new construction, a known quantity.

The financial sector foresaw all of these problems and more. The assumed difficulty in setting rehabilitation budgets means that project costs and time schedules are uncertain. Market receptivity to space in rehabilitated buildings also is not well established. These uncertainties mean unpredictable income streams and endangered debt service. In many cases, rehabilitation projects are also too small to satisfy the appetite of the financial community, especially those institutional lenders with a nationwide presence and large real estate portfolios. Those banks and financiers most willing to make rehabilitation loans consequently are those with smaller investment budgets and a stake in the health of a local economy. Many at first participated in rehabilitation projects as a civic contribution and non-standard investment. With time and the growing familiarity, this thinking usually turned around.

Federal Tax Incentives and the For-Profit Sector

Perhaps more than any other single factor the federal tax incentives for historic rehabilitation provided the spark to ignite urban revitalization. Beginning with the Tax Reform Act of 1976, rehabilitation became an attractive prospect to developers and investors. Each subsequent change in the law, up to the Tax Reform Act of 1986, only increased its appeal.

These credits involved the real estate community in virtually every kind of rehabilitation project and began the large-scale improvement of many American downtowns. The results are impressive: over a 10-year period, nearly 17,000 rehabilitation projects, representing a private investment of an estimated $11 billion, qualified for tax benefits. The breadth in location and kind of project is all the more notable, because virtually every corner of the country, every size of city and every kind of structure was involved. The top 50 cities using the tax incentives ranged from large to small, from Baltimore, Maryland, to Guthrie, Oklahoma. More than 50 percent of the projects since 1982 have been residential rental properties involving approximately 83,500 housing units. Sixty-two percent are newly created units and 19 percent, or more than 15,200, are targeted at low and moderate-income tenants. Almost 20 percent of these projects combine commercial, office and residential uses. Among the most popular kinds of rehabilitation projects are conversions of surplus schools into housing for the elderly.

A direct impact on the business community was the creation of a corps of building trade professionals sensitive to the structural and aesthetic demands of old buildings. The Secretary of the Interior's Standards for Rehabilitation, to which all projects seeking tax credits must conform, have ensured a high level of craftsmanship. While many projects initially encountered difficulty in meeting these standards, growing sophistication in the building trades has largely solved this problem. New materials and products appropriate to historic structures emerged and achieved widespread recognition. The Secretary's Standards earned widespread respect and acceptance as the industry standard for all rehabilitation work, whether or not otherwise qualifying for the tax credits. They also have ensured a high quality of work.

Tax credits also caused the proliferation of professionals who are conversant with historic rehabilitation in every real estate-related field. The volume of tax-credit work spawned architects, lawyers and accountants, who specialize in the intricacies of structuring a project. Mortgage bankers and financial institutions across the country who backed these projects understand their implications. If for no other reason than self-interest, these professionals became important supporters of historic preservation and their role in the successful effort to retain the tax credits in the Tax Reform Act of 1986 proved their commitment. The credits heightened the ties between preservationists and the real estate community.

A wide range of profit-making ventures also developed. Many organizations duplicate the commercial operations of nonprofit preservation groups, such as tours of historic areas. The public's taste for old houses also encouraged vendors to recreate an almost endless variety of items related to living in historic houses and neighborhoods. Catalogues and advertisements in most historical publications offer, for example, reproduction cabinet and furniture hardware for old doors and patterns for 19th-century dresses. The *Old House Journal* established its profitable niche as the magazine for the old house owner and restorer, while at least one publishing house, Dover Publications, identified a market for reissued architectural classics. Entrepreneurs in all parts of the country now specialize in dismantling historic houses and reconstructing them in other locations, often surrounded by modern reproductions. A sizeable trade arose furthermore, in old architectural artifacts, such as ornate mantlepieces and stained glass windows salvaged from demolished buildings.

Preservation Professionals

The number of professionals following historic preservation careers in the private sector has risen dramatically during the past 10 years. Again, tax credits are partly responsible. A new title, historic preservation consultant, describes many of them whose work ranges from conducting municipal architectural surveys to advising developers on the architectural hurdles involved in qualifying for the rehabilitation tax credits. As private preservation organizations grew in number and size, so too did their staffs. The more than 30 degree-granting programs in historic preservation at American universities have opened up educational opportunities for scholars and professionals in this new field of concentration.

Unresolved Issues

The success enjoyed by the historic preservation community in its range of programs has not been without conflict. One problem centers on the aesthetic integrity of both new and old buildings. As historic preservationists reach out to embrace a larger public, they are inevitably called upon to balance their goals with those of other groups. The extent to which the preservation community should compromise was a divisive problem in many cases. A related issue arose from the movement's own success: Will historic preservation breed aesthetic excesses that in the end lead to its rejection? These problems concern all preservationists whether involved in the public or private sphere. The private sector perhaps faces them most directly because they are on the front line.

How Much to Save?

The issue of aesthetic integrity arises most often where a downtown development proposal seeks to combine new construction and an old building. These plans vary greatly in the manner and extent to which the fabric of the old is preserved and reused. Extensive alteration of the interior of a historic building is a common objective in the process of rehabilitation and the standards for obtaining the federal preservation tax credits do not, in many cases, discourage it. Typically, controversy appears where designs go even further and call for the retention of only a portion of a building's original features. To save old buildings, preservationists increasingly find that compromise is necessary on this issue. One result is that preservation communities in many cities find themselves divided about the extent to which original building fabric may be sacrificed while still calling the result historic preservation.

Developers justify these exercises in partial preservation on many grounds. Their arguments usually focus on the extreme deterioration of the historic building or its inability to meet modern standards for commercial space. The reasonableness of their claims varies greatly from one situation to another. In the end, preservationists are often still divided, their opponents now being the very municipal officials and the real estate people whom they sought to cultivate.

Facadectomies, where virtually the only surviving original component is the historic facade, occurred nationwide and are a well-known example of this phenomenon. Of several examples in Washington, D.C., the most controversial was the incorporation of the facade and one bay of the early 20th-century Keith-Albee Theatre into the one-block Metropolitan Square project. Two projects currently underway in Hartford, Connecticut, also are illustrative. In one, a 30-story revivalist skyscraper will rise behind the elaborate terra cotta facade of the late 19th-century Goodwin Building, one of the city's few downtown apartment buildings. The other will superimpose the facade of a Greek Revival bank onto a modern glass and stone panel office building. A replica of the old facade will be reconstructed on its original site.

Other projects are even more sweeping in their effect and have earned the label of "bits and pieces" preservation. The Commission on Chicago's Historical and Architectural Landmarks has divided the preservation community in that city by approving a plan to incorporate remnants of the city's last remaining Neoclassical Revival train station into a 25-story downtown office complex. Some of the building's original features will be saved, while others will be relocated or demolished. In Riverside, California, a proposal would save the facade of the 1908 Greek Revival Masonic Temple as free-standing art.

The "Commercialization" of Historic Preservation

Another concern among some preservationists is the increasing attention given to the commercial side of historic preservation, by both the nonprofit and profit-making sectors, which will have a detrimental long-term impact. The question arises whether the deeper and more enduring message of historic preservation will be lost in the process of exploiting its commercial potential. To borrow a phrase, "will success spoil historic preservation?"

The American tendency to turn popular phenomena into fads through overexposure is a threat facing the private sector and the entire movement. Some critics have zeroed in on the festival marketplace concept, for example, which has successfully utilized historic buildings for impressive downtown revitalization, as a formula that starts to pall through repetition. The first such example, Fanueil Hall Marketplace in Boston, Massachusetts, achieved unparalleled commercial success and critical acclaim because of its inventive combination of retail and commercial uses, creative and innovative design and worthy adaptive use of deteriorating waterfront warehouses. With the passage of time and creation of numerous imitations in other cities, some critics complained of the programmed quaintness of this technique.

A variation of this phenomenon that is even more clearly a function of historic architecture is the proliferation of new buildings, in certain historic districts around the country, that are stylistic copies of the old. In Alexandria, Virginia, an unwritten understanding exists that a mixture of the colonial and Federal styles is the acceptable style for new construction. The result has proven to be commercially successful and does preserve the 18th and early 19th-century atmosphere of the city center. On the other hand, the new buildings generally are not the equal, in design and quality of materials, of the originals and run the risk of cheapening the district through a false sense of historic integrity and a stifling of high-quality modern architecture.

The wide assortment of goods having some association with historic preservation that is now on the market may also have detrimental effects. Their extraordinary volume and vast range of quality may well create two problems. First, it is possible that much of the general public will view these items as the substance of historic preservation. Unfortunately, unlike the historic rehabilitation projects using the investment tax credits, no quality control governs the appearance and taste. Objects such as lighting fixtures that "recreate the nostalgia of a bygone era" run the risk of overwhelming historic preservation in superficiality. Secondly, these goods may lead to overexposure and eventual rejection by the public. Once they lose their commercial appeal, as marketing history indicates they will, preservationists must guard against allowing them to impair the public response toward historic preservation in general.

A fine line exists between appropriate and inappropriate commercialization of historic preservation. The private sector is justified in deriving gain from the public's current enthusiasm for history and architecture and the existence of many nonprofit historic preservation organizations depends on it. The preservation community almost inevitably will suffer differences among its adherents about the virtues of its commercial aspects. All unite, however, in their concern that the business of historic preservation will continue to prosper in a sensitive and effective manner.

A Look at the Future

By virtually all standards of measurement, the private sector of the historic preservation community has enjoyed remarkable progress over the 20 years since the enactment of the National Historic Preservation Act of 1966. Its nonprofit organizations have experienced unparalleled growth in numbers and influence and their voice is now a widely respected one. They have expanded and refined their programs to broaden their support and respond effectively to changing issues. The significant and broad contributions of historic preservation to the quality of American life are now generally appreciated, in part through the direct role that these organizations have played in the revitalization of many cities and towns.

The emergence of a substantial profit-making preservation sector is testimony both to the success of the nonprofit preservation community and to the vital role that preservation has come to play in the basic economic life of the United States. Resulting in a large part from the existence of rehabilitation tax credits and the complete reversal of the impact of federal tax laws on old buildings, the nation's architectural and historical resources have economic and aesthetic value that they have never before enjoyed.

The future prospects for private sector historic preservation appear brighter than ever before. It is vital, however, for members of the American preservation community to recognize the problems that exist and that may threaten its continued progress.

A number of aspects of historic preservation as it is currently practiced and understood may, over time, conspire to trivialize and demean its message and impact on American society. Perhaps the one most central to the operation of nonprofit organizations themselves is the question of commercialization in the name of fiscal responsibility. Preservation groups embraced a variety of commercial opportunities to improve their financial position and their impressive creativity in this regard has had a significant and positive effect on their balance sheets. In many cases, these efforts also served important educational ends. Care must be taken, however, that these opportunities do not adversely affect the cause of historic preservation, either by having an undue influence on the validity of program priorities or by appearing to emphasize commercial gain at the expense of the basic message of historic preservation.

Preservationists have achieved notable success in reaching out and finding common ground with many other groups in American society. The attendant risk for the future is that the message of preservation may become diluted in the process. Compromises over fates of endangered old buildings often serve legitimate social and economic goals. Without proper care, however, such agreements may fail to respect the integrity of these vital resources. Bits and pieces historic preservation, whether it involves the preservation of architectural details in situ as part of a new project or the incorporation of salvaged ornamentation in an entirely new setting, usually transmit an entirely inappropriate message about the meaning of preservation.

A third danger facing the preservation community is complacency, particularly as it concerns the long-term commitment to its goals by the profit-making sector. The widespread economic benefits being reaped by developers and many other members of the business sector are not necessarily permanent. Tax incentives may be repealed. Numerous studies and polls demonstrate that, in most cases, developers would not have undertaken rehabilitation projects without the existence of these tax credits. Their present commitment to historic preservation is not a future certainty. The historic preservation community must take this into account when developing plans and priorities.

CHAPTER EIGHT

PREHISTORY AND BEYOND: THE PLACE OF ARCHAEOLOGY

THOMAS F. KING

Prehistory and Beyond: The Place of Archaeology

THOMAS F. KING

Introduction

The academic discipline of archaeology and the historic preservation movement evolved separately in the United States during the 19th and early 20th centuries. It was not until after the passage of the National Historic Preservation Act in 1966, in fact, that the two began to be tied together in a significant way, and to influence one another.

As the practice of archaeology and historic preservation became more intertwined, archaeologists have adopted a preservationist or conservationist ethic that demands the preservation of archaeological sites in place and left undisturbed where possible. This is a dramatic break with the past, when the central purpose of archaeology was understood to be the excavation of ancient sites. Archaeologists are now deeply engrossed in land use planning as a way to rationalize the treatment of archaeological sites and to understand them in regional contexts. They are active in the national historic preservation program, and often occupy significant administrative positions at the state and national levels.

Archaeology has had a significant influence on the practice of historic preservation in the United States. The regional perspective that archaeologists bring to their work, seeking to understand the sites that they study in the context of regional environmental processes and settlement systems, added a distinctive intellectual dimension to preservation practice. This perspective led archaeologists into leadership roles in the development of systems for large-scale preservation planning. These leadership roles are central to many preservation programs at the state level and are reflected in national standards and guidelines. By contrast with other parts of the world where archaeology is based in art history or classical studies, in the United States archaeology is firmly embedded in the discipline of anthropology, the study of human cultural systems living and dead. As a result, archaeologists bring anthropological perspectives to their work in preservation. They tend to support and influence efforts to make historic preservation relate positively to the preservation of intangible cultural values and traditional social practices.

236

The place of archaeology in preservation and the place of preservation in archaeology continue to be somewhat uncertainly defined, however, and the relationship is not always a comfortable one. The future of archaeology in historic preservation in the United States, and the role that archaeology will play in defining and working out major issues that will confront the preservation movement in the coming decades can be only glimpsed and guessed at today.

This chapter explores the history of American archaeology's relationship with historic preservation, the nature of the relationship today, and some issues that will be faced in the future.

Beginnings

The practice of archaeology in the United States is almost as old as the nation itself. The first archaeologist known to have explored the nation's past was its third President and author of the Declaration of Independence, Thomas Jefferson. In 1784 Jefferson excavated Indian burial mounds on Monticello, his plantation in Virginia. In his characteristically meticulous manner, he recorded the soil strata in which he found different kinds of artifacts. In doing so, he added to his long list of intellectual accomplishments what has been called the first scientific excavation in the history of archaeology.

During the next century, archaeologists in the United States, not yet identified as practitioners of a named discipline, were preoccupied with research and, often, simple speculation into the origins of the Native Americans (Indians) and their civilizations. As exploring parties pushed west into the continent, they came upon spectacular ruins. Great complexes of mounds were found in the valleys of the Ohio, the Illinois, the Missouri and the Mississippi Rivers that were clearly the remains of temples and tombs. In the desert Southwest, the pueblos were discovered, some of which were still occupied, but most deserted and in ruins. Towers, huge subterranean rooms and complexes of stone-walled apartments covered the equivalent of many city blocks. Americans of the time, mostly of European descent, had difficulty believing that the fierce warrior societies with whom they were often locked in combat could have been responsible for the ruined cities of the Midwest and Southwest. It was easier, and less threatening intellectually, to imagine the ruins to be the products of wandering refugees from the old civilizations of the Mediterranean. For years, mounds were opened and pueblos explored for the purpose of demonstrating that they were built by Egyptians, Phoenicians, Romans or the Lost Tribes of Israel.

Interest persists in possible prehistoric connections between the Americas and Europe, Asia and Africa, and responsible researchers have produced evidence suggesting that such contacts did take place. By early in the 20th century, however, the bulk of scientific evidence supported a conclusion now widely accepted that American Indians were responsible for all of the New World's prehistoric ruins and that their ancestors had come out of Asia many thousands of years ago. The Indians crossed the Bering Strait into Alaska and then went southward to people the continent.

It may be no accident that the decline in belief that the old civilizations of Europe and the Middle East were responsible for the New World's archaeological remains coincided with their accelerated destruction. As the pace of westward expansion and industrialization increased, remains of America's pre-history, alien to the continent's new masters, were not allowed to stand in the way of progress. During the late 19th and early 20th centuries, there was widespread, largely undocumented and seldom lamented destruction of Indian archaeological sites by expanding cities, road networks, railroads and military bases.

The late 19th and early 20th century also saw the slow growth of an archaeological discipline in the United States, which ultimately would awaken to and confront the destruction of the nation's patrimony. Initially, archaeologists in the United States were little involved in preservation, instead pursuing the study of sites that for the most part were relatively safe from destruction. Excitement was stirred, however, when artifact collectors began large-scale excavations in the desert Southwest to stock European museums. This stimulated passage of the first preservation law in the United States, the Antiquities Act of 1906. This law is much like preservation legislation in most Latin American nations today, except that it applies only to land owned by the federal government and Indian tribes. While prohibiting the excavation of archaeological sites without a permit from the government, on pain of fines and jail terms, it does nothing about the destruction of such sites by the government or its agents in their development and use of the land.

Salvage Archaeology versus Preservation

During the Great Depression of the 1930s, government economic relief officials found that archaeology had the potential of being highly labor-intensive. Hundreds of people could be put to work digging an archaeological site and cleaning, sorting, counting and labeling the recovered artifacts. Throughout the nation, but particularly in the Southeast, large crews were mobilized under the direction of academic archaeologists and their students. The first large-scale, albeit sometimes haphazard, archaeological research campaign in the United States was launched.

Much of the archaeological work was done in river valleys soon to be flooded by the reservoirs of the Tennessee Valley Authority, it having been created to stimulate economic development and generate power in the financially devastated South. Thus was created an archaeological preoccupation with reservoir projects that would long persist, as well as a characteristic archaeological dilemma between the remains of the past and the needs of modern society: salvage archaeology.

Salvage archaeology, called rescue archaeology in many other nations, involves the excavation and study of sites scheduled for destruction by the forces of development or, more rarely, those subject to damage by erosion, vandalism and similar causes. Salvage archaeology is based on an important premise that the site in question will be destroyed, that the forces of destruction cannot be turned aside and that preservation of the site in its original location cannot occur. Typically, salvage sites are scheduled for destruction by some sort of construction project. Before destruction occurs, however, archaeologists conduct excavations to learn what they can from the contents. For decades, this premise served to set archaeologists apart from the growing American historic preservation movement, whose raison d'etre was, and is, the preservation of historic places in situ by slowing, redirecting and more recently coopting progress.

The salvage premise was not the only thing to set archaeologists apart from their colleagues-to-be in historic preservation. Until recently, archaeologists were predominantly concerned with prehistory, which in the United States means the millennia before the European invasion of the continent. They thus tended to pay little attention to the more recent sites and structures with which preservationists are preoccupied. Archaeology's major purpose, moreover, is to learn from the remains of the past. This usually requires that such remains be excavated and, therefore, to a large extent, destroyed. As one prominent archaeologist has put it: "Archaeology is the only branch of anthropology where we kill our informants." Preserving archaeological sites in situ had little appeal to archaeologists until recently, when it was realized that within a few years or decades the archaeological record of whole cultures and time periods might be lost forever.

Furthermore, archaeologists in the United States come from a scholarly tradition quite different from those of historians, architects and other preservation professionals. In many nations, archaeology is practiced by individuals who, like historians and architectural historians, are trained in the arts and humanities. This is not the case in this country, where archaeology is firmly established as a subdiscipline of anthropology, a social science concerned with the systematic study of human society and culture. Archaeologists are defensive of their claim to be scientists. They tend to align themselves with social and behavioral sciences where in universities they are grouped administratively.

Finally, archaeologists often perceive themselves as psychologically distinct from preservationists, and the perception is generally reciprocated. The image conveyed by the cinematic character, Indiana Jones, is comfortable to archaeologists who, according to a controlled sociological study done in the late 1970s, see themselves as being "more masculine, more active, more favorable and stronger" than preservationists.

Cowboys of Science: The Growth of Salvage Archaeology

Salvage archaeology projects gained in scope and numbers after World War II, when the United States embarked on large programs to construct dams and interstate highways. Drawing on the experience of the Great Depression era, the Smithsonian Institution and the National Park Service jointly launched the River Basin Salvage Program, sending teams into the river valleys ahead (though often not far ahead) of the dam builders to snatch whatever could be gotten before the waters rose to wash away the sites or cover them, presumably forever. In some states, similar salvage programs were launched in connection with highway construction. The salvage era stretched into the late 1960s. Finances were stabilized somewhat by the Reservoir Salvage Act of 1960, which authorized appropriations to the National Park Service for salvage purposes. The Smithsonian gradually withdrew from the program, and the National Park Service began to acquire salvage funds from the U.S. Congress, generally a few million dollars each year. These were parceled out through contracts with academic institutions and museums.

This period was both an exciting and frustrating time, when many practitioners now in preservation-oriented archaeology received their initial training. Most projects were badly underfunded and were conducted in an atmosphere of crisis and impending doom. They were often carried out in locations that had not been explored by archaeologists, resulting in unexpected discoveries and the need to reconsider existing ideas about prehistory. Often these areas were physically remote from urban centers, and archaeologists shared use of the land, riverbank campsites and small town bars with cowboys and construction workers. The self-image of archaeologists as rough-and-ready cowboys of science (as a bumper sticker widely sold at archaeological conventions proclaims them to be) grew apace and not without reason.

The Development of a Preservation Consciousness

But amid the swaggering and excitement, there was an uneasiness bordering at times on anguish. Participating in the destruction of archaeological sites was disquieting. Archaeologists seldom, if ever, excavated a threatened site in its entirety; in almost all cases the great bulk of the remains was left for destruction by the reservoir or highway. At the same time, the scientific techniques that could be applied to the archaeological record grew rapidly in number and sophistication. Scientific techniques included radiocarbon age determination; trace element analysis to identify the sources of materials; chemical analysis and special photographic techniques to identify areas, within sites, where particular activities took place and to discriminate between minute soil strata; and the application of computers to study artifact distribution. All these and many more were opening up new possibilities and the potential to address hitherto unimagined research problems. The pace of technological change was expected to continue, bringing with it still more new research possibilities. But how could these new possibilities be exploited if, in the present, archaeologists dug up all the sites or abetted their destruction by the forces of development? The answer was obvious: it was necessary to begin banking sites, in effect putting them away for future study. Archaeologists began to call for the practice of a conservation ethic, which meant, in essence, that archaeologists had to become preservationists.

The Convergence of Archaeology with Historic Preservation, 1966–86

Archaeology's new awareness of the desirability of preserving the object of its study coincided with several important new laws. These are discussed in Chapter 2. By the early 1970s, the National Historic Preservation Act of 1966 had created a preservation infrastructure at both the federal and state levels. Executive Order l1593 issued by President Nixon in 1972, the procedures for Section 106 review issued by the Advisory Council on Historic Preservation and a program of Executive Order consultation launched by the National Park Service to acquaint federal agencies with their new legal responsibilities, all created a basis for urging agencies to find whatever archaeological sites were threatened by their actions and to give strong consideration to their protection.

The National Environmental Policy Act of 1969 also contributed to this legal base, requiring the conduct of interdisciplinary studies to define the environmental impacts of federal projects and programs. Archaeological sites were obviously part of the environment that needed to be considered, and archaeologists wasted no time in reminding offending agencies of the fact. Some participated in litigation challenging the adequacy of environmental impact statements (EISs) prepared by federal agencies; others pressed for the preservation of archaeological sites in the context of Section 106 review by the Advisory Council. The spirit of the times is summed up in a bit of doggerel composed during a 1974 archaeological conclave:

> "We must now learn all the tricks
> to be found in 106
> when we find a fed whose EIS is lacking.
> We must look 'em in the eye,
> holler FAILURE TO COMPLY,
> and the legions of the Council start attacking."

The year 1974 produced more than bad poetry. It also saw the passage, after five years of effort, of the Archeological and Historic Preservation Act, usually referred to after its sponsors as the Moss-Bennett Act. Moss-Bennett amends the Reservoir Salvage Act of 1960, extending its provisions beyond reservoirs to all forms of federal, federally assisted and federally licensed projects. It authorizes all federal agencies—not just the National Park Service, as had hitherto been the case—to expend funds on archaeological work. It is indicative of the continuing estrangement of archaeology from historic preservation in the 1970s that Moss-Bennett was in no way coordinated with the provisions of the National Historic Preservation Act of 1966. The criteria for listing in the National Register of Historic Places are not used as measures of archaeological significance, no role is given to the state historic preservation officer (SHPO) and no connection is made with Section 106 review.

Moss-Bennett is important to the convergence of archaeology with historic preservation, however, because it unequivocally authorized and implicitly directed agencies to spend their money on archaeology. In addition, the administration of its provisions was assigned by the Secretary of the Interior to the Office of Archeology and Historic Preservation (OAHP) in the National Park Service. The office also administered the National Register, the Historic American Buildings Survey, Historic American Engineering Record and the program of grants to the states. Within the office, a deliberate effort was made to make the implementation of Moss-Bennett an integrated part of the national historic preservation program.

From the standpoint of other preservation disciplines, this effort may have worked too well. The federal agencies were now authorized to spend money on archaeology; they were encouraged by the Office of Archeology and Historic Preservation to create integrated preservation programs; they were under pressure from the office, the Advisory Council and the states to come into compliance with Section 106 and Executive Order 11593; and they were badgered by litigious and otherwise aggressive archaeologists, many pursuing their newfound conservation ethic with a near-religious fervor. Many agencies responded by hiring archaeologists in large numbers to manage their preservation affairs. In 1966, perhaps 100 archaeologists were employed by federal agencies, most of them by the National Park Service and the Smithsonian Institution; by 1980 this number had grown to at least 600, and most were employed by agencies, such as the Corps of Engineers and the Forest Service. They were also employed in all state historic preservation offices and a great many were working as independent contractors. In 1966, there were no more than three private archaeological contracting firms in the nation—that is, businesses operating outside and in competition with the academic institutions and museums. By 1980, there were estimated to be 500, employing perhaps 2,000 archaeologists on a full-time basis and many more temporarily or seasonally. As a result, by the late 1970s, historians and architectural historians expressed alarm at the "archaeologization" of the federal historic preservation program.

The Conservation Ethic

The desirability of preserving archaeological sites in place became so internalized by archaeologists during the 1970s that by the mid-1980s salvage archaeology was a dirty word. It is still done, of course, and on a larger scale than ever, but only when options for in situ preservation are exhausted. It is now called data recovery.

In the first explicit articulation of what archaeologists refer to as the conservation ethic, William Lipe asserted in 1974 that "we need not only to discuss how to do salvage archaeology but how not to do it. . . . If our field is to last beyond a few more decades, we need to shift to resource conservation as a primary model, and treat salvage . . . as a last resort, to be undertaken only after other avenues of protecting the resource have failed." Although Lipe added the caveat that "we must, of course, continue to excavate enough to pursue the problems raised by the discipline and to keep the field intellectually healthy," his model has been taken by many archaeologists working in preservation as a rationale for never even contemplating the conduct of excavations if archaeological sites could possibly be preserved in place.

This new archaeological priority created problems. Government agencies were not always understanding. "How are you ever going to learn anything," they ask, "if you don't dig? We thought you wanted to excavate sites!" The responses, rendered with greater and lesser degrees of pomposity, and based on greater or smaller amounts of knowledge of the law and the discipline, range from: "The law doesn't allow us to do excavation, except as a last resort," to "We do want to excavate, but we also want to save something for those who come after us, who will surely have questions to ask that are different from those we ask today, and who will surely have better intellectual and technological tools to use in answering them." The first response is by no means true; the law says nothing about giving priority to preservation in place. The second response is the real message of Lipe's paper; it implies striking a balance between preservation for the future and use in the present, not unlike the balance that must be struck between preserving the historic fabric of a building and adapting it for modern use.

The priority given to preservation in-place over excavation is helped along by the development of federal procedures for compliance with Section 106 of the Preservation Act of 1966 and related laws. Before a site can be committed to salvage excavation and destruction by a federal or federally assisted project, the Advisory Council's regulations require that its treatment be reviewed by the federal agency, the SHPO, the Advisory Council and other interested parties. This review provides an important opportunity to explore options for preservation in place.

Before the review itself can take place, a judgment must be made as to whether the site is eligible for inclusion in the National Register of Historic Places (See Chapter 2). This can be a time-consuming and expensive process, requiring the development of detailed descriptive and analytic data about the site, which in turn may often require test excavations. Faced with the alternatives of carrying out these operations or simply bypassing or avoiding a site altogether, it is easy for a federal agency to regard avoidance as the better part of valor, whatever the historical or scientific significance of the site in question might be. As a result, many agencies are comfortable with the notion of avoiding archaeological sites wherever possible, often with little study of their significance.

Broadening the Field of Inquiry

During the 1960s and early 1970s, coincidental with the rise of modern preservation, archaeology underwent a far-reaching intellectual revolution. Since the time of Jefferson, archaeological research was preoccupied with what amounted to the reconstruction of narrative history, trying to determine when human occupation of a given region began and the basic history of that region's occupants. Typically, research was focused on large sites with as many soil strata as possible, which archaeologists boasted they could read like books to decipher the history of the area.

By the late 1950s, dissatisfaction was growing with this approach. Archaeologists worried about the possibility that by excavating only the large central places of a given prehistoric society, they were ignoring the lives and histories of the bulk of its population. Their leavings were more likely to be found in modest sites representing suburbs, hamlets, villages and temporary camps. The idea of studying these kinds of sites, in the context of whole regions, led to the notion of settlement archaeology, in which the regional settlement pattern of a society, rather than its individual great sites, became the focus of attention.

A more profound revolution was developing, however. In 1962, in an article entitled, "Archeology as Anthropology," Lewis R. Binford argues that by falling into the study of narrow historical questions, archaeology was failing to realize its promise as an anthropological discipline. Binford proposes that instead of excavating to reconstruct the narrative history of regions, archaeologists should study the past in order to deal with large questions about social process, seeking fundamental truths about how and why societies change, develop, collapse or remain stable through time. To do this, he argued, archaeologists should adopt a hypothetical-deductive approach to their research, in which hypotheses are deduced about social processes, based on general anthropological theory and then tested through controlled fieldwork. Binford's work, and that of his colleagues and supporters, became known as the New Archaeology. Though controversial, and resisted by many traditional practitioners, the concept swept the

Archaeologists excavate the sites they study in carefully mapped, controlled units, usually square or rectangular in shape so that each item found can be located in three-dimensional space. These excavations, conducted in 1983 at the Medicine House Site in Wyoming, revealed the remains of a prehistoric residential structure some 5,300 years old. (Rawlins District Office, Bureau of Land Management)

Archaeology is labor-intensive work. During most excavations, all soil is sifted or washed through wire-mesh screens so that each artifact, fragment of bone or shell or other items of interest can be found and recorded. (Ronald Anzalone, Advisory Council on Historic Preservation)

The conservation ethic demands that where possible, archaeological sites be preserved for future use, rather than excavated. These employees of the Bureau of Land Management have just finished assembling a steel grate over the entrance to a cave that contains extensive archaeological deposits to deter vandals and pothunters. (California State Office, Bureau of Land Management)

Historical archaeologists often find that outdoor toilets and wells, like this one at the South Street Seaport project in New York City, are rich storehouses of information. Used as trash dumps after they outlived their original purposes, they are filled with stratified deposits of material that represents the life and times of past residents. (Ronald Anzalone, Advisory Council on Historic Preservation)

Archaeological programs in America's cities make copious use of volunteers from the community. Here in Alexandria, Virginia, volunteers carry out the painstaking task of cleaning, conserving, identifying and labeling artifacts from an excavation. (Alexandria Archeology, Alexandria, Virginia)

discipline. Its rise to prominence had two important implications for archaeology in a historic preservation context.

First, the idea of focusing attention on the study of large anthropological issues, rather than on the reconstruction of culture-history in a localized setting, converged with precepts of settlement archaeology to emphasize the importance of small sites and whole settlement systems. If interested simply in the historical questions of when different cultures entered a region and under what circumstances, one could study only the big, central sites and look for changes in artifact styles or architectural forms indicating major periods of culture-change. However, if interested in using the archaeology of an area to address larger issues, such as how and why human societies increase in social complexity, one is likely to have to reconstruct and study complex relationships among things such as population size, the economic base and the natural environment. These relationships are revealed not only in the major sites, but in the total settlement system and the environment in which it exists. Thus, small sites and groups of sites in a natural environment, which in the terminology of the National Register of Historic Places are now called "districts" took on more significance than had previously been attributed to them.

In some areas, for example Hawaii, where prehistoric social groups practiced their activities over broad land areas, the study of individual sites could reveal little, but the study of whole areas could reveal much. In the arid Southwest, where remains tend to be well-preserved and relatively visible on the landscape, the focus of attention shifted toward field systems, irrigation systems, trails, roads and the distribution of small sites, structures and even individual artifacts through the environment. In 1975, David Hurst Thomas proposed that "nonsite archaeology" should be the order of the day, arguing that by studying the distribution of individual artifacts and other objects across the landscape one could get a more true picture of prehistoric human behavior than by focusing attention on sites where such materials are aggregated.

Nonsite archaeology was difficult to integrate into the historic preservation system. It inevitably attends best to individual properties and groups of properties whose boundaries and locations can be firmly and permanently established. However, the growing emphasis on regional studies gave archaeologists a new way to judge significance. At the same time, archaeology's new regional and theoretical emphases established points of agreement and intellectual discourse with historians and architectural historians in preservation, who were becoming increasingly interested in the study and preservation of districts, as opposed to individual landmark buildings.

The New Archaeology gave intellectual legitimacy to the study of historical archaeology, industrial archaeology and the archaeology of buildings and structures, bringing archaeologists into contact with their colleagues in other preservation disciplines. Previously, archaeological reconstructions of narrative history were preoccupied with prehistoric cultures. In the Americas, these were the native societies that ruled the continents before the arrival of Europeans. There was little interest in the archaeology of Euro-American groups or other historical immigrants, because their history, ostensibly, had already been written down. Historical archaeology was practiced, but it was largely directed toward contributing details to the reconstruction of historical buildings and sites for purposes of public interpretation.

The interest of the New Archaeologists in social process changed all this. For the study of social process, historical archaeology offers unique opportunities. Major events that triggered historical transformations in modern American society and its constituent social and ethnic groups are more or less well-documented. We know when the Civil War occurred, for example, and have historical records of events reflecting the course of the Industrial Revolution. The processes by which events actually transformed society are seldom well understood, particularly from the perspectives of those most intimately involved. These are the common soldiers in the American Revolution, slaves and free blacks in the South and Chinese miners during the California Gold Rush. Archaeology could provide access to information about such groups, through the study of their physical leavings, gaining unique insights into the processes involved in the development of modern American social, economic and industrial systems.

Recognizing this potential, archaeologists in the last two decades assigned new intellectual respectability to the study of historical, and even quite modern, social groups and to historical industrial complexes. Thought-provoking work is being done to address issues, such as economic differentiation among free black social groups before the Civil War and interaction among ethnic groups in mid-19th century California gold camps. Relatively recent history, for example, that surrounding World War II, became a legitimate subject of inquiry; archaeological studies of World War II battlefields and installations are being undertaken; and an organization devoted to the study of the war's remains was formed. Even contemporary society is now being subjected to archaeological scrutiny. The Projet du Garbage in Tucson, Arizona, is shedding new light on issues such as the response of different social groups to inflation and recession through the study of just-discarded trash.

Long before the New Archaeology revolution, historical archaeology had established a place for itself in historic preservation. It was important in the reconstruction of Williamsburg, Virginia, for example, and was used earlier as an essential part of reconstruction at many historical sites in the West. As both historical archaeology and historic preservation itself were transformed in the late 1960s and early 1970s, this relationship broadened and deepened. Historic and prehistoric archaeological sites are now routinely accorded equal treatment in most historic preservation programs carried out by states and federal agencies.

As historical archaeology matured, archaeologists also began to realize that their skills and techniques could be applied to things other than the study of sites. Sometimes to the annoyance of historians and architectural historians, archaeologists began to talk and write about the anthropological research significance of historic buildings and structures.

As in other nations, a specialized subfield of historical archaeology developed in the United States to address the archaeological remains of industrial history. Industrial archaeology brings archaeologists, historians and engineers together in identifying and documenting early facilities such as mills, waterworks, power plants and mines. The growth of industrial archaeology in the United States paralleled and is closely related to the growing recognition in historic preservation that America's industrial heritage was worth preserving, which led to the creation of the Historic American Engineering Record in 1969.

An important result of the increased attention given historical and industrial archaeology, and their integration into historic preservation projects, is increased collaboration between archaeologists and historians. Predicting where one will find historic archaeological sites, and what they will look like, naturally requires historical research before field surveys begin. Evaluating the significance of discovered sites and structures and developing research programs to document them when they must be destroyed or modified by construction projects require additional historical expertise. After some initial conflicts between archaeologists who seemed to believe that they could do without historians and historians who objected to being left out of historical research, interdisciplinary collaboration has increased steadily in recent years, with positive results for both fields.

Technological Change

The last 20 years have seen widespread technological change in the practice of archaeology, and much of this change took place in the context of preservation-oriented work. The use of computers revolutionized the field, permitting the management of vastly increased quantities of information and the mobilization of this information to address large and complicated research questions. Some of the major applications of computer-based technology were in studies of regional settlement patterns. These studies were often explicitly designed to meet the needs of federal land management agencies in compliance with the Preservation Act of 1966. In other cases they were promptly seized upon and used for such purposes. High level aerial photography, false-color infrared imagery and digitized imaging data provided by satellites were used increasingly in archaeological work for research and preservation. On the ground, archaeologists gained access to a wide array of devices that permit prospecting in advance of excavation. For example, under some conditions, ground-penetrating radar can be used before excavation to plot the locations of structures, hearths and graves buried within a site. Such technology can be of great value in preservation-oriented field surveys, allowing archaeologists to judge the complexity and organization of a site without excavating it, and to better judge the impact that a given use of land will have on it.

At sea, tools developed for the energy industry and for military purposes opened up vast unexplored areas for archaeological study, and made it possible, though often difficult, to manage archaeological sites. Because the sea level has risen substantially since human beings arrived in North America, it is probable that some of the earliest prehistoric sites on the continent are now far offshore and under water. Such sites would be of intense research interest if they could be found and studied. At the same time, however, their probable existence and the known existence of archaeologically valuable shipwrecks pose significant management problems for those who use or regulate the use of the off-shore continental shelf for purposes such as oil and gas exploration and national defense.

Various agencies of the U.S. Department of the Interior lead in applying technology to problems of prehistoric site and shipwreck identification on the continental shelf, with promising results. Modern navigation systems, using satellites and computers, make it possible for the underwater explorer to plot locations precisely on the seabed. Magnetometers, robot and manned submarines and side-scan sonar can be employed in the search for historic shipwrecks. Sub-bottom profilers, which reveal submarine terrain even if buried under many meters of silt, are employed in locating likely prehistoric sites.

Change has also occurred in the laboratory. Many techniques are now available for determining when objects found in an archaeological site were made or obtained, and for determining the sources of stones, wood products and clays used in prehistoric trade systems. Sophisticated procedures and facilities now exist for reconstructing prehistoric environments, changes in environments, and for plotting physical and chemical changes across sites and among buried soil strata. These are important aids in mapping where specific activities occurred in the past and in establishing the origin of particular soils in a site. The development or application of these techniques to archaeology were in many cases stimulated by the needs of large, well-financed preservation-related archaeological projects.

Research Results

Archaeological projects carried out under the authority of the preservation laws made important contributions to our knowledge of United States history and pre-history. For example, in Phoenix, Arizona, excavations in advance of express-way construction funded by the Federal Highway Administration revealed the first evidence of prehistoric barley cultivation in the New World, amid the remains of elaborate canal irrigation systems and two major population centers of the Hohokam, a cultural system that disappeared from the area about 1500 A.D. In the San Juan Basin of northwestern New Mexico, planning studies carried out by the Bureau of Land Management in connection with surface mining, oil and gas exploration and other land management activities traced a network of pre-historic roads, up to 12 meters wide and running arrow-straight out from the great urban center at Chaco Canyon, in the middle of the Basin. Since the pre-historic people of the San Juan Basin did not have the wheel, the purpose of these roads is a mystery. It is thought that they were used, in part, to transport building materials; more than 200,000 trees were used in the construction of just one of Chaco Canyon's major villages, some brought from mountain ranges on the distant fringes of the Basin.

In cities such as Alexandria, Virginia; Philadelphia, Pennsylvania; and Atlanta, Georgia, archaeological surveys and excavations carried out in advance of housing construction, highway expansion and urban railway construction revealed evidence of the early growth of the cities, including the remains of buildings, trash deposits, trash-filled outhouse pits and long-lost cemeteries. Study of these remains made it possible to reconstruct something of the social and economic organization of early residents. Particular attention was given to the study of early urban black communities, about whom little written record exists. It is becoming abundantly clear that such communities were essential participants in and contributors to the economy of early United States cities.

These are a few of many examples. The integration of archaeology into historic preservation resulted in the exploration of new areas, the development and application of new techniques and the investigation of new research problems, substantially increasing scholarly understanding of America's past.

Personnel and Money

Archaeologists moved into leadership roles in the American preservation movement. Several key management positions in the Bureau of Land Management, the Forest Service, the National Park Service and the Advisory Council on Historic Preservation are now occupied by archaeologists. Others serve as SHPOs in several states. In most states, an archaeologist oversees the state historic preservation office's participation in Section 106 review. The major federal landholding agencies employ almost 400 archaeologists and several major Army installations have archaeologists on duty.

It is estimated that up to $300,000,000 is spent annually on archaeology by federal agencies, recipients of federal assistance and regulated industries, most of it paid to private firms and academic institutions on a contract basis. Approximately half of the projects reviewed by the Advisory Council involve archaeology in some way, and one fourth involve only archaeological sites. It is likely that in terms of money spent, the number of people employed and the general level of activity, only tax benefit-driven rehabilitation claims a larger share of the American preservation program.

Impact of Historic Preservation on Archaeology

Archaeologists express mixed feelings about the effects of historic preservation on their discipline. On the positive side, it is recognized that preservation laws and programs stimulated a remarkable increase in archaeological work, preserved large numbers of sites for future research and stimulated scholarly inquiry into areas, both geographic and of the mind, that would otherwise have gone unexplored. On the negative side, many researchers and regulators perceive that the rapid growth of archaeology-in-preservation created employment opportunities for people with poor credentials and little ability, dragging down the overall quality of work performed. Practitioners in the field sometimes complain that federal and state standards, guidelines and regulations concerning archaeology are overly restrictive and tend to smother creativity.

Concern about what rapid growth might do to the discipline was expressed early in archaeology's movement into preservation. Professors responsible for major academic training programs fretted that they simply could not produce enough high-quality scholars to meet needs that would develop if federal agencies actually began to comply with environmental and historic preservation laws passed during the 1960s. Some of those involved in promoting the laws and their implementation belittled this concern, saying that the profession would be extremely lucky if sufficient compliance occurred to make much difference. Then if it did, ways would doubtless be found to cross the bridge of insufficient personnel when it came into view.

Even with the benefit of hindsight, it is difficult to imagine what could have been done to improve the situation, but it is now clear that the critics and worriers of the late 1960s and early 1970s had a good point. Although the record of federal agency compliance with the Preservation Act of 1966 and its related authorities remains rather uneven, virtually every agency responsible for substantial management of archaeological resources, or for programs that affect such resources, initiated some kind of program to contend with new laws. Agencies were prodded and cajoled into establishing such programs by the National Park Service and the SHPOs, who added archaeologists to their staffs in order to carry out their new responsibilities. The new programs generated a need for archaeologists within agencies, and a greatly increased volume of archaeological contracts. Contract archaeologists were needed to conduct surveys in advance of planned construction and land use projects, to test-excavate discovered sites to determine their eligibility for the National Register and to conduct salvage work.

On the whole, the university and museum-based archaeological research units that were formed before the agency preservation programs came into being did not mesh well with agency needs. Agencies required work done on schedule and with reference to specific legal requirements. The university-based research units, on the other hand, were accustomed to scheduling their work around the academic year, usually concentrating their research activities in summer months. Few of them knew or cared about federal legal and procedural requirements. As a result, a large number of service groups loosely affiliated with academic institutions and museums, and even more private consulting firms, sprang up to serve agency needs. Some of these were headed or staffed by highly trained, experienced professionals, but others provided employment opportunities to less qualified individuals.

The profession had never worried about competition for project funding between qualified and unqualified people, so standards by which a competent professional could be recognized were vaguely defined at best. A graduate degree in anthropology was generally regarded as at least desirable, but for years anthropology departments awarded masters degrees not only to those who earned them, but as consolation prizes to people who for one reason or another, after admission to Ph.D. programs, could not complete their courses of study. Experience was generally recognized as important, but field experience in archaeology does not necessarily equate with ability to make intellectual contributions to the field. During the archaeological salvage era of the 1950 and 1960s, a caste of people referred to in the field as shovel-bums grew up, individuals who worked on field crews for many years and knew how to dig carefully, survey sites, fill out recording forms and measure artifacts, but who were seldom challenged or trained to put their work in scholarly perspective. Thus it was, and to some extent still is, possible to create an archaeological consulting organization whose staff members have advanced degrees and extensive field experience, but who are neither equipped to participate in the advancement of archaeology as a scholarly discipline nor particularly inclined to do so.

Many private consulting archaeologists, who needed to capture business reacted to what they viewed as the arrogant unwillingness of universities and museums to come down out of the ivory tower and address real-world needs. They adopted the premise that contract work was different from traditional archaeological research, that it was driven by the need to meet minimum legal standards rather than, and indeed to the exclusion of, the need to contribute to scholarship. They believed that they, rather than the academics, were best equipped to meet these needs. This attitude came to be called client-oriented archaeology, and it generated substantial debate in the field. One client-oriented archaeologist who wrote extensively and thoughtfully on the subject, James Fitting, argued that it was unethical to take a client's money while serving another master, even if that master was archaeology. He believed that a contract archaeologist's first, and only, duty was to provide professional advice that would aid the client in finding a way through federal law requirements and moving the project forward. Critics of client-oriented archaeology claimed that it served to justify doing essentially meaningless archaeological work. If one's studies did not contribute to scholarship, what good were they? It was also suggested that an orientation toward client needs could lead archaeologists into what amounted to conspiracy with agencies whose missions were fundamentally destructive of archaeological resources.

Debate over client-oriented archaeology cooled substantially over recent years, although some contracting archaeologists apparently continue to practice it. Similarly, the last few years have seen a decrease in expressions of alarm about the quality of work being done under contract, and about professional abilities of the archaeologists conducting such work. It is not clear whether this indicates improvement in the quality of contract archaeology, abandonment of the field by disgusted critics or the preoccupation of practitioners with other, more pressing problems.

Academic archaeologists who chose not to participate in preservation-related work seldom write about the reasons for their choice, but they do express their criticisms in conversation and in the messages that they convey to students. It is widely perceived among academicians that agencies and SHPOs often employ archaeologists with inadequate training and experience, and with little knowledge of or commitment to the needs of archaeological scholarship. Academicians believe also that consultants who work under contract for agencies are similarly underqualified and espouse a philosophy that is explicitly inimical to the conduct of research. Preservation-related work, according to these critics, demeans the discipline and results in the conduct of activities in the name of archaeology that lack scholarly merit and wastes resources.

This grim view of the condition of archaeology in preservation is not without some factual basis. There are both poorly qualified and badly motivated individuals at work as archaeologists in federal agencies, state historic preservation offices and consulting firms. The dynamics of employment in a federal or state agency, or in a consulting firm, inevitably promote fast, rote work rather than exemplary scholarship. There is a widespread and self-fulfilling belief among agency employees and consultants that work done in compliance with the historic preservation laws cannot and even should not contribute to the advancement of archaeological research.

On the other hand, there are excellent scholars in the agencies and in consulting firms. There are others who have carefully crafted niches for themselves as administrators who try to ensure that scholarly skills are well matched with preservation needs. Not all of these people possess high academic degrees, but this does not necessarily reflect badly on their work quality. Agencies responsible for setting standards in preservation-related archaeological work made efforts to design standards to insure that preservation needs and scholarly research interests are mutually supportive. Academic critics also tend to undervalue intellectual contributions that preservation-oriented archaeology has made. Work in preservation produced important research results, as noted earlier. Moreover, efforts to relate archaeology to the preservation planning needs of land-management agencies, such as the Forest Service and the Bureau of Land Management, and to those of major regulated private industries, such as surface coal mining, stimulated major regional studies of prehistoric and historic settlement systems. Often these studies involve technological or methodological innovations. The desire to preserve archaeological sites in place led to the development of a new field of scholarly inquiry and experimentation, involving efforts to find out what happens to a site when its management involves burial, inundation, being burned over or having its trees cut in the course of logging operations.

The need to justify one's opinions about the importance of a given archaeological site, in order to demonstrate its eligibility for nomination to the National Register of Historic Places and hence for consideration in planning, drove archaeological thinking in another new direction. Before 1966, determining the significance of a site was an ad hoc affair. An archaeologist would survey an area and select certain sites to excavate which were believed to yield information relevant to the person's research interests. These sites were obviously significant to the archaeologist who selected them; there was no presumption that they were significant to any other archaeologist or to anyone else. Because the sites selected were the ones excavated, however, they tended to become those upon which scholarly attention centered and, ipso facto, they came to define the important archaeology of the area. In the context of salvage archaeology, sites not determined significant were usually destroyed without investigation. The validity of the archaeologist's judgment about significance was thus central, but no organized system existed to evaluate, question and, if necessary, correct such judgments. The National Register changed all this, at least in theory, by requiring that judgments about significance or nonsignificance be supported with concrete information and explicit arguments. This material is reviewed by agency officials, state historic preservation office archaeologists and the National Register staff. The system, at least potentially, introduces intellectual rigor into the evaluation process.

Some archaeologists object to the National Register as overly bureaucratic, insulting to their professional judgment and epistemologically unsound. None of these objections is entirely without merit, and the last is particularly interesting. It is argued that archaeological significance can be defined only in relation to research problems, which change through time as old questions are answered and new ones arise. This being the case, it is argued that it is illusory to attempt to define significance using broad criteria of the kind used by the National Register. It is also considered unrealistic to expect archaeological sites to retain their significance or lack of significance in perpetuity. This proposition is the subject of continuing debate in archaeology. While it calls the National Register concept of significance into doubt, the fact that it is debated shows how the existence of the National Register stimulated intellectual discourse about an important and long-neglected aspect of archaeological practice.

As the practice of archaeology in preservation expanded, its attendant costs and increasing influence on planning and land use decisions raised basic questions about the need for archaeology, its values and approaches to it. Before 1966, for example, archaeologists might have worried about the fact that field surveys carried out in adjoining river valleys might be done by different scholars and according to such different procedures that their results would not be comparable. No one, however, beyond the archaeological community was concerned about it, and no system existed to address the problem. When the adequacy and reliability of such surveys became factors to be considered by feder-

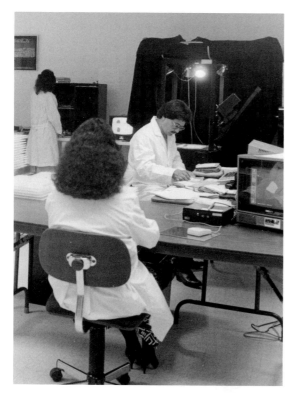

Revolutionary changes are occurring in the archaeological laboratory as the result of new technology. In this fully computerized laboratory, artifacts are scanned by color video cameras, weighed and measured, with all data recorded by computer and stored on laser disc. (Goodyear/Celeron Archeological Laboratory, Las Cruces, New Mexico)

Modern technology is extending the range of archaeological exploration to previously inaccessible areas. Robot submersibles similar to this one, armed with television cameras, sensitive controls and computerized recording devices, are used to explore shipwrecks and other submerged sites on the seabed. (Richard Hughes, Maryland Historical Trust)

This stone rabbit was uncovered in Samburg, Tennessee, during a Soil Conservation Service-sponsored excavation of an early Mississippian burial mound at the Effigy Rabbit Site. (Gene Alexander, Soil Conservation Service)

Among the most remarkable archaeological phenomenon in North America is the Chaco road system, a network of arrow-straight roads radiating out across the desert San Juan Basin of New Mexico, Arizona, Colorado and Utah from the great prehistoric center at Chaco Canyon. It was recorded as part of an ongoing study of the system by the Bureau of Land Management. (New Mexico State Office, Bureau of Land Management)

Sites of archaeological importance are sometimes of even more cultural and religious significance to native groups. This ancient "tsektsel" or prayer seat, on Doctor Rock, a high peak in the Helkau Historic District of northern California, is still used by Indian religious practitioners. (Theodoratus Cultural Research, Fair Oaks, California)

al agencies in project planning, the need for standards quickly became apparent. Similarly, before 1966, the amount and kind of excavation that an archaeologist might carry out, the research questions to be addressed and the techniques to be used were determined by the individual archaeologist and the sponsor. When federal agencies received authorization to fund archaeological work in advance of their projects, and were strongly encouraged to do so by the Preservation Act of 1966 and other statutes, it immediately became necessary to establish standards for the conduct of such work, to protect archaeologists and sites from impecunious agencies and to protect agencies from unscrupulous archaeologists.

Standard-setting can lead to intellectual stultification if the standards established are too rigid. The Advisory Council, the National Park Service and the state historic preservation offices were for the most part sensitive to this danger. They tried to establish standards for the conduct of surveys and excavations in full consultation with archaeologists and others concerned with sites.

Widely used national standards now exist and are currently undergoing review and revision. Many state offices adopted their own standards and guidelines as well. Recognition that standards applicable to one region or jurisdiction may not be applicable to another led to the development of preservation plans for cities and large rural land areas. Among other things, these establish contexts for the evaluation of archaeological sites and for making decisions about their treatment. They have the added benefit of encouraging the organization of archaeological data on a regional basis, and they establish specific directions for archaeological research.

Some archaeologists take the organization of data and research a step further, developing research topics at a national or even international level to provide major foci for their work carried out under the preservation laws. It is argued that the pursuit of major topics—questions such as "how and why do civilizations collapse?" and "how and why has the climate in North America changed over the last 10,000 years?" would give coherence and relevance to the conduct of archaeological work. This would in turn provide a better basis for making wise decisions about which sites to excavate and how. Although the idea was initially greeted with some suspicion and alarm by archaeologists who saw in it the potential for government restrictions on their traditional scholarly freedom, it is gradually gaining greater acceptance.

Impact of Archaeology on Historic Preservation

The integration of archaeology into historic preservation had three major conceptual effects on preservation itself. Firstly, it contributed substantially to the federal government's approach to what is generally referred to as preservation planning. Secondly, it brought a more disciplined perspective to the process of making judgments about the significance of historic properties. Thirdly, it brought anthropological views to bear on historic preservation issues, notably on how to address preservation interests of local communities, ethnic groups and American Indian religious practitioners.

Perhaps the best-known contribution of archaeology to preservation is promoting and strongly influencing the federal government's approach to preservation planning. Archaeology's influence in this area is based on the revolution in its theory and method that began in the decades preceding enactment of the Preservation Act of 1966.

At least since the rise of settlement archaeology in the 1950s, most archaeologists attempted to look beyond the limits of the site they happened to be excavating, orienting their research toward physiographic regions. As students of material remains, believing that artifacts reflect social and cultural behavior, they naturally tend toward materialist, economic explanations of culture change. This leads to research emphasizing human interactions with the environment. By the 1960s, it was virtually an article of faith among American archaeologists that to understand a society's history, one had to study how its relationships with the land and the natural environment had changed through time. Such changes can seldom be studied in a single site. One needs to look at many sites throughout a region to see how settlement location, trade patterns and use of environmental resources are reflected in the archaeological record.

When archaeologists moved into preservation, they brought with them their emphasis on regional studies. The use of a regional perspective promised to help in confronting one of the major strategic problems that accompanied the growth of preservation in the 1970s. This problem was how to rationalize the evaluation of specific properties for inclusion in the National Register of Historic Places. In order to cope with the great architectural and cultural diversity of the nation, the criteria used in determining eligibility for nomination to the National Register were written broadly. As the criteria were applied the perception developed, rightly or wrongly, that practically anything might meet the National Register's criteria. This was true, especially among federal agency administrators whose projects were encumbered by the need to consider impacts on what they perceived to be ordinary old buildings or unspectacular archaeological sites.

Archaeologists quickly realized that their regional perspective could help them alleviate this criticism. Simply stated, understanding the archaeology of a region does not necessarily require study of all its sites. One can instead select a sample of sites representing different aspects of the settlement system of the region as it existed at different times, and from study of this sample generalize about the whole. It follows that sites making up the regional sample should be placed on the National Register and given maximum protection. Similarly, one can define research questions or problems on a regional basis and determine National Register eligibility for those sites whose study is likely to contribute to addressing the questions. Ideally, both approaches would be combined in such a way that a representative sample of sites is preserved for future research while sites useful in contemporary research are recognized as eligible for the National Register but may be committed to data recovery (salvage archaeology).

The concept of looking at the archaeology of a region as the basis for making decisions about the preservation of archaeological resources coincided with the passage of legislation that encouraged embedding preservation in the project planning processes of federal land management agencies and state governments. Efforts were made by planners, cultural geographers and preservationists to improve these planning processes. The scope of such planning is generally compatible with archaeology's regional perspective. In theory at least, it is in the context of such a plan that long-term decisions can be made about the future of archaeological sites within the planning area.

Archaeologists sought the integration of their interests into planning at a variety of levels, including city planning, small-region planning by federal land managing agencies, such as the Forest Service, the Bureau of Land Management, the U.S. Army and multi-agency planning at the state and large regional levels. Techniques were developed for predicting the distribution of archaeological sites in a region based on historical, ethnographic, archaeological and environmental data and on field surveys of sample tracts. Research problems were set forth in regional terms to guide survey and data recovery efforts.

As archaeologists moved into increasingly influential administrative positions in the National Park Service, they sought to extend their ideas about planning to the preservation field as a whole. Based initially on a requirement of the Preservation Act of 1966 that each state historic preservation office prepare and implement a comprehensive statewide historic preservation plan, the National Park Service promoted the establishment of historic preservation planning processes at the state level. By the late 1970s, the Resource Protection Planning Process—RP3 for short—was urged by the National Park Service on states and federal agencies alike.

RP3 begins with a compilation of available information on a region's history, prehistory, culture, economics and environment, and the organization of data about these areas into study units or historical contexts. Each context is a bounded unit of time and space, with particular social or economic characteristics. The early colonial period in the greater Boston area would be one example; industrial development along the Savannah River another; the Paleo-Indian period in the Powder River basin a third. With reference to each such unit, data gaps and research problems are defined. An ideal operating plan is established that will allow one to fill the gaps and address the problems. The process then turns to the real-world constraints that may keep one from realizing the ideal operating plan. For example, in the study of Paleo-Indian sites in the Powder River Basin of Wyoming, the biggest data gap to be filled might be located in the northern part of the basin, but major coal strip mining may be taking place in the southern part, forcing one's attention to be focused on threatened sites there. Based on an analysis of gaps and constraints, the operating plan is adjusted to establish a realistic process that can be used in guiding survey, evaluation and preservation decisions.

As discussed later, there is reason to believe that RP3 may lead preservation planning in directions that are not always desirable. There is little doubt about its influence, however. By 1985, according to a National Park Service tally, at least 5 states had RP3-based planning processes in place while 25 had them under development.

A second impact of archaeology on preservation has to do with the evaluation and treatment of specific historic buildings, structures and other architectural and engineering phenomena. Although traditionally viewed as the province of the historian, architectural historian or historian of industry, these kinds of historic properties came under archaeological scrutiny when archaeologists began working in preservation. As federal agencies and archaeologists whom they employed attempted to meet their new responsibilities under the Preservation Act of 1966 and the National Environmental Policy Act of 1969, they had to concern themselves with all kinds of historic properties, not just with prehistoric and underground archaeological sites. No matter what archaeologists might have wanted to do, when assisting federal agencies to comply with new laws, they were not in a position to ignore historic properties that did not happen to be archaeological sites. Archaeologists brought their anthropological training to bear on the significance of things other than archaeological sites, contributing new perspectives to the analysis and appreciation of standing structures.

The application of anthropological concepts and techniques to historic preservation had a third and potentially more far-reaching consequence. Because their discipline is a part of the larger field of anthropology and because of the kinds of properties they study, archaeologists often work with and become spokesmen for the interests of Indians and other ethnic groups, such as native Pacific Islanders. They argue for the significance of places that have cultural or religious value to such groups and for the appropriateness of their consideration under the historic preservation laws. Archaeological surveys and data recovery projects increasingly serve as conduits through which cultural anthropologists and folklorists apply their skills and concepts to historic properties. Thus archaeologists and their anthropological colleagues are important parts of the growing movement that seeks to address intangible cultural values, as discussed in Chapter 7. Traditional cultural values are the basis for National Register nominations and eligibility determinations. Such values figured regularly in cases considered under Section 106 and generated controversies that continue as this is written.

Issues in Preservation Archaeology

The integration of archaeology into the national historic preservation program brought to the surface a number of issues and problems, both for archaeologists and for preservation in general. Sorting them out will continue to be a major challenge for the next decade.

The Price of Success

The employment of archaeologists in federal and state agencies and the development of a large market for archaeological work done under contract inevitably generates costs to federal, state and local governments, and to the regulated industries that must comply with the historic preservation laws in order to get licenses, permits and federal financial assistance. Not only is more archaeology being done in the United States today than ever before as the result of historic preservation laws but it is more costly. There are two reasons for this. Firstly, most of the work is no longer done free or at subsidized costs by universities and museums. Now it is done as a business, by organizations that charge for what they know or believe their services to be worth. Secondly, the Archeological and Historic Preservation Act of 1974 authorized agencies to spend up to one percent of the cost of a construction project on archaeological salvage. There is some tendency to accept this figure as appropriate in developing a project budget, whether it is needed or not. Needless to say, one percent of the budget for a large dam, highway segment or federal office building can be a substantial amount of money.

As the cost of archaeology increased, per acre surveyed and per hole dug, stories appeared in the media to the effect that archaeologists were extracting large fees from clients for identifying and in some cases salvaging insignificant sites. When examined, most of these claims were found to lack specific merit. Some that have apparent merit simply reflect a failure by archaeologists to communicate the value of the properties in which they are interested. Others have the ring of truth, however. Justified or not, the belief that insignificant sites are judged significant in order to generate money for archaeologists resulted in occasional efforts to stiffen National Register criteria, or even to change or do away with the Preservation Act of 1966.

Efforts to contend with this problem took two forms. Firstly, staff of the National Register tended over time to become more conservative in their assessment of significance and required more extensive documentation to back up judgments about significance. Secondly, the Advisory Council initiated cost effectiveness review, under Section 106, looking critically at archaeological budgets for ways to reduce costs without reducing quality. The Advisory Council expressed increased willingness to accept the destruction of some archaeological sites without salvage if solid research-based justification for their excavation could not be demonstrated.

Both of these approaches are only sporadically successful, and each may have unintended and adverse consequences. The National Register's approach may generate paperwork and create delays. In the end, it may deprive historic properties of the attention they should receive in federal project planning. The Advisory Council's approach has the potential for playing into the hands of agencies that want to avoid responsibility for archaeological sites because of budget constraints. In the absence of a more comprehensive solution, however, neither agency has much choice but to pursue the strategies it has adopted.

Quality Control

Coupled with the concern about costs is a rising concern about the quality of work performed under archaeological contract. Ezra Zubrow, in a study of contract archaeology survey reports, in New York and Colorado, for example, found that about 5 percent of the contractors did not even report the locations in which the work was conducted; an average of more than 30 percent failed to report the size of the area surveyed; and the majority were deficient in their reporting of fieldwork methods. In Colorado, reports indicate that an average of 158.1 acres were surveyed per person per day, a figure that would literally require surveyors to perform their work at a dead run.

By the late 1970s, charges by archaeologists that their colleagues were doing bad work were widespread and began to be detailed and discussed in the professional literature. Although as noted above, charges of malfeasance appear to be less frequent in recent years, there is no evidence that the problem is solved.

The most visible response to the new concern with research quality is the formation of the Society of Professional Archeologists (SOPA). SOPA reviews the qualifications of applicant archaeologists and certifies them as professionals in a variety of subfields. Each person certified must agree to abide by a written code of ethics and statement of professional standards. Upon receipt of a complaint about misbehavior by a certified archaeologist, SOPA investigates and, if the charge is borne out, withdraws the archaeologist's certification. SOPA offers what is probably the best hope for overall self-improvement by the archaeological community. However, only a few practicing archaeologists are certified, and few government agencies make SOPA certification the threshold over which an archaeologist must pass in order to receive a contract. For that matter, relatively few government-based archaeologists are themselves certified by SOPA.

Irrelevant Research Results

An important aspect of the quality control problem is the possibility that much of the information generated by contracted archaeological surveys and data recovery is of little use to science or the public. As noted above, there is a belief, among both contract archaeologists and academics, that work done to achieve compliance with federal laws somehow cannot, or even should not, contribute to scholarship. As a result, some federal agencies prepare scope-of-work documents for salvage projects that tell contractors precisely how many holes they will dig, how big they will be and what size wire-mesh all soil will be passed through, without discussing the kinds of research questions that should be addressed by the excavation.

Taking their lead from such agencies, some archaeologists prepare proposals that address particulars without concern for purpose. Where research questions are articulated, they are often vague at best. They sometimes appear to have been stored in a word-processor for rote regurgitation into every proposal. Since settlement archaeology and the New Archaeology give a special legitimacy to their study, it is almost de rigueur to assert that one intends to investigate settlement and subsistence systems. This is done regardless of whether the work proposed has anything to do with how people in the past arranged their settlements and obtained their food and other necessities, and without bothering to demonstrate why the settlement and subsistence practices of the vanished group being investigated are of any scholarly importance whatsoever.

Approaches to this issue generally involve proposals to establish broad-scale research topics to be addressed by archaeologists in a given state, region or the nation. For example, this author and others proposed the establishment of National Archeological Research Topics. The Society for American Archeology sponsored a series of regional seminars to encourage archaeologists to exchange information on regional research problems and questions. While none of these efforts has yet borne much fruit, some are making progress. Each must confront three problems. Firstly, the archaeological community tends to be cautious in its support for such attempts, which are regarded as suspect both because government control of scholarly inquiry would be highly inappropriate in a free society and because they risk stifling innovation and new discoveries. Secondly, and largely in response to the first problem, most efforts, such as the Society for American Archeology initiatives, are made by or in cooperation with state or regional groups of archaeologists who seek to reach consensus on topics to be addressed. This tends to produce unsorted laundry lists of topics that archaeologists find interesting, but whose relative importance to scholarly research in general may not be clear. Thirdly, even where research priorities are established, there is no organized way to pursue them. Presently, there is no way to ensure that federal agencies require contractors to address agreed-upon research topics. Even if such requirements could be established in individual cases, the pursuit of most large-scale research topics requires comparative study and synthesis of data. There are at present few systems for mobilizing results of numerous studies in a region, typically sponsored by numerous agencies, in order to address a given topic in a coherent way.

The Conservation Ethic Run Wild

As noted above, the idea of preserving archaeological sites in place, in preference to excavating them, was a revolutionary one when William Lipe proposed it over a decade ago. Today, it is so widely accepted that many are beginning to wonder if it is not being carried to extremes. For example, it is standard practice in the regulation of oil and gas exploration and timber harvesting on federal lands to require that all archaeological sites be avoided, and left in place for future study. This is usually done without evaluating them to determine their eligibility for the National Register, because evaluation would require studies whose costs, it is thought, cannot be justified if the sites are not going to be damaged or destroyed. As a result, many of the sites avoided are recorded with the SHPO and the land management agency as little more than dots on the map. Unfortunately, little is learned about the nature of the sites or their research potential. This in turn inhibits both research and good management.

In some cases, archaeological sites may be avoided that are not really worth preservation, generating unnecessary costs and complicating oil, gas or timber operations. Since it is now widely accepted that even small sites may be important for research purposes, sites that are avoided are often no more than small concentrations of stone flakes on the surface of the ground, representing places where prehistoric people camped briefly and worked on stone tools. Other sites may be isolated tepee rings, where a Plains Indian group once erected a shelter, or pot drops where a scatter of pottery fragments on the surface of the ground marks the scene of a prehistoric stumble. Such sites may not be of much importance at all. It is impossible to know in the absence of agreed-upon research priorities. Even if they are important, it may be more useful and cost-effective simply to record them and pick up their constituent parts than to route a road, drilling site or timber cut around them.

Finally, it is by no means certain, even when a site is avoided, that it has really been protected. When a timber cut is sprinkled with clumps of uncut trees, each marking an archaeological site, or when a road to an oil rig takes a strange jog, a signal is sent to artifact collectors that something is there to be found, and the site may not long survive.

The problem of over enthusiasm for the preservation of sites in place can be overcome through the development and application of large-scale research topics and plans. For example, if it were determined that in order to address an established set of research topics, every pot-drop in a region should be recorded in place and picked up, then archaeological surveyors could simply do this whenever they come upon such a site, rather than leaving it in place. However, this approach troubles those who hold closely to the conservation ethic. It can also be a problem for strict constructionist interpreters of preservation regulations, who believe that compliance requires the evaluation for National Register eligibility of each and every property found, before decisions are made about its treatment.

Vandalism and Relations with Amateurs

Many people other than professional archaeologists explore and exploit archaeological sites. Amateur archaeologists, often organized into local or state societies, conduct surveys and excavations, sometimes in cooperation with professionals, sometimes on their own. Many such projects are responsibly done and add importantly to research and preservation. Others, called pothunters by archaeologists, are irresponsible and destructive. Private artifact collectors, more interested in the beauty or rarity of individual artifacts than in the information they can impart, seek and excavate sites or pay others to excavate them, in destructive ways. A commercial market for artifacts has developed with links to art dealers in this country and abroad, creating powerful economic incentives for artifact looting. Finally, some people vandalize archaeological sites for reasons of sheer wantonness, digging up graves for the thrill of grave robbing, or blasting centuries-old rock paintings with spray cans simply to announce their presence.

Like archaeologists, artifact seekers and vandals benefited from the last 20 years of technological change and innovation. Metal detectors, off-road vehicles and earth-moving equipment are employed in the search for treasures on land. Even more sophisticated detection equipment is used to seek treasure under the sea. These changes, coupled with population increase, increased leisure time and a growing international interest in aboriginal art has elevated the problem of vandalism and pothunting to crisis proportions. With few exceptions, it is not illegal to vandalize or pothunt archaeological sites on private land in the United States. On federal land, however, the Antiquities Act of 1906 defines the excavation of a site and removal of its artifacts without a permit as a misdemeanor. The Archeological Resources Protection Act of 1979 sets forth more specific terms and increased penalties for violations. Police action against pothunters has become more aggressive in recent years, and a modest record of convictions is developing.

Many uncertainties remain about the effectiveness and appropriateness of current approaches to the pothunter problem. Is it possible to deal with the problem through police action, considering the vastness of federal lands, the tremendous number of recorded and unrecorded sites and the small number of federal agents available to do the job? The answer certainly is no. If it were possible, would it be desirable to protect all sites on federal land, if the result were to drive pothunters onto private lands, where they could pursue their depredations without interference?

Artifact collectors argue that laws such as the Archeological Resources Protection Act of 1979 which permit professional archaeologists to excavate while prohibiting nonprofessional excavations of all kinds, are unfair, and that responsible amateurs should be allowed to pursue their hobby if their work is helpful to science or preservation. The collectors' position deserves more respect than many archaeologists give it. Is it reasonable for archaeologists to salvage 10 or 20 percent of the sites in a reservoir area, or to excavate only part of a site to be destroyed by a highway? To forbid artifact collectors from digging in

The involvement of archaeology in historic preservation has brought archaeological perspectives and techniques to bear on a wide range of properties that are not archaeological sites in the traditional sense. Buildings such as this trapper's or prospector's cabin in Alaska, built in the 1930s, are now routinely studied and documented by archaeologists. (Alaska State Office, Bureau of Land Management)

These excavations, carried out by the New Mexico State University in advance of auto parking facility construction in El Paso, Texas, revealed the remains of a community of overseas Chinese who occupied the area during the 19th century. (Department of Sociology and Anthropology, New Mexico State University)

*The development of industrial
archaeology since the 1970s has
resulted in the preservation of many
purely functional structures. This
1886 truss bridge at Allegan,
Michigan, is the only one-lane
bridge in the nation to be
rehabilitated using Federal
Highway Administration funds.*
(Bureau of History, Michigan
Department of State)

*In Dunn County, North Dakota, a
team from the University of North
Dakota undertook a study of the
Nordsven Quarry site to investigate
prehistoric quarries in advance of
the development of coal mining
planned for the west central part of
the state.* (Matthew J. Root,
Department of Anthropology,
University of North Dakota)

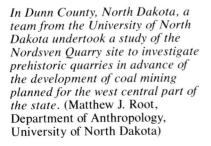

the remainder of the site that is to be destroyed by bulldozers or rising water? Is it necessarily wrong for an individual to want a beautiful pot to display at home? If thousands of such pots are in storage in museums, should there not be some legitimate way for a private individual to acquire or enjoy them?

Some archaeologists believe that legitimizing the private ownership of artifacts obtained under controlled conditions would strike effectively at the economic underpinnings of the antiquities market. Others think this would only encourage pothunting. They accept police action on federal land as a half-loaf that they are glad to have and loathe to place in peril by exploring other approaches to the problem.

What To Do With All The Artifacts?

An archaeological excavation, or even a surface survey, can generate a tremendous volume of material that must be cared for after the fieldwork is done. Behind every artifact appearing in a museum, there are hundreds, sometimes thousands of others, held in archives for future research. These include pottery fragments, broken spearpoints, seed grinding tools and animal skinning tools from prehistoric sites. There are rusty metal and fragments of glass or crockery from historic sites. Besides objects purposefully shaped by human hand, there are often tons of items that are not strictly artifacts but nonetheless critical to research, such as samples of rock, soil, charcoal, animal bone, marine shell and plant pollen.

Archaeological sites have yielded unwieldy objects such as whole ships or boats, which not only are large but require special handling to prevent deterioration once out of the ground. Wet sites often preserve wood and leather that must be treated with laborious laboratory processes in order to keep them intact following excavation. Dry desert sites produce basketry, featherwork or even human excrement, an important source of information on diet. These also require special handling in a humidity-controlled environment. Another product of archaeological fieldwork is records; including field notes, plans, maps and photographs, which must be retained in good order if future scholars are to understand the work performed and gain new insights.

The increase in archaeological work resulting from various preservation laws naturally placed a special strain on the curatorial facilities caring for the things found. By the mid-1970s, academic institutions and museums alike complained about being unable to handle the material that federal projects were sending in from the field. A study sponsored by the Department of the Interior in 1977 concluded that federal policy regarding the care of collections was inadequate, and that a wide range of guidelines and improved procedures was needed. In a few regions a particular institution or the SHPO took the matter in hand and obtained funds to develop improved facilities, but generally, the problem persists unresolved.

Treatment of Human Remains

A special aspect of the curatorial problem that gained recent prominence is the treatment of human skeletal material. Cemeteries are important sources of information on social organization, population structure, disease and social interaction. For this reason, and in order to avoid their destruction by modern projects, it is often necessary to exhume skeletons, often in substantial numbers, from some sites. Since the great majority of such skeletons now being stored in curatorial facilities represent the mortal remains of deceased American Indians, this is of special concern to contemporary Indian groups. Indian organizations are lobbying at all levels of government for the return of their ancestors' bones, and for their reinternment in a manner respectful of cultural and religious values. They charge that it is discriminatory to retain the bones of their ancestors as scientific specimens, while routinely reburying the remains of whites, blacks and orientals whenever they are excavated. They argue that the exhumation and retention of such remains has a continuing influence on the practice of their religion and on their culture.

Archaeologists and their colleagues in physical anthropology who study human skeletal remains are of two minds regarding this issue. Some insist that the remains are vital sources of information that must be retained for future study. They point out that the new research questions that constantly arise can be adequately addressed only if collections of skeletal remains are available. Also new techniques are constantly developed that can be fruitfully applied to such collections. Others believe that out of respect for both the dead and the living, the retention of such collections must be foregone, and that archaeologists and physical anthropologists should content themselves with addressing only research questions that can be answered during a specified period after a given set of remains is exhumed.

The Resource Protection Planning Process

As noted earlier, one of archaeology's contributions to preservation is the development of an approach to preservation planning known as the Resource Protection Planning Process or RP3. Thirty states and several federal agencies developed, or are in the process of developing, plans based to some extent on RP3. The Department of the Interior has issued national planning standards and guidelines that embody its concepts.

Discontent with RP3 has emerged, however. Some who have wrestled with the process believe that it requires a great deal of work without producing much planning. This results from the fact that RP3 efforts to date seldom progressed beyond the creation of contexts for evaluating the significance of properties. They thus may help rationalize the evaluation process, but they do not address the central planning problem of influencing development decisions.

A peculiarly archaeological concern about RP3 is its emphasis on filling information gaps. As discussed earlier, RP3 is based on the creation of study units or historical contexts, each representing a block of time and space reflecting a major cultural pattern in, or influence on, the history or prehistory of the area under study. Significance is then ascribed to those properties that can provide information to fill information gaps of each historical context. Archaeologists who are influenced by the New Archaeology of the 1960s and its intellectual descendants find this approach suspiciously akin to that against which the New Archaeologists revolted. They perceive the gap-filling approach to be antithetical to the development of large-scale research questions and the generation of hypotheses about the past. The National Park Service responded to this concern by directing, in its standards and guidelines for preservation planning, that research questions be established as part of historical context development. In practice, however, the overall emphasis of RP3 continues to be on gap-filling.

A more general question about RP3 which is beginning to trouble preservationists is whether it fundamentally misdirects the evaluation of historic properties. Because of its origins in archaeology, RP3 is too often oriented toward the information value of historic properties. However, there are many kinds of historical significance beyond those related to information, and often many reasons to preserve a historic property that have little to do with its information content. The Preservation Act of 1966 is explicitly oriented toward preserving historic properties as living parts of modern community life, regarding them as parts of the environment that contribute to the quality of life in communities. The research value of such properties was of relatively minor concern to the drafters of the act. Ironically, the tendency by some to emphasize information value can be interpreted as a throwback to the way historic preservation was practiced before 1966, when the emphasis at all levels of government was on the identification, preservation and protection of properties illustrative of major historical themes. These were primarily historic buildings and sites that could be used for public interpretation and commemoration. To the extent that RP3 tends to drive us back toward this narrow pedagogical kind of preservation, at the expense of recognizing the social and cultural values ascribed to historic properties by local people, RP3 is antithetical to the purposes of the act.

Cultural Values

The anthropological backgrounds of virtually all North American archaeologists give them a special interest in and, in theory at least, sympathy for the cultural values of American Indians, other ethnic groups and small-scale communities. In recent years, these values have become increasingly prominent in American preservation. The ways in which they were or were not addressed by preservationists and federal agencies generated substantial controversy. As preservationists and employees of federal and state agencies, archaeologists often find themselves at the heart of these controversies.

An example of such a cultural controversy is the case of the Gasquet-Orleans Road, the GO Road for short, on which the Forest Service began construction in the late 1970s. The GO Road was routed over the top of the northern California Coast Range, to open rich interior timberlands to sawmills on the coast. The road was to pass through a high-country area used by several local Indian tribes for religious purposes, a place where practitioners of native religions went to meditate, receive visions and prepare medicine. After years of trying to ignore the problem while continuing construction on the road, the Forest Service conducted a detailed archaeological and ethnographic study of the area resulting in a decision by the Keeper of the National Register that a substantial part of the high country, called the Helkau Historic District, was eligible for the Register because of its association with traditional American Indian cultural practices. By this time, the road was built to each side of the district. The Indians halted construction, not on historic preservation grounds, but on the concern that construction through the district violated their constitutional rights to the free exercise of religion.

While the GO Road case was being litigated, another group of Indians sought to halt expansion of a ski resort on land administered by the Forest Service on the San Francisco Peaks of New Mexico. The Peaks are of religious importance to the Navajo, Hopi and other groups in the area. Here the Forest Service successfully avoided seeking a determination from the Keeper of the National Register as to whether the Peaks might be eligible for the National Register, despite urging by both the National Park Service and the Advisory Council that such a determination be sought. The Forest Service relied on its own determination, concurred in by the SHPO, that the Peaks were not eligible because there was no archaeological evidence of Indian activity on them. They also concluded that to consider their religious value would purportedly violate the constitutional separation of church and state.

In another case from the early 1980s the entire Hawaiian Island of Kaho'olawe, used by the U.S. Navy as a target range, was determined eligible for the National Register in part because of its stated cultural importance to native Hawaiians. This was one basis for an out-of-court settlement requiring the Navy to constrain its bombardment activities and to provide access to native Hawaiians who wish to use the island for cultural and religious purposes.

In another case, where litigation was averted, plans to expand an airport within the Tonaachow Historic District in the State of Truk, within what was then the U.S. administered Trust Territory of the Pacific Islands, was strongly opposed by the two villages that made up the district. Their opposition was based in part on the damage the expansion would do to the district's central feature, a mountain important in traditional Trukese history and culture. Here the Trust Territory government used archaeological and anthropological services to mediate the dispute, including the strictly historic preservation issues and problems such as the airport's impact on traditional fishing grounds and the need generated by its construction for installing a sanitary sewer system.

Federal agencies are seldom well prepared to deal with cases involving traditional cultural values. Because such values are often foreign to those on which the United States legal system is based, addressing them can be a vexing problem for administrators. Archaeologists and their anthropological colleagues can sometimes offer solutions to these conflicts by virtue of the anthropological discipline's tradition of analyzing and seeking to understand both sides of cultural conflict situations. This role can be a dangerous one, however. Too close an identification with the interests of a native group can destroy one's credibility in administrative circles, and too close an identification with the government can close off communication with the native group.

Some archaeologists and other preservationists backed away from the issue, arguing that traditional cultural values have no place in historic preservation. This proposition reflects a reactionary view that is expressed with reference to other aspects of historic preservation as well. A not-insubstantial element in the American preservation establishment believes that the scope of the national preservation program should be narrow, concluding that the breadth of property types and kinds of significance embraced by the National Register are too great. This may be the single most important issue the American historic preservation movement will have to face during the next decade or two. Are we to be concerned primarily with specific landmarks, to be preserved to commemorate and instruct upon the great events and processes of American history? Or should we be primarily concerned with the places people treasure for their cultural associations and for the enjoyment of life today in the local areas where they spend their lives? If the latter is central to our mission, we cannot ignore the traditional cultural values of native Americans and other minorities without discriminating against them on the basis of their race and religion.

Conclusion

The field of archaeology has experienced extraordinary growth since 1966 as part of the American historic preservation program. Today, archaeologists are employed in all sectors of the program and at all administrative levels. Archaeological concepts are now embedded in the intellectual life of preservation, and preservation philosophy has in turn had profound effects on the practice of archaeology.

Archaeologists bring with them the basic philosophy of their parent discipline, anthropology, contributing to the idea that American preservation should address the histories, the artifacts and the intangible cultural values of all of the nation's diverse ethnic and social groups. Archaeological emphasis on understanding the past in the context of larger physiographic regions and the natural environment supports the idea that preservation should take a broad, comprehensive view of its subject matter.

Archaeology's integration into historic preservation has not been without its negative aspects, however, and many problems remain to be resolved. The quality of archaeological work done for preservation must be improved. The results of archaeological research must be made more meaningful to the public and to international scholarship. Ways must be found to develop fruitful cooperation between professional archaeologists and responsible amateurs, and to reduce the economic incentives that bring about the destruction of archaeological sites. Archaeology's interest in the information value of historic properties must be more carefully balanced with other values in the conduct of preservation planning. Perhaps most important, archaeologists have important potential roles to play in establishing a direction for American preservation as the 20th century comes to a close. As a science, archaeology can help bring rigor and discipline to the national historic preservation movement, but it can also encourage a narrow-minded emphasis on the information value of historic properties to the exclusion of other aspects of significance. This danger can be averted, however, through greater attention to archaeology's place as a subdiscipline of anthropology, which in turn emphasizes respect for all of human history and culture in all their manifestations.

CHAPTER NINE

THE NEXT TWENTY YEARS

ROBERT E. STIPE

THE NEXT TWENTY YEARS

ROBERT E. STIPE

Introduction

The 20 years since 1966 have seen electrifying growth and progress in the American preservation movement. Thousands of buildings and neighborhoods have been officially designated and placed under some form of protection. A national survey of buildings and sites is well under way, and an official monuments list has been established. Threatened buildings have been saved and restored to productive use, and the worst ravages of federal construction projects have been slowed or stopped. Public awareness of historic preservation has been raised considerably as a result of the Bicentennial celebrations of the American Revolution and the U.S. Constitution, and the restoration of the Statue of Liberty. A national partnership of federal, state and local governments, led by one of the most competent government preservation offices anywhere in the world, has been put in place. Within and without this partnership, state and local governments have accepted increasingly greater levels of responsibility for preservation. Much has been accomplished. All of the recommendations of the 1965 Special Committee of the U.S. Conference of Mayors are now in place in one form or another. Perhaps no cause in American history has accomplished so much in such a short time.

At the same time, it is difficult to reconcile these accomplishments with the air of concern that hangs over many of the recent meetings of American preservationists, especially those involving professionals. The litany is familiar. For seven consecutive years of the Reagan administration, the Department of the Interior has recommended no federal appropriations. The preservation community has undergone an annual uphill battle to persuade the U.S. Congress to restore even a modest appropriation. Fearing the demise of a truly national preservation system, state historic preservation offices have been skeptical about announced federal intentions to focus effort and attention on nationally significant properties and to divert preservation authority back to states. Enthusiastic but unproven new partners in the preservation enterprise, certified local governments, have begun to assume new responsibilities for preservation that hitherto have been the duty of the states.

Concern is expressed about the rapidly expanding scope of the preservation field and the speed with which traditional concepts have changed. The subject matter of preservation has been democratized and is no longer focused entirely on the oldest and the best. Now there is talk of preserving cultural and designed landscapes, the intangible cultural heritage, ethnic tradition and conservation areas. There is a new sense of responsibility and concern for any preservation activity resulting in the gentrification of neighborhoods and harm to the poor and elderly. An expanded federal preservation planning effort has resulted in accusations of widget counting. This, taken with recommendations for reduced funding, resulted in proposals for the establishment of a new federal preservation agency. Direct federal funding of preservation has been substantially reduced over recent years and questions raised about the problems arising from the privatization of preservation resulting from federal tax subsidies.

One wonders, is the glass half full or half empty? Is the preservation movement still moving up? Is it stuck on a plateau? Or is it heading downward? This closing chapter attempts to discuss some of the more urgent issues, to place the movement in the context of larger events in American domestic life and to suggest a few alternatives for regaining the strong forward momentum of 20 years ago. Notwithstanding the atmosphere of concern expressed above, the basic premise is one of optimism.

Reading the preceding chapters of this book, one must be struck by the extraordinary complexity of any system that operates simultaneously on three levels of government and in both the public and private sectors of the economy. In a real sense, there is no single preservation issue that is not demonstrably linked to many others. This is further complicated by the fact that the underlying values and motives that drive the American preservation movement are almost limitless. This chapter seeks to impose some order on both problems and opportunities confronting the American preservation movement, and the order of presentation follows as closely as possible the overall structure of the book. The first part deals with the roles of the actors in the federal partnership: federal, state and local governments. Next it deals with issues related to historic resources themselves and changing concepts about what is important to preserve—what we seek to preserve and why. A third section speaks to a newer dimension of historic preservation that emphasizes people as well as the buildings and other artifacts with which Americans have traditionally been concerned. A fourth attempts to place the preservation movement in the current context of American social, political and economic life. The concluding section attempts to pose a few questions of overriding importance to the future of the preservation movement.

The Partnership

One must look at the overall structure of the American preservation partnership from two standpoints. One is the position of each level of government working alone and exercising its defined responsibilities. The other arises from interactions among the three—federal, state and local. Each partner confronts certain internal problems at its own level, but must also deal with situations arising from its relationships with each of the others. While each perspective reveals problems and tensions, each also presents opportunities.

The Federal Establishment

The principal agencies of the federal establishment are the National Park Service in the Department of the Interior and the Advisory Council on Historic Preservation. Supplementing their activities are private sector agencies, such as Preservation Action and the National Trust for Historic Preservation. Here we are concerned primarily with the first two.

The great strength of the preservation program in the National Park Service lies in the experience, excellence and dedication of its professional staff and the care with which it gives direction and leadership to the national preservation effort. Particularly notable accomplishments are the National Register and its criteria, which define for many practical as well as legal purposes what is worth preserving in the United States. Implicitly or explicitly, the criteria have become the national standard against which historic resources are measured. In addition, the Park Service also has established national standards for preservation and restoration through the *Secretary of the Interior's Standards for Rehabilitation*, prepared in connection with the tax subsidy program first created by the U.S. Congress in 1976. The Park Service also serves as the conduit through which funds appropriated by the U.S. Congress for preservation are passed to state governments, the National Trust and local governments.

The heart of the problem is that while the national preservation program has been lodged within the Park Service from its beginnings at the time of World War I, it does not regard historic preservation as its most critical or important function. If forced to make a choice, the Park Service will first turn its attention, priorities and resources to the national parks. Administratively, the national preservation program and preservation of cultural resources outside the boundaries of national parks are regarded as external functions.

Exacerbating these problems has been diminished federal financial support in the U.S. Congress for the national preservation program. What the federal government does best is to create a climate within which states and local governments will be encouraged to establish and administer programs considered by the U.S. Congress to be important to the country as a whole. This is done through the power of the purse. In real or adjusted dollar terms, the purse began to shrink during the Carter administration. Since the beginning of the Reagan administration, the Department of the Interior itself requested that the national preservation program not be funded by the U.S. Congress. The shrinkage in federal funding resulted in a greater need for the National Park Service to allocate funds to states through a demonstrably rational and fair system. Contemporaneously with the shrinkage, the Park Service required states to initiate a complex but necessary planning process, which, they complain, places more emphasis on points, paperwork and administration than on preservation. This is done through periodic audits of state programs by the Park Service based on a point-scoring system. This tends, by its nature, to imply a master-servant relationship between the federal program and the states and has resulted in accusations of federal widget counting. All these factors have left the states, which are still heavily dependent on the National Park Service in many ways, in an unhappy, almost rebellious, frame of mind in recent years.

If the National Park Service is the standard-setter, the ultimate provider of technical services and the administrator of the national preservation program, the Advisory Council on Historic Preservation is its conscience. It monitors the performance of federal agencies, states and the private sector, occasionally undertaking special studies and recommending new preservation initiatives to the U.S. Congress. It also administers the Section 106 review and comment process. The Council is not only free to review, comment and criticize the performance of other agencies: it is required by law to do so.

The Advisory Council, as an independent executive agency, has the capability to be the quintessential protagonist for preservation. In actual practice it is known for seeking balanced solutions to the cases that come before it, on the one hand to advance the cause of preservation and on the other recognizing the reality of agency missions. At the same time, it has not been shy in reviewing the programs of federal agencies, admonishing them to tighten up procedures and to take a more aggressive stand on preservation issues when necessary.

Over the years since 1966, the Advisory Council appears to many to have gone beyond the merely reactive posture implied by the words review and comment. Correctly or not, it is widely regarded as a regulatory agency and the mitigation process, which in the end produces a piece of paper enforceable in court, gives it that appearance. Unlike the national preservation program, which is lodged within the larger institutional setting of the National Park Service and the Department of the Interior, the Advisory Council is a relatively small, independent agency, less subject to the internal political constraints of a large bureaucracy. The nature of its task is that it is damned if it does a good job and damned if it does not. It goes without saying that fundamental differences in the purpose, structure and setting of the two agencies would almost inevitably produce occasional frictions, but it would be a mistake to make too much of them.

The private sector in preservation is represented in Washington, D.C., by the National Trust for Historic Preservation, created in 1949 for the purpose of facilitating public participation in historic preservation. Although it represents the private sector, a substantial part of its budget comes from congressional appropriations that are funneled to it by the National Park Service. Many in the professional preservation community lament publicly that the Trust's educational, legal and technical assistance programs have declined in recent years; however, the Trust has been a significant source of innovation in preservation; especially during the 1970s and early 1980s. Its support for such activities as maritime preservation and Main Street, its Critical Issues and Inner Cities Ventures Funds, and preservation loan and easement programs were first-class attempts at innovation, experiment and demonstration that would have been too politically risky, for a government agency. However, as a broad-based membership organization that hangs somewhere between the public and private sectors, it must confront the question of whether in seeking to satisfy such a wide spectrum of specialized preservation interests, it can avoid becoming spread so thinly that it alienates important sectors of the very membership on which it depends. A related issue is whether its educational mission (always modest by comparison with the need for it) should not be given higher priority and be better coordinated with educational tasks assigned by the U.S. Congress to the National Park Service and the Advisory Council. The argument is sometimes also heard that the National Trust's museum properties program could be handled by the Park Service, as could its grant-in-aid programs to state and local, public and private agencies. One recent suggestion is to combine the preservation programs of the Park Service, the Advisory Council and the National Trust within a single new federal agency.

Do we need a new, reconstituted national preservation agency? This suggestion first appeared in the report of Thomas O. Schneider, whose recommendations to Secretary Ickes during the Roosevelt administration laid the foundation for the Historic Sites Act of 1935. The proposal was taken up again in the late 1970s when proposals for a new national heritage program were being considered. Such has been the growing tension between the states and the federal preservation offices during the last several years that the suggestion has been seriously advanced once again. The state preservation offices have argued that a new agency, outside the National Park Service and perhaps folding the functions of the Park Service and the Advisory Council into one super-agency, would be the best answer.

Such a course of action seems ill-advised. One reason is that any such agency would inevitably be headed by a presidential appointee no less subject to political considerations or administration policies than any other cabinet officer. Another is that to create such an agency would combine in one organization those who make the rules and those who enforce them—long held to be a bad idea in our system of government. However, the most telling argument against the proposal is that the National Park Service is the national government service most highly regarded by the American taxpayer. Since the allocation of resources for any governmental function is the result of a highly political process in which taxpayer preferences count strongly, there is much more to be gained by improving the status of the program within the Park Service than by creating a new agency. This suggests that the most urgent requirement of the national preservation community is to raise preservation as a priority within the Department of the Interior by every appropriate means.

The State Preservation Establishments

As a direct consequence of the Preservation Act of 1966, all of the states have historic preservation programs headed by a state historic preservation officer (SHPO). The position of the SHPO, without regard to individual personalities, presents certain tensions because of the way the system operates.

As is the case at the federal level, historic preservation is widely regarded by the states as a less important function of government. If not at the very bottom, it is far from the top of the list of priorities, where programs such as highways, prisons, education and industrial development predominate. In addition, state government reorganizations during the early 1970s tended to diminish the direct access of preservation agencies to governors and legislatures by combining them to create larger agencies of cultural resources, or by integrating them with existing departments of transportation, parks and recreation or natural resources. The net result was that some formerly strong and independent state preservation agencies now work through politically appointed cabinet members, thus losing influence and, politicizing a hitherto professional operation.

These difficulties are compounded by the position of the SHPO. Appointed by the governor and paid by the state to carry out the state preservation program, the officer spends most of the time administering the federal program within the state. Thus, the central question is whether the SHPO is the branch manager of a Washington program, placed in the state to carry out federal program policies and enforce federal regulations, or whether that official is an employee of the state, appointed by the state and responsible primarily to it? There are also problems within the office itself, where the SHPO is sometimes seen as a mixed blessing. Professional staff may see the officer as a gutless compromiser who will all too easily succumb to political pressures to sign off on questionable nominations or accede to other demands. Real estate developers may perceive the SHPO as a roadblock standing in the way of a project; and the federal establishment tends to look upon the SHPO as a federal enforcer. This is too many hats for anyone to wear at one time, but the nature of any federal-state preservation partnership requires it.

As implied earlier, these problems are compounded by the nature of state governments, which address themselves to programs that are perceived to bring in more development, money and jobs—but only reluctantly to conservation and preservation issues, which more often are seen as standing in the way of progress. The principal problem in 1987 is money for state programs. If the experience of the last decade is a portent for the future, it is clear that state and local preservation interests will themselves have to find funds for the greatly expanded programs that resulted from the federal-state partnership of the last 20 years. But given the relatively weak position of the SHPO and the potential for conflicts noted above, this will require almost superhuman political skills. The SHPO who takes a tough line on Section 106 cases, who holds developers to strict and high standards on Tax Act projects or who relies heavily on the prescriptions of a federally approved planning model—in short, one who puts preservation principles above politics—will not be successful at the state appropriations game. In fact, such a SHPO will probably not keep the job long. The central issue now, as it was in 1966, is whether the SHPO is a state employee hired by and responsible to the governor to implement state policies, or whether the officer is the resident agent of the federal government engaged to maintain the standards of a national program removed from the state political arena.

A most troublesome aspect of the current situation is that state legislators who perceive historic preservation as a federal responsibility now have, in the face of declining federal appropriations, an excuse to cut rather than increase state support. Whether the federal government or states should bear the ultimate responsibility for funding preservation in the future is discussed later. However, anticipating the eventual withdrawal of the federal government, for whatever reasons, many states are now reviewing their enabling legislation with a view to establishing or re-establishing state registers, authorizing state grant and loan programs, creating state-level Section 106 programs and state preservation trust funds. For the moment an uneasy standoff has been achieved in the tensions between states and the federal government, and an uneasy truce is in effect.

Preservation at the Local Level

As a result of the national program, historic preservation has been so well and so widely accepted as a public activity since 1966 that it is probably a fair guess, in the absence of hard data, that virtually all of the larger metropolitan governments and most of the smaller cities with a population of more than 200,000 population now have one or more professional, full-time staff employee to administer local historic preservation programs. With an estimated 2,000 local zoning historic districts around the country and hundreds of Certified Local Government programs now beginning, it is certain that preservation is in for substantial growth over the next decade. Again, while the priority accorded preservation by local governments is partly a matter of tradition and available resources, in the end it is always dependent on the attitude of local citizens. This is especially true at the local level, where, as the result of the close contact between voters and their elected representatives, public policy tends to be more closely linked to citizen attitudes than at any other level of government.

Perhaps the critical problem of a more structural nature is whether local preservation interests, which tend (especially in the smaller towns) to limit their interest to architectural resources and merely respond to current crises as they emerge, can broaden their view and join forces with programs and activities to which they do not normally relate, such as neighborhood rehabilitation, urban design and housing. The problem is partly a matter of perception. Preservationists tend to value their independence of local politics (often seen as dirty), in much the same way as did the first planning boards, recreation commissions, hospital boards, library trustees, urban redevelopment and other groups in the early stages of moving from the private sector into government. American political tradition tends to place these newcomers to one side of the local government structure. To maintain a certain distance between local preservation and older, better accepted local government programs is still the order of the day in many of the smaller communities where preservation programs are relatively new.

Thus, independent preservation commissions still operate outside the city hall family, frequently make their own budgets and appoint their own staffs. Some even possess the authority to designate or list landmark properties on their own. To be sure, this kind of organizational structure does tend to insulate preservation from the day-to-day world of local politics, but at the same time it also effectively isolates and marks it as a less than full participant in local government activities. This is unfortunate, because many of these activities—capital improvements planning and budgeting, land use regulation and the incorporation of preservation goals into both long and short-term public planning programs and strategies—are the keys to the success of preservation programs in the long run. This is a structural problem of magnitude.

A local problem of growing seriousness has evolved from the splendid success of the national program in articulating, through the National Register standards and in illustrating, through the *Secretary of the Interior's Standards for Rehabilitation,* what should and should not be done to the fabric of a historic building. Many local governments, either on their own or pursuant to state law, adopted these federal definitions and guidelines as the standard for other local actions, resulting in problems that are sometimes best described as horrendous.

Many cities and towns possess two—occasionally more—types of historic districts, the boundaries of which are not necessary coterminous with one another. Or there may exist National Register or National Historic Landmark buildings that may or may not match the list of those designated as landmarks pursuant to a local ordinance. The federal designation is aimed at protecting local buildings or environments from the harmful effects of federal projects via Section 106 or by providing federal tax benefits. The local designation is aimed at regulating, usually through local zoning, the design and construction, moving and demolition of buildings through uncompensated regulations adopted by the city. Local property owners in one, another, or both districts cannot always understand why they qualify in one case but not the other. Nor can they contain themselves easily when they receive one decision regarding a certificate of appropriateness to proceed with construction from a local board, and another decision from the state and federal preservation apparatus denying a Tax Act certification especially when applications are based on identical plans.

The problem is made more serious by the American tradition, now firmly established in state laws, of handing over the task of administering local regulations involving the use of property to part-time volunteer officials appointed by a governing board. This is a serious problem in smaller towns and other jurisdictions where professional planning, legal or other technical assistance is not readily available to the board. The result is often a pronounced tendency toward arbitrary or casual decisions, unaccompanied by the procedural assurances and documentation that the courts insist upon when appeals are taken from local decisions. In many states, appeals from a local historic district or landmark decision would normally be to a court, and limited to procedural grounds alone. However, both the initial review and appeals on Tax Act applications are made by full time professionals in state historic preservation offices and in the regional and Washington, D.C., offices of the National Park Service, not so much on procedural but on substantive and design grounds. In such a setting it is not at all surprising that a property owner might receive conflicting signals regarding the same project.

There are other problems. For example, the purpose of local historic district regulations is the preservation of the entire district or neighborhood, the tout ensemble or the entire scene. However, the *Secretary of the Interior's Standards for Rehabilitation,* which put almost all their emphasis on the building and have little to say about the larger environment, are not very helpful. The point is that standards and guidelines prepared for one purpose by one level of government will often fail to work very well when applied to another purpose by another level of government.

The state-local areas of tension and conflict are thus not very different from those afflicting the state-federal scene, and again are based as much on perceptions and attitudes as on anything else. Whether perceived down the line as mere paternalism or as an exercise of raw authority from a superior, the consequences can be serious and lasting. The conflict originates, in many instances, in state laws providing for the review or approval of local preservation regulatory activities or state grant-in-aid projects. In all these situations, local preservationists and property owners often readily become impatient, and find the required reviews and approvals slow, tedious and picky. The local attitude about this problem is summed up in the much-worn aphorism still heard often at local preservation meetings that "The federal government has the money, the states have the power and the local governments have the problems."

It is too early to determine what will come of the new certified local government program. It remains to be seen, for example, whether the states, which have been saying "trust us" to the managers of the federal program, can develop a comparable degree of trust toward local preservation efforts and thereby freely delegate to cities and counties the real authority and responsibility needed under the expanded partnership. It is also no secret that local politics can be even more intense and manipulative than those at state and federal levels. Consequently the outlook for local preservation policy decisions based on sheer rationality is even worse than elsewhere, notwithstanding the extra federal money allocated under the program to pay for professional services.

The Changing Scope of Historic Preservation

"Well, what *is* preservation? Lemme tell you, it's this thing what you folks out there don't unnerstand. . . ."

This charming assertion, describing historic preservation in Hoboken, New Jersey, and spoken with a heavy New Jersey accent, is the opening line in one segment of the 1975 National Trust film, "A Place in Time." It never fails to draw a smile or a laugh from its audience. Like the sequence in that same film of California tourists at Lake Havasu, Arizona, exclaiming over the beauty of a relocated, rebuilt (and relatively late model) London Bridge from the vantage point of a pedal boat on an artificial lake—which also draws laughs—these scenes and commentary tell us much about the contemporary American preservation movement. They mark it as expansive, ebullient, optimistic and tolerant of change. They also stand in stark contrast to the more serious, almost crisis-oriented text of the 1966 edition of *With Heritage So Rich*, the report of the Special Committee responsible for the Preservation Act of 1966. The American preservation scene has changed to an extent undreamed of by authors of the act. Many of the issues that will have to be faced during the next 20 years have their origins in the extent and speed of that change.

In 1966, there was little interest in the preservation of 20th-century buildings, either among the public at large or among the preservation community. Public interest in old buildings stopped at a period just following the end of the Civil War or a bit later, and serious scholarly interest in buildings of the Victorian era was just beginning to emerge. Christopher Tunnard noted in *With Heritage So Rich* that "Most people think poorly of their parents' wedding presents, and some even turn up their noses at their grandparents' notions of interior decoration, but when buildings or objects are three or more generations away, they begin to be treated with respect. Thus buildings less than a century old, in styles currently unfashionable, often are victims of neglect, if not downright antagonism."

By 1966, however, buildings of the World War I era were beginning to come under scrutiny, and today a progressive preservationist might speak with enthusiasm of buildings from the 1930s and sometimes a bit later—a continuing span of roughly 50 years, which remains as the general standard for inclusion in the National Register. In 1966 the principal concerns of preservationists were described as "Architecture with an A and Art with an A." In 1966, history as an associative value continued to emphasize great events and important people, but the seeds of change were beginning to show there, too, as the civil rights movement progressed.

By 1986, the subject matter of preservation was thoroughly democratized, and topics such as vernacular architecture, and industrial and commercial archaeology, were routine and popular topics at preservation meetings everywhere. Industrial and commercial structures found a growing number of enthusiastic supporters. Small case "a" architecture was in. The word "heritage" came increasingly into common usage, even as a brief and controversial reference to the federal preservation program when, during the Carter administration, it was reorganized within the Department of the Interior as the Heritage Conservation and Recreation Service.

Now, in 1987, the time span of preservation interest has been compressed and the subject matter broadened. The time period has been foreshortened to 40 years or less. The subject matter now includes things such as designed and cultural landscapes, ships and harbors, railroads and roundhouses and other buildings and structures illustrative of our recent commercial and industrial growth. Neighborhoods of ethnic significance, which have as much to do with people as with architecture, are increasingly accepted as important to preserve. Many preservationists advocate that our intangible cultural resources, music, stories, skills and life styles, should also somehow be preserved, as is done in both European and Asian societies.

Significantly, recent years have seen intensified interest throughout the American preservation community in the concept of conservation and conservation areas. As applied to individual buildings and structures, the term appears to be almost indistinguishable from the concept of preservation, except that it tends to imply a special emphasis on continuing maintenance and preventive measures to keep a place or a building standing in the first place—a protective emphasis. Interesting applications of the concept, not always clearly articulated but nonetheless real, are beginning to show up in practice. For example, the boundaries of a 1966 zoning historic district would almost certainly have been drawn tightly, almost as a protective fence around the very heart of an architectural or period set-piece. Today those boundaries are drawn in locations generously distant from that same center, to give as much protection as possible to outer, more recent portions of the neighborhood that will one day assume its own special importance.

In conservation areas, the time span to achieve significance is also compressed. Conservation areas are not limited to neighborhoods of obvious age, certifiable historic importance or obvious architectural value, but include places that are merely middle-aged and which have only begun to acquire the patina of age. The essential associative values have as much to do with the landscape, pathways and spatial structure of the place as with buildings. Design guidelines are more often derived from the work of designers such as Christopher Alexander than any architectural style book. The emphasis is on creating respected and familiar places to be used and enjoyed by people. The hope for such districts is that if protected early enough, an area of merely potential importance will one day become, as one writer has put it, a "genuine" historic district. He refers to these areas in their present state as pre-natal historic districts.

It would be easy to dismiss such a modern concept as impractical, foppish and unscholarly were it not for the fact that other countries such as Great Britain have made it—since the passage by Parliament in 1966 of the Civic Amenities Act—a matter of standard preservation practice. More than 5,000 Conservation Areas have been designated in Great Britain under this act.

As this concept takes hold in the United States, it is interesting to note what is beginning to happen to the traditional associative values used to define places that are important to us. A bill presented to the North Carolina General Assembly several years ago defined conservation areas legally as ". . .

[areas] that possess form, character, and visual qualities derived from arrangements or combinations of topography, vegetation, space, scenic vistas, architecture, appurtenant features, distinctive natural habitats, natural formations, or places of natural or cultural significance, that create an image of stability, comfort, local identity, and livable atmosphere." Note that architecture takes a proper place within a larger context, and that history as an associative value—except as a place of cultural significance—is not specifically mentioned.

Old hands in the preservation movement, brought up on early editions of Sir Banister Fletcher's *A History of Architecture on the Comparative Method*, decry such encompassing, modernist approaches that de-emphasize buildings. And given the business and commercializing influences on preservation during the last decade, it is not surprising to hear the plea of historians to put the history back in historic preservation. Others belittle the alliance between preservation and planning. Each innovation has its detractors. But just as the American preservation movement of 1966 was not that of the time of Ann Pamela Cunningham and Mount Vernon, so it is not the same today as it was in 1966. New ideas—this one an obvious outgrowth of the environmental conservation ethic that had its rise in the 1960s and 70s—have come along to supplement or take the place of old ones. The concept of conservation and conservation areas is beginning to take root.

Some New Issues in Preservation: People

Not only has the American preservation movement been opened up and democratized since 1966, it has added a social conscience to its traditional concern for the physical world and material culture. In retrospect, this can be seen as an almost inevitable outcome of the Great Society days of the 1960s. Even though the eventual shape of this new interest is not yet clear in terms of practical application, it poses some fundamental questions for the preservation movement 20 years from today.

Firstly, it must be obvious that the earlier concept of the United States as the melting pot had begun to disappear by the time of the Preservation Act of 1966. Also, a new emphasis on separateness, ethnic pride and distinct racial identity—as embodied in such slogans as "Black is Beautiful!"—had already begun to appear. This approach was seen as a challenge to traditional American cultural expectations of an eventual, evolutionary national cultural homogeneity. Many probably still see it as a challenge to national unity as well. It began to have an effect on preservation from the first years of its appearance following 1966. The ethnic history, settlement and character of neighborhoods has always been a factor of significance in National Register district nominations, although not a dominant one. The Little Italys and Chinatowns of the country are the most obvious. The consideration of ethnicity as an associative value of increasing importance was facilitated by the emergence of thematic and multiple resource nomination procedures during the mid-70s. Presently, it is estimated that there are approximately 250 National Register districts and more than 1,000 individual nominations having ethnic character. Whether this is too many or too few remains a personal judgment.

276

The addition of ethnic and social factors to an evaluation process that has hitherto emphasized a more narrowly defined architectural tradition presents conceptual as well as practical problems. The National Register criteria of significance are broad enough to take in such considerations. There is, however, a substantial question as to whether the local zoning historic district enabling legislation in 50 states and the territories would have to be amended or changed to include the ethnic and social fabric as a proper basis for district or landmark designation as most acts are addressed to the physical corpus of neighborhoods and districts. A related question is the extent to which individual state courts would support such a rationale, accustomed as they are to justifying historic district legislation on grounds of aesthetics, the maintenance of property values and tourism.

The problems of preserving the ethnic and social flavor of a place arise most often and most readily in the displacement issue—gentrification as it has come to be called, wherein low-income and minority families and the elderly are displaced as the result of increased property values resulting from the new popularity of inner city neighborhoods. As learned from the experience of cities such as Savannah, Georgia; Charleston, South Carolina; Pittsburgh, Pennsylvania; and elsewhere, it is possible to reduce the problem to some extent, but rarely with unqualified success.

While it goes without saying that a humane and caring society should strive to insure absolutely that its most defenseless citizens should not be harmed, other basic protections are also involved. Displacement is directly related to the transitory nature of American life. Fashion in neighborhoods as preferred places to live is no less transitory an event than fashion in food, clothing and entertainment. Viewed in this light, the right to be secure in one's neighborhood must be balanced against what has been asserted in federal court to be a constitutional right to travel. In other words, the right held by all citizens, according to their circumstances, to move freely from place to place without a permit from the authorities and to live wherever they choose according to their circumstances.

Thus, if we seek to preserve ethnicity as well as physical fabric, difficult questions arise. At what point does an ethnic neighborhood lose its integrity as a specially designated and protected place when the original population dies, disappears or is diluted by newcomers to the point where factors that led to its designation no longer exist? Must such a neighborhood or district maintain a certain percentage of certifiably ethnic residents to maintain its eligibility? What percentage? Who decides? And the most troubling question of all: could such standards operate in the manner of a quota system under which minorities have been the first and worst sufferers? It has been said that attempting to put social policy in place through planning and regulatory measures is roughly equivalent to trying to nail a chiffon pie to a wall. In this area there clearly remain unresolved issues to which neither the preservation community nor any level or unit of government yet have acceptable answers.

A moment's thought also reveals that the question of gentrification is closely related to problems of tourism in historic cities and towns. It is clear that historic neighborhoods, just like environmentally sensitive natural areas, have a finite capacity for use. A carnival atmosphere, tourist buses, excess commercialization and unwanted visitors in the garden can have the same harmful effect on a neighborhood that hikers may have on an ecologically sensitive trail in a national park. But the underlying question again, is: "Whose neighborhood is this, anyway?" Does it belong to the residents—or does it belong in part to a larger community, which, arguably, must retain the right to invade it temporarily as tourists, or more permanently as new residents, who by definition become displacers. If we believe that everyone who enters a neighborhood, whether as a tourist or as a resident, is a temporary occupant, the length of the stay being the only discernable difference between the two, the importance of concentrating preservation efforts on the physical fabric of the place is clear.

The last two decades have seen a massive shift away from the preservation of the best of the high-style American building and design tradition toward the common and the vernacular. What of historical traditions? Will we see a corresponding turn in interest away from the highest and noblest aspects of our young history to those that portray the more common and the mean? Slave quarters and slave auction houses in the South have been preserved and displayed for many years. But how, given the limits of our existing preservation machinery, do we preserve the memory of a once-black neighborhood when the only remaining physical attribute is that its street pattern isolates it from surrounding white neighborhoods? Ford's Theatre, in Washington, D.C., the place of Lincoln's assassination, is a leading historic attraction; but what of the Book Depository in Dallas, Texas, from which President John F. Kennedy was shot? Do we need to preserve a World War II Japanese internment camp in California, for perhaps the same reasons it is necessary to preserve Auschwitz? The Watergate in Washington, D.C.? We are not too many years away from having to make decisions about which of these and similar remains to place on an official list of some kind.

That recent years have seen an emerging interest in preserving some of the more mundane, everyday aspects of American life and tradition openly and honestly portrayed is unmistakably clear. These range from the steaming pile of manure in the parking lot at Harpers Ferry, to proposals for a bare bones portrayal of the utter misery of Plimouth Plantation in Massachusetts to street theater and the asylum at Williamsburg, Virginia. Unlike the more widely revered, high-style examples that portray our highest and best design and historical traditions, these less glamorous places and themes will find it more difficult to attract the public and financial support necessary to their preservation. An even more difficult problem is that the preservation system finds it difficult to make rational choices about which of these more common artifacts should be saved when there are so many from which to choose.

A final problem to which there are also, as yet, no clear future directions, has to do with the preservation of the intangible cultural heritage—folkways and folklife. Although a number of west European countries, the Netherlands, the Federal Republic of Germany and Switzerland among them have had ambitious, well-financed and broadly supported programs in this area for many years, the American preservation community has only recently begun to consider the concept.

The 1980 amendments to the Preservation Act of 1966 directed the American Folklife Center in the Library of Congress, with the help of the Department of the Interior, to investigate the feasibility of a national folklife preservation program. An interdisciplinary committee of individuals representing historic preservation, archaeology, folklife studies, anthropology and related fields submitted recommendations for a modest survey and documentation effort built upon existing programs in the Library of Congress, the National Endowments for the Arts and Humanities, the Department of the Interior and other government departments. While there is general agreement that the full spectrum of cultural resources is far from being treated adequately, there is also deep concern about the practical problems of preserving anything as dynamic as folklife and folkways, which are potentially subject to harmful change (or, worse, arrested development) by the mere fact of designation of any kind. It is thought to be politically and administratively unfeasible to designate individuals as national living treasures as is done in Japan and a few other countries. Whether the National Register of Historic Places, a list of essentially static resources not subject to much change over time, and the protective processes it engenders, could accommodate such an expanded concept is open to serious question.

Other straws in the wind, which suggest that programs to preserve the physical remnants of American tradition will expand to accommodate a new emphasis on people and lifeways, are the growth of social impact assessments under the Environmental Act of 1969, the rise in importance and influence of ethnographic specialists within the National Park Service, and the spread of the concept of cultural equity among archaeologists. This is all the idea that preservation programs have a special responsibility to under-represented native, minority and ethnic groups to insure the protection of established traditions and the places that support them.

Preservation in the Larger World

Much that happens in the world of preservation is the result of events quite beyond the control of the preservation community and many, if not most, of these events ultimately take place in a political setting or are strongly influenced by political factors. Notwithstanding that the concept of historic preservation is now more widely understood than in 1966, and that many in the population at large support the idea, it is dangerous to assume that the historic preservation movement has achieved the status of a popular cause.

A Gallup Poll, conducted for the Urban Land Institute in 1986, purported to show that Americans strongly favor historic preservation and believe that local community groups should have a central role in decisions about preservation. While there is no reason to disbelieve the numbers presented, it is obvious that public support for preservation or any other program will vary with the locality. A poll taken in a mall in an upper-middle class suburb near a historic town outside Washington, D.C., will almost certainly produce different results from one taken on the street in the South Bronx or the barrio of San Antonio. Public subsidy for preservation is still the most critical issue to be faced, and whether increases in that subsidy for any preservation purpose is politically realistic depends on whether one is talking about the U.S. Congress, which operates in one setting, or the legislatures of such widely different states as New York (relatively wealthy) or Mississippi (relatively poor).

This is another way of stating the obvious: that each political jurisdiction will have its own priorities, and that, at any level of government, support for preservation comes down to a question of whether the underlying votes are those of reasonably well-off white Anglo-Saxons whose basic needs for food, shelter and education are already met, or whether the votes are those of minority interests or the ethnic poor on the lower rungs of the economic ladder to whom a job and a roof are the highest priorities. Development and real estate interests presently support preservation. But as others have pointed out, it is money that is important and the support of that sector is not necessarily enduring. For reasons having everything to do with interest rate changes and technical distinctions between passive and earned income appearing in the 1986 tax reform law, and nothing to do with historic preservation, applications for tax act certifications are already down by 46 percent or more in 1987. The political reality is that historic preservation has always been, and will probably always remain, the frosting on the political cake in almost every political venue. This will be so unless or until the preservation movement can bring the public and politicians in turn to a better understanding of both the business and the social opportunities into better focus. Much has been done since 1966, but creating this understanding remains the principal incompleted task.

If there is uncertainty about the viability of funding preservation activity through tax credits, look for the possibility of a resumption of substantial congressional appropriations for preservation following the 1988 elections. Again, that will depend in part on the larger political drift—either toward or away from a Democratic administration and the U.S. Congress who tend to be more generous with domestic programs. If, as some observers have suggested, the country has drifted toward the conservative right for almost two decades and the Carter administration was merely a momentary reaction to Watergate, preservation is in trouble.

Viewed thus, the two terms of the Reagan administration are no more than the predictable continuation of a long-term political phenomenon. The signs of federal withdrawal (or decentralization, depending on one's point of view) from traditional responsibility for many domestic programs, not just preservation, are well advanced, some of them dating back to the beginning of revenue-sharing in 1972. This is partly a matter of budgetary necessity and partly a matter of political philosophy. Assuming that the federal government will continue to disengage from many domestic programs, whatever the reasons, the preservation community must necessarily look for salvation to state and local governments as the best sources of political opportunity.

A reasonable challenge at this point would be, "Why all this long-winded speculation about politics?" The answer is that since our national preservation program is a public program, driven even in the private sector by government policies (of which the Tax Act is the perfect example), some speculation about the larger political drift of the country at large is better than sitting back and waiting to be overtaken by events over which we have no control.

Carry the argument a step further before leaving the national scene, by asking where preservation is headed in the courts? The U.S. Supreme Court has essentially stayed away from the field of land use regulation ever since its first favorable pronouncement in *Euclid v. Ambler* more than a half-century ago. The re-entry of the court by way of Justice Douglas' dictum in *Berman v. Parker* in 1954 and *Penn Central* in 1978 proved fortuitous for the preservation movement, as did many decisions of the state courts over this long period. But two 1987 California decisions, *First English Evangelical Lutheran Church v.*

County of Los Angeles and *Nollan v. California Coastal Commission*, while not directly adverse to preservation, may or may not be signs of the court's reluctance to remain on the sidelines in the future. Our continuing euphoria over *Penn Central* may lead us in the wrong direction. The addition of another conservative justice during the remainder of the Reagan administration may tip the scales in an alternate direction. It is clear from a number of state court decisions that older limitations regarding aesthetic regulation are rapidly disappearing. Many cases confirm, on the other hand, that America has entered an era in which the impact of preservation procedures will be scrutinized more carefully by the court. Again, many of the cases affecting preservation programs arise in other contexts with which the preservation community must be familiar. Already in 1987 it is fairly predictable that there will be fewer significant innovations in preservation law at the state and local level than in the past, and that administrative procedures must come in for a relatively greater share of attention.

The Localization of Preservation

It is clear that most of the action in preservation over the next decade or so is going to be at the local level. As noted earlier, the medium-size cities and large metropolitan areas will unquestionably absorb increased preservation responsibilities with a minimum of difficulty. Small cities, towns and rural areas will have a more difficult time as they are inherently more dependent on outside money and technical assistance. Independent preservation commissions will inevitably come into the local government family and take their places as accepted, even routine, aspects of local planning and management. But that scene is changing, too, and in a sense preservation activity will have to follow.

Until recently, the administration of land use controls and growth management schemes were seen as a local matter, best approached through zoning, annexation, extraterritorial land development controls and other familiar techniques, all based on powers delegated to local governments by the state. This is changing, if not rapidly, at least steadily. There is an increasing number of states that are in effect repossessing conservation and development controls, delegated but not used effectively by them. This is especially true in coastal and other environmentally sensitive areas, and in situations where new developments are regarded as so large or substantial as to have a regional impact. It is fair to speculate that within a decade many local regulatory and public investment programs will be given by the states to regional planning authorities or shared with them. These changes will happen whether or not the preservation community considers it desirable. It is at these new levels where preservation is going to have to be effective.

There has been much good preservation work at regional levels already. The Georgia state preservation office has provided technical preservation assistance for many years to localities through regional planning agencies. In an increasing number of states, cultural resource inventories and surveys are increasingly important aspects of regional land use planning efforts. Vermont, Florida, California, Kentucky and others recently began to approach growth management and planning on a regional basis, with historic preservation as an important component.

To pursue preservation objectives as integral parts of local planning programs will be important in a general way, but critically important to the problem of preserving rural areas and landscapes, now emerging as one of the most essential but difficult of all preservation tasks for the next 20 years. Central to the problem is that the outlook for the profitable, adaptive use of many important rural buildings and landscapes throughout the country ranges from poor to terrible. The planning and regulatory jurisdiction of cities do not cover rural areas, and most rural governments have limited fiscal resources, extensive obligations, and limited technical and administrative resources. They also have fundamentally different views about land use regulation and preservation.

Faced with heavy burdens of responsibility for schools, roads, care of the poor and other basic services, yet lacking prosperity, tax base or federal subsidies to support them, rural governments, must be considered unlikely partners in the preservation endeavor. Worse, this is an area where federal programs and policies seriously adverse to preservation are still in effect.

If preservation is to be localized to an even greater extent over the next 20 years, whether through the withdrawal of the federal government or the success of Certified Local Governments, there is the danger that local governments will not maintain the high standards of the National Register. As the content of local programs expands to incorporate new ideas about culture and heritage, it may be tempting to stray from the standards to use the Register to protect buildings, places or areas of lesser quality but nonetheless important to local citizens. This is responding, in a sense, to the same kinds of pressures created by the tax incentives program to use the Register for extraneous purposes. The concept of conservation areas, clearly offers a broader vision and a better coordinated set of strategies. But an overall effort that seeks to deal with townscape and landscape values in addition to traditional historic resources will occasionally blur administrative and professional lines. Without careful educational and promotional efforts at the local level, there will be the risk of further confusing the property owners and voters, leading ultimately to loss of support for both objectives. There is the potential of real problems with the *Secretary of the Interior's Standards for Rehabilitation*. These will arise not only as a result of the continuing problem of inconsistent application, noted earlier, but also from the absence of any real guidance in them for dealing with larger environmental design issues.

Some Imperatives for the '90s and Beyond
A Preservation Philosophy

An eminent foreign preservationist was once heard to remark that preservation in America has no book, no established philosophy, no guiding principles. To some extent this was true in 1966. Unlike preservation movements in other western countries, Americans are not particularly interested in doctrine or philosophy. The tendency of the American preservation movement over the years has been to take advantage of opportunities as they arise: to meet problems head on and to try to solve them after they have become problems. We have not relied on instruments such as the 1964 ICOMOS *Venice Charter for the Conservation and Restoration of Monuments and Sites* or the 1976 UNESCO *Recommendation*

Concerning the Safeguarding and Contemporary Role of Historic Areas as guidelines to a preservation philosophy. By 1966, our basic guidelines, aside from some technical specifications in use by restoration architects, were from the days of William Morris and simply stated as, "Better to preserve than to repair; better to repair than restore; better to restore than reconstruct."

But we do have a book, one created essentially by the federal program. Its first chapter contains the National Register criteria, which has come to define for almost all practical purposes—many going far beyond the boundaries of the program itself—what is worth saving. Increasingly, the National Register is the basic threshold over which a historic resource must pass if it is to gain attention. A number of state and local governments have adopted it literally or by reference for their own purposes.

The second chapter in the book is found in the fine print of Title 36, Part 800 of the Code of Federal Regulations, widely referred to as "36 CFR 800." It is a short paragraph written by the Advisory Council on Historic Preservation defining the criteria of adverse effect, or the outer limits of good manners with respect to historic resources. This underlying philosophy is, "You should not move it or tear it down, you should not alter its essential character, and you should not permit harmful intrusions of any kind—visual, audible or atmospheric—to intrude upon its immediate surroundings."

The third chapter of the book is found in the *Secretary of the Interior's Standards for Rehabilitation*, created about a decade ago for the purpose of defining what is and what is not acceptable treatment of historic fabric. Because the standards and guidelines were established for purposes of administering the Tax Act of 1976, which in turn is written for buildings, the standards and guidelines emphasize buildings and structures and have less relevance to the larger environment of the buildings.

Taken together these three chapters are perhaps the most significant achievements of the national program since 1966. The trick during the next decade will be to take the principles they represent and with appropriate modifications put them to work as standard operating procedure in programs that will be increasingly local and less federal in both origin and purpose. Equally important will be the writing of a fourth chapter that addresses with equal purpose and effect, neighborhoods and the larger environment.

Local preservation programs will have the difficult task of following two seemingly divergent paths simultaneously. One will be to maintain the integrity of the lists and the listing process, in other words, maintain established norms of artistic, design and craft tradition in buildings. It will be difficult to maintain the integrity of the National Register as more and more authority is turned over to states (and, thereby to local governments through the operation of the political process). At the same time, national, state and local preservation programs—especially the latter—will have to develop and display increased sensitivity to changing concepts of significance that have less to do with maintaining the artistic and stylistic integrity of buildings than they do with enhancing the quality of the larger environment for the daily living purposes of people. This is not to say that one objective may be substituted for the other; both will have to be pursued at the same time.

One task will have to be approached with special care as the scope of things worth preserving is broadened. Choosing something to be preserved is relatively easy when there is only one surviving Greek Revival building in the county. It is a more difficult achievement when the local inventory contains more than 50 Art Deco buildings and the politics or economics of the situation permit the listing of only 10. Not only will the range of important historic resources be more inclusive stylistically but the supply of resources may be more plentiful and the choices more difficult. And as the concept of significance broadens, as surely it will, to include, for example, ethnic values, the choices will be increasingly influenced by political factors and less by scholarly ones. Complex judgments involving skills not possessed by traditional custodians of our existing preservation machinery will be required to decide which cultural, scenic or historic landscapes should be singled out for special treatment. Developing and maintaining standards, while at the same time carefully defining a broader range of environmental values to be preserved will be the most challenging task of all.

Several other things are involved. Preserving anything involves some element of public expenditure, regulation or other governmental process affecting citizens and their traditional rights to reasonable freedom in the use of their property. As we saw earlier, there is a level of importance, defined by state and federal constitutions as public purpose or public use that must be attained before public subsidy or intervention will be tolerated by courts. If it is decided, for example, that a particular rural landscape is to be preserved through regulation, there must be compelling evidence of a public purpose or benefit. Translated, this means that there must be strong and demonstrable public support for actions of the preservation community. Presently neither the public nor the courts would be easily persuaded that a 1950s diner or roadside tourist cabin is worth preserving through regulation or public subsidy. Much of the public still regard preservationists as wanting to save everything. Educational efforts and campaigns aimed at gathering public support for preservation are no less necessary now than they were in 1966. They will be more important as time goes on. For the same reasons, preservation, heritage and environmental education programs aimed at children may in the long run prove to be crucial.

As procedures become more important to the courts, the question "Who says so?!" becomes an even more important one. Who is expertly qualified to testify about the intrinsic value of a building or neighborhood will have to be answered to the satisfaction of a court if these tests of public purpose and public benefit are to be met. For example, architectural historians with experience and advanced degrees would clearly be qualified to say which buildings are important, which are not and why. They must also be qualified to speak to the issue of which restoration techniques might be best for a building. They would not, however, necessarily be qualified to speak to the issue of what contemporary additions are appropriate to be made to the fabric of a historic building, to speak to the design quality of contemporary buildings in historic neighborhoods or to issues involving spatial structure or landscape qualities of the larger environment. By the same token, architects and environmental designers must learn to give greater respect to historical qualities of older buildings and avoid the urge to express their design individuality on established historic building fabric. Some of our present preservation procedures at all three levels of government make it both too easy and too tempting for experts in one field to step over lines of professional expertise and make judgments in subject areas for which they are not qualified.

Research, Education and Training

It is not possible to speak of the need for a preservation philosophy without confronting the underlying need for research, education and training required across the board to make that philosophy work.

If these new interests in the areas of ethnic tradition, commercial and industrial archaeology, and the outer fringes of material culture mentioned throughout this book are ever to take a serious and respected place in the American preservation movement, the preservation community will, in turn, have to take a look at the underlying scholarly base that sorts out and codifies those interests. This process, backed by scholarly tradition and professional judgment, is essential if the preservation movement is to be taken seriously by the public, and, even more important, have the necessary credibility in legislatures and courts.

This is perhaps a long-winded way of saying that Americans will have to ask whether the research, education and training programs in fields pertinent to these new interests are available and sufficient in number, quality and direction to serve the historic preservation movement 20 years hence. It would be misleading to point to the expansion of preservation courses and curricula in American universities since 1966 and assume that all is well or that the problem will take care of itself. Like other university programs, the increase in historic preservation courses and curricula in universities since 1966 has had more to do with growth in the preservation job market than an inherent scholarly interest in preservation on the part of academics. Intangible heritage, ethnic tradition and the more recent aspects of domestic history are relatively new fields and have special requirements of their own, not the least of which are incentive funds to attract Indian and other minority students to the field of preservation and to support research in these areas. Research and documentation in fields, such as ethnic studies, folklife, conservation and vernacular architecture—to say nothing of the high-tech specialties and applications now required in the field of archaeology—require untraditional skills and approaches, and can be expensive. Conservation studies are as yet an untapped field, even in the more traditional schools of architecture, design and landscape architecture.

How these requirements in the fields of material culture, American studies and the like can be balanced with the continuing and unmet needs of historians and architectural historians in the more traditional aspects of preservation is a question that has generally been ignored by institutional leaders of the movement. Equally important aspects of the field, such as public school education in preservation, beginning with the earliest years, also receive much less attention than they should command.

A critical problem much discussed since 1966 and for which no real solutions are yet in sight is the training of volunteers. One special need that has grown in importance to the critical stage is for the training of local leadership. There is little instruction available to tell the leadership of a local society how to manage a business meeting, raise money, speak in public, maintain corporate records and accounts, work with the press and the Internal Revenue Service, effectively pressure politicians, and motivate and supervise volunteers. For a movement so heavily dependent on volunteers, the failure to provide leadership and administrative training can only be described as tragic.

The special educational needs of preservation commission members, especially in matters related to legal procedure and design decision-making, have been discussed for many years, but nothing more than sporadic, ad hoc efforts have been made to fill this need. The Park Service, the Advisory Council and many state historic preservation offices have attempted to meet some of these requirements as best they can with limited resources, but the national organizations with responsibilities in this area have simply not produced what is required. Given the insistence of courts for ever-higher standards of performance in procedural matters related to design review, there remains a vast gap between what is needed and what is being done. By default the preservation movement must now look to the statewide nonprofit organizations for intensified efforts in this area, perhaps in cooperation with government preservation agencies. If indeed there is a crisis of confidence in the delivery systems of some of the national organizations, it arises largely from failures in the area of public education.

Finally, there is the larger issue of changing the burden of proof with respect to preservation and development issues generally. In American society this burden remains on those who want to preserve something from the past; there is a presumption that what is new is progressive and therefore better. The principal task of the preservation movement is to reverse that burden of proof, so that it says, in effect, what is already here should remain, in the absence of convincing evidence that what will replace it improves the human environment and the human condition. This is the basic message of the larger world of environmental conversation. Until preservation can join forces with that larger world to turn public opinion around, preservationists will remain pretty much at Square One, always on the defensive, winning battles here and there, but never winning the war.

Tightening Up the Preservation Process

The weak points in the preservation process at every level of government still rest, as they did two decades ago, in the areas of planning, regulation and funding.

Planning

The basic purpose of any well-grounded planning system, whatever the effort, is to ensure that program goals and objectives remain in sight and serve as a point of reference against which progress toward those goals can be met. A planning system becomes even more important in the political process of allocating scarce dollars fairly to all players in the game. The Resource Protection Planning Process (RP3, recently renamed "comprehensive planning") about which so much controversy has swirled in recent years is an excellent start in the right direction for both purposes. However, any federal planning process must also recognize and respect the tender political situation of the state historic preservation office in the larger setting of state government, and the increasingly important role of politics as government moves further from the federal level and closer to decentralization. The process must also accept the necessity for a substantial degree of freedom from constraints of the plan. If it is to be useful, it must recognize that once past national historic landmarks, and perhaps historic resources of state-wide significance, what is worth saving can only be defined by local preferences, with or without the help of scholarly or expert judgment. Both federal and state governments still have much to learn about trusting the judgment of local people. Perhaps what local people believe should be preserved should be preserved, whether or not local preferences fit neatly into the preconceived historical themes or study units prescribed by planners. The question has been raised whether state historic preservation offices are branch offices of the National Park Service in Washington, D.C., or full-service preservation assistance centers for local programs. The answer is that they are both. If they remain part of the national partnership, they must be at least the former, and they must have unfettered freedom as well as adequate resources to serve as the latter if they so choose.

It should be noted parenthetically at this point that much of the confusion and frustration arising from the federal planning process is more a matter of confusion about terminology and the meaning of the word "planning" than anything else. Land use planning, particularly at the local level, has come to refer to a process that has as its objective enhancing the quality of life through the better arrangement and spatial distribution of land use. It differs in many essential respects from the kind of resource protection planning envisioned by federal and state programs under RP3, Section 106, the Environmental Act of 1969 and similar programs. Sorting out some of this confusion would be a major step forward for the preservation community.

The Listing Process

The major imperative here is to roll back the line regarding owner consent with respect to National Register listing. Ours is virtually the only preservation system in the world that gives preference to the wishes of the temporary owner rather than to expert scholarly judgment. The underlying issue, however, has less to do with expertise than with trust. The American political system simply does not repose full or sole trust in government experts. An argument can be made that the best answer lies not with allowing experts to make the judgment for some purposes and the owner for others, as at present, but with the establishment of a process in which both the owner, experts and perhaps the community itself arrive at a consensus. This is the evaluation system established pretty much everywhere with respect to local landmark and historic district commissions and with state professional review boards for National Register nominations.

The Protective Processes: Regulation

The first requirement here is to do a better job with local regulatory programs. If, in the future, public funding for preservation, direct or indirect, is going to be harder and harder to come by, it stands to reason that we are increasingly dependent on the less expensive alternatives of planning and uncompensated regulation. We now have many more zoning historic districts than in 1966, but their administration is not necessarily better. The inherent weaknesses in a regulatory approach are no different here than elsewhere around the world. The most obvious of these are that the process is essentially benign; nothing happens until the owner needs a permit to do something on the property. Hardship variances are often too easy to obtain and, in many cases, the regulations cannot govern the inside of the building to save valuable interiors. All too often, design standards and criteria are mindlessly copied from one place to another without regard for the local situation. A more troubling problem stems from the exasperatingly high procedural standards demanded by the courts of a quasi-judicial agency to be met by local boards composed of part-time, volunteer, lay citizens. Clearly, the principal unmet need in this area is for extensive and continuing training of lay board members in both design and procedural matters. Looking at the delivery systems of national organizations and agencies, both public and private, which might be expected to take on this task, one comes quickly to the conclusion that there is a major educational task here for the statewide nonprofit organizations, perhaps in tandem with university design schools, institutes of government and state historic preservation offices.

The Protective Processes: Planning

Whether the essentially negative task presented by landmark and historic district regulations of merely reviewing and responding to proposals of individual owners can ever take a more positive turn and begin to feed into the public investment and day-to-day environmental maintenance operations of local governments, will depend on the extent to which these independent agencies can be brought more closely into the local government family.

Earlier it was mentioned that local preservation programs must become more aggressive and active partners in local land use planning processes. However, this is a two-way street. Much more might be required of the local planning programs themselves. One glaring area of weakness almost everywhere has been the failure to require developers to identify and respect archaeological and historic sites before site design, engineering and construction processes begin. In almost every state this is simply a matter of will, requiring no additional enabling authority.

The Protective Processes: Disclosure and Review

The consumerist approaches of advance disclosure and review of plans for public projects embodied in the Environmental Act of 1969, with the added feature of opportunities for negotiated mitigation embodied in Section 106, have generally served well. The compliance record of many federal agencies is good and getting better, and, of course, one answer over time is accelerated and expanded survey, inventory and nomination processes. The touchstone for bringing Section 106 into play is still federal involvement by way of licensing, funding or other participation. Some states provide a modicum of protection following the pattern of Section 106 where state funds or state licensing is involved. In these states, the last remaining gap is thus locally funded projects. Unfortunately, local governments themselves, along with churches and universities, still tend to be unsympathetic to preservation.

As noted earlier, the Section 106 process has been notched up bit by bit since 1966, moving beyond mere comment and into the arena of negotiated agreement, and Section 4(f) planning procedures have nominally, at least, been extended since 1980 to the most significant buildings. Whether 20 years from now these procedures will or should go beyond the progressively more stern measures of review, comment, mitigation and planning to an absolute veto or outright prohibition is an unresolved question. Who should have the environmental review responsibilities required for some programs, particularly the Urban Development Action Grant and Community Development Block Grant programs, which have demonstrated capacity for trouble, is also an open question. The process, begun in 1974, of designating the local government sponsor-beneficiary of these projects as the responsible agent for environmental review purposes has always smacked of putting the fox in charge of the chickens.

Paying for Preservation

The last 20 years have seen a major shift in thinking about public funding for preservation—one with serious implications for the future. Prior to the Tax Reform Act of 1976, the principal funding for preservation was direct loans and grants to the owners of needy properties. In 1976, the balance shifted radically in favor of back door subsidies through the taxing system. While welcomed as a device for putting preservation and rehabilitation in the same market with new construction, some public administrators and tax policy analysts argued against this approach, saying that the tax system should be used only for the purpose of raising money to run the government. It is also argued that using it to favor particular segments of the private market, no matter how desirable the goal, enabled politicians to make expenditure choices without the necessity for having clear priorities.

These arguments notwithstanding (they were heard again and prevailed in many areas in the tax reform effort in 1986), a modified version of the tax credits embedded in the Economic Recovery Tax Act of 1981 came through the latest round of reform relatively unscathed as one of the few remaining tax shelters.

Such has been the success of the tax incentives created in 1976 and 1981 that they are now seen in and out of the U.S. Congress as an appropriate substitute for the former system of direct grants. The problem created by this tremendous success in the market is that non-income producing properties, archaeological sites and other important properties are left with few sources of public support. And it seems unlikely, in the face of staggering fixed costs for social security and debt service, heavy expenditures for defense and an array of higher priority domestic programs, that direct funding for preservation will be resumed by the U.S. Congress in the future. Indeed, there has been almost a decade of federal policy that redirects many domestic programs back to the states for funding. There is even the possibility that the modest appropriations from 1980 through 1987 for state survey and planning programs will be further reduced or terminated.

Some hope that state and local governments will enter the breach, but this is extremely unlikely, since they, too, are in the midst of a fiscal crunch. Presently (summer 1987) state and local governments face their largest revenue shortfall since the 1975 recession. A fourth quarter 1986 surplus of $1.2 billion has become a $5.7 billion annualized deficit in the first quarter of 1987. Twenty-four states are cutting their budgets as a result, while proposals for tax increases abound at state and local levels. While some states are clearly better off than others, the energy and farm states are having an especially tough time of it. In short, states are not likely to be of much help to preservation.

Notwithstanding the objections noted above, there have been recurring suggestions that back door subsidies for preservation using state and local tax systems should be used to create preservation incentives. The difficulty with this suggestion, however, is that state income taxes represent a much smaller portion of the total tax burden borne by individuals than does the federal tax on income, now capped at 28 percent (33 percent and more in a few cases). State income taxes tend to run less than 10 percent of adjusted gross income and at this level provide much less of an incentive than the federal program. Local property taxes are also a relatively small percentage of the total tax burden and have the additional disadvantage of being perceived (incorrectly) as a disincentive for preservation, since assessed property values rise following a restoration or preservation project. Worse, local officials are apt (again incorrectly) to look upon preservation incentives based on the property tax as potentially eroding the tax base itself and to oppose them.

Again, it seems unlikely that state and local taxing systems, even assuming that political reluctance to use them for preservation purposes could be overcome, can match existing federal incentives. This suggests that the gaps will have to be filled through the creative use of publicly subsidized trust or revolving funds, perhaps funded through tax-exempt bonds where permissible, or possibly through below-market-rate loans. There is obviously a vastly expanded role for statewide revolving funds in both the near and long-term future.

To close on a somewhat more optimistic note, one special aspect of the privatization of preservation over the last decade requires special mention, and that is the potential of the private financial sector as a major force for preservation in years to come. Local and statewide revolving fund experience to date reveals that when properly approached with a solid financial plan, foundation and corporate support for preservation is available to a far greater extent than ever supposed. While individual preservation projects will always be at the mercy of prevailing interest rates, tax considerations and other market factors, corporations, foundations and local endowments have the potential to produce a reliable source and stream of income for preservation. Educating those who control institutional wealth to preservation values and having those resources available for preservation, is not all that difficult. It is a field where much digging remains to be done.

Making Preservation Policy Better

Again, the challenge: Why a long, gloomy analysis of long-term funding possibilities at this point in the book? The answer: to introduce the idea that for all the success enjoyed by the American preservation movement during the last two decades, there has been an utter failure to develop long-term, continuing strategies for the preservation movement as a whole, and to recognize the importance of doing so. As Jerry Rogers, the Associate Director for Cultural Affairs of the National Park Service, put it in 1986, "When you're playing defense, you don't strategize very well."

Viewed over time, the American preservation movement has grown and expanded more by adding incrementally to existing programs and responding defensively to external events than by consciously attempting to direct its own future. It began with a concern for the lessons of history and a need to preserve the best of a rapidly disappearing architectural tradition. Archaeology entered the picture at the turn of the century, and in the mid-30s Americans began to think seriously about preserving the physical fabric of neighborhoods and whole towns. In the 1960s and 70s preservationists tagged on to the environmental movement and a growing concern for the use and enjoyment of historic buildings and places by people. About the same time we began to recognize more fully the potential of the human and social dimensions of preservation. Largely as a result of the civil rights movement, the American melting pot contains beef stew rather than cream soup. The vision contained in *With Heritage So Rich* sees buildings and places that emphasize people in addition to information and tradition.

On the whole, though, the preservation movement progressed as much if not more by responding to opportunities than by plotting a future course for itself as a matter of deliberate purpose. The Special Committee on Historic Preservation (1965) set forth the directions that have brought us to the present state, and the National Trust's *Goals and Programs, A Summary of the Study Committee Report* (1973) and its Williamsburg *Preservation: Toward An Ethic in the 1980s* conference (1979), defined important new directions. But though the preservation movement has grown in scope and numbers, the people and institutions who comprise it do not yet have an independent journal of critical thought or a forum in which these broader interests can propose or debate long-term strategies. While sometimes shrugged off as poorly led, the late 70s attempt to create a formal alliance of larger preservation and conservation interests was an important turning point. The reasons for such an effort are no less relevant or important to the future of the preservation movement now than then. The arguments for creating that alliance remain valid. The principal obstacles to achieving it, existing turfs and competition, are also still in place.

Perhaps the time has come for the formation of a broad-based national preservation policy group as a permanent institution that goes beyond narrow interests. It would not, however, be a super-agency like those proposed recently as the result of state dissatisfaction with federal programs. What is needed is a neutral forum in which new ideas can be explored, where consultation can be taken with a wide variety of related interests on a continuing basis and existing roles examined in ways that stress long-range planning and true leadership rather than the mere protection of turf. One would hope that such an atmosphere would be creative and expansive and broadly inclusive of a wide variety of preservation interests. The present system of friendly but competing organizational interests, each with its own staff, budget and program, and specific interests competing for prestige may be the best that can be done. However, it is likely that the events of the next 20 years will demand a more structured, studied and coherent approach to advance policy formulation. Given the increased competition for diminishing federal resources and the existing limitations of state and local governments to fill the gap, the size of the task and the increasing numbers of new players creating a new structure for leadership appears as an urgent task. There is much to be said for a movement that can present itself to the larger world as one with a good sense of where it has come from and where it is going.

RECOMMENDED READINGS

Adler, Leopold, II, Kidney, Walter C. and Ziegler, Arthur P., Jr., *Revolving Funds for Historic Preservation: A Manual of Practice*. Pittsburgh: Ober Park Associates, Inc., 1975.

Advisory Council on Historic Preservation. *Annual Report to the President and the Congress of the United States*. Washington, D.C.: U.S. Government Printing Office, 1968–1986.

Advisory Council on Historic Preservation. *Assessing the Energy Conservation Benefits of Historic Preservation*. Washington, D.C.: U.S. Government Printing Office, 1979.

Advisory Council on Historic Preservation. *The Contribution of Historic Preservation to Urban Revitalization*. Washington, D.C.: U.S. Government Printing Office, 1979.

Advisory Council on Historic Preservation. *The National Historic Preservation Act of 1966: An Assessment of Its Implementation Over Twenty Years*. Washington, D.C.: Advisory Council on Historic Preservation, September 1986.

Albright, Horace M. *The Birth of the National Park Service: The Founding Years, 1913–33*. Salt Lake City: Howe Brothers, 1985.

Albright, Horace M. *Origins of National Park Service Administration of Historic Sites*. Philadelphia: Eastern National Park and Monument Association, 1971.

Alexander, Christopher. *The Timeless Way of Building*. New York: Oxford University Press, 1979.

Alexander, Christopher, Sara Ishikawa, and Murray Silverstein. *A Pattern Language*. New York: Oxford University Press, 1977.

Andrews, Gregory E., editor. *Tax Incentives for Historic Preservation*. Washington, D.C.: Preservation Press, 1980.

Barnett, Jonathan. *Urban Design as Public Policy*. New York: Architectural Record Books, 1974.

Binford, Sally R. and Lewis R. Binford, editors. *New Perspective in Archeology*. Chicago: Aldine Publishing Co., 1968.

Bosselman, Fred P. *In the Wake of the Tourist*. Washington, D.C.: The Conservation Foundation, 1978.

Bowsher, Alice Meriwether. *Design Review in Historic Districts: A Handbook for Virginia Review Boards*. 1978. "Business Ventures for Non-Profits," *Conserve Neighborhoods*, No. 59, June 1986.

Chang, Kwang-chih, editor. *Settlement Archeology*. Palo Alto, California: National Press, 1968.

Chittenden, Betsy. *Tax Incentives for Rehabilitating Historic Buildings—Fiscal Year 1986 Analysis*. Washington, D.C.: U. S. Department of the Interior, National Park Service, 1987.

Chittenden, Betsy and Jacques Gordon. *Older and Historic Buildings and The Preservation Industry*, Preservation Policy Research Series. Washington, D.C.: National Trust for Historic Preservation, March 1984 (revised).

Clay, Grady. *Close-Up, How to Read the American City*. Chicago: University of Chicago Press, 1980.

The Conservation Foundation. *National Parks for a New Generation: Visions, Realities, Prospects*. Washington, D.C.: The Conservation Foundation, 1985.

Costonis, John J. *Space Adrift: Landmark Preservation and the Marketplace*. Urbana: National Trust for Historic Preservation by the University of Illinois Press, 1974.

Cullen, Gordon. *The Concise Townscape*. New York: Van Nostrand Reinhold Company, 1961.

Dale, Antony. *Historic Preservation in Foreign Countries* (France, Great Britain, Ireland, the Netherlands, Denmark), Vol. I. Robert E. Stipe, editor of the series. Washington, D.C.: U.S. Committee of the International Council on Monuments and Sites, 1982. And *Supplement*, 1986.

Dennis, Stephen N., editor. *Preservation Law Update* (serial). Washington, D.C.: National Center for Preservation Law, 1986– .

Duerksen, Christopher A. *A Handbook on Historic Preservation Law*. Washington, D.C.: The Conservation Foundation, 1983.

Favretti, Rudy J. and Joy Putman Favretti. *Landscapes and Gardens for Historic Buildings*. Nashville, Tennessee: American Association for State and Local History, 1978.

Finley, David E. *History of the National Trust for Historic Preservation, 1947–1963*. Washington, D.C.: National Trust for Historic Preservation, 1963.

Fitch, James Marston. *Historic Preservation: Curatorial Management of the Built World*. New York: McGraw-Hill Book Company, 1982.

Gardner, James B. and George Rollie Adams, editors. *Ordinary People and Everyday Life: Perspectives on the New Social History*. Nashville, Tennessee: American Association for State and Local History, 1983.

Greiff, Constance M. *Lost America: From the Atlantic to the Mississippi*. Princeton, New Jersey: The Pyne Press, 1971.

Greiff, Constance M. *Lost America: From the Mississippi to the Pacific*. Princeton, New Jersey: The Pyne Press, 1972.

Hosmer, Charles B., Jr. *Presence of the Past: The History of the Preservation Movement in the United States before Williamsburg*. New York: G. P. Putnam's Sons, 1965.

Hosmer, Charles B., Jr. *Preservation Comes of Age: From Williamsburg to the National Trust, 1926–1949*, 2 vols. Charlottesville, Virginia: Preservation Press by the University Press of Virginia, 1981.

Huxtable, Ada Louise. *Goodbye History, Hello Hamburger*. Washington, D.C.: Preservation Press, 1986.

International Council on Monuments and Sites. *Monumentum*, Vol. XIII, 1976. Washington, D.C.: The Preservation Press and the U.S. Committee for ICOMOS.

Jackson, John Brinckerhoff. *Discovering the Vernacular Landscape*. New Haven: Yale University Press, 1984.

Johnson, Ronald W. and Michael G. Schene. *Cultural Resources Management*. Malabar, Florida: Robert E. Krieger Publishing Company, 1987.

Keune, Russell V., editor. *The Historic Preservation Yearbook*. Bethesda, Maryland: Adler & Adler, 1984.

King, Thomas F., Patricia L. Parker and Gary Berg. *Anthropology in Historic Preservation: Caring for Culture's Clutter*. New York: Academic Press, 1977.

Kyvig, David E. and Myron A. Marty. *Nearby History: Exploring the Past Around You*. Nashville, Tennessee: American Association for State and Local History, 1982.

Longstreth, Richard. *The Buildings of Main Street*. Washington, D.C.: Preservation Press, 1987.

Lottman, Herbert R. *How Cities Are Saved*. New York: Universe Books, 1976.

Lowenthal, David. *The Past is a Foreign Country*. Cambridge: Cambridge University Press, 1985.

Lowenthal, David and Marcus Binney. *Our Past before Us: Why Do We Save It?* London: Temple Smith, 1981.

Lynch, Kevin. *Managing the Sense of A Region*. Cambridge, Massachusetts: MIT Press, 1976.

Lynch, Kevin. *What Time Is This Place?* Cambridge, Massachusetts: MIT Press, 1972.

Mackintosh, Barry. *The Historic Sites Survey and the National Historic Landmarks Program: A History*. Washington, D.C.: National Park Service, 1985.

Mackintosh, Barry. *The National Parks: Shaping the System*. Washington, D.C.: U. S. Department of the Interior, 1985.

Mackintosh, Barry. *The National Historic Preservation Act and the National Park Service: A History*. Washington, D.C.: The National Park Service, 1986.

Maddex, Diane, editor. *All About Old Buildings: The Whole Preservation Catalog*. Washington, D.C.: The Preservation Press, 1985.

McGimsey, Charles R., III. *Public Archeology*. New York: Seminar Press, 1972.

McHargue, Georgess and Michael Roberts. *A Field Guide to Conservation Archeology in North America*. Philadelphia: Lippincott, 1977.

Meinig, D. W., editor. *The Interpretation of Ordinary Landscapes: Geographical Essays*. New York: Oxford University Press, 1979.

Merritt, Carole. *Historic Black Resources: A Handbook for the Identification, Documentation, and Evaluation of Historic African-American Properties in*

Georgia. Atlanta, Georgia: Historic Preservation Section, Georgia Department of Natural Resources, 1984.

Metcalf, Fay D. and Matthew T. Downey. *Using Local History in the Classroom*. Nashville, Tennessee: American Association for State and Local History, 1982.

Middleton, Michael. *Man Made the Town*. London: The Bodley Head, 1987.

Myers, Phyllis and Gordon Binder. *Neighborhood Conservation: Lessons from Three Cities*. Washington, D.C.: The Conservation Foundation, 1977.

National Park Service. *Promised Land on the Solomon: Black Settlement at Nicodemus, Kansas*. Washington, D.C.: U. S. Government Printing Office, n.d.

"The National Park Service and Historic Preservation," *The Public Historian: A Journal of Public History*. Vol. 9, Spring 1987.

National Trust for Historic Preservation, Tony P. Wrenn, and Elizabeth D. Mulloy. *America's Forgotten Architecture*. Washington, D.C.: National Trust for Historic Preservation, 1976.

National Trust for Historic Preservation. *A Guide to State Historic Preservation Programs*. Washington, D.C.: Preservation Press, 1976.

National Trust for Historic Preservation. *Historic Preservation Today*. Charlottesville, Virginia: University Press of Virginia, 1966.

National Trust for Historic Preservation. *Historic Preservation Tomorrow*. Washington, D.C.: National Trust for Historic Preservation, 1967.

National Trust for Historic Preservation. *Old and New Architecture: Design Relationship*. Washington, D.C.: Preservation Press, 1980.

National Trust for Historic Preservation. *Preservation: Toward an Ethic in the 1980s*. Washington, D.C.: Preservation Press, 1980.

Newton, Norman T. *Design on the Land: The Development of Landscape Architecture*. Cambridge, Massachusetts: The Belknap Press of Harvard University, 1971.

Quick, Polly McW., editor. *Proceedings: Conference on Reburial Issues*. Washington, D.C.: Society for American Archaeology and Society of Professional Archeologists, 1985.

"Renovation, Rehabilitation, and Recycling," *National Real Estate Investor*, Vol. 22, No. 8, July 1980.

Rettig, Robert B. "Conserving the Man-Made Environment: Planning for the Protection of Historic and Cultural Resources in the United States." Manuscript prepared for the U.S. Department of the Interior, September 1, 1975.

"Revolving Funds—Recycling Resources for Neighborhoods," *Conserve Neighborhoods*, No. 18, May/June 1981.

Schiffer, Michael B. and George J. Gumerman. *Conservation Archeology: A Guide for Cultural Resource Management Studies*. New York: Academic Press, 1977.

Schlereth, Thomas J. *Artifacts and the American Past*. Nashville, Tennessee: American Association for State and Local History, 1980.

Schlereth, Thomas J., editor. *Material Culture Studies in America*. Nashville, Tennessee: American Association for State and Local History, 1982.

The Secretary of the Interior's 20th Anniversary Report on the National Historic Preservation Act. Washington, D.C.: U. S. Department of the Interior 1986.

Society of Architectural Historians. *The Forum: Bulletin of the Committee on Preservation* (serial). Philadelphia: Society of Architectural, 1979– .

South, Stanley. *Method and Theory in Historical Archeology*. New York: Academic Press, 1977.

Sowell, Thomas. *Ethnic America: A History*. New York: Basic Books, Inc., Publishers, 1981.

Stilgoe, John R. *Common Landscape of America, 1580 to 1845*. New Haven: Yale University Press, 1982.

Stipe, Robert E. for the Heritage Conservation and Recreation Service, U.S. Department of the Interior. *New Directions in Rural Preservation*. Washington, D.C.: U.S. Government Printing Office, 1980.

Timmons, Sharon. *Preservation and Conservation: Principles and Practices*. Washington, D.C.: Preservation Press, 1976.

Upton, Dell, editor. *America's Architectural Roots: Ethnic Groups that Built America*. Washington, D.C.: The Preservation Press, 1986.

Weinberg, Nathan. *Preservation in American Towns and Cities*. Boulder, Colorado: Westview Press, 1979.

Will, Margaret T. *Historic Preservation in Foreign Countries* (Federal Republic of Germany, Switzerland, Austria), Vol. II. Robert E. Stipe, editor of the series. Washington, D.C.: U.S. Committee of the International Council on Monuments and Sites, 1984.

Willey, Gordon R. and Jeremy A. Sabloff. *A History of American Archeology*. London: Thames and Hudson, 1974.

Wilson, Rex L. and Gloria Loyola, editors. *Rescue Archeology: Papers from the New World Conference on Rescue Archeology*. Washington, D.C.: The Preservation Press, 1982.

With Heritage So Rich, A Report of a Special Committee on Historic Preservation under the Auspices of the United States Conference of Mayors with a Grant from the Ford Foundation. New York: Random House, 1965.

"With Heritage Still So Rich, Special National Park Service Supplement," *Preservation News*, October 1986.

Worskett, Roy. *The Character of Towns, An Approach to Conservation*. London: Architectural Press, 1969.

Ziegler, Arthur P. Jr. and Walter C. Kidney. *Historic Preservation in Small Towns: A Manual of Practice*. Nashville, Tennessee: American Association for State and Local History, 1980.

EDITORS AND AUTHORS

Gregory E. Andrews is a real estate appraiser and consultant specializing in historic preservation projects and architectural history. Previous work includes four years as an attorney in the investment law department of CIGNA Corporation, four years as an attorney at the National Trust for Historic Preservation and as an attorney in private practice. He was general editor and contributing author of *Tax Incentives for Historic Preservation* (The Preservation Press, 1980) and has written articles on state preservation legislation and historic preservation law. He serves on the boards of the Hartford Architecture Conservancy, Connecticut Preservation Action (President, 1981–83), the West Hartford Historic District Commission and is chairman of the West Hartford Architectural Heritage Committee. Currently, he is a consultant to the Connecticut Historical Commission and to the Connecticut Historical Society.

John M. Fowler is deputy executive director/general counsel of the Advisory Council on Historic Preservation. Upon receiving his law degree from Yale Law School, he was associated with Henry M. Fowler in the general practice of law. He began his career at the Advisory Council in 1972 and over the following decade served as associate legal counsel, director of the Office of Intergovernmental Programs and Planning and general counsel. He has authored several chapters on historic preservation and environmental law and served as a faculty member and speaker at the Nantucket Preservation Institute, Harvard School of Design and Yale Law School.

J. Myrick Howard is the executive director of the Historic Preservation Foundation of North Carolina, Inc., one of the nation's oldest and largest statewide preservation organizations. The Foundation created the first American statewide revolving fund in 1975, which he has directed since 1978. The revolving fund has directly generated more than $20 million in private investment in North Carolina's historic properties. He holds a master's degree in urban planning in addition to a law degree from the University of North Carolina at Chapel Hill. He has served as a member of the Chapel Hill Historic District Commission and as chairman of the Raleigh Appearance Commission. He has traveled extensively around the United States to assist preservationists with revolving funds, historic districts and other preservation programs. He is co-chairman of the North Carolina Attorney General's Preservation Law Revisions Committee and serves on the boards of preservation organizations, both within and outside North Carolina.

Thomas F. King is director of the Office of Cultural Resource Protection at the Advisory Council on Historic Preservation. Previous work includes positions as consultant in historic preservation to the High Commissioner, Trust Territory of the Pacific Islands; archaeologist with Interagency Archeological Services, Department of the Interior; and executive director of the Archeological

Resource Management Service, New York Archeological Council. He has also worked as an archaeologist with the University of California in Riverside and Los Angeles and with San Francisco State University, and holds a Ph.D. in anthropology from the University of California in Riverside. He has written many books, monographs and reports on archaeological investigations, historic preservation law as it affects archaeological resources and traditional cultural values, and methods of archaeological survey. He is co-author of *Anthropology in Historic Preservation: Caring for Culture's Clutter* (The Academic Press, 1977).

Antoinette J. Lee is an independent architectural historian and a historic preservation consultant and holds a Ph.D. degree in American Civilization from George Washington University. Since 1969, she has undertaken numerous projects, including the preparation of manuscripts on the history of planning in Washington, D.C.; reports on the preservation system in Great Britain; and articles and essays on cast iron in architecture, preservation education and civil engineering history. She has served as consultant to the U.S. Committee, International Council on Monuments and Sites and the Architectural League in New York and as contract historian to the Midwest Regional Office, National Park Service. She is completing a manuscript on the history of the Office of the Supervising Architect of the U.S. Treasury Department. She serves on the Arlington County, Virginia, Historic Affairs and Landmark Review Board and on the board of directors of the Society of Architectural Historians.

Elizabeth A. Lyon is chief of the Historic Preservation Section within the Parks, Recreation and Historic Sites Division of the Georgia Department of Natural Resources where she has worked since 1976. She received her Ph.D. degree from Emory University and was a member of the faculty there from 1965 to 1975. She served as a lecturer in the American Studies program of the Graduate Institute of the Liberal Arts and in the Department of the History of Art where she offered courses in architectural and urban design history. Since joining the state historic preservation office, she has published several articles and presented papers on historic preservation and the relationship of public historic preservation programs to the history and architectural history professions. She has served as an officer, board member and committee chairperson for the National Conference of State Historic Preservation Officers, the professional organization that represents the state historic preservation programs.

W. Brown Morton III is assistant professor at the Mary Washington College Department of Historic Preservation and a historic preservation consultant active in investigations of properties abroad and in the United States. Between 1975 and 1978, he was departmental consultant for historic architecture and chief of the technical preservation services division with the Department of the Interior. In this position, he administered the nationwide technical historic preservation programs of the Secretary of the Interior. He is co-author of *The Secretary of the Interior's Standards for Historic Preservation Projects.* He also served as conservation architect with the International Centre for the Study of the Preservation and Restoration of Cultural Property in Rome; architect with the National Historic Landmark Program, Department of the Interior; principal architect with the Historic American Buildings Survey, Department of the Interior; and architect in the office of Jean-Pierre Paquet, Architecte-en-Chef, Service des Monuments Historiques, Hotel des Invalides in Paris. He has undertaken international missions to Indonesia, China, Italy, Japan, Nepal and Vietnam, and served as chairman, U.S. Committee, International Council on Monuments and Sites from 1975 to 1979.

Robert E. Stipe is professor of design in the landscape architecture program at the School of Design, North Carolina State University at Raleigh. Trained in law and urban planning, he has been active in legal and governmental aspects of historic preservation. A former state historic preservation officer for North Carolina, he is a trustee emeritus of the National Trust for Historic Preservation and has served on the boards of many national, state and local preservation organizations. He is a fellow of US/ICOMOS and in 1978 received the Secretary of the Interior's Conservation Service Award. He has authored many state and local preservation statutes and ordinances and published widely on the subject of historic preservation and amenity planning. In 1968 to 1969, he was a senior Fulbright research scholar at the University of London. His teaching has included design studios and courses in planning law, historic preservation law, community design policy and the legal aspects of landscape and townscape conservation.